NUMBER TWO HUNDRED AND TWENTY-SEVEN

THE OLD FARMER'S ALMANAC

CALCULATED ON A NEW AND IMPROVED PLAN FOR THE YEAR OF OUR LORD

2019

Being 3rd after Leap Year and (until July 4) 243rd year of American Independence

FITTED FOR BOSTON AND THE NEW ENGLAND STATES, WITH SPECIAL CORRECTIONS AND CALCULATIONS TO ANSWER FOR ALL THE UNITED STATES.

Containing, besides the large number of Astronomical Calculations and the Farmer's Calendar for every month in the year, a variety of NEW, USEFUL, & ENTERTAINING MATTER.

ESTABLISHED IN 1792
BY ROBERT B. THOMAS (1766–1846)

Learn to make the most of life, / Lose no happy day, /
Time will never bring thee back / Chances swept away!
–"The Lesson of the Water-Mill," Sarah Doudney, English writer (1841–1926)

Cover design registered U.S. Trademark Office · Copyright © 2018 by Yankee Publishing Incorporated · ISSN 0078-4516 · Library of Congress Card No. 56-29681

Cover illustration by Steven Noble • Original wood engraving (above) by Randy Miller

THE OLD FARMER'S ALMANAC • DUBLIN, NH 03444 • 603-563-8111 • ALMANAC.COM

CONTENTS

7

8

13

2019 TRENDS
Forecasts, Facts, and Fascinating Ideas 6

190

84

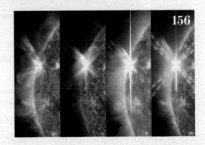

156

GLAD "TIDINGS"

Good news, Patrons! We may be "Old," but every year we also bring you the "new"—and 2019 is no exception.

In the Calendar Page spreads (120–147), you'll find on the left-hand pages our customary "calendar of the heavens," replete with its galaxy of celestial information and sea of tidal data, the latter now back on these pages after a year's hiatus.

On the right-hand pages, as you enjoy discovering each month's special days and Moon phases intermixed with trivia that is trivial even by trivia standards, don't overlook the "doggerel"—longtime writer Tim Clark's amusing, italicized, vertical weather rhyme—which is usually an uncannily accurate forecast!

Please join us in welcoming Vermonter Julia Shipley, award-winning writer and poet, as the first woman in 227 years to pen our Farmer's Calendar essays. A keen observer of nature, Julia is a farmer, too, having raised cows, sheep, chickens, turkeys, and vegetables on her 6-acre homestead.

Speaking of farmers, we're always interested in hearing from hard-working farm families about how they are successfully meeting today's challenges. If you're a farmer or rancher (or you know one), young or old, in the United States or Canada, with a story to share, please let us know at Almanac.com/Feedback.

Really good news for us is that you continue to send us questions, comments, and observations via snail mail, email (Almanac.com/Feedback), social media, and telephone. That's right: When the phone rings, we, the editors, actually answer it—or we call you back (if you leave a number). We appreciate that you care enough to let us know how we're doing.

We'd love to meet you. If your travels take you to New Hampshire, do drop in! We'll personally sign your Almanac, show you around our headquarters, and regale you with Almanacky tales. Or visit from home via Almanac.com/Webcam and view our barn-red office building in Dublin, with the church steeple, Police Department, and Town Hall behind it.

In closing this opening, we send you glad tidings, wish you a new year filled with good news, and thank you for your trust in this Almanac. We're here for you and because of you.

–J. S., JUNE 2018

However, it is by our works and not our words that we would be judged. These, we hope, will sustain us in the humble though proud station we have so long held in the name of

Your obedient servant,

Robt. B. Thomas.

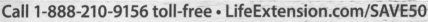

2019 TRENDS

WHAT'S COOKING?

Instead of scheduling our days around mealtimes, we're scheduling our meals around everything else going on in our days.

–Laurie Demeritt, CEO, The Hartman Group, Bellevue, Washington

SMART FOODS

Consumers are seeking potent energy sources to power their brains.

–Kara Nielsen, VP, trends and marketing, CCD Innovation, Emeryville, California

- coffee creamer made with grass-fed butter

- beverages made with reishi mushrooms

PEOPLE ARE TALKING ABOUT . . .

- nutritionists in restaurants to help patrons choose healthy foods

BUZZWORD
Eatertainment: a restaurant that offers board games or arcades

- commuters bringing cutlery and ingredients to work to create gourmet lunches

- exercising at grocery stores

- DNA kits that help us to choose foods based on genetics

MENUS ARE GOING MEATLESS

Top-end restaurants used to serve steak and potatoes, but now they have lentil dishes and other plant-based proteins.

–Mike von Massow, associate professor, University of Guelph, Ontario

- **43%** of Canadians plan to eat more plant-based proteins (soya, lentils, and chia seeds are growing in popularity)

PROOF IS A PRIORITY

People want proof of food sources:

- scannable packages linking to videos of producer animals being well treated

- ice cream made with "traceable" milk (to identify the source farm)

• restaurants certified as "green" that, e.g., use recyclable containers, solar panels, food from local sources; reduce waste and water use; compost

• menus "augmented" with apps that show food prep and/or ingredients used

restaurants, then served to diners.

• Mini-farms are appearing in grocery store aisles and on rooftops.

• Greenhouses are being built adjacent to supermarkets.

FROM DISCARDED TO DELICIOUS
• Imperfect fruit is being pressed into juice.

• Fruit pulp is being made into chips.

• Plant leaves and stems are being used in "root-to-stem" cooking.

FLAVORS WE CRAVE
• sugar-free syrups made from dates, sorghum, and yacon root

• banana milk and flour

• fish-free tomato "sushi"

• bacon-flavor seaweed

"GROCERANT" GROWTH
Convenience has more currency than ever, with restaurants and food markets colliding in the ready-to-eat spaces at grocery stores.

–Sylvain Charlebois, professor, Dalhousie University, Halifax, Nova Scotia

(continued)

BY THE NUMBERS
22%
of U.S. vegetable buyers want produce grown on store premises

20%
of Canadians trust health claims on food packages

40%
of Canadians have fallen victim to "food fraud" (e.g., honey, saffron, or olive oil diluted with cheaper ingredients)

70%
of U.S. consumers want to understand an ingredients list

EATING IS EXTRA
Average time spent preparing, presenting, and cleaning up food each day by generation (in minutes):
• Traditionalists: **101**
• Baby boomers: **136**
• Gen Xers: **143**
• Millennials: **88**

FRESHNESS FIRST
• Produce is being grown indoors at

IN THE GARDEN

People want plant-related projects that are easy and lifestyle-friendly—adaptive to short attention spans, hectic schedules, and smaller spaces.

–Tom Soulsby, senior horticulturist, Chicago Botanic Garden

GETTING TO GROUND ZERO

Gardeners are composting, gardening, and reducing their footprint, as zero-waste living becomes aspirational.

–Katie Dubow, creative director, Garden Marketing Group

PEOPLE ARE TALKING ABOUT . . .

• DNA testing used on plants displayed at public botanical gardens to prove that certain species still exist, even though they're no longer found in the wild

• the future of growing indoors hydroponically in Internet-connected, refrigerator-size boxes

GROW TO SHOW

• Succulents are fleshy, compact, colorful, and low-maintenance—and fun to have a bowl-full of on a coffee table.

–Dave Forehand, VP of gardens, Dallas Arboretum and Botanical Gardens

• Edible flowers are everywhere— in salads: pansies and nasturtiums; in water pitchers: roses, lavender, and lilacs; in ice cubes: marigolds and impatiens.

–Jennifer Smock, outdoor supervisor, Kemper Center for Home Gardening, Missouri Botanical Garden

• Gardeners want plants that are social media–shareable: displays of bold tropical foliage with unique colors, shapes, patterns, and variations, indoors and out.

–Soulsby *(continued)*

HARDINESS IS IN HIGH DEMAND

Gardeners want plants that stand up to extreme weather, e.g.:

- high winds: native grasses, evergreens, yarrow, and sedum
- drought: date palm, euphorbia, fennel, iris, poppy
- flood: black chokeberry, meadowsweet shrubs, bayberry, ferns
- frost: spruce, birch, and maple trees; hellebore and hosta

–Garden Media Group

YARROW

NATURAL IS NORMAL

- We're partnering with "pests," letting rabbits eat dandelions, parasitoid wasps control caterpillar populations, and tachinid flies manage insects.

–Nancy Lawson, author,
The Humane Gardener
(Princeton Architectural Press, 2017)

BY THE NUMBERS

7.2%:
average reduction in home energy use due to trees

52%
of Americans use indoor plants to clean the air

$503
is the average spent on lawn and garden products and services per U.S. household

30 million
households purchased food preservation products in 2016

- We're planting pollinator gardens on "hellstrips"—patches of grass between roads and sidewalks.

THE PROS' PICKS

- Dwarf produce: 'Raspberry Shortcake' raspberry, 'Little Miss Figgy' fig, 'Peach Sorbet' blueberry, 'Patio Pride' pea
- Ornamental hot peppers (to eat and for visual interest):

'Midnight Fire', 'Hot Pops Purple', 'Sedona Sun', 'Paracho', 'Joker', 'Salsa' series
–Smock

'HOT POPS PURPLE'

- Burpee's Space Saver series: 'Patio Baby' eggplant, 'Tangerine Dream' sweet pepper, 'Tidy Treats' small-fruited tomato
–Forehand

- For patio containers and small spaces: 'Atlas' beefsteak tomato, shrublike 'Confetti' pepper with variegated foliage, 'Jungle Parrot' snack-size bell pepper, and 'Fioretto' cauliflower, which produces small florets that stay crunchy when cooked and are sweeter than those from large-head varieties
–Venelin Dimitrov, senior product manager, W. Atlee Burpee and Company

(continued)

OUR ANIMAL FRIENDS

It's a go-anywhere, mobile world—
and that includes our pets.

–David Dorman, publisher, Pets Magazine

PEOPLE ARE TALKING ABOUT . . .

- "yappy hours" at bars for dogs and their owners or for people looking for pets

- pet doors operated with microchips to allow entry only to authorized animals

- paid "pawternity leave" to allow new pet owners time to spend with their animals

- wearing matching pajamas with their pets

COUNTING CATS AND DOGS

Pets in the U.S.:

- Cats: **94.2 million**
- Dogs: **89.7 million**

–American Pet Products Association National Pet Owners Survey

In Canada:

- Cats: **8.8 million**
- Dogs: **7.6 million**

–Canadian Animal Health Institute

PET PERKS FOR GOOD HEALTH

- dog walkers sending postwalk photos to owners and providing GPS tracking of routes

- food made with pet-friendly grains and vegetables

- portable systems to wash dogs in any room of the house

- touch screen computer games and TV shows to keep pets mentally sharp

BY THE NUMBERS

10%
of pets have social media accounts

$1 billion
is the annual revenue of the dog-walking industry

$5.76 billion
is spent annually on pet services (e.g., pet-sitting, boarding, grooming, training)

$2.8 billion
is spent annually on U.S. sales of cat litter

12%
of pet dogs are under 8 pounds

- workouts on in-home treadmills alongside owners

- mouse-shape food containers, hidden around the house, to encourage domestic felines to hunt

PET CONVENIENCES

Products will perform more and more daily pet care tasks for us.
–David Lummis, market research analyst, Packaged Facts

- Cats and small litter-trained dogs will use automatic-flush toilets.

- Robots will launch tennis balls for dogs to chase when home alone.

- Balls will track how fast a dog can fetch.

- We'll see home-delivered veterinary care, grooming, oral health care, and train-ing, as well as doggie day care pickup.

- Self-propelled devices will clean aquariums while photographing the fish.

MONEY MATTERS

The lifestyle of minimalism and intentionally owning less will continue to grow.
–Joshua Becker, author, The More of Less *(WaterBrook, 2016)*

WE WANT IT OUR WAY

In order to succeed in the new age of commerce, retailers must include profound experiences, product and brand curation, and a frictionless shopping journey.
–Oliver Chen, senior equity research analyst, Cowen

SIGNS OF SKEPTICISM

According to Kit Yarrow, author, *Decoding the New Consumer Mind* (Jossey-Bass, 2014) . . .

- We're overloaded with info: "Shoppers are looking for trustwor-thy partners, whether retailers or vloggers [video bloggers], to help them make good choices by doing the research for them."

- We're wary of company claims: "We're looking for cues that businesses are worthy, that go beyond the products we're consid-ering."   *(continued)*

BY THE NUMBERS

14% of Americans carry no cash

52% of U.S. adults say that their current finances are "excellent" or "good"

$17.2 billion: the estimated e-commerce taxes that go uncollected annually

Photos, from top: pixdeluxe/Getty Images; gracethang/Getty Images

COLLECTIBLES

Attendance at flea markets and online bidding at decor
and design auctions have reached all-time highs.

–Kathleen Guzman, appraiser, Heritage Auctions

THE NEXT BIG THING?

A younger genera-
tion is seeking iconic
original movie props,
rare autographs, and
unique objects
representing key
points in mass culture.
*–Eric Bradley, editor,
Antique Trader Antiques &
Collectibles Price Guide*

FANDOM FAVES

• Comic book and film
fans are dressing up as
characters ("cosplay")
to search for accesso-
ries at antique shops.

• Harry Potter fans
fancy vintage brooms,
neckties, and eyeglass
frames.

SOLD FOR . . .

$4,025:
1930s children's
barbershop chair

$8,625:
1950s Roy Rogers
"Ride Trigger"
coin-operated
kiddie ride

$158,600:
original town
plan for the city
of Pittsburgh, Pa.

$432,500:
telescope owned
by Albert Einstein

$708,000:
original map used
to secure funding
for Disneyland
in 1953

• *Star Wars* fans
quest for military
surplus backpacks,
belts, and straps.

• *Totoro* fans love
vintage umbrellas and
straw hats.
*–Gary Piattoni, appraiser,
Evanston, Illinois*

COMPETING INTERESTS

While older collectors
crave nostalgia,
younger buyers seek
simple technology:

• rotary phones

• film cameras

• manual typewriters

• View-Masters
–Piattoni

(continued)

Consumer Cellular®

UNLIMITED TALK & TEXT FOR JUST $25/MONTH

✓ Choose a Data Plan That Fits Your Needs, From Small to Large

✓ No Contracts ✓ Nationwide Coverage

WIRELESS THE WAY YOU LIKE IT—SWITCH TODAY!

LOW PRICES

Plans start as low as $15/month, and activation is free!

VARIETY OF PHONES & DEVICES

Select any device, from flip phones to smartphones—including the latest iPhones.

RANKED #1 BY J.D. POWER

"Highest in Customer Service among Non-Contract Value Wireless Providers, 4 Times in a Row!"

Member-Advantages

AARP MEMBER BENEFITS

AARP members receive a 5% discount on service and usage every month.

CALL CONSUMER CELLULAR AT
(888) 270-8608

VISIT US ONLINE AT
ConsumerCellular.com/8608

AVAILABLE AT  **TARGET**

AROUND THE HOUSE

As baby boomers age and environmentally conscious millennials begin settling into homes, the demand for smaller houses will begin to exceed the demand for larger ones.
–*Joshua Becker, author,* The More of Less *(WaterBrook, 2016)*

WE'RE GREENER WITH . . .
- "breathing rooms" filled with plants to clean the air and clear our minds
- plants as art: "statement" plants in pots and staghorn ferns in driftwood hung like paintings

WALLPAPER POSSIBILITIES
- impregnated with scratch-and-sniff fragrances
- lighting up when you touch it
- made with naturally shed peacock feathers

THE INSIDE STORY
We'll see a rise in minimalism, tiny furniture, and clever storage spaces.
–*Patty Shapiro, Montreal-based trend forecaster*

- televisions mounted on easels, toilets that flush when told, showers programmed for a specific temperature and timed to save water, and glass garage doors used as walls in houses
- homes with "flex space," wired for home offices
- apartment buildings with shared workspaces for communal offices

STYLE NOTES
Decorators are mixing patterns together for a rich and layered look.
–*Eugenia Santiesteban Soto, senior style editor,* Better Homes & Gardens

LIGHT UP YOUR LIFE!
We'll see paintings made from bioluminescent bacteria: The images glow for 2 weeks.
(continued)

BY THE NUMBERS

32: median age of first-time home buyers

33% of Americans would consider living in a haunted house

$16,000: cost of integrating a laundry-folding robot into a home's walls

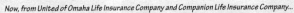

HEALTH CHECK

Municipal governments are investing in urban nature, spurred by growing evidence of how greenspace affects our social health and physical well-being.

–Holli-Anne Passmore, psychology researcher, University of British Columbia

BY THE NUMBERS

4.38: servings of fruit and vegetables consumed by Canadians each day, on average

10 minutes: aerobic activity needed to improve mental focus

90% of medical school curricula include spiritual health

$4.39 billion: estimated annual health care costs incurred in Canada due to citizens not eating enough fruit and vegetables

NATURE IS NURTURE

"Ecotherapy," a process of growth and healing by interacting with nature, is being used to treat a range of conditions such as anxiety, depression, diabetes, and high blood pressure.

–Jennifer Lennox, spokesperson, The Davey Tree Expert Company, Kent, Ohio

BUZZWORD
Emodiversity: the ability to feel a wide range of healthful, positive emotions (enthusiasm, determination, pride, inspiration, and strength)

PEOPLE ARE TALKING ABOUT . . .

- falling asleep to movies of sheep grazing in a field
- consuming collagen-infused foods for better complexions
- gym workouts based on children's games (e.g., relay races, dodgeball)

COMING SOON . . .

- self-healing cavity fillings: If a crack develops, a little capsule of material opens up to seal it.
- shoes with vibrating insoles to improve balance *(continued)*

FARMING TODAY

Young people are cutting their teeth as urban farmers in the cities, then moving to rural areas into a more traditional model of small-scale farming.

–Georgia Stanley, manager of membership, British Columbia Association of Farmers' Markets

FARMS GROW HEALTHY KIDS

• Environmental exposures or other elements of the farming lifestyle help kids to be resistant to both allergies and viral respiratory illnesses.
–James Gern, MD, researcher, University of Wisconsin

PEOPLE ARE TALKING ABOUT . . .

• computer games in which players sample an agricultural career

• "renting" a farm animal, beehive, or maple tree; getting photos of its growth cycles; and, eventually, consuming its harvest

CONSUMER CONNECTIONS

• **114,801** U.S. farms sell direct-to-consumer

• **24,510** Canadian farms sell direct-to-consumer

BY THE NUMBERS

69% of new farmers have college degrees

267,500: number of U.S. cows dedicated to producing organic milk in one recent year

39% of U.S. farmland is rented

820 acres: average size of a Canadian farm

GROWERS ARE PRODUCING . . .

• "exotic" vegetables (Asian greens, okra) for culturally diverse customers
–Stanley

• in cities, indoors: "Indoor farming technology will continue to evolve and develop urban agriculture."
–Michael Levenston, executive director, City Farmer Society, Vancouver, British Columbia

• Top 5 veggies surging in sales in Canada:
1. kale
2. yams
3. artichokes
4. okra
5. gingerroot
–Canadian Produce Marketing Association (continued)

CLOTHING UP CLOSE

We will continue to see an expansion of women renting fashion and thinning out their closets.

–Leonard Schlesinger, Baker Foundation Professor, Harvard Business School

MULTITASKING TOGS INCLUDE . . .

- patch pockets to snap off and wear on other garments
- shirtsleeves to take off and attach to outerwear
- coats to use as backpacks, sleeping bags, or blankets

DISRUPTION IN THE RAG TRADE

If it is not local, online, or off-price, it is not happening.

–Jan Rogers Kniffen, retail consultant, Greenwich, Connecticut

BY THE NUMBERS

15%
of consumers have ordered apparel using subscription boxes

79%
of women own at least one unworn pair of shoes

$323:
average amount spent on clothing annually, by men

$571: average amount spent on clothing annually, by women

INDIVIDUALITY IS US

We want a wardrobe that lets us create more garments, such as jacket linings to wear as blouses.

–Steven Faerm, associate professor of fashion, Parsons School of Design

LADIES' WEAR DAILY

- one-shoulder dresses evoking Grecian statuary
- sheer patterned socks, worn with sneakers or sandals

MEN'S WEAR DAILY

- modern kimonos, in muted blues and grays
- dress pants with athletic stripes

RETAILERS ARE REVVED UP BY . . .

- steaming out wrinkles so that items can be immediately worn
- opening early to repair commuters' ripped buttons, torn cuffs, or stains
- turning clothing "stores" into gathering spots, with spa services, juice bars, classes, and tailors

CULTURE CUES

Hundreds of thousands of people are joining citizen science projects which collectively lead to discoveries that would be impossible with conventional science.

–Caren Cooper, assistant head, Biodiversity Research Lab, North Carolina Museum of Natural Sciences

who were given money and told to buy a gift for someone were happier than those who were instructed to spend it on themselves.

QUIET, PLEASE!
Shhhh! for . . .
- stores with "quiet hours"
- self-imposed smartphone-free time periods
- fold-up, portable pods for privacy in crowded spaces ∎

- "cargo" bikes with detachable hand trucks for toting up to 50 pounds
- "citizen scientists" counting urban trees

PICK-ME-UPS
- **1,456:** number of times U.S. moms and dads pick up after their children annually
- **71%** of parents have been injured by stepping on a toy

GIVING IS GOOD
- Study participants

PEOPLE ARE TALKING ABOUT . . .
- movies of laundry being washed
- hobbyhorse rider competitions
- playing shorter rounds of golf and tennis matches because they are time-stressed

BY THE NUMBERS

16% of Americans celebrate Thanksgiving on a date other than the holiday to save travel costs

94% of the U.S. population has a recycling program available to them

Choose Life
Grow Young with HGH

From the landmark book Grow Young with HGH comes the most powerful, over-the-counter health supplement in the history of man. Human growth hormone was first discovered in 1920 and has long been thought by the medical community to be necessary only to stimulate the body to full adult size and therefore unnecessary past the age of 20. Recent studies, however, have overturned this notion completely, discovering instead that the natural decline of Human Growth Hormone (HGH), from ages 21 to 61 (the average age at which there is only a trace left in the body) and is the main reason why the body ages and fails to regenerate itself to its 25 year-old biological age.

Like a picked flower cut from the source, we gradually wilt physically and mentally and become vulnerable to a host of degenerative diseases, that we simply weren't susceptible to in our early adult years.

Modern medical science now regards aging as a disease that is treatable and preventable and that "aging", the disease, is actually a compilation of various diseases and pathologies, from everything, like a rise in blood glucose and pressure to diabetes, skin wrinkling and so on. All of these aging symptoms can be stopped and rolled back by maintaining Growth Hormone levels in the blood at the same levels HGH existed in the blood when we were 25 years old.

There is a receptor site in almost every

cell in the human body for HGH, so its regenerative and healing effects are very comprehensive.

Growth Hormone, first synthesized in 1985 under the Reagan Orphan drug act, to treat dwarfism, was quickly recognized to stop aging in its tracks and reverse it to a remarkable degree. Since then, only the lucky and the rich have had access to it at the cost of $10,000 US per year.

The next big breakthrough was to come in 1997 when a group of doctors and scientists, developed an all-natural source product which would cause your own natural HGH to be released again and do all the remarkable things it did for you in your 20's. Now available to every adult for about the price of a coffee and donut a day.

GHR now available in America, just in time for the aging Baby Boomers and everyone else from age 30 to 90 who doesn't want to age rapidly but would rather stay young, beautiful and healthy all of the time.

The new HGH releasers are winning converts from the synthetic HGH users as well, since GHR is just as effective, is oral instead of self-injectable and is very affordable.

GHR is a natural releaser, has no known side effects, unlike the synthetic version and has no known drug interactions. Progressive doctors admit that this is the direction medicine is seeking to go, to get the body to heal itself instead of employing drugs. GHR is truly a revolutionary paradigm shift in medicine and, like any modern leap frog advance, many others will be left in the dust holding their limited, or useless drugs and remedies.

It is now thought that HGH is so comprehensive in its healing and regenerative powers that it is today, where the computer industry was twenty years ago, that it will displace so many prescription and non-prescription drugs and health remedies that it is staggering to think of.

The president of BIE Health Products stated in a recent interview, I've been waiting for these products since the 70's. We knew they would come, if only we could stay healthy and live long enough to see them! If you want to stay on top of your game, physically and mentally as you age, this product is a boon, especially for the highly skilled professionals who have made large investments in their education, and experience. Also with the failure of Congress to honor our seniors with pharmaceutical coverage policy, it's more important than ever to take pro-active steps to safeguard your health. Continued use of GHR will make a radical difference in your health, HGH is particularly helpful to the elderly who, given a choice, would rather stay independent in their own home, strong, healthy and alert enough to manage their own affairs, exercise and stay involved in their communities. Frank, age 85, walks two miles a day, plays golf, belongs to a dance club for seniors, had a girl friend again and doesn't need Viagra, passed his drivers test and is hardly ever home when we call - GHR delivers.

HGH is known to relieve symptoms of Asthma, Angina, Chronic Fatigue, Constipation, Lower back pain and Sciatica, Cataracts and Macular Degeneration, Menopause, Fibromyalgia, Regular and Diabetic Neuropathy, Hepatitis, helps Kidney Dialysis and Heart and Stroke recovery.

For more information or to order call
877-849-4777
www.biehealth.us

These statements have not been evaluated by the FDA. Copyright © 2000. Code OFA.

●

FOOLPROOF ADVICE FOR BEGINNERS, "BLACK THUMBS," AND ANYONE TRYING TO GROW FOOD.

JOIN THE

BY SUSAN PEERY

Remember back to last fall or maybe winter. You were thinking, *"I want a garden!"* You scrutinized seed catalogs and ordered beautiful things, some with Latin names that you couldn't pronounce. You strolled down nursery aisles and arrived home with trays of cute, tender seedlings.

When the days got warmer, you marked off a spot, cleared the ground, and turned over the dirt with muscles you didn't know that you had. Dropped seeds into knuckle-deep holes in neat rows. Tamped the earth around the eager seedlings to help them settle into their new digs.

Through the summer, you yanked weeds, beat back bugs, cursed rampaging rabbits or woodchucks, and toted watering cans or hoses (how much is enough?). You got dirty, sweaty, hungry, and tired, watching and waiting for your plot to become . . . picture-perfect. Like those in magazines and on Facebook and Pinterest.

Then, in August—or maybe even earlier, in July—you bought vegetables at a farm stand, thinking: *"Why aren't my tomatoes* (beans, carrots, squash—whatever) *like this?"*

Sound familiar? Feeling frustrated just thinking about it?

Take a deep breath. We've all been there. This season will be different. Follow this guidance to go from grief to glory in the garden!

(continued)

You waited for your plot to become picture-perfect, like this one.

GREEN THUMB CLUB

SUN

IF YOU GROW IT FOR THE FRUIT OR THE ROOT, YOU NEED FULL SUN. IF YOU GROW IT FOR THE LEAVES, PARTIAL SHADE IS ALL YOU NEED.

—GARDENING ADAGE

Most vegetables and herbs require about 8 hours of sunlight each day to thrive. Exceptions include shade-tolerant leafy greens and a few herbs. (In the high heat of summer or if a late spring frost threatens, protect tender plants with floating row covers.) Choose a garden site that gets 8 hours of sunlight, ideally with southern exposure unhindered by shade from trees or buildings, a plot into which you can put the tallest plants on the north end so that they do not cast shade on smaller plants to their south.

Soil is slower to warm than air. If you plant seedlings and certain seeds in cold soil, you might as well throw them away. Sure, peas will sprout and thrive when the soil temperature is in the low 40s°F and the days are cool and damp, but melons, most squashes, pumpkins, and tomatoes require soil temperature above 50°F and warm days.

A warm Sun dries out the soil, and plants require frequent watering. This is best done in early morning or evening; water in midday, and much of the moisture may be lost to evaporation. If water is costly, use a hose or watering can at the base of plants instead of broadcasting it with sprinklers.

(continued)

Watering is best done in early morning or evening.

Photo: Westbury/Getty Images

Few of us are naturally blessed with loamy, fertile soil at a pH of 5.5–6.5, the ideal range for most herbs and vegetables. Soil pH (a measure of acidity or alkalinity), together with soil chemistry and structure, will greatly affect the health and vigor of your plants. If your tomatoes are plagued with blossom end rot, this may be due to a calcium deficiency in the soil—something you can easily fix.

Get your soil tested. For most thorough results and specific recommendations, contact your local Cooperative Extension service. Make the advised amendments, adding compost, manure, peat, lime, and other organic material as necessary. *(continued)*

The ideal pH range for growing most herbs and vegetables is 5.5–6.5.

IN SPRING AT THE END OF THE DAY, YOU SHOULD SMELL LIKE DIRT.
–MARGARET ATWOOD, CANADIAN WRITER (B. 1939)

I t takes self-control not to overplant a garden—but we've all done it and then struggled to thin seedlings without uprooting their neighbors. Sometimes we've left plants to crowd only to see that none mature to full size. Map out your garden plot, noting the space advised on the seed packet or plant stick. Or try the easy app at Almanac.com/GardenPlanner.

Think again before tucking an extra cherry tomato plant over here, adding another row of green beans there. If a friend gives you two zucchini (cuke, eggplant, pepper—whatever) plants, give them away or plant them in a pot. You'll be glad that you did in July, when your garden is a jungle, with plants competing for sunlight and nutrients.

Develop a spare, minimalist mentality. Leave space: Good air circulation helps to ward off mildew and blight. Plan walkways and spread wood chips or other mulch on the paths. Allow at least 6 feet between indeterminate tomato plants and stake them well. Plant sprawlers like zucchini or pumpkins on the garden's edge and encourage their vines away from the other crops.

Weed as needed and mulch. Well. Mulch helps to minimize weeds and retain moisture. *(continued)*

Good air circulation helps to ward off mildew and blight.

TO NURTURE A GARDEN IS TO FEED NOT JUST THE BODY, BUT THE SOUL.
–ALFRED AUSTIN, ENGLISH POET (1835–1913)

SPACE

SUCCESS

GARDENING IS LEARNING, LEARNING, LEARNING. THAT'S THE FUN OF THEM. YOU'RE ALWAYS LEARNING.
–HELEN MIRREN, ENGLISH ACTRESS (B. 1945)

Gardening is an experiment. No one (so far) can control the weather, the bugs, or any other force of nature. You can make good choices and educated guesses and adopt best practices and still experience crop failures. But if you follow this guidance, embrace the surprises and uncertainties of each gardening season, and look forward to the next, you are on the road from grief to glory.

SEEDS VS. SEEDLINGS

Which plants should you seed directly into the soil and which should you purchase as seedlings?

Buy seedlings if you do not have a good setup for starting seeds, if you have a short growing season, and/or if you want only two or three plants of a certain crop, such as squashes or tomatoes. Choose stocky, sturdy-looking plants over large, leggy ones. Plant at the depth and spacing recommended on the label.

When sowing seeds directly, follow the directions: If a seed packet says to space seeds 2 inches apart, do it. If a packet says to sow "sparsely," allow at least 1 inch between seeds.   *(continued)*

Buy seedlings if you do not have a good setup for starting seeds.

Mortise & Tenon Red Cedar Quality Wood Shutters

Interior & Exterior Custom Wood Shutters

(203) 245-2608 • www.shuttercraft.com

Endless Cutouts • All Types & Sizes • Full Painting Services
Authentic Hardware • Shipped Nationwide
Family-owned since 1986 • Madison, CT 06443

INCINOLET® SIMPLY THE BEST

electric incinerating toilets

PROBLEM SOLVED!
Need a toilet located conveniently?
Home, cabin, barn, boat, or dock—
INCINOLET is your best solution!

SIMPLE to install & maintain.
ULTRA CLEAN Waste reduced to ash.
TOP QUALITY stainless steel, quality controls.

www.incinolet.com

Call 1-800-527-5551 for information, prices, and personal attention.

RESEARCH PRODUCTS/Blankenship
2639 Andjon • Dallas, Texas 75220

10 EASY EDIBLES

Most gardeners find these to be the most reliable and rewarding edibles to grow:

1. *Basil, any variety:* Needs warm air and soil; pinch off flowers to encourage leaves. A hint of a frost will finish it.

2. *Beans:* Need 60°F soil; space seeds as directed; choose 'Provider' or 'Blue Lake' (bush varieties) for heavy harvests.

3. *Carrots:* Need light, well-draining soil; sow sparsely to avoid thinning later; tolerate light frost; choose 'Chantenay' and 'Nantes', which keep well.

4. *Cherry tomatoes:* No plot? Put in a large container; especially sweet and productive 'Sun Gold'.

5. *Chives:* Use this hardy perennial herb as a great garnish; eat its flowers; divide in fall.

6. *Garlic:* Plant individual cloves in fall, mulch with hay; rake off mulch in spring; when scapes curl around once, cut off and make pesto; harvest when leaves wither. Save the biggest bulbs for your next crop.

7. *Greens:* Can be planted early; full sun not needed; especially arugula, mesclun, loose-leaf lettuces. Go from seed to salad bowl in 6 weeks!

8. *Parsley:* Seeds are slow to germinate, so buy little plants; especially curly, which is slower to bolt than flatleaf and will last into fall; needs space to put down deep roots.

9. *Peas:* Love cool weather; may need support; especially snap, which outyield shelling peas.

10. *Potatoes:* Plant chunks of sprouted seed potatoes, especially russets, early reds, and yellow-flesh varieties, with eyes upward in a trench; fill in; mulch well. Dig (carefully!) when tops die down. *(continued)*

GARDENING IS JUST ANOTHER DAY AT THE PLANT.
—GARDENING ADAGE

THERE ARE NO GARDENING MISTAKES, ONLY EXPERIMENTS.

–Janet Kilburn Phillips, English cottage garden designer

These plants need specific (perfect) conditions. Proceed with careful attention to the advice below.

1. *Cantaloupes* and *watermelons* need warmth: hot days, warm nights, and a long growing season. A plastic hoop house may help.

2. *Sweet corn* needs rich soil, warm sun, and a lot of moisture.

3. *Tomatillos* need a long growing season; cool August nights stop them. Homegrown are much better than the store-bought specimens.

4. *Asparagus* requires a rich, weed-free, undisturbed bed. Control slugs and asparagus beetles. Harvest in the third year, and, yes, it's worth the wait: Homegrown spears are ambrosial to asparagus lovers.

Get more information on how to grow in pots at Almanac.com.

GOOD, BETTER, BEST

Never let it rest, till your good is better and your better is the best! Get more information on the edibles mentioned here (including how to grow in pots), plus read stories from growers like you at Almanac.com/Gardening. ■

Susan Peery gardens in Nelson, New Hampshire, where she loves to experiment with traditional gardening methods and plants. Like all gardeners, she invokes the mantra "Wait 'til next year!"

Ask the Expert

THE TRUTH ABOUT COCHLEAR IMPLANTS

Straining to hear each day, even when using powerful hearing aids?

Feeling frustrated and sometimes even exhausted from listening? Whether it happens suddenly or gradually over time, hearing loss can affect you physically and emotionally. Being unable to hear impacts your ability to communicate with your loved ones, hear in noisy environments, talk on the phone, and may force you to become more reliant on your family members to interpret for you.

David C. Kelsall, M.D.,
Cochlear Medical Advisor

Cochlear implants work differently than hearing aids. Rather than amplifying sound, they use state-of-the-art software and electronic components to provide access to the sounds you've been missing. They are designed to help you hear better and understand speech in all situations, including noisy environments.

Dr. David C. Kelsall, a cochlear implant surgeon and medical advisor to Cochlear, the world leader in cochlear implants, answers questions about cochlear implants and how they are different from hearing aids.

Q: How are cochlear implants different than hearing aids?
A: Hearing aids help many people by making the sounds they hear louder. Unfortunately, as hearing loss progresses, sounds need to not only be made louder, they need to be made clearer. Cochlear implants can help give you that clarity, especially in noisy environments. Be sure to discuss your options with a Hearing Implant Specialist in your area.

Q: Are cochlear implants covered by Medicare?
A: Yes, by Medicare and most private insurance plans.*

Q: How do I know a cochlear implant will work for me?
A: Cochlear hearing implant technology is very reliable. In fact, it has been around for over 30 years and has helped change the lives of over 450,000 people worldwide.

Q: Is it major surgery?
A: No, not at all. In fact, the procedure is often done on an outpatient basis and typically takes just a couple hours.

Q: Am I too old to get a cochlear implant?
A: No, it's never too late to regain access to the sounds you're missing.

Call **800 805 3530** to find a Hearing Implant Specialist near you.

Visit **Cochlear.com/US/Almanac** for a free guide about cochlear implants.

Cochlear®

PLATE YOUR PETALS

Edible flowers are blossoming into an old-is-new-again culinary trend.

BY JODI HELMER

In garden beds and window boxes, the colorful blossoms of begonias, calendula, nasturtiums, and roses can be dazzling. Did you know that they are also delicious?

Edible flowers have figured in ancient culinary traditions for centuries. Over time, the practice of and interest in using flowers as food fell out of favor. *(continued)*

Photo: Iryna Melnyk/Getty Images

EDIBLE FLOWERS LOOK GREAT BOTH ON THE PLATE AND IN THE GARDEN.

Apple blossoms

Rosalind Creasy, author of *The Edible Flower Garden,* attributes the shift to a misguided (but prevalent) belief that flowers are so beautiful that "only the eyes should feast on them."

Today, the other "ayes" have it: Edible flowers look great both on the plate and in the

Calendula

garden. As you plan your vegetable plots and ornamental beds, add a few of these flowering plants—and double your pleasure.

APPLE BLOSSOMS (*Malus* spp.): Pick from apple trees in late spring; trimming out some flowers helps to maximize fruit

production. Use the petals for a mild apple flavor at mealtime: Sprinkle a few in a Waldorf salad or greens dressed with apple cider vinegar. Steep petals in cream to pour on apple pie, crepes, or pastries. (Use in moderation; low levels of cyanide are present in apple wood, bark, and seeds.)

CALENDULA/POT MARIGOLDS *(Calendula officinalis):* These cool-season annuals produce bright orange or yellow flowers. Used in ancient Rome as an inexpensive substitute for saffron, the petals of varieties such as 'Fiesta' and 'Radio' have a tangy taste. Cut the

Daylilies

petals off the flower and dry them in a warm (100°F) oven. Sprinkle the crushed petals on cheese dishes, omelets, and rice.

Carnations

HANDLE WITH CARE
- Harvest flowers in the morning. Flower petal oils are strongest in cooler temperatures.
- Remove stamens, pistils, and leaflike sepals at the base of blossoms.
- Use and consume flowers on the day of harvest.
- Avoid flowers from plants, gardens, landscapes, roadsides, and florist shops that have been treated with chemicals, pesticides, or other hazardous material.

CARNATIONS (*Dianthus* spp.): The clove-flavor petals of the 300-plus varieties of annual, biennial, and perennial carnations are edible (be sure to remove the bitter white base). Add to cake mixes, candies (especially chocolate), and teas. Sprinkle minced fresh petals over a bowl of berries.

CHRYSANTHEMUMS (*Chrysanthemum* x *morifolium, Dendranthema* x *grandiflora*): Piquant-flavor "mums" make a colorful herb in chowders and egg dishes. Dry the petals in a warm oven (100°F) for several hours until they are crunchy but still colorful.

DAYLILIES (*Hemerocallis* spp.): Use only the *Hemerocallis* genus. Some other lilies contain poisonous alkaloids. Harvest blossoms on the day after they bloom. (Taste as you pick: Pale petals

FOR A LEMONY FLAVOR, HARVEST LILAC FLOWERS JUST AFTER THEY OPEN.

Lilacs

Impatiens

Gladiolus

tend to be sweeter, while darker petals tend to have stronger flavor.) Remove petals from the flower base. Add to salads or stir-fried dishes moments before serving. Dried petals are used in Chinese Sweet and Sour Soup. In the spring, gather 2- to 3-inch-tall shoots to try in pesto.

IMPATIENS *(Impatiens walleriana):* Use the sweet-tasting blossoms of this annual as garnish on plates or in beverages and salads.

GLADIOLUS *(Gladiolus* spp.): Glads taste vaguely like lettuce. Remove the flowers' pistils and stamens and toss a few whole blossoms into green salads for a dash of color. Or, use to hold dip (see "Tulips").

LILACS *(Syringa vulgaris):* For a distinct lemony flavor, harvest these spring flowers immediately after they open. Candied lilac

Photos, from top: Vlad_Losh/Getty Images; itasun/Getty Images; prill/Getty Images

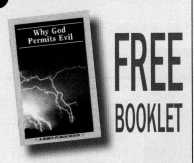

NASTURTIUMS LOOK LOVELY FLOATING IN A BOWL OF PUNCH.

flowerets make charming cake decorations. Separate individual flowers and use tweezers to dip each one into a beaten egg white, reconstituted egg white powder, or packaged egg whites. Then dip each flower into finely granulated sugar and set it aside to dry before placing on a cake.

NASTURTIUMS *(Tropaeolum majus):* This plant is a member of the Brassica family, and dozens of varieties can be grown from seed. Try 'Empress of India' for its deep red-orange flowers and dark blue-green leaves, which impart a peppery or sweet mustard flavor to salad

Nasturtiums

dressings or vinegars and look lovely floating in a tureen of soup or bowl of punch. Be sure to remove the spur

behind the bloom as it may shelter insects.

ROSES (*Rosa* spp.): Roses are famously edible flowers. Note that lighter flowers have a mild flavor; the darker a rose's color, the more likely that it will have a strong metallic taste. Remove the white base.

THYME (*Thymus* spp.): The tiny pink or lavender flowers on this Mediterranean herb are often overlooked in favor of its aromatic leaves. The lavender flowers of French thyme (*T. vulgaris)* embody the earthiness of the herb (sprinkle them on top of baked mushroom caps), while the pink flowers on lemon thyme

Roses

Oleander

LOVELY TO LOOK UPON, FATAL AS FOOD

Caladium (*Caladium bicolor*), clematis, foxglove (*Digitalis purpurea*), oleander (*Nerium oleander*), sweet pea (*Lathyrus odoratus*), and larkspur (*Delphinium*) are poisonous. To be safe, before planning to eat flowers, identify the plant—using its Latin name—and research it to make sure that it is safe for consumption.

(*T. citriodorus*) add a citrusy zing.

TUBEROUS BEGONIAS (*Begonia* x *tuberhybrida*): Brilliant orange, white, pink, red, and yellow tuberous begonia flowers bring light lemon flavor to salads and tea sandwiches. (Avoid if you have kidney stones, gout, or rheumatism: The flowers contain oxalic acid.)

TULIPS (*Tulipa* spp.): Spring's darlings taste a little like fresh baby peas and make a stunning presentation: Remove the pistils and stamens and fill the empty cups with luncheon salad or dip.

ZUCCHINI (*Cucurbita pepo* var. *cylindrica*): This vegetable's yellow blossoms, when stuffed with cheese, bacon, and mushrooms, make for flavorful and fun appetizers. The flowers have a mild squash flavor that also pairs well with salads and omelets. (If a squash harvest is desired, harvest only male flowers to eat.) ■

Jodi Helmer is a North Carolina–based garden writer.

Tulips

The ABCs of Pickling

ASPARAGUS, BEETS, CORN–AND CUKES!

by Mare-Anne Jarvela

Pickling is an age-old method of preserving food, sure, but it's also a technique to alter the flavor of familiar vegetables and fruit with herbs and spices and enjoy them in new and delicious ways. Conveniently, these A–B–C vegetables are harvested at different times, so pick a peck and pickle!

BEFORE YOU BEGIN . . .

Wash and sterilize all jars and lids: Set the empty jars right-side up on the rack in a boiling-water canner. Fill the canner and jars with hot water to 1 inch above the tops of the jars. Bring the water to a boil for 15 minutes. Sterilize the lids by boiling in water for 5 minutes.

(continued)

Photo: Oksana Slepko/Shutterstock

FOR PERFECT PICKLES

- Use the most uniform and unspoiled produce.
- Pickle fresh produce as soon as possible after it is harvested.
- Use pickling salt. Iodized salt makes the brine cloudy and may change the color and texture of the produce.
- Use distilled white or cider vinegar with 5 percent acidity. Use distilled white vinegar when a light color is desirable.
- For best flavor and nutritional value, eat processed pickled produce within a year, unless otherwise directed.
- Glass canning jars can be reused and will last many years if washed and stored properly.
- Never reuse canning jar lids. After the first use, a lid will no longer seal effectively.

THE ACID INFLUENCE

Pickles are made by immersing fresh vegetables and fruit into an acidic liquid—for example, vinegar. Vinegar keeps pickles crisp and prevents the growth of unwanted bacteria. Unprocessed pickles made with vinegar can be refrigerated and should be eaten within a couple of weeks.

For longer storage, process jars in a boiling-water bath. Start by placing sterilized, filled, and sealed jars into the canner. Cover with boiling water and follow instructions in the recipe for how long to process the jars in the boiling water. This method is used for "high acid" foods. Vinegar makes pickled foods "high acid."

Pressure canning, during which trapped steam increases the pressure and temperature inside the canner, is the safe way to preserve "low-acid" foods. You do not need to pressure-can pickles. ■

Mare-Anne Jarvela's favorite pickles are crunchy cucumber pickles made from her garden's bounty in Munsonville, New Hampshire.

PLEASE TURN TO PAGE 200 FOR PICKLING RECIPES.

2018 ORANGE RECIPE CONTEST WINNERS

Many thanks to the hundreds of you who submitted recipes!

PHOTOS BY LORI PEDRICK · STYLING BY CATRINE KELLY

FIRST PRIZE: $300

CRAN-ORANGE COUSCOUS SALAD

SALAD:
3 cups pearl couscous, cooked
   according to package directions
1 cup goat cheese
¾ cup dried cranberries
½ cup chopped pecans
2 cans (15.5 ounces each) chickpeas,
   drained and rinsed
5 basil leaves, chopped
2 large oranges, peeled and chopped
1 small red onion, chopped

VINAIGRETTE:
½ cup olive oil
¼ cup balsamic vinegar
4 tablespoons orange juice
1 tablespoon orange zest
2 teaspoons honey
salt and freshly ground black pepper,
   to taste

1. *For salad:* Place couscous in a bowl. Add goat cheese, cranberries, pecans, chickpeas, basil, oranges, and onions. Mix well.

2. *For vinaigrette:* In a small bowl, whisk together oil, vinegar, orange juice, orange zest, honey, and salt and pepper.

3. Pour vinaigrette over salad and stir to coat.

Makes 8 servings.

–Kristen Heigl, Staten Island, New York

(continued)

ENTER THE 2019 RECIPE CONTEST: PASTA

Got a great recipe using pasta that's loved by family and friends? It could win! See contest rules on page 251.

SECOND PRIZE: $200

SPICED ORANGE SALMON WITH CARAMEL EDAMAME CORN SAUCE

2 navel oranges

1 tablespoon soy sauce

1 tablespoon mirin

1 tablespoon white wine

½ teaspoon ground cumin

¼ teaspoon garlic powder

⅛ teaspoon ground thyme

2 fresh salmon fillets (4 ounces each)

salt and freshly ground black pepper, to taste

1 tablespoon olive oil

1 tablespoon brown sugar

½ cup frozen shelled edamame, thawed

3 tablespoons frozen corn, thawed

1 scallion, thinly sliced, for garnish

1. Remove zest and juice from oranges (measure out ½ cup of orange juice). Set zest aside for garnish.

2. In a zip-top bag, combine orange juice, soy sauce, mirin, wine, cumin, garlic powder, and thyme.

3. Pat salmon dry with paper towels and season with salt and pepper. Put salmon into marinade bag and place in refrigerator for 30 minutes.

4. About 10 minutes before cook time, remove bag from refrigerator.

5. In a cast iron skillet, heat oil over medium-high. Remove salmon from bag and reserve marinade. Put salmon, skin side down, into skillet. Cook until skins are crisp and brown, about 3 minutes. Flip salmon, reduce heat to medium, and cook until flesh is firm and flakes easily, about 4 minutes.

6. In a separate skillet over medium heat, combine brown sugar and 1 teaspoon of water. After 1 minute, add reserved marinade. Reduce heat to medium-low and add edamame and corn. Cook, stirring occasionally, until slightly thickened, about 5 minutes. Season with salt and pepper.

7. To serve, spread edamame and corn on two plates. Place salmon on top and sprinkle with orange zest and scallions.

Makes 2 servings.

–Hidemi Walsh, Greenfield, Indiana

(continued)

THIRD PRIZE: $100

ORANGE AND BACON BRUSSELS SPROUTS

6 tablespoons extra-virgin olive oil, divided

2 small oranges, cut in half, then into ½-inch slices

kosher salt, to taste

3 or 4 strips thick-cut bacon, cut into ¼-inch pieces

1½ pounds brussels sprouts, trimmed and halved

1. Preheat oven to 425°F. Brush a rimmed baking sheet with 1 tablespoon of oil.

2. Place oranges in a single layer on prepared baking sheet, turning to coat. Season with salt and drizzle with 1 tablespoon of oil. Roast for 15 minutes, remove from oven, and stir in bacon. Roast until crisp, about 12 minutes.

3. Toss brussels sprouts with remaining 4 tablespoons of oil and season with salt. Add to baking sheet and toss to combine. Roast, stirring once, for 20 to 25 minutes, or until sprouts are tender and browning at edges and oranges are caramelized.

Makes 6 servings.

–Jennifer Miessau, East Haven, Connecticut

HONORABLE MENTION

ORANGE-GLAZED GRILLED CHICKEN WITH CHUNKY ORANGE SALSA

1 cup orange juice

½ cup light brown sugar

2 tablespoons Worcestershire sauce

1 container (6 ounces) orange cream yogurt

4 cooked chicken breast halves

2 cups cooked brown rice

1 lime, quartered, for garnish

1. In a skillet over medium heat, combine orange juice, brown sugar, Worcestershire sauce, and yogurt. Whisk together until smooth and creamy.

2. Place chicken in orange sauce and reduce heat to low. Simmer, turning chicken occasionally until warmed and coated with sauce. Remove chicken from skillet and let sauce continue to simmer until thick.

3. To serve, place a piece of chicken on a bed of brown rice, pour orange sauce over chicken, and top with salsa. Garnish with a slice of lime.

For Chunky Orange Salsa recipe, please turn to page 201.

DUCK STAMP
DYNASTY

by Benjamin Kilbride

This 2017 entry by wildlife
artist Bob Hautman was his third
federal duck stamp win.

Eighty-five years ago, the first federal duck stamp was issued, beginning an era of conservation, collaboration, and—in at least one family—fraternal competition.

Every migratory waterfowl hunter age 16 and older in the United States must purchase a $25, 1¾×1½-inch duck stamp to be properly licensed. The stamp also serves as a free admission pass to National Wildlife Refuges. Over 1 million stamps are sold every year, most of them slipped into waterproof bags and unceremoniously shoved into pockets and glove compartments. However, a rising number of stamps are purchased by nonhunters who stick them on cars and laptops; some even frame them.

Why do people buy these stamps if they don't hunt? It's for the birds, of course.

In 1934, during the Great Depression, conservationists and naturalists became concerned about the increasing destruction of wetlands vital to the survival of waterfowl. At the considerable encouragement of Jay "Ding" Darling, a cartoonist, artist, and conservationist, Congress passed and President Franklin D. Roosevelt signed the Migratory Bird Hunting Stamp Act, aka the "Duck Stamp Act."

This act made the possession of a stamp mandatory for hunters of migratory waterfowl and created a fund for the proceeds of those stamps. Ninety-eight cents of every dollar raised from the sale of duck stamps is used to purchase and conserve waterfowl habitat. The program has raised over $800 million and protected over 6.5 million acres of wetlands since the passing of the Duck Stamp Act.

Today's duck stamp program has a component that Darling and

Stamp © U.S. Fish and Wildlife Service

Roosevelt may not have envisioned: It has become an art competition. Until 1949, the image was drawn or painted by an artist chosen by the U.S. Department of the Interior. Today, a panel of judges chooses the winning design.

The duck stamp program remains the only federally funded art contest still in existence. The competition has captured the attention of collectors far and wide, made and broken friendships, and spawned family legacies.

Unlike some art competitions, the duck stamp contest offers no cash prize. Instead, the winning artist receives publicity, recognition by the media, and fame in the wildlife and conservation community.

The artist can also sell reproductions of the winning image and other work with the prestigious title "by the Federal Duck Stamp artist." For example, Jim Hautman sells prints of his 2017 winning image for from $189 (10,500 printed) to $1,295 each (300 printed). There is a huge market for art from the stamp contest among supporters of national parks and wildlife refuges, the National Audubon Society, and stamp collectors, so there is a good chance that fortune will follow in the wake of fame.

Over a 50-year span, renowned stamp collector Jeanette Cantrell Rudy assembled the world's largest collection of federal duck stamps, which includes rare misprints and early

One day prior to the competition, the judges review all entries (above). The actual judging consists of three rounds, the first being a simple "In" or "Out" vote (below), while the last two rounds are judged numerically.

Thanks to BetterWOMAN, I'm winning the battle for
Bladder Control.

All Natural
Clinically-Tested
Herbal Supplement

- Reduces Bladder Leaks
- Reduces Bathroom Trips
- Sleep Better All Night
- Safe and Effective – No Known Side Effects
- Costs Less than Traditional Bladder Control Options
- **Live Free of Worry, Embarrassment, and Inconvenience**

You don't have to let bladder control problems control you.
Call now!

Frequent nighttime trips to the bathroom, embarrassing leaks and the inconvenience of constantly searching for rest rooms in public – for years, I struggled with bladder control problems. After trying expensive medications with horrible side effects, ineffective exercises and uncomfortable liners and pads, I was ready to resign myself to a life of bladder leaks, isolation and depression. But then I tried **BetterWOMAN**.

When I first saw the ad for BetterWOMAN, I was skeptical. So many products claim they can set you free from leaks, frequency and worry, only to deliver disappointment. When I finally tried BetterWOMAN, I found that it actually works! It changed my life. Even my friends have noticed that I'm a new person. And because it's all natural, I can enjoy the results without the worry of dangerous side effects. Thanks to BetterWOMAN, I finally fought bladder control problems and I won!

Also Available: **BetterMAN**®
The 3-in-1 Formula Every Man Needs –
Better **BLADDER**, Better **PROSTATE**, and Better **STAMINA!**
Order online at **www.BetterMANnow.com**.

Limited Time Offer

Call Now & Ask How To Get A
FREE BONUS BOTTLE
CALL TOLL-FREE 1-888-256-5507
or order online: www.BetterWOMANnow.com

In 1985, Robert Bateman's painting *Mallard Pair–Early Winter* appeared on the WHC Duck Stamp (top left). In 2018, artist Pierre Girard took the top prize with his painting *Autumn Colours–Wood Duck* (bottom left).

sketches. The collection also features the very first duck stamp ever sold, which had originally been bought for $1 by its artist, Ding Darling, who then had co-signed it along with William Mooney, the Washington, D.C., postmaster. Today, that first issue is among the rarest stamps in the series, with an estimated value of $450,000. Rudy's collection is on display at the Smithsonian National Postal Museum in Washington, D.C.

To enter the 2019 duck stamp competition (for the 2020–2021 stamp), you need to be a citizen or resident of the United States and at least 18 years old. Submit your work to the U.S. Fish and Wildlife Service headquarters in Virginia by June 1, 2019. For more information, visit www.fws.gov/birds.

The Canadian Wildlife Habitat Conservation Stamp program is run by Wildlife Habitat Canada [WHC]. While each Migratory Game Bird Hunting Permit must carry a stamp, the stamps and prints are also sold to stamp collectors and wildlife art lovers and for gifts, presentations, and fund-raisers.

Since 1985, $50 million has been generated for habitat conservation and stewardship projects across Canada under WHC's grant program.

From 1985 to 1989, the stamps featured commissioned works from renowned artists such as Robert Bateman. Since 1990, WHC has held an annual competition to depict a chosen bird species. The 2018 winner was Pierre Girard's *Autumn Colours-Wood Duck*. WHC's choice for the 2019 stamp is the canvasback *(Aythya valisineria)*. These beautiful artworks are available at whc.org.

(continued)

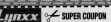

A Family With Its Ducks in a Row

One family in particular has risen to prominence in the duck stamp community—the Hautman brothers. As of 2017, Jim, Joe, and Bob Hautman of Minnesota had won a combined 13 duck stamp contests since 1990, including the last three in a row. In 2015, Joe's migrating trumpeter swans painting (top right) was his fifth win; in 2016, Jim's Canada geese in flight entry (right) was also his fifth win; and in 2017, Bob's pair of mallard ducks artwork (pages 62–63) was his third win. ∎

Benjamin Kilbride is an editorial assistant at *The Old Farmer's Almanac.*

From left, brothers Jim, Joe, and Bob Hautman dominate the federal competition.

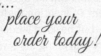

BY STACEY KUSTERBECK

FARMER

Farmers share their stories, inspirations, and dreams in an occasional series featuring folks who grow our food.

BRYAN HARPER, HARPER FARMS
JUNCTION CITY, OREGON

In 2016, when a decision had to be made about Harper Farms, Bryan Harper saw it as his chance: "There was nobody else to take over. If I didn't do it, then we were going to sell out."

Born in Kenya, Harper moved to the United States as a child and grew up on the farm, hoeing and pulling weeds. Encouraged by his father to pursue a more profitable career, he went to aviation flight school and graduated from the University of Oregon—but he soon landed back at the farm. "I fell in love with living in the country and being my own boss," says the now fifth-generation family farm manager.

He converted the farm from diversified crops to a single one: hazelnuts. "It's one of the more versatile tree nuts on the market," Harper notes, "because you can eat it raw, roast it, cream it, butter it. You can even put it in a confectionary product."

Gradually, he is replacing the orchard's older, established trees with newer, ready-to-eat kernel varieties that don't require cracking—"a superior nut to what we produced a few generations ago."

Still, Harper knows that his plan has inherent risks: "There's always the threat of losing everything if the market were to fall out." To increase his crop's security, he is moving from raw production (with outsourced cleaning, dividing, processing, and packaging) to vertical integration and higher returns. "Farmers are typically price takers. I want to move to price making," he adds. "I want to bring the farm into the 21st century." *(continued)*

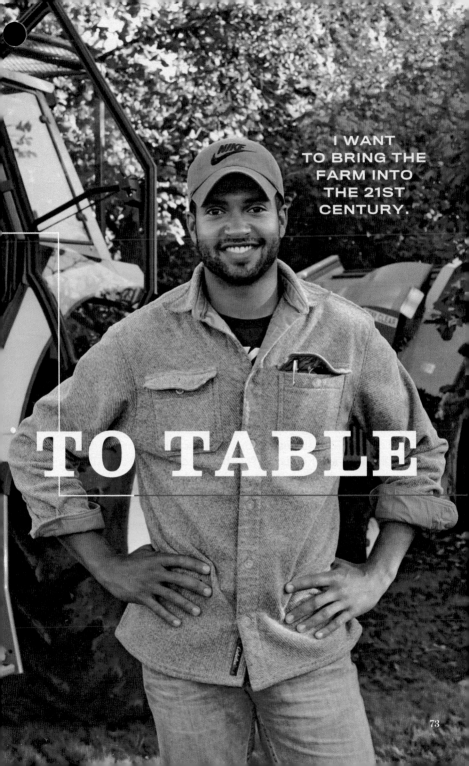

I WANT
TO BRING THE
FARM INTO
THE 21ST
CENTURY.

TO TABLE

BUYING USED EQUIPMENT HAS BEEN A KEY TO OUR SURVIVAL.

ANA AND GREG KELLY, DAYSPRING DAIRY
GALLANT, ALABAMA

Cow milk, goat milk, or sheep milk? This was the question for Ana and Greg Kelly, who felt a calling to become cheese makers. After visiting a sheep dairy in Tennessee, they got the answer. "As we researched all of the different types of cheeses that we could make with sheep milk, we were more intrigued," says Ana.

In 2011, they purchased a 30-acre property in northeast Alabama and sold their home near Birmingham. Ana took cheese-making courses, and Greg attended animal husbandry and sheep-dairying classes.

Their first flock consisted of Gulf Coast sheep accustomed to the hot, humid climate. Soon thereafter, they brought in East Friesian dairy sheep from Oklahoma and Kentucky. They built a barn complex with housing for the animals, a milking parlor, and a cheese plant.

Maintaining off-farm income for the first few years and buying used equipment allowed them to expand incrementally. "That's been the key to our survival," says Ana. In 2013, Dayspring Dairy, with its 25 milking ewes, became Alabama's first licensed sheep dairy. Today, the flock numbers about 160.

Sheep reward keepers with nutritionally rich, sweet milk. The Kellys use it to make eight varieties of cheese, both fresh and aged and all by hand, which they sell wholesale and at local farmers' markets. Specialties include raw-milk Gouda, creamy feta, and grillable Halloumi cheese. Spreadable cheese flavors include lemon fig, basil peppercorn, pimento garlic, and caramel.

New customers are sometimes surprised to learn that sheep can be milked. Many exclaim that they've never had sheep cheese, but Ana disavows them of this notion: "I ask them, 'Have you ever had Roquefort or Romano? How about feta?' They've had it. They just didn't realize that it was sheep cheese." *(continued)*

MARIAH AND GREG ANDERSON, TRIPLE M FARM
CLINTON, ILLINOIS

I n 2009, Mariah and Greg Anderson noticed the local food movement taking off—but not near them. "Greg saw a need for a grower in our area," says Mariah. "No one else was doing it."

Getting into farming was exciting but financially risky. "I told him that I'd give it 1 year and then we'd revisit it," she says.

The couple owned 5 acres of land and leased 7 more. They extended the growing season with a high-tunnel greenhouse, started a community-supported agriculture (CSA) operation, and offered their produce at their own farm stand.

Farmer mentors at the University of Illinois Extension Service offered advice and opportunities. For example, the Andersons swapped market produce with a farmer they had met in a neighboring county. He traded water- and muskmelons for their sweet corn, which added variety to both farm stands. The couple also works with a local high school ag program and the FFA chapter to find members who need supervised agriculture education.

Soon, grocery stores became customers in response to their customers' demand for locally grown food. Plus, through a survey of the CSA members, the couple learned that "people wanted more time with us," says Mariah. They made time to talk with customers, many of whom were also gardeners, and they had a Farm to Fork dinner. "Our community wants more things like this," she reports. *(continued)*

GREG SAW
A NEED FOR
A GROWER
IN OUR AREA.

Photo: Mariah's Mums & More/Facebook

YOU'VE GOT
TO THINK
LONG-TERM.

SANTANNA AND RYAN BAY
MOUND, TEXAS

In 2009, Santanna and Ryan Bay bought a run-down pecan orchard in rural Texas. "Neither one of us knew anything about pecans," says Santanna. "We thought, 'Maybe we can make it profitable.'"

In a farming course at Texas A&M, they learned they had made a commitment. "Pecans are not like corn, where you can plant it and it matures in 100 days and you harvest it. You've got to think long-term," notes Ryan.

They set about clearing the overgrown orchard. "We did it every night and weekend," says Santanna. (Both worked full-time at the family business, a feed and supply store.) With the first harvest came a hard lesson: Doing things by hand was impractical. They bought a used harvester and shaker and an old tractor that continually broke down. Then, they learned the value of a cleaning table. "We thought that we'd just dump the pecans in the back of the truck and clean them by hand. But there was no way that you could do it," says Santanna. "Each thing that we had, we thought, 'This is the bees' knees,' and then we'd find out that we needed one more thing."

Or a better thing. They had to replace the used shaker, but the "new" (used) one enabled Ryan to earn money harvesting neighbors' orchards.

The couple now grows, harvests, processes, and shells pecans, selling them both wholesale and direct to consumers. They planted over 300 new disease-resistant trees, but disease is not the only adversary. One squirrel can eat up to 50 pounds of pecans a year, and hungry crows consume even more profits.

Ryan, however, points to the benefits: "It's a multiyear crop. You don't need to do any tillage or anything like that. You don't worry about keeping livestock fenced in. The trees just sit there and grow."

Photos: above, courtesy of Santanna and Ryan Bay; opposite, Mike Hazard/Flickr

PAKOU HANG, HMONG AMERICAN FARMERS ASSOCIATION
VERMILLION TOWNSHIP, MINNESOTA

Growing up, Pakou Hang and her siblings spent long hours working on their family's farm. They did it to survive. Today, Hang and her parents farm 10 acres, growing more than 60 varieties of fruit, vegetables, and flowers. She loves the life.

Farming taught Hang important skills: "It's about not abandoning a job until it's done. And planning. If you miss planting time, you have to wait a whole year."

Her personal success made her determined to improve life for local Hmong farmers who did not have access to affordable land. She thought that they might pool their resources, but she was initially turned down for a loan. "People never thought about a bunch of farmers buying land together," she says.

She persisted and in 2013 started a land cooperative. Today, the Hmong American Farmers Association (HAFA) farm consists of 155 acres, with 24 farmers sharing an irrigation system, a walk-in cooler, a wash station, storage, a packinghouse, and other resources. They practice sustainable agriculture, such as composting, succession planting, installing grass roadways, and laying erosion blankets.

The cooperative provides a livelihood, and it has united generations. "There is a lot of social capital among farming communities, and a certain civic-minded culture is created," observes Hang. "You can not do farming alone."

"I wanted farmers to have access to land," she continues. "But I never thought that I'd be seeing grandchildren look at their grandparents and say, 'I want to be a farmer one day.'" *(continued)*

IT'S ABOUT
NOT ABANDONING
A JOB UNTIL
IT'S DONE.

79

DAVID ARANT JR., DELTA BLUES RICE
RULEVILLE, MISSISSIPPI

In the 1970s, David Arant Jr.'s grandfather bought an antique rice mill machine. For many years, it was used to produce 5-gallon buckets of homegrown rice as holiday gifts for family members.

Arant spent childhood summers working on his uncle's farm. He loved the life but took a job as a civil engineer after college. "I thought that somehow, some way, I'd end up back on the farm," he says.

As the farmers' market movement spread, memories of those early days came back to mind: "I could relate to the farmers who were out there selling. I felt like I had a connection to them."

Arant met many farmers through his role as an engineer. One once observed, "Farming is hard work, but it's one of the best things that I've ever done." This simple remark led Arant to return to the family's 4,000-acre farm to work alongside his uncle and father, thus becoming the fourth generation in his family to do so. (Happily, he applies his civil engineering skills to the farm's technology, such as its irrigation systems.)

In 2014, the family rice gifts inspired the Arants to sell their Delta Blues Rice directly to consumers. They purchased a bigger, more efficient mill and now sell the grain wholesale, too. "We are still growing the business," says Arant. "It gives us a way to really show what the American farmer does." *(continued)*

EVERYONE AGREES: FRESH IS BEST!

THE OLD FARMER'S ALMANAC
FIELD TO FORK

MORE THAN 100 "FRESH INGREDIENT–BASED" SEASONAL RECIPES

$19.95

GO TO ALMANAC.COM/FORK

ANDREW GIBSON, SUNRISE ORGANIC FARM
LOMPOC, CALIFORNIA

For 35 years, Jesus Salas has been a farmer. In 2015, he partnered with his son, Chuy, and Andrew Gibson to establish 70-acre Sunrise Organic Farm. They grow 210 different kinds of produce organically, a crop diversity that has generated a customer base of stores, restaurants, farm stands, juiceries, and pickling companies.

The trio is committed. "It's 7 days a week, 14 hours a day," Gibson says. "We've come across a lot of unexpected challenges." Until recently, they did much of the work by hand. To improve efficiencies, they began automating and mechanizing every process (weeding, planting, irrigating, and picking), buying the equipment at auction and doing repairs and maintenance themselves. "A dollar saved is a dollar earned," observes Gibson. "At this stage, we are not even paying ourselves. It's not a money-motivated quest—we believe in organic farming."

The farmer partners are gratified to have achieved commercial success, but interacting with customers at farmers' markets brings them genuine joy. Locals come hungry for information as well as exotic edibles, and the farmers field myriad questions. Watching people sample their produce makes all of the work worthwhile: "People are so stoked when they taste that cherry tomato or sugar snap pea," says Gibson. "It just blows their mind, because they've never had something that sweet or that fresh." ■

Stacey Kusterbeck compiles our annual Trends section and resides in New York State.

Are you a farmer with a story to share or do you know a farmer whom we should contact? Tell us briefly about yourself or a farmer you know at Almanac .com/Feedback. Include your name and address and the farmer's name and address. We may reach out for a future edition of the Almanac.

IT'S 7 DAYS A WEEK, 14 HOURS A DAY.

FROM LEFT: CHUY SALAS, ANDREW GIBSON, AND JESUS SALAS

ADVENTURES IN THE ZODIAC ZONE

WHAT'S BEHIND THE SUN AND MOON?

BY BOB BERMAN

Throughout millennia, civilizations have paid great attention to the Moon, Sun, and planets, yes, but also to the stars and constellations behind them—in particular, the zodiac. Those background bodies and patterns matter, but in different ways for astronomers and astrologers. Here's how and why.

THE STELLAR ZOO

As Earth performs its yearly orbit, we view the Sun from a slightly different direction each day. As a result, a stream of background stars parades behind the Sun. Ancient astronomers figured out what lurked behind the Sun on each day of the year. They realized that the Sun's annual circuit never varied and called this solar path the *ecliptic,* because whenever eclipses appeared, they occurred along this imaginary line in the sky. The ecliptic passed through, or in front of, 13 constellations, although most ancient civilizations recognized only 12.

Since the Moon orbits Earth in almost the same flat plane in which we circle the Sun, the Moon also roughly travels along this same celestial road (the deviation is a paltry 5 degrees). All of the planets in our solar system

tably Scorpius, Taurus, and Leo—really do resemble these animals. Others, like Aries, the Ram, require a vivid imagination to envisage.

There are 12 traditional members of the zodiac, but the Sun also spends 18 days every year in front of the stars of Ophiuchus (ah-fee-YOU-kuss), sometimes called the 13th zodiacal constellation. Since the Moon and planets have those slight inclinations in their orbits, they occasionally skirt the edges of a few other star patterns like Ce-

---

THERE ARE 12 TRADITIONAL MEMBERS OF THE ZODIAC, BUT THE SUN ALSO SPENDS 18 DAYS EVERY YEAR IN FRONT OF THE STARS OF OPHIUCHUS, SOMETIMES CALLED THE 13TH ZODIACAL CONSTELLATION.

---

also orbit in pretty much the same flat ring, so they, too, appear against these same stars.

Because the orbits of the Moon and planets are slightly tilted, the ancients conceived of an 18-degree-wide ribbon centered on the ecliptic, wide enough to embrace the paths of all of these bodies. They called this roadway across the sky the *zodiac,* derived from the Greek word for "circle of animals," because more than half of the constellations behind the Sun, Moon, and planets were perceived as animals (e.g., Cancer, the Crab; Taurus, the Bull). Some of these figures—notably

tus, the Whale, and Orion, the Hunter. (This Almanac often gives the positions occupied by the Sun, Moon, and planets. See "Visible Planets" on page 108, as well as "Sky Watch" and "Moon's Astron. Place" on the Left-Hand Calendar Pages, 120–146.)

The zodiacal constellations are different sizes. (The exact boundaries between one constellation and another were not precisely defined until 1930.) Some are huge, some small, and each planet traverses the zodiac path at its own speed. Thus, the amount of time that a celestial body spends in each constellation varies. The Sun lingers for 45 days each year in Virgo but spends only 20 days in

THE OLD
FARMER'S STORE

GIFTS FOR ANY OCCASION!

⚜ PURVEYORS OF ⚜

ALMANACS ☼ CALENDARS ☼ COOKBOOKS

KITCHEN APRONS • COUNTER STORAGE SOLUTIONS

OUTDOOR THERMOMETERS	GARDEN STAKES	WIND BELLS AND SPINNERS	RAIN GAUGES	GARDEN SIGNAGE

GLASS SUN CATCHERS • HOME GOODS

DECORATIVE OUTDOOR LIGHTING ☼ DOORMATS

WALL DECORATIONS	HAND SOAP	HARVEST BASKETS	NIGHT LIGHTS	COAT RACKS	BALSAM FIR PILLOWS

RAIN CHAINS • DOORSTOPS • READING MAGNIFIERS

CANDLES ☼ ALPACA SOCKS ☼ AND MORE!

Genuine Old Farmer's Almanac–Branded Merchandise

Exclusive Almanac Publications & Offers

⚜ CONTINUOUS PROPRIETORSHIP SINCE 1792 ⚜

Open Daily | Immense Assortment

WWW.ALMANAC.COM/SHOP • 1-877-717-8924

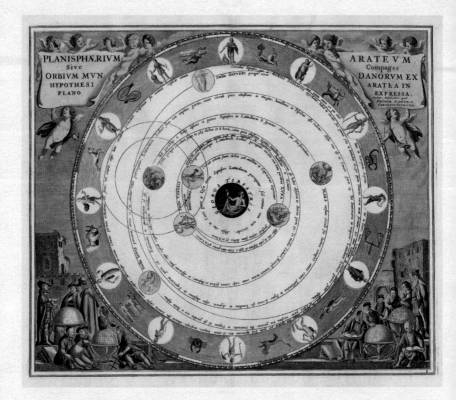

ASTROLOGY'S "SIGNS" EACH OCCUPY 30-DEGREE-WIDE "SLICES" OF SPACE.

Cancer. Mercury changes position rapidly, while Saturn requires almost 30 years to make one full circuit.

THE ASTRONOMER'S VIEW

Today, every serious backyard astronomer can trace out the zodiac, the imaginary ribbon that circles the sky. Watching the sky nightly, modern astronomers can see that the Moon moves rapidly along this path, one Moon diameter per hour. (Remember, the Moon completes a full circuit in just a month.)

On many nights, observers see the zodiac aglow, with the Moon lurking in one part of the sky and planets lighting up other parts. This year, for example, on July 4, we should easily observe the Moon, Mars, and Mercury gathered together in Cancer, Jupiter against the stars of Ophiuchus, and Saturn in Sagittarius.

(continued)

WEEKENDS
WITH YANKEE

EXPLORE THE BEST OF
NEW ENGLAND TRAVEL,
FOOD, AND LIFESTYLE

Airing on public television
stations across the
country and online at
WeekendsWithYankee.com

BROUGHT TO YOU BY:

WGBH · YANKEE · American Public Television

FUNDED BY:

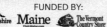
New Hampshire LIVE FREE · Maine VisitMaine.com · The Vermont Country Store · AMERICAN CRUISE LINES

THE ASTROLOGER'S VIEW

Astrologers, too, use the terms "zodiac," "ecliptic," "retrograde motion," and all of the constellation names, except for Scorpius, which astrologers call Scorpio.

Astrologers in India follow the actual constellations of the night sky, but European and American astrology instead uses imaginary signs that do not correspond with the visible star patterns. Moreover, astrology's "signs" each occupy 30-degree-wide overhead on that day are said to lie on the Tropic of Cancer. A few thousand years ago, the actual constellations and the astrological signs more or less coincided, although never exactly. Today, due to Earth's axis having a 26,000-year-long wobble, the star pattern behind the Sun on the solstice is at the Gemini–Taurus boundary. It is nowhere near Cancer.

So it is that the Moon's Place given in the Almanac's Left-Hand Calendar Pages (120–146) does not coincide with

RETROGRADE REVISITED

The Sun and planets move rather slowly against the background stars. A totally separate and much faster sky-motion is the daily whooshing of stars and planets alike, as they rise, cross the sky toward the west, and then set—the effect of being viewed from rapidly spinning (rotating) Earth.

Because everything in the solar system orbits in the same direction, the Sun, Moon, and planets are all usually observed to move east- ward along the zodiac. The only exceptions are when the speedy innermost planets Mercury and Venus are on the side of their orbits nearest to Earth; they then appear to move backward—in what is called "retrograde motion"—for a short time. (Think of a truck seemingly moving backward as we pass it on the highway.) Similarly, whenever Earth passes the slower outer planets, they too temporarily appear to travel in retrograde.

"slices" of space, whereas, as noted, the actual star patterns' sizes vary greatly. Thus, any night's *astrological* location of Jupiter will not match Jupiter's actual *(astronomical)* location in the night sky—the area at which you might aim a telescope.

Consider this: On June 21, the day of the summer solstice, astrology places the Sun in the zodiac sign of Cancer, which explains why all places on Earth where the Sun is directly its place in the "Secrets of the Zodiac" pages (224–225). The Calendar Pages are astronomical; the "Secrets of the Zodiac" are astrological. This seeming discrepancy is never a mistake. It's the ancient legacy of very different ways of perceiving the heavens. ∎

Bob Berman, the *Old Farmer's Almanac* astronomy editor, is the director of Overlook Observatory in Woodstock and Storm King Observatory in Cornwall, both in New York.

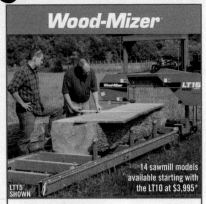

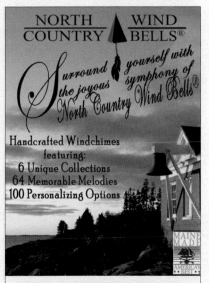

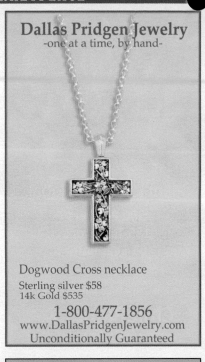
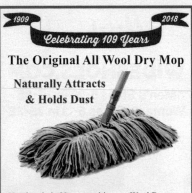
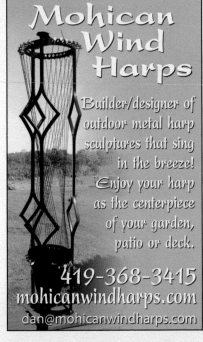

WINTER 2018–19

Mild, snowy

Warm, dry

Warm, dry

Warm, wet

Warm, wet

Cold, wet

Normal temps, snowy

Mild, snowy

Warm, dry

Mild, snowy

Warm, wet

Warm, wet

Warm, dry

Cold, wet

Warm, dry

Mild, normal precip

Cold, dry

Cold, snowy

Warm, dry

Warm, wet

Warm, dry

Warm, dry

Warm, wet

These weather maps correspond to the winter (November through March) and summer (June through August) predictions in the General Weather Forecast (opposite). Forecast terms here represent deviations from the normals; learn more on page 202.

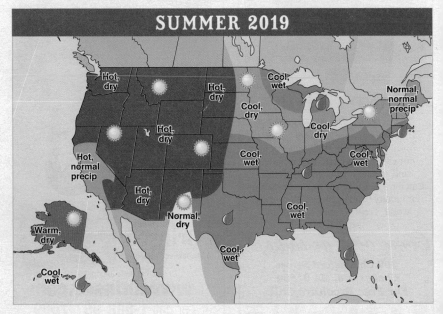

SUMMER 2019

Hot, dry

Hot, dry

Cool, wet

Normal, normal precip

Cool, dry

Hot, dry

Cool, dry

Hot, normal precip

Cool, wet

Cool, wet

Hot, dry

Cool, wet

Warm, dry

Normal, dry

Cool, wet

Cool, wet

THE GENERAL WEATHER REPORT AND FORECAST

FOR REGIONAL FORECASTS, SEE PAGES 206-223.

What's shaping the weather? Solar Cycle 24, the smallest in more than 100 years, is well into its declining phase after reaching double peaks in late 2011 and early 2014. As solar activity continues to decline from these low peaks toward the minima in 2019, we expect temperatures during the winter of 2018–19 to be milder than normal in most of the nation, with only the Southwest being colder than normal. Snowfall will be below normal in most places that usually receive snow, with only the interior West and a small area near the nation's midsection experiencing above-normal snowfall.

With last winter's weak La Niña most likely to be replaced by a weak El Niño this winter, cold air masses will have difficulty making any prolonged inroads into the northern Plains, the Great Lakes, or northeastern states. Other important factors in the coming weather pattern include the Atlantic Multidecadal Oscillation (AMO) in a continued warm phase, the North Atlantic Oscillation (NAO) in a neutral phase, and the Pacific Decadal Oscillation (PDO) in the early stages of its warm cycle. Oscillations are linked ocean–atmosphere patterns that influence the weather over periods of weeks to years.

WINTER temperatures will be colder than normal in the southwestern part of the nation, but above-normal temperatures will be the rule elsewhere. Precipitation will be above normal in most of the country, although the Southeast, southern California, the nation's midsection, and parts of Alaska and Hawaii will have below-normal precipitation. Snowfall will be greater than normal in most of the Intermountain region, parts of the Southwest, and the nation's midsection, but below normal in most other areas that receive snow.

SPRING will be cooler than normal in the Northeast, Appalachians, Upper Midwest, Pacific Southwest, and northern Intermountain region and warmer than normal elsewhere. Precipitation will be below normal in the Atlantic Corridor, Appalachians, Intermountain region, Desert Southwest, Pacific Northwest, Pacific Southwest, and western Hawaii and above normal elsewhere.

SUMMER temperatures will be below normal, on average, in most of the eastern half of the nation and state of Hawaii and hotter than normal in the West. Rainfall will be above normal from Texas northward to Kansas and eastward to the Atlantic Ocean, in the northern Great Lakes area, and along the spine of the Appalachians and near or below normal elsewhere.

The best chance for a major **HURRICANE** strike is in early September in Louisiana or eastern Texas. Watch for threats of tropical storms or hurricanes in Florida in June, September, and early October and of tropical storms in Texas in August.

AUTUMN temperatures will be cooler than normal in the Northeast, Deep South, Texas–Oklahoma, New Mexico, parts of southern California, northern Alaska, and western Hawaii and near or above normal elsewhere. Precipitation will be above normal in the Upper Midwest, Texas–Oklahoma, the Desert Southwest, Pacific Southwest, and Hawaii and near or above normal elsewhere.

TO LEARN HOW WE MAKE OUR WEATHER PREDICTIONS, TURN TO PAGE 202;
TO GET A SUMMARY OF THE RESULTS OF OUR FORECAST FOR LAST WINTER, TURN TO PAGE 204.

WEATHER

THE OLD
FARMER'S ALMANAC

Established in 1792 and published every year thereafter
ROBERT B. THOMAS, *founder* (1766–1846)

YANKEE PUBLISHING INC.

EDITORIAL AND PUBLISHING OFFICES
P.O. Box 520, 1121 Main Street, Dublin, NH 03444
Phone: 603-563-8111 • Fax: 603-563-8252

EDITOR *(13th since 1792)*: Janice Stillman
ART DIRECTOR: Colleen Quinnell
MANAGING EDITOR: Jack Burnett
SENIOR EDITORS: Sarah Perreault, Heidi Stonehill
EDITORIAL ASSISTANTS: Tim Clark,
Benjamin Kilbride
WEATHER GRAPHICS AND CONSULTATION:
AccuWeather, Inc.

V.P., NEW MEDIA AND PRODUCTION:
Paul Belliveau
PRODUCTION DIRECTORS:
Susan Gross, David Ziarnowski
SENIOR PRODUCTION ARTISTS:
Rachel Kipka, Jennifer Freeman, Janet Selle

WEB SITE: ALMANAC.COM
DIGITAL EDITOR: Catherine Boeckmann
DIGITAL ASSISTANT EDITOR: Christopher Burnett
NEW MEDIA DESIGNERS: Lou S. Eastman, Amy O'Brien
E-COMMERCE DIRECTOR: Alan Henning
PROGRAMMING: Peter Rukavina

CONTACT US

We welcome your questions and comments about articles in and topics for this Almanac. Mail all editorial correspondence to Editor, The Old Farmer's Almanac, P.O. Box 520, Dublin, NH 03444-0520; fax us at 603-563-8252; or contact us through Almanac.com/Feedback. *The Old Farmer's Almanac* can not accept responsibility for unsolicited manuscripts and will not acknowledge any hard-copy queries or manuscripts that do not include a stamped and addressed return envelope.

Thank you for buying this Almanac! We hope that you find it "useful, with a pleasant degree of humor." Thanks, too, to everyone who had a hand in it, including advertisers, distributors, printers, and sales and delivery people.

OUR CONTRIBUTORS

Bob Berman, our astronomy editor, is the director of Overlook Observatory in Woodstock and Storm King Observatory in Cornwall, both in New York. In 1976, he founded the Catskill Astronomical Society. Bob has led many aurora and eclipse expeditions, venturing as far as the Arctic and Antarctic.

Julia Shipley, a journalist and poet, wrote the Farmer's Calendar essays that appear in this edition. She raises animals and vegetables on a small farm in Northern Vermont. Her recordings of the essays are available free at Almanac.com/Podcast.

Tim Clark, a retired English teacher from New Hampshire, has composed the weather doggerel on the Calendar Pages since 1980.

Bethany E. Cobb, our astronomer, is an Associate Professor of Honors and Physics at George Washington University. She conducts research on gamma-ray bursts and specializes in teaching astronomy and physics to non–science majoring students. When she is not scanning the sky, she enjoys rock climbing, figure skating, and reading science fiction.

Celeste Longacre, our astrologer, often refers to astrology as "a study of timing, and timing is everything." A New Hampshire native, she has been a practicing astrologer for more than 25 years. Her book, *Celeste's Garden Delights* (2015), is available for sale on her Web site, www .celestelongacre.com.

Michael Steinberg, our meteorologist, has been forecasting weather for the Almanac since 1996. In addition to college degrees in atmospheric science and meteorology, he brings a lifetime of experience to the task: He began predicting weather when he attended the only high school in the world with weather Teletypes and radar.

THE OLD
FARMER'S ALMANAC

Established in 1792 and published every year thereafter
Robert B. Thomas, *founder* (1766–1846)

YANKEE PUBLISHING INC.
P.O. Box 520, 1121 Main Street, Dublin, NH 03444
Phone: 603-563-8111 • Fax: 603-563-8252

PUBLISHER *(23rd since 1792):* Sherin Pierce
EDITOR IN CHIEF: Judson D. Hale Sr.

YANKEE PUBLISHING INCORPORATED
Jamie Trowbridge, *President;* Judson D. Hale Sr., *Senior Vice President;* Paul Belliveau, Jody Bugbee, Judson D. Hale Jr., Brook Holmberg, Sherin Pierce, *Vice Presidents.*

Leading Acid Reflux Pill Becomes an Anti-Aging Phenomenon

Clinical studies show breakthrough acid reflux treatment also helps maintain vital health and helps protect users from the serious conditions that accompany aging such as fatigue and poor cardiovascular health

"ACCIDENTAL" ANTI-AGING BREAKTHROUGH: Originally developed for digestive issues, AloeCure not only ends digestion nightmares... it revitalizes the entire body. Some are calling it the greatest accidental discovery in decades.

Stewart Blum
Health Correspondence

Seattle, WA – A clinical study on a leading acid reflux pill shows that its key ingredient relieves digestive symptoms while suppressing the inflammation that contributes to premature aging in men and women.

And, if consumer sales are any indication of a product's effectiveness, this 'acid reflux pill turned anti-aging phenomenon' is nothing short of a miracle.

Sold under the brand name AloeCure, it was already backed by clinical data documenting its ability to provide all day and night relief from heartburn, acid reflux, constipation, irritable bowel, gas, bloating, and more.

But soon doctors started reporting some incredible results...

"With AloeCure, my patients started reporting less joint pain, more energy, better sleep, and even less stress and better skin, hair, and nails" explains Dr. Liza Leal; a leading integrative health specialist and company spokesperson.

AloeCure contains an active ingredient that helps improve digestion by acting as a natural acid-buffer that improves the pH balance of your stomach.

Scientists now believe that this acid imbalance is what contributes to painful inflammation throughout the rest of the body.

The daily allowance of AloeCure has shown to calm this inflammation which is why AloeCure is so effective.

Relieving other stressful symptoms related to GI health like pain, bloating, fatigue, cramping, constipation, diarrhea, heartburn, and nausea.

Now, backed with new clinical studies, AloeCure is being recommended by doctors everywhere to help improve digestion, calm painful inflammation, soothe joint pain, and even reduce the appearance of wrinkles – helping patients to look and feel decades younger.

FIX YOUR GUT & FIGHT INFLAMMATION

Since hitting the market, sales for AloeCure have taken off and there are some very good reasons why.

To start, the clinical studies have been impressive. Participants taking the active ingredient in AloeCure saw a stunning 100% improvement in digestive symptoms, which includes fast and lasting relief from reflux.

Users also experienced higher energy levels and endurance, relief from chronic discomfort and better sleep. Some even reported healthier looking skin, hair, and nails.

Doctors are calling AloeCure the greatest accidental health discovery in decades!

EXCITING RESULTS FROM PATIENTS

To date over 5 million bottles of AloeCure have been sold, and the community seeking non-pharma therapy for their GI health continues to grow.

According to Dr. Leal, her patients are absolutely thrilled with their results and are often shocked by how fast it works.

"For the first time in years, they are free from concerns about their digestion and almost every other aspect of their health," says Dr. Leal, "and I recommend it to everyone who wants to improve GI health

without resorting to drugs, surgery, or OTC medications."

With so much positive feedback, it's easy to see why the community of believers is growing and sales for the new pill are soaring.

THE SCIENCE BEHIND ALOECURE

AloeCure is a pill that's taken just once daily. The pill is small. Easy to swallow. There are no harmful side effects and it does not require a prescription.

The active ingredient is a rare Aloe Vera component known as acemannan.

Made from of 100% organic Aloe Vera, AloeCure uses a proprietary process that results in the highest quality, most bioavailable levels of acemannan known to exist.

According to Dr. Leal and several of her colleagues, improving the pH balance of your stomach and restoring gut health is the key to revitalizing your entire body.

When your digestive system isn't healthy, it causes unwanted stress on your immune system, which results in inflammation in the rest of the body.

The recommended daily allowance of acemannan in AloeCure has been proven to support digestive health, and calm painful inflammation without side effects or drugs.

This would explain why so many users are experiencing impressive results so quickly.

HOW TO GET ALOECURE

In order to get the word out about AloeCure, the company is offering special introductory discounts to all who call. Discounts will automatically be applied to all callers, but don't wait. This offer may not last forever. Call toll-free: 1-800-547-0173

ECLIPSES

There will be five eclipses in 2019, three of the Sun and two of the Moon. Solar eclipses are visible only in certain areas and require eye protection to be viewed safely. Lunar eclipses are technically visible from the entire night side of Earth, but during a penumbral eclipse, the dimming of the Moon's illumination is slight. See the **Astronomical Glossary, page 110,** for explanations of the different types of eclipses.

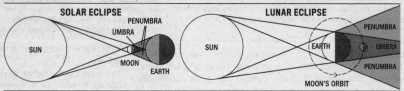

JANUARY 5: PARTIAL ECLIPSE OF THE SUN. This eclipse is visible from North America only in westernmost Alaska. (It is also visible from northeastern China, Mongolia, Japan, eastern Russia, and northern Micronesia.) In Bethel, Alaska, for example, the eclipse will begin at 3:25 P.M. AKST, reach a maximum (obscuring about 60% of the Sun) at 4:51 P.M. AKST, and end at 6:16 P.M. AKST, with the Sun being very low on the horizon for the entire duration of the partial eclipse.

JANUARY 20-21: TOTAL ECLIPSE OF THE MOON. This eclipse is visible from North America. The Moon will enter the penumbra at 9:35 P.M. EST on January 20 (6:25 P.M. PST on January 20) and leave the penumbra at 2:50 A.M. EST on January 21 (11:50 P.M. PST on January 20).

JULY 2: TOTAL ECLIPSE OF THE SUN. This eclipse is not visible from North America. (It is visible only from eastern Oceania and most of South America.)

JULY 16-17: PARTIAL ECLIPSE OF THE MOON. This eclipse is not visible from North America. (It is visible only from Australasia, most of Asia, Africa, all of Europe except for northernmost Scandinavia, and most of South America.)

DECEMBER 26: ANNULAR ECLIPSE OF THE SUN. This eclipse is not visible from North America. (It is visible only from the Middle East, northeastern Africa, Asia except for northern and eastern Russia, northern and western Australia, Micronesia, and the Solomon Islands.)

TRANSIT OF MERCURY. Mercury will pass directly between Earth and the Sun on November 11. Because Mercury is so small relative to the observed disk of the Sun, the transit is not visible with just a filter over the naked eye—appropriately filtered telescopes or binoculars are necessary for viewing. The transit will be visible from most of North America from 7:35 A.M. EST to 1:04 P.M. EST (4:35 A.M. PST to 10:04 A.M. PST; it will be in progress at sunrise in mid– to western North America).

THE MOON'S PATH

The Moon's path across the sky changes with the seasons. Full Moons are very high in the sky (at midnight) between November and February and very low in the sky between May and July.

FULL-MOON DATES (ET)				
	2019	2020	2021	2022	2023
JAN.	21	10	28	17	6
FEB.	19	9	27	16	5
MAR.	20	9	28	18	7
APR.	19	7	26	16	6
MAY	18	7	26	16	5
JUNE	17	5	24	14	3
JULY	16	5	23	13	3
AUG.	15	3	22	11	1 & 30
SEPT.	14	2	20	10	29
OCT.	13	1 & 31	20	9	28
NOV.	12	30	19	8	27
DEC.	12	29	18	7	26

"To you, it's the perfect lift chair. To me, it's the best sleep chair I've ever had."

— J. Fitzgerald, VA

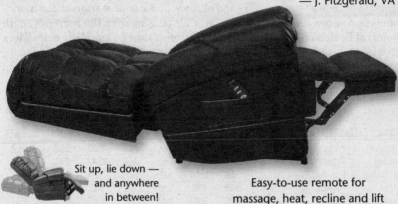

Sit up, lie down — and anywhere in between!

Easy-to-use remote for massage, heat, recline and lift

Our Perfect Sleep Chair® is just the chair to do it all. It's a chair, true – the finest of lift chairs – but this chair is so much more! It's designed to provide total comfort and relaxation not found in other chairs. It can't be beat for comfortable, long-term sitting, TV viewing, relaxed reclining and – yes! – peaceful sleep. Our chair's recline technology allows you to pause the chair in an infinite number of positions, including the Trendelenburg position and the zero gravity position where your body experiences a minimum of internal and external stresses. You'll love the other benefits, too: It helps with correct spinal alignment, promotes back pressure relief, and encourages better posture to prevent back and muscle pain.

And there's more! The overstuffed, oversized biscuit style back and unique seat design will cradle you in comfort. Generously filled, wide armrests provide enhanced arm support when sitting or reclining. The high and low heat settings along with the multiple massage settings, can provide a soothing relaxation you might get at a spa – just imagine getting all that in a lift chair! It even has a battery backup in case of a power outage. Shipping charge includes white glove delivery. Professionals will deliver the chair to the exact spot in your home where you want it, unpack it, inspect it, test it, position it, and even carry the packaging away! You get your choice of fabrics and colors – **Call now!**

This lift chair puts you safely on your feet!

The Perfect Sleep Chair®
1-888-602-3060

Please mention code 109424 when ordering.

© 2018 *first*STREET for Boomers and Beyond, Inc.

46471

BRIGHT STARS

TRANSIT TIMES

This table shows the time (ET) and altitude of a star as it transits the meridian (i.e., reaches its highest elevation while passing over the horizon's south point) at Boston on the dates shown. The transit time on any other date differs from that of the nearest date listed by approximately 4 minutes per day. To find the time of a star's transit for your location, convert its time at Boston using Key Letter C (see Time Corrections, page 238).

STAR	CONSTELLATION	MAGNITUDE	TIME OF TRANSIT (ET) BOLD = P.M. LIGHT = A.M.						ALTITUDE (DEGREES)
			JAN. 1	MAR. 1	MAY 1	JULY 1	SEPT. 1	NOV. 1	
Altair	Aquila	0.8	**12:52**	9:00	6:00	2:00	**9:52**	**5:52**	56.3
Deneb	Cygnus	1.3	**1:42**	9:50	6:50	2:50	**10:42**	**6:43**	92.8
Fomalhaut	Psc. Aus.	1.2	**3:58**	**12:06**	9:06	5:06	1:03	**8:59**	17.8
Algol	Perseus	2.2	**8:08**	**4:16**	**1:16**	9:16	5:13	1:13	88.5
Aldebaran	Taurus	0.9	**9:35**	**5:43**	**2:44**	10:44	6:40	2:40	64.1
Rigel	Orion	0.1	**10:14**	**6:22**	**3:22**	11:22	7:18	3:19	39.4
Capella	Auriga	0.1	**10:16**	**6:24**	**3:25**	11:25	7:21	3:21	93.6
Bellatrix	Orion	1.6	**10:24**	**6:32**	**3:33**	11:33	7:29	3:29	54.0
Betelgeuse	Orion	var. 0.4	**10:54**	**7:02**	**4:03**	**12:03**	7:59	3:59	55.0
Sirius	Can. Maj.	-1.4	**11:44**	**7:52**	**4:52**	**12:52**	8:49	4:49	31.0
Procyon	Can. Min.	0.4	12:42	**8:46**	**5:46**	**1:47**	9:43	5:43	52.9
Pollux	Gemini	1.2	12:48	**8:52**	**5:53**	**1:53**	9:49	5:49	75.7
Regulus	Leo	1.4	3:11	**11:15**	**8:15**	**4:15**	**12:11**	8:12	59.7
Spica	Virgo	var. 1.0	6:27	2:35	**11:31**	**7:32**	**3:28**	11:28	36.6
Arcturus	Boötes	-0.1	7:17	3:25	12:26	**8:22**	**4:18**	**12:18**	66.9
Antares	Scorpius	var. 0.9	9:31	5:39	2:39	**10:35**	**6:32**	**2:32**	21.3
Vega	Lyra	0	11:38	7:46	4:46	12:46	**8:38**	**4:38**	86.4

RISE AND SET TIMES

To find the time of a star's rising at Boston on any date, subtract the interval shown at right from the star's transit time on that date; add the interval to find the star's setting time. To find the rising and setting times for your city, convert the Boston transit times above using the Key Letter shown at right before applying the interval (see Time Corrections, page 238). Deneb, Algol, Capella, and Vega are circumpolar stars—they never set but appear to circle the celestial north pole.

STAR	INTERVAL (H. M.)	RISING KEY	DIR.*	SETTING KEY	DIR.*
Altair	6 36	B	EbN	E	WbN
Fomalhaut	3 59	E	SE	D	SW
Aldebaran	7 06	B	ENE	D	WNW
Rigel	5 33	D	EbS	B	WbS
Bellatrix	6 27	B	EbN	D	WbN
Betelgeuse	6 31	B	EbN	D	WbN
Sirius	5 00	D	ESE	B	WSW
Procyon	6 23	B	EbN	D	WbN
Pollux	8 01	A	NE	E	NW
Regulus	6 49	B	EbN	D	WbN
Spica	5 23	D	EbS	B	WbS
Arcturus	7 19	A	ENE	E	WNW
Antares	4 17	E	SEbE	A	SWbW

*b = "by"

New Arthritis Painkiller Works on Contact and Numbs the Pain in Minutes

New cream works faster and is more targeted than oral medications. Key ingredients penetrate the skin within minutes to relieve joint arthritis pain. Users report significant immediate relief.

Apeaz™: Quick Acting Pain and Arthritis Cream is Now Available Without a Prescription

By Robert Ward
Associated Health Press

BOSTON – Innovus Pharmaceuticals has introduced a new arthritis pain relief treatment that works in minutes.

Sold under the brand name Apeaz™, the new pain relief cream numbs the nerves right below the skin.

When applied to an arthritic joint, or a painful area on the body, it delivers immediate relief that lasts for hours and hours.

The powerful painkilling effect is created by the creams active ingredients, three special medical compounds.

Anesthetics are used in hospitals during surgery. They block nerve signals from the brain so that patients don't feel pain and they work fast.

The anesthetic found in Apeaz™ is the strongest available without a prescription.

The cream form allows users to directly target their area of pain. It works where it is applied. The company says this is why the product is so effective and fast acting.

"Users can expect to start feeling relief immediately after applying," explains Dr. Bassam Damaj, President of Innovus Pharmaceuticals.

"There will be a pleasant warming sensation that is followed by a cool, soothing one. This is how you know that the active ingredients have reached the affected joint and tissue."

Works In Minutes

For arthritis suffers, Apeaz™ offers impressive advantages over traditional medications. The most obvious is how quickly it relieves pain discomfort.

The cream contains the maximum approved OTC dose of a top anesthetic, which penetrates the skin in a matter of minutes to numb the area that's in pain. This relief lasts for several hours.

Published pre-clinical animal studies have shown that the ingredients in Apeaz™ can also prevent further bone and cartilage destruction.

There are also no negative side effects like from oral medication. Apeaz™ delivers its ingredients through the skin. Oral medications are absorbed in the digestive tract. Overtime, the chemicals in pills can tear the delicate lining of the stomach, causing ulcers and bleeding.

When compared to other arthritis medications, Apeaz™ is a fraction of the cost. At less than $2 a day, the cream quickly is becoming a household name.

Those with terrible arthritis in their hands and fingers, love how easy Apeaz™ is to open. The jar fits in the palm of the hand, which makes it much easier to use.

Instant Pain Relief Without a Prescription

Many Apeaz™ users report significant improvements in daily aches and pain. Many more report increased flexibility and less stiffness. They are moving with less pain for the first time in years, like Henry Esber, an early user of Apeaz™.

"I've tried more pills than I can count. I've also had a handful of cortisone shots. Nothing is as effective as this product. With Apeaz™, I get relief right away. I rub a little on my hands. It keeps the pain away. It also prevents the pain from getting really bad. It's completely changed my life."

How It Works

Apeaz™ contains the highest, non-prescription OTC dose of a medical compound that fights pain on contact. When applied to the skin it goes to work within minutes by penetrating right to the source of your pain, numbing the nerve endings.

"This is why Apeaz™ is so effective for people with arthritis pain. It reduces pain while adding an additional potential layer of joint support," explains Damaj.

How to Get Apeaz™

In order to get the word out about Apeaz™, the company is offering special introductory discounts to all who call. Discounts will automatically be applied to all callers, but don't wait. This offer may not last forever. Call toll-free: 1-800-411-8480.

THE TWILIGHT ZONE/METEOR SHOWERS

Twilight is the time when the sky is partially illuminated preceding sunrise and again following sunset. The ranges of twilight are defined according to the Sun's position below the horizon. **Civil twilight** occurs when the Sun's center is between the horizon and 6 degrees below the horizon (visually, the horizon is clearly defined). **Nautical twilight** occurs when the center is between 6 and 12 degrees below the horizon (the horizon is distinct). **Astronomical twilight** occurs when the center is between 12 and 18 degrees below the horizon (sky illumination is imperceptible). When the center is at 18 degrees (**dawn** or **dark**) or below, there is no illumination.

LENGTH OF ASTRONOMICAL TWILIGHT (HOURS AND MINUTES)

LATITUDE	JAN. 1– APR. 10	APR. 11– MAY 2	MAY 3– MAY 14	MAY 15– MAY 25	MAY 26– JULY 22	JULY 23– AUG. 3	AUG. 4– AUG. 14	AUG. 15– SEPT. 5	SEPT. 6– DEC. 31
25°N to 30°N	1 20	1 23	1 26	1 29	1 32	1 29	1 26	1 23	1 20
31°N to 36°N	1 26	1 28	1 34	1 38	1 43	1 38	1 34	1 28	1 26
37°N to 42°N	1 33	1 39	1 47	1 52	1 59	1 52	1 47	1 39	1 33
43°N to 47°N	1 42	1 51	2 02	2 13	2 27	2 13	2 02	1 51	1 42
48°N to 49°N	1 50	2 04	2 22	2 42	–	2 42	2 22	2 04	1 50

TO DETERMINE THE LENGTH OF TWILIGHT: The length of twilight changes with latitude and the time of year. See the **Time Corrections, page 238,** to find the latitude of your city or the city nearest you. Use that figure in the chart above with the appropriate date to calculate the length of twilight in your area.

TO DETERMINE ARRIVAL OF DAWN OR DARK: Calculate the sunrise/sunset times for your locality using the instructions in **How to Use This Almanac, page 116.**

Subtract the length of twilight from the time of sunrise to determine when dawn breaks. Add the length of twilight to the time of sunset to determine when dark descends.

EXAMPLE:
BOSTON, MASS. (LATITUDE 42°22')

Sunrise, August 1	5:36 A.M. ET
Length of twilight	– 1 52
Dawn breaks	3:44 A.M.
Sunset, August 1	8:04 P.M. ET
Length of twilight	+1 52
Dark descends	9:56 P.M.

PRINCIPAL METEOR SHOWERS

SHOWER	BEST VIEWING	POINT OF ORIGIN	DATE OF MAXIMUM*	NO. PER HOUR**	ASSOCIATED COMET
Quadrantid	Predawn	N	Jan. 4	25	–
Lyrid	Predawn	S	Apr. 22	10	Thatcher
Eta Aquarid	Predawn	SE	May 4	10	Halley
Delta Aquarid	Predawn	S	July 30	10	–
Perseid	**Predawn**	**NE**	**Aug. 11–13**	**50**	**Swift-Tuttle**
Draconid	Late evening	NW	Oct. 9	6	Giacobini-Zinner
Orionid	Predawn	S	Oct. 21–22	15	Halley
Taurid	Late evening	S	Nov. 9	3	Encke
Leonid	Predawn	S	Nov. 17–18	10	Tempel-Tuttle
Andromedid	Late evening	S	Nov. 25–27	5	Biela
Geminid	**All night**	**NE**	**Dec. 13–14**	**75**	**–**
Ursid	Predawn	N	Dec. 22	5	Tuttle

*May vary by 1 or 2 days   **In a moonless, rural sky   **Bold** = most prominent

THE VISIBLE PLANETS

Listed here for Boston are viewing suggestions for and the rise and set times (ET) of Venus, Mars, Jupiter, and Saturn on specific days each month, as well as when it is best to view Mercury. Approximate rise and set times for other days can be found by interpolation. Use the Key Letters at the right of each listing to convert the times for other localities **(see pages 116 and 238).**

FOR ALL PLANET RISE AND SET TIMES BY ZIP CODE, VISIT ALMANAC.COM/ASTRONOMY.

VENUS

The cloud-covered planet starts 2019 at its brightest of the entire year, dominating the predawn east. It gets lower and less luminous thereafter, yet remains visible throughout winter and most of spring. It's low starting in May, but can be glimpsed before dawn in July. Its superior conjunction behind the Sun occurs on August 14, after which it can be seen low in the west 40 minutes after sunset in late September. A month later, Venus is an easier viewing target, and in November and December it becomes even more striking as it gets higher and brighter. It's near the Moon on April 2, June 1, and December 28; meets Jupiter from November 23 to 25; and joins Saturn on December 10 and 11.

Jan. 1	rise	3:26	D	Apr. 1	rise	5:15	D	July 1	rise	4:20	A	Oct. 1	set	6:59	C
Jan. 11	rise	3:37	E	Apr. 11	rise	5:05	D	July 11	rise	4:33	A	Oct. 11	set	6:48	B
Jan. 21	rise	3:50	E	Apr. 21	rise	4:54	C	July 21	rise	4:52	A	Oct. 21	set	6:40	B
Feb. 1	rise	4:04	E	May 1	rise	4:42	C	Aug. 1	rise	5:17	A	Nov. 1	set	6:36	A
Feb. 11	rise	4:16	E	May 11	rise	4:31	B	Aug. 11	rise	5:41	B	Nov. 11	set	5:37	A
Feb. 21	rise	4:23	E	May 21	rise	4:21	B	Aug. 21	set	7:47	D	Nov. 21	set	5:45	A
Mar. 1	rise	4:27	E	June 1	rise	4:13	B	Sept. 1	set	7:36	D	Dec. 1	set	5:59	A
Mar. 11	rise	5:27	E	June 11	rise	4:10	B	Sept. 11	set	7:24	C	Dec. 11	set	6:19	A
Mar. 21	rise	5:23	D	June 21	rise	4:12	A	Sept. 21	set	7:11	C	Dec. 21	set	6:42	A
												Dec. 31	set	7:07	B

MARS

Mars has an off-year in 2019, with no opposition. The Red Planet is highest and brightest on the year's first day as a zero-magnitude "star" in Pisces, high in the south at nightfall with a tiny 7-arcsecond disk for telescope users. Sinking lower in the west, Mars enters Aries in mid-February, Taurus in late March, and Gemini in mid-May. It's lost in solar glare for most of the summer, in conjunction with the Sun on September 2, and low in the October morning sky. Mars is above the Moon on January 12, February 9 and 10, April 8, and May 7. It meets Mercury from June 12 to 22 and is near Virgo's blue star Spica from November 1 to 17. Mars is just to the right of Uranus from February 10 to 12 and above it from February 13 to 16.

Jan. 1	set	11:04	C	Apr. 1	set	11:26	E	July 1	set	9:42	E	Oct. 1	rise	5:51	C
Jan. 11	set	11:00	C	Apr. 11	set	11:20	E	July 11	set	9:22	E	Oct. 11	rise	5:45	C
Jan. 21	set	10:56	D	Apr. 21	set	11:14	E	July 21	set	9:01	E	Oct. 21	rise	5:38	C
Feb. 1	set	10:51	D	May 1	set	11:06	E	Aug. 1	set	8:37	E	Nov. 1	rise	5:32	D
Feb. 11	set	10:47	D	May 11	set	10:56	E	Aug. 11	set	8:14	D	Nov. 11	rise	4:26	D
Feb. 21	set	10:43	D	May 21	set	10:45	E	Aug. 21	set	7:50	D	Nov. 21	rise	4:20	D
Mar. 1	set	10:40	E	June 1	set	10:31	E	Sept. 1	set	7:23	D	Dec. 1	rise	4:15	D
Mar. 11	set	11:36	E	June 11	set	10:16	E	Sept. 11	rise	6:04	B	Dec. 11	rise	4:10	E
Mar. 21	set	11:31	E	June 21	set	10:00	E	Sept. 21	rise	5:57	C	Dec. 21	rise	4:05	E
												Dec. 31	rise	4:01	E

BOLD = P.M. LIGHT = A.M.

JUPITER

The largest planet spends 2019 in the "13th zodiac constellation," Ophiuchus, the Serpent Bearer. It starts the year low in the east before dawn, forming a line with the Moon, Venus, and Mercury. Jupiter is a bit higher and brighter each morning as it rises 2 hours earlier each month. Jove rises before midnight in late March and reaches its opposition on June 10, when it rises at sunset. All summer, Jupiter remains well placed, although it never ascends more than one-third of the way up the sky. It's seen only during the first half of the night in autumn and becomes low in the west in November at nightfall. Lost in solar glare, it passes behind the Sun in conjunction on December 27.

Jan. 1	rise	5:04	E	Apr. 1	rise	1:08	E	July 1	set	3:47	A	Oct. 1	set	**9:46**	A
Jan. 11	rise	4:35	E	Apr. 11	rise	12:29	E	July 11	set	3:04	A	Oct. 11	set	**9:12**	A
Jan. 21	rise	4:04	E	Apr. 21	**rise**	**11:45**	E	July 21	set	2:22	A	Oct. 21	set	**8:39**	A
Feb. 1	rise	3:31	E	May 1	**rise**	**11:04**	E	Aug. 1	set	1:36	A	Nov. 1	set	**8:04**	A
Feb. 11	rise	2:59	E	May 11	**rise**	**10:21**	E	Aug. 11	set	1:00	A	Nov. 11	set	**6:33**	A
Feb. 21	rise	2:26	E	May 21	**rise**	**9:37**	E	Aug. 21	set	12:17	A	Nov. 21	set	**6:03**	A
Mar. 1	rise	1:59	E	June 1	**rise**	**8:48**	E	Sept. 1	set	**11:32**	A	Dec. 1	set	**5:33**	A
Mar. 11	rise	2:25	E	June 11	**rise**	**8:03**	E	Sept. 11	set	**10:56**	A	Dec. 11	set	**5:03**	A
Mar. 21	rise	1:49	E	June 21	set	4:31	A	Sept. 21	set	**10:20**	A	Dec. 21	set	**4:34**	A
												Dec. 31	rise	7:03	E

SATURN

The Ringed Planet is parked in Sagittarius all year, which keeps it from getting very high up in 2019. Saturn first appears as a low morning star before sunrise in February. It rises at 1:00 A.M. in May and at sunset on July 9, when it reaches opposition. It's out all night throughout the summer, bright at magnitude +0.1. Its rings, slightly less "open" than during the past few years but still far from edgewise, are gorgeous through any telescope using more than 30×. Saturn is the "star" near the Moon on July 15, August 11 and 12, and September 7.

Jan. 1	rise	7:15	E	Apr. 1	rise	2:53	E	July 1	**rise**	**8:45**	E	Oct. 1	set	**11:38**	A
Jan. 11	rise	6:41	E	Apr. 11	rise	2:15	E	July 11	**rise**	**8:03**	E	Oct. 11	set	**11:00**	A
Jan. 21	rise	6:06	E	Apr. 21	rise	1:37	E	July 21	set	4:36	A	Oct. 21	set	**10:23**	A
Feb. 1	rise	5:27	E	May 1	rise	1:02	E	Aug. 1	set	3:49	A	Nov. 1	set	**9:42**	A
Feb. 11	rise	4:52	E	May 11	rise	12:18	E	Aug. 11	set	3:07	A	Nov. 11	set	**8:07**	A
Feb. 21	rise	4:16	E	May 21	**rise**	**11:34**	E	Aug. 21	set	2:25	A	Nov. 21	set	**7:32**	A
Mar. 1	rise	3:48	E	June 1	**rise**	**10:49**	E	Sept. 1	set	1:40	A	Dec. 1	set	**6:57**	A
Mar. 11	rise	4:11	E	June 11	**rise**	**10:08**	E	Sept. 11	set	1:04	A	Dec. 11	set	**6:23**	A
Mar. 21	rise	3:35	E	June 21	**rise**	**9:26**	E	Sept. 21	set	12:20	A	Dec. 21	set	**5:49**	A
												Dec. 31	set	**5:15**	A

MERCURY

The innermost planet whirls so closely around the Sun that we see it only in twilight. As an evening star low in fading western twilight in 2019, Mercury is marginally visible in the last half of February and October but well seen throughout June. As a morning star, Mercury can be glimpsed during the first halves of January and April but is best seen in August, except for at the very end of that month, and from mid-November through mid-December. Mercury hovers below the Moon and Mars on November 24 and between them the next evening.

DO NOT CONFUSE: *Mercury and Mars on June 18, low in evening twilight: Mercury is brighter.* • *Jupiter and Saturn low in the south throughout summer: Jupiter is more brilliant.* • *Mercury with a sunspot during its Nov. 11 transit, through a solar telescope: Mercury is uniformly round and black.* • *Venus and Jupiter on Nov. 23 and 24, low in western twilight: Venus is brighter.*

ASTRONOMICAL GLOSSARY

APHELION (APH.): The point in a planet's orbit that is farthest from the Sun.

APOGEE (APO.): The point in the Moon's orbit that is farthest from Earth.

CELESTIAL EQUATOR (EQ.): The imaginary circle around the celestial sphere that can be thought of as the plane of Earth's equator projected out onto the sphere.

CELESTIAL SPHERE: An imaginary sphere projected into space that represents the entire sky, with an observer on Earth at its center. All celestial bodies other than Earth are imagined as being on its inside surface.

CIRCUMPOLAR: Always visible above the horizon, such as a circumpolar star.

CONJUNCTION: The time at which two or more celestial bodies appear closest in the sky. **Inferior (Inf.):** Mercury or Venus is between the Sun and Earth. **Superior (Sup.):** The Sun is between a planet and Earth. Actual dates for conjunctions are given on the **Right-Hand Calendar Pages, 121–147;** the best times for viewing the closely aligned bodies are given in **Sky Watch** on the **Left-Hand Calendar Pages, 120–146.**

DECLINATION: The celestial latitude of an object in the sky, measured in degrees north or south of the celestial equator; comparable to latitude on Earth. This Almanac gives the Sun's declination at noon.

ECLIPSE, LUNAR: The full Moon enters the shadow of Earth, which cuts off all or part of the sunlight reflected off the Moon. **Total:** The Moon passes completely through the umbra (central dark part) of Earth's shadow. **Partial:** Only part of the Moon passes through the umbra. **Penumbral:** The Moon passes through only the penumbra (area of partial darkness surrounding the umbra). **See page 102** for more information about eclipses.

ECLIPSE, SOLAR: Earth enters the shadow of the new Moon, which cuts off all or part of the Sun's light. **Total:** Earth passes through the umbra (central dark part) of the Moon's shadow, resulting in totality for observers within a narrow band on Earth. **Annular:** The Moon appears silhouetted against the Sun, with a ring of sunlight showing around it. **Partial:** The Moon blocks only part of the Sun.

ECLIPTIC: The apparent annual path of the Sun around the celestial sphere. The plane of the ecliptic is tipped 23½° from the celestial equator.

ELONGATION: The difference in degrees between the celestial longitudes of a planet and the Sun. **Greatest Elongation (Gr. Elong.):** The greatest apparent distance of a planet from the Sun, as seen from Earth.

EPACT: A number from 1 to 30 that indicates the Moon's age on January 1 at Greenwich, England; used in determining the date of Easter.

EQUINOX: When the Sun crosses the celestial equator. This event occurs two times each year: **Vernal** is around March 20 and **Autumnal** is around September 22.

EVENING STAR: A planet that is above the western horizon at sunset and less than 180° east of the Sun in right ascension.

GOLDEN NUMBER: A number in the 19-year Metonic cycle of the Moon, used in determining the date of Easter. See **page 150** for this year's Golden Number.

MAGNITUDE: A measure of a celestial object's brightness. **Apparent magnitude** measures the brightness of an object as seen from Earth. Objects with an apparent magnitude of 6 or less are observable to the naked eye. The lower the magnitude, the greater the brightness; an object with a magnitude of –1, e.g., is

New Pill Can Relieve the Need for Adult Diapers and Padded Underwear

According to Dr. Seipel, Leaking, Squirming, Squeezing, and Night Time Bathroom Trips... Even Accidents Can Now be a Thing of the Past!

Finally a clinically proven pill solution to ease all your bladder problems, without a prescription

NEW YORK, NEW YORK — If life isn't hard enough, now you have to worry about making it to the bathroom in time. The feeling of your bladder bursting and the down right panic of "not making it" in time can be absolutely overwhelming.

Don't even dare to laugh, cough or sneeze at the "wrong" time and when did you start to become scared to take a big sip of tea, coffee or water? You're not alone in your battle to control your bladder. According to The National Institute of Health, as many as 33 million Americans are affected by bladder control issues described above.

The Family Secret Even the Family Doesn't Know

"Most people who have overactive bladders choose to keep their problem a secret," says Dr. Tracey Seipel, a longtime clinician who is one of the world's leading experts in natural urological healthcare.

"They don't even tell their spouse or families about it. It affects their lives in every way, influencing where they go, and even what they will wear in case they have an accident."

A 100% natural, drug-free aid developed by Dr. Seipel is now available in a remarkable, fast-acting natural formula called UriVarx™ featuring urox. This sophisticated patented herbal compound has been shown in clinical studies to help improve UriVarx™ with reductions in bladder frequency, nocturia (having to urinate at night), urgency, and bladder discomfort, sometimes in as little as two weeks.

Dr. Seipel's formula has made a believer out of 45-year-old, mother of three, Brandy W., from Brisbane, Australia. A friend told her about Dr. Seipel's formula. "I was finding that although I felt I needed to urinate, I wasn't as desperate to run to

the toilet. Now, when I get up in the morning," she adds, "I'm able to make the coffee and even have a cup before needing to go, which is a great improvement!"

How Does It Work?

"UriVarx™ helps support bladder health by revitalizing bladder tone and function, and by helping support the kidney. UriVarx™ promotes normal urinary frequency, and reduces urgency, nocturia and those embarrassing, away-from-home bladder accidents," says Dr. Seipel. "The compound invigorates the tone of the bladder wall, assisting a healthy level of firmness by enhancing the bladder's muscular elasticity. This reduces the frequent urge to urinate."

Positive Clinical Trial

This natural, drug-free UriVarx™ formula has performed well in a clinical study. Thirty days later 77% of participants were experiencing benefits. Results like these are not surprising to Dr. Seipel who single-handedly pioneered the bladder care category in the early 2000's, receiving an award from the prestigious US Nutrition Business Journal for her work.

Her patented formula consisting of select, synergistically paired botanicals like Crateva nurvala, Equisetum arvense and Lindera aggregata, was 15 years in the making.

No More Diapers

Insiders in the adult diaper industry are keeping a close eye on Dr. Seipel's bladder support breakthrough because of people like 78-year-old retired teacher, Glenda B. from Gold Coast, Australia.

Glenda wore adult diapers every day to guard against accidents. "My bladder capacity was good but the leakage and accidents would occur without warning." Since Glenda discovered Dr. Seipel's UriVarx™ formula, you won't find her shopping in the adult diaper section of the store anymore.

Prostate or Bladder? Hard to Tell

Many men confuse the symptoms of overactive bladder syndrome with prostate woes. Dr. Seipel explains, "Prostate enlargement restricts urine flow. The bladder compensates for this by trying harder and harder to push the urine out." As bladder pressure increases, so does instances of urinary frequency and urgency. Long after a man's prostate woes are relieved, he may still experience the same symptoms thanks to his now-overactive bladder.

"It's a his-and-her formula," she smiles. David M., age 46, can attest to this. "I was having to go to the toilet every hour or so and I had to go to the toilet at least four times per night."

How to Get UriVarx™

If you're ready to alleviate your go-now urination urges, and if you are looking for the confidence and security that a healthy bladder can bring to your life, here's your risk-free opportunity.

Experience the life-changing effect UriVarx™ can have, and get a special introductory discount – **Call Toll-Free: 1-800-736-4601.**

brighter than one with a magnitude of +1.

MIDNIGHT: Astronomically, the time when the Sun is opposite its highest point in the sky. Both 12 hours before and after noon (so, technically, both A.M. and P.M.), midnight in civil time is usually treated as the beginning of the day. It is displayed as 12:00 A.M. on 12-hour digital clocks. On a 24-hour cycle, 00:00, not 24:00, usually indicates midnight.

MOON ON EQUATOR: The Moon is on the celestial equator.

MOON RIDES HIGH/RUNS LOW: The Moon is highest above or farthest below the celestial equator.

MOONRISE/MOONSET: When the Moon rises above or sets below the horizon.

MOON'S PHASES: The changing appearance of the Moon, caused by the different angles at which it is illuminated by the Sun. **First Quarter:** Right half of the Moon is illuminated. **Full:** The Sun and the Moon are in opposition; the entire disk of the Moon is illuminated. **Last Quarter:** Left half of the Moon is illuminated. **New:** The Sun and the Moon are in conjunction; the Moon is darkened because it lines up between Earth and the Sun.

MOON'S PLACE, Astronomical: The position of the Moon within the constellations on the celestial sphere at midnight. **Astrological:** The position of the Moon within the tropical zodiac, whose twelve 30° segments (signs) along the ecliptic were named more than 2,000 years ago after constellations within each area. Because of precession and other factors, the zodiac signs no longer match actual constellation positions.

MORNING STAR: A planet that is above the eastern horizon at sunrise and less than 180° west of the Sun in right ascension.

NODE: Either of the two points where a celestial body's orbit intersects the ecliptic. **Ascending:** When the body is moving from south to north of the ecliptic. **Descending:** When the body is moving from north to south of the ecliptic.

OPPOSITION: The Moon or a planet appears on the opposite side of the sky from the Sun (elongation 180°).

PERIGEE (PERIG.): The point in the Moon's orbit that is closest to Earth.

PERIHELION (PERIH.): The point in a planet's orbit that is closest to the Sun.

PRECESSION: The slowly changing position of the stars and equinoxes in the sky caused by a slight wobble as Earth rotates around its axis.

RIGHT ASCENSION (R.A.): The celestial longitude of an object in the sky, measured eastward along the celestial equator in hours of time from the vernal equinox; comparable to longitude on Earth.

SOLSTICE, Summer: When the Sun reaches its greatest declination (23½°) north of the celestial equator, around June 21. **Winter:** When the Sun reaches its greatest declination (23½°) south of the celestial equator, around December 21.

STATIONARY (STAT.): The brief period of apparent halted movement of a planet against the background of the stars shortly before it appears to move backward/westward (retrograde motion) or forward/eastward (direct motion).

SUN FAST/SLOW: When a sundial is ahead of (fast) or behind (slow) clock time.

SUNRISE/SUNSET: The visible rising/setting of the upper edge of the Sun's disk across the unobstructed horizon of an observer whose eyes are 15 feet above ground level.

TWILIGHT: See page 106. ■

2018

JANUARY
S	M	T	W	T	F	S
		1	2	3	4	5	6
7	8	9	10	11	12	13
14	15	16	17	18	19	20
21	22	23	24	25	26	27
28	29	30	31			

FEBRUARY
S	M	T	W	T	F	S
				1	2	3
4	5	6	7	8	9	10
11	12	13	14	15	16	17
18	19	20	21	22	23	24
25	26	27	28			

MARCH
S	M	T	W	T	F	S
				1	2	3
4	5	6	7	8	9	10
11	12	13	14	15	16	17
18	19	20	21	22	23	24
25	26	27	28	29	30	31

APRIL
S	M	T	W	T	F	S
1	2	3	4	5	6	7
8	9	10	11	12	13	14
15	16	17	18	19	20	21
22	23	24	25	26	27	28
29	30					

MAY
S	M	T	W	T	F	S
		1	2	3	4	5
6	7	8	9	10	11	12
13	14	15	16	17	18	19
20	21	22	23	24	25	26
27	28	29	30	31		

JUNE
S	M	T	W	T	F	S
					1	2
3	4	5	6	7	8	9
10	11	12	13	14	15	16
17	18	19	20	21	22	23
24	25	26	27	28	29	30

JULY
S	M	T	W	T	F	S
1	2	3	4	5	6	7
8	9	10	11	12	13	14
15	16	17	18	19	20	21
22	23	24	25	26	27	28
29	30	31				

AUGUST
S	M	T	W	T	F	S
			1	2	3	4
5	6	7	8	9	10	11
12	13	14	15	16	17	18
19	20	21	22	23	24	25
26	27	28	29	30	31	

SEPTEMBER
S	M	T	W	T	F	S
						1
2	3	4	5	6	7	8
9	10	11	12	13	14	15
16	17	18	19	20	21	22
23	24	25	26	27	28	29
30						

OCTOBER
S	M	T	W	T	F	S
	1	2	3	4	5	6
7	8	9	10	11	12	13
14	15	16	17	18	19	20
21	22	23	24	25	26	27
28	29	30	31			

NOVEMBER
S	M	T	W	T	F	S
				1	2	3
4	5	6	7	8	9	10
11	12	13	14	15	16	17
18	19	20	21	22	23	24
25	26	27	28	29	30	

DECEMBER
S	M	T	W	T	F	S
						1
2	3	4	5	6	7	8
9	10	11	12	13	14	15
16	17	18	19	20	21	22
23	24	25	26	27	28	29
30	31					

2019

JANUARY
S	M	T	W	T	F	S
		1	2	3	4	5
6	7	8	9	10	11	12
13	14	15	16	17	18	19
20	21	22	23	24	25	26
27	28	29	30	31		

FEBRUARY
S	M	T	W	T	F	S
					1	2
3	4	5	6	7	8	9
10	11	12	13	14	15	16
17	18	19	20	21	22	23
24	25	26	27	28		

MARCH
S	M	T	W	T	F	S
					1	2
3	4	5	6	7	8	9
10	11	12	13	14	15	16
17	18	19	20	21	22	23
24	25	26	27	28	29	30
31						

APRIL
S	M	T	W	T	F	S
	1	2	3	4	5	6
7	8	9	10	11	12	13
14	15	16	17	18	19	20
21	22	23	24	25	26	27
28	29	30				

MAY
S	M	T	W	T	F	S
			1	2	3	4
5	6	7	8	9	10	11
12	13	14	15	16	17	18
19	20	21	22	23	24	25
26	27	28	29	30	31	

JUNE
S	M	T	W	T	F	S
						1
2	3	4	5	6	7	8
9	10	11	12	13	14	15
16	17	18	19	20	21	22
23	24	25	26	27	28	29
30						

JULY
S	M	T	W	T	F	S
	1	2	3	4	5	6
7	8	9	10	11	12	13
14	15	16	17	18	19	20
21	22	23	24	25	26	27
28	29	30	31			

AUGUST
S	M	T	W	T	F	S
				1	2	3
4	5	6	7	8	9	10
11	12	13	14	15	16	17
18	19	20	21	22	23	24
25	26	27	28	29	30	31

SEPTEMBER
S	M	T	W	T	F	S
1	2	3	4	5	6	7
8	9	10	11	12	13	14
15	16	17	18	19	20	21
22	23	24	25	26	27	28
29	30					

OCTOBER
S	M	T	W	T	F	S
		1	2	3	4	5
6	7	8	9	10	11	12
13	14	15	16	17	18	19
20	21	22	23	24	25	26
27	28	29	30	31		

NOVEMBER
S	M	T	W	T	F	S
					1	2
3	4	5	6	7	8	9
10	11	12	13	14	15	16
17	18	19	20	21	22	23
24	25	26	27	28	29	30

DECEMBER
S	M	T	W	T	F	S
1	2	3	4	5	6	7
8	9	10	11	12	13	14
15	16	17	18	19	20	21
22	23	24	25	26	27	28
29	30	31				

2020

JANUARY
S	M	T	W	T	F	S
			1	2	3	4
5	6	7	8	9	10	11
12	13	14	15	16	17	18
19	20	21	22	23	24	25
26	27	28	29	30	31	

FEBRUARY
S	M	T	W	T	F	S
						1
2	3	4	5	6	7	8
9	10	11	12	13	14	15
16	17	18	19	20	21	22
23	24	25	26	27	28	29

MARCH
S	M	T	W	T	F	S
1	2	3	4	5	6	7
8	9	10	11	12	13	14
15	16	17	18	19	20	21
22	23	24	25	26	27	28
29	30	31				

APRIL
S	M	T	W	T	F	S
			1	2	3	4
5	6	7	8	9	10	11
12	13	14	15	16	17	18
19	20	21	22	23	24	25
26	27	28	29	30		

MAY
S	M	T	W	T	F	S
					1	2
3	4	5	6	7	8	9
10	11	12	13	14	15	16
17	18	19	20	21	22	23
24	25	26	27	28	29	30
31						

JUNE
S	M	T	W	T	F	S
	1	2	3	4	5	6
7	8	9	10	11	12	13
14	15	16	17	18	19	20
21	22	23	24	25	26	27
28	29	30				

JULY
S	M	T	W	T	F	S
			1	2	3	4
5	6	7	8	9	10	11
12	13	14	15	16	17	18
19	20	21	22	23	24	25
26	27	28	29	30	31	

AUGUST
S	M	T	W	T	F	S
						1
2	3	4	5	6	7	8
9	10	11	12	13	14	15
16	17	18	19	20	21	22
23	24	25	26	27	28	29
30	31					

SEPTEMBER
S	M	T	W	T	F	S
		1	2	3	4	5
6	7	8	9	10	11	12
13	14	15	16	17	18	19
20	21	22	23	24	25	26
27	28	29	30			

OCTOBER
S	M	T	W	T	F	S
				1	2	3
4	5	6	7	8	9	10
11	12	13	14	15	16	17
18	19	20	21	22	23	24
25	26	27	28	29	30	31

NOVEMBER
S	M	T	W	T	F	S
1	2	3	4	5	6	7
8	9	10	11	12	13	14
15	16	17	18	19	20	21
22	23	24	25	26	27	28
29	30					

DECEMBER
S	M	T	W	T	F	S
		1	2	3	4	5
6	7	8	9	10	11	12
13	14	15	16	17	18	19
20	21	22	23	24	25	26
27	28	29	30	31		

Love calendar lore? Find more at Almanac.com.

A CALENDAR OF THE HEAVENS FOR 2019

–Beth Krommes

The Calendar Pages (120–147) are the heart of *The Old Farmer's Almanac*. They present sky sightings and astronomical data for the entire year and are what make this book a true almanac, a "calendar of the heavens." In essence, these pages are unchanged since 1792, when Robert B. Thomas published his first edition. The long columns of numbers and symbols reveal all of nature's precision, rhythm, and glory, providing an astronomical look at the year 2019.

HOW TO USE THE CALENDAR PAGES

The astronomical data on the **Calendar Pages (120–147)** are calculated for Boston (where Robert B. Thomas learned to calculate the data for his first Almanac). Guidance for calculating the times of these events for your locale appears on **pages 116–117.** Note that the results will be *approximate*. For the *exact* time of any astronomical event at your locale, go to **Almanac.com/ Astronomy** and enter your zip code. While you're there, print the month's "Sky Map," useful for viewing with "Sky Watch" in the Calendar Pages.

For a list of 2019 holidays and observances, see **pages 148 and 150.** Also check out the **Glossary of Almanac Oddities** on **pages 152 and 154,** which describes some of the more obscure entries traditionally found on the **Right-Hand Calendar Pages (121–147).**

ABOUT THE TIMES: All times are given in ET (Eastern Time), except where otherwise noted as AT (Atlantic Time, +1 hour), CT (Central Time, –1), MT (Mountain Time, –2), PT (Pacific Time, –3), AKT (Alaska Time, –4), or HAT (Hawaii-Aleutian Time, –5). Between 2:00 A.M., March 10, and 2:00 A.M., November 3, Daylight Saving Time is assumed in those locales where it is observed.

ABOUT THE TIDES: Tide times for Boston appear on **pages 120–146;** for Boston tide heights, see **pages 121–147.** Tide Corrections for East Coast locations appear on **pages 236–237.** Tide heights and times for locations across the United States and Canada are available at **Almanac.com/Tides.**

The Left-Hand Calendar Pages, 120 to 146

On these pages are the year's astronomical predictions for Boston. Learn how to calculate the times of these events for your locale here or go to **Almanac .com/Rise** and enter your zip code.

A SAMPLE MONTH

SKY WATCH: The paragraph at the top of each Left-Hand Calendar Page describes the best times to view conjunctions, meteor showers, planets, and more. (Also see **How to Use the Right-Hand Calendar Pages, p. 118.**)

			1		2		3	4	5		6		7	8
DAY OF YEAR	DAY OF MONTH	DAY OF WEEK	☼ RISES H. M.	RISE KEY	☼ SETS H. M.	SET KEY	LENGTH OF DAY H. M.	SUN FAST M.	SUN DECLINATION ° ′	HIGH TIDE TIMES BOSTON	☾ RISES H. M.	RISE KEY	☾ SETS H. M.	SET KEY	ASTRON. PLACE	☾ AGE
60	1	Fr.	6:20	D	5:34	C	11 14	4	7 s. 30	7¼ 8	3:30	E	12:58	B	SAG	25
61	2	Sa.	6:18	D	5:35	C	11 17	4	7 s. 07	8¼ 9	4:16	E	1:51	B	SAG	26
62	3	**F**	6:17	D	5:36	C	11 19	4	6 s. 44	9¼ 9¾	4:56	E	2:47	B	CAP	27
63	4	M.	6:15	D	5:37	C	11 22	4	6 s. 21	10 10½	5:31	E	3:45	C	CAP	28

1. To calculate the sunrise time in your locale: Choose a day. Note its Sun Rise Key Letter. Find your (nearest) city on **page 238**. Add or subtract the minutes that correspond to the Sun Rise Key Letter to/from the sunrise time for Boston.

EXAMPLE:

To calculate the sunrise time in Denver, Colorado, on day 1:

Sunrise, Boston, with Key Letter D (above)	6:20 A.M. ET
Value of Key Letter D for Denver (p. 238)	+ 11 minutes
Sunrise, Denver	6:31 A.M. MT

To calculate your sunset time, repeat, using Boston's sunset time and its Sun Set Key Letter value.

2. To calculate the length of day: Choose a day. Note the Sun Rise and Sun Set Key Letters. Find your (nearest) city on **page 238**. Add or subtract the minutes that correspond to the Sun Set Key Letter to/from Boston's length of day. *Reverse* the sign (e.g., minus to plus) of the

Sun Rise Key Letter minutes. Add or subtract it to/from the first result.

EXAMPLE:

To calculate the length of day in Richmond, Virginia, on day 1:

Length of day, Boston (above)	11h.14m.
Sunset Key Letter C for Richmond (p. 242)	+ 25m.
	11h.39m.
Reverse sunrise Key Letter D for Richmond (p. 242, +17 to -17)	- 17m.
Length of day, Richmond	11h.22m.

3. Use Sun Fast to change sundial time to clock time. A sundial reads natural (Sun) time, which is neither Standard nor Daylight time. To calculate clock time on a sundial in Boston, subtract the minutes given in this column; add the minutes when preceded by an asterisk [*].

-Beth Krommes

To convert the time to your (nearest) city, use Key Letter C on **page 238.**

EXAMPLE:

To change sundial to clock time in Boston or Salem, Oregon, on day 1:

Sundial reading (Boston or Salem)	12:00 noon
Subtract Sun Fast (p. 116)	− 4 minutes
Clock time, Boston	11:56 A.M. ET
Use Key Letter C for Salem (p. 241)	+ 27 minutes
Clock time, Salem	12:23 P.M. PT

4. This column gives the degrees and minutes of the Sun from the celestial equator at noon ET.

5. This column gives the approximate times of high tide in Boston. For example, the first high tide occurs at 7:15 A.M. and the second occurs at 8:00 P.M. the same day. (A dash indicates that high tide occurs on or after midnight and is recorded on the next day.) Figures for calculating approximate high tide times for localities other than Boston are given in the **Tide Corrections** table on page **236.**

6. To calculate the moonrise time in your locale: Choose a day. Note the Moon Rise Key Letter. Find your (nearest) city on **page 238.** Add or subtract the minutes that correspond to the Moon Rise Key Letter to/from the moonrise time given for Boston. (A dash indicates that the moonrise occurs on/after midnight and is recorded on the next day.) Find the longitude of your (nearest) city on **page 238.** Add a correction in minutes for your city's longitude (see table, bottom left). Use the same procedure with Boston's moonset time and the Moon Set Key Letter value to calculate the time of moonset in your locale.

EXAMPLE:

To calculate the time of moonset in Lansing, Michigan, on day 1:

Moonset, Boston, with Key Letter B (p. 116)	12:58 P.M. ET
Value of Key Letter B for Lansing (p. 240)	+ 53 minutes
Correction for Lansing longitude, 84°33'	+ 1 minute
Moonset, Lansing	1:52 P.M. ET

7. This column gives the Moon's *astronomical* position among the constellations (not zodiac) at midnight. For *astrological* data, see **pages 224–227.**

Constellations have irregular borders; on successive nights, the midnight Moon may enter one, cross into another, and then move to a new area of the previous. It visits the 12 zodiacal constellations, as well as Auriga **(AUR),** a northern constellation between Perseus and Gemini; Cetus **(CET),** which lies south of the zodiac, just south of Pisces and Aries; Ophiuchus **(OPH),** primarily north of the zodiac but with a small corner between Scorpius and Sagittarius; Orion **(ORI),** whose northern limit first reaches the zodiac between Taurus and Gemini; and Sextans **(SEX),** which lies south of the zodiac except for a corner that just touches it near Leo.

8. This column gives the Moon's age: the number of days since the previous new Moon. (The average length of the lunar month is 29.53 days.) *(continued)*

LONGITUDE OF CITY	CORRECTION MINUTES	LONGITUDE OF CITY	CORRECTION MINUTES
58°–76°	0	116°–127°	+4
77°–89°	+1	128°–141°	+5
90°–102°	+2	142°–155°	+6
103°–115°	+3		

The Right-Hand Calendar Pages, 121 to 147

The Right-Hand Calendar Pages contain celestial events; religious observances; proverbs and poems; civil holidays; historical events; folklore; tide heights; weather prediction rhymes; Farmer's Calendar essays; and more.

A SAMPLE MONTH

1 2 3 4 5 6 7 8 9 10

1	Fr.	ALL FOOLS' • *If you want to make a fool of yourself, you'll find a lot of people ready to help you.*	*Flakes*	an inch long, who w
2	Sa.	Tap dancer Charles "Honi" Coles born, 1911 • Tides {9.5 9.0	*alive!*	in fresh water, pro
3	**B**	2nd S. of Easter • Writer F. Scott Fitzgerald married Zelda Sayre, 1920	*Spring's*	pond across the r
4	M.	Annunciation[T] • ☌♆☾ • *Ben Hur* won 11 Academy Awards, 1960	*arrived!*	emerged a month o
5	Tu.	☾ AT ☋ • Blizzard left 27.2" snow, St. John's, Nfld., 1999 • Tides {10.8 10.8	*Or is this*	to spend the next 3 on land before ret their wet world.
6	W.	☾ ON EQ. • ☌♀☾ • Twin mongoose lemurs born, Busch Gardens, Tampa, Fla., 2012	*warmth*	You can't mis

1. The bold letter is the Dominical Letter (from A to G), a traditional ecclesiastical designation for Sunday determined by the date on which the year's first Sunday falls. For 2019, the Dominical Letter is **F.**

2. Civil holidays and astronomical events.

3. Religious feasts: A[T] indicates a major feast that the church has this year temporarily transferred to a date other than its usual one.

4. Sundays and special holy days.

5. Symbols for notable celestial events. For example, ☌♆☾ on the 4th day means that a conjunction (☌) of Neptune (♆) and the Moon (☾) occurs: They are aligned along the same celestial longitude and appear to be closest together in the sky. See "Celestial Symbols" below.

6. Proverbs, poems, and adages.

7. Noteworthy historical events, folklore, and legends.

8. High tide heights, in feet, at Boston Massachusetts.

9. Weather prediction rhyme.

10. Farmer's Calendar essay.

Celestial Symbols

☉ Sun
○●☾ Moon
☿ Mercury
♀ Venus
⊕ Earth
♂ Mars
♃ Jupiter
♄ Saturn
⛢ Uranus
♆ Neptune
♇ Pluto
☌ Conjunction (on the same celestial longitude)
☊ Ascending node
☋ Descending node
☍ Opposition (180 degrees from Sun)

PREDICTING EARTHQUAKES

Note the dates in the Right-Hand Calendar Pages when the Moon rides high or runs low. The date of the high begins the most likely 5-day period of earthquakes in the Northern Hemisphere; the date of the low indicates a similar 5-day period in the Southern Hemisphere. Also noted are the 2 days each month when the Moon is on the celestial equator, indicating the most likely time for earthquakes in either hemisphere.

EARTH AT PERIHELION AND APHELION

Perihelion: January 3, 2019 (ET). Earth will be 91,403,554 miles from the Sun. **Aphelion:** July 4, 2019 (ET). Earth will be 94,513,221 miles from the Sun.

Why We Have Seasons

The seasons occur because as Earth revolves around the Sun, its axis remains tilted at 23.5 degrees from the perpendicular. This tilt causes different latitudes on Earth to receive varying amounts of sunlight throughout the year.

In the Northern Hemisphere, the summer solstice marks the beginning of summer and occurs when the North Pole is tilted toward the Sun. The winter solstice marks the beginning of winter and occurs when the North Pole is tilted away from the Sun.

The equinoxes occur when the hemispheres equally face the Sun. At this time, the Sun rises due east and sets due west. The vernal equinox marks the beginning of spring; the autumnal equinox marks the beginning of autumn.

In the Southern Hemisphere, the seasons are the reverse of those in the Northern Hemisphere.

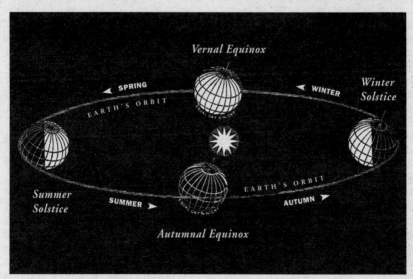

THE FIRST DAYS OF THE 2019 SEASONS

VERNAL (SPRING) EQUINOX: March 20, 5:58 P.M. EDT	
SUMMER SOLSTICE: June 21, 11:54 A.M. EDT	
AUTUMNAL (FALL) EQUINOX: Sept. 23, 3:50 A.M. EDT	
WINTER SOLSTICE: Dec. 21, 11:19 P.M. EST	

NOVEMBER

SKY WATCH: Mars, having resumed its normal eastward motion against the stars, speeds from Capricornus into Aquarius, gaining elevation to stand about a third of the way up the southern sky at nightfall. Just 12 arcseconds wide and at magnitude zero, it's lost half its width and is now too small to show useful detail in telescopes. On the 1st, Jupiter meets Mercury low in the west; both soon vanish. The Moon floats left of ever-lower Saturn on the 11th, close below Mars on the 15th, and to the left of Taurus's main star, Aldebaran, on the 23rd. The action switches to the predawn sky, where the Moon meets returning Venus on the 6th. Venus hovers near Virgo's Spica from the 6th to the 12th and stands 25 degrees high by month's end.

● **NEW MOON** 7th day 11:02 A.M.   ○ **FULL MOON** 23rd day 12:39 A.M.
◐ **FIRST QUARTER** 15th day 9:54 A.M.   ◑ **LAST QUARTER** 29th day 7:19 P.M.

After 2:00 A.M. on November 4, Eastern Standard Time is given.

GET THESE PAGES WITH TIMES SET TO YOUR ZIP CODE AT ALMANAC.COM/ACCESS.

DAY OF YEAR	DAY OF MONTH	DAY OF WEEK	☼ RISES H.M.	RISE KEY	☼ SETS H.M.	SET KEY	LENGTH OF DAY H.M.	SUN FAST M.	SUN DECLINATION ° '	HIGH TIDE TIMES BOSTON		☾ RISES H.M.	RISE KEY	☾ SETS H.M.	SET KEY	☾ ASTRON. PLACE	☾ AGE
305	1	Th.	7:17	D	**5:38**	B	10 21	32	14 s. 33	6	6¼	12:07	B	**2:44**	E	CAN	24
306	2	Fr.	7:19	D	**5:36**	B	10 17	32	14 s. 52	7	7½	1:18	C	**3:21**	E	LEO	25
307	3	Sa.	7:20	D	**5:35**	B	10 15	32	15 s. 11	8	8½	2:29	C	**3:54**	D	LEO	26
308	4	**G**	6:21	D	**4:34**	B	10 13	32	15 s. 30	8	8½	2:39	D	**3:25**	D	VIR	27
309	5	M.	6:22	D	**4:33**	B	10 11	32	15 s. 48	9	9½	3:49	D	**3:55**	C	VIR	28
310	6	Tu.	6:24	D	**4:31**	B	10 07	32	16 s. 06	9¾	10¼	4:57	E	**4:25**	C	VIR	29
311	7	W.	6:25	E	**4:30**	B	10 05	32	16 s. 24	10½	11	6:05	E	**4:57**	C	LIB	0
312	8	Th.	6:26	E	**4:29**	B	10 03	32	16 s. 41	11¼	11¾	7:11	E	**5:32**	B	LIB	1
313	9	Fr.	6:27	E	**4:28**	B	10 01	32	16 s. 58	12	—	8:15	E	**6:11**	B	SCO	2
314	10	Sa.	6:29	E	**4:27**	B	9 58	32	17 s. 15	12½	12¾	9:15	E	**6:53**	B	OPH	3
315	11	**G**	6:30	E	**4:26**	B	9 56	32	17 s. 32	1¼	1½	10:10	E	**7:41**	B	SAG	4
316	12	M.	6:31	E	**4:25**	B	9 54	32	17 s. 48	2	2¼	10:59	E	**8:32**	B	SAG	5
317	13	Tu.	6:32	E	**4:24**	B	9 52	31	18 s. 04	2¾	3	11:43	E	**9:27**	B	SAG	6
318	14	W.	6:34	E	**4:23**	B	9 49	31	18 s. 20	3¾	3¾	2:21	E	**10:24**	B	CAP	7
319	15	Th.	6:35	E	**4:22**	B	9 47	31	18 s. 35	4½	4¾	12:55	E	**11:22**	C	CAP	8
320	16	Fr.	6:36	E	**4:21**	B	9 45	31	18 s. 50	5½	5¾	1:25	E	—	-	AQU	9
321	17	Sa.	6:37	E	**4:21**	B	9 44	31	19 s. 05	6¼	6½	1:53	D	12:21	C	AQU	10
322	18	**G**	6:39	E	**4:20**	B	9 41	31	19 s. 19	7¼	7½	2:20	D	1:22	D	AQU	11
323	19	M.	6:40	E	**4:19**	B	9 39	30	19 s. 33	8	8¼	2:47	C	2:24	D	CET	12
324	20	Tu.	6:41	E	**4:18**	B	9 37	30	19 s. 46	8¾	9	3:15	C	3:27	E	PSC	13
325	21	W.	6:42	E	**4:18**	B	9 36	30	20 s. 00	9¼	9¾	3:46	C	4:33	E	CET	14
326	22	Th.	6:43	E	**4:17**	A	9 34	30	20 s. 13	10	10½	4:21	B	5:42	E	ARI	15
327	23	Fr.	6:45	E	**4:16**	A	9 31	29	20 s. 25	10¾	11¼	5:02	B	6:52	E	TAU	16
328	24	Sa.	6:46	E	**4:16**	A	9 30	29	20 s. 37	11½	—	5:50	B	8:02	E	TAU	17
329	25	**G**	6:47	E	**4:15**	A	9 28	29	20 s. 49	12¼	12¼	6:46	B	9:08	E	ORI	18
330	26	M.	6:48	E	**4:15**	A	9 27	28	21 s. 00	1	1	7:49	B	10:09	E	GEM	19
331	27	Tu.	6:49	E	**4:14**	A	9 25	28	21 s. 11	1¾	2	8:58	B	11:01	E	CAN	20
332	28	W.	6:50	E	**4:14**	A	9 24	28	21 s. 22	2¾	3	10:09	C	11:46	E	CAN	21
333	29	Th.	6:51	E	**4:13**	A	9 22	27	21 s. 32	3¾	4	11:20	C	12:24	E	LEO	22
334	30	Fr.	6:53	E	**4:13**	A	9 20	27	21 s. 42	4¾	5	—	-	12:58	D	LEO	23

NOVEMBER

Shorter and shorter now the twilight clips
The days, as through the sunset gate they crowd . . .
–Alice Cary

DAY OF MONTH	DAY OF WEEK	DATES, FEASTS, FASTS, ASPECTS, TIDE HEIGHTS, AND WEATHER	
1	Th.	All Saints' • Architect James Renwick Jr. born, 1818 • First direct flight from Canada to USSR, 1966	*Dank*
2	Fr.	All Souls' • Storm blocked Ben Franklin's view of lunar eclipse, Philadelphia, 1743 • {9.6 10.3	*and*
3	Sa.	Sadie Hawkins Day • *Mariner 10* spacecraft launched, Cape Canaveral, Fla., 1973 • {10.0 10.3	*dismal,*
4	**G**	**24th S. af. P.** • DAYLIGHT SAVING TIME ENDS, 2:00 A.M. • ☾ ON EQ.	*dearie.*
5	M.	☌♀☾ • *In the evening, one may praise the day.* • {10.8 10.5	*Just*
6	Tu.	ELECTION DAY • ☿ GR. ELONG. (23° EAST) • Composer Pyotr Ilyich Tchaikovsky died, 1893	*short*
7	W.	NEW ● • Evangelist Billy Graham born, 1918 • Tides {11.2 10.4	*of*
8	Th.	☌♃☾ • Black bears head to winter dens now. • Tides {11.2 10.2	*abysmal;*
9	Fr.	☌☿☾ • Worst day of storm that caused 12 major shipwrecks on Great Lakes, U.S. and Canada, 1913	
10	Sa.	Statue of Our Lady of Prompt Succor first in U.S. to be canonically crowned, New Orleans, La., 1895	*hardly what*
11	**G**	**25th S. af. P.** • VETERANS DAY • ☾ RUNS LOW • ☌♄☾	*we'd*
12	M.	Indian Summer • ☌♇☾ • 208-mile-long, 60-mile-wide iceberg discovered, 1956 • {9.2 9.9	*call*
13	Tu.	☾ AT ☋ • ♀ STAT. • Lobsters move to offshore waters.	*cheery.*
14	W.	☾ AT APO. • Yale U. announced will admit women following fall, 1968 • {8.6 9.2	*Rain*
15	Th.	☌♂☾ • First gas-turbine electric locomotive in U.S. track-tested, Erie, Pa., 1948 • Tides {8.5 8.9	*comes*
16	Fr.	Louis Riel, Métis leader and founder of Man., died, 1885 • Tides {8.5 8.8	*and*
17	Sa.	St. Hugh of Lincoln • ☌♆☾ • ☿ STAT. • Tides {8.7 8.9	*goes:*
18	**G**	**26th S. af. P.** • Crab apples are ripe now. • {9.0 9.0	*dreary!*
19	M.	☾ ON EQ. • Columbus first saw what is now Puerto Rico, 1493 • Tides {9.4 9.3	*At*
20	Tu.	☌⛢☾ • *One sesame seed won't make oil.* • Tides {9.9 9.5	*least*
21	W.	Actress Marlo Thomas born, 1937 • Actor Bill Bixby died, 1993 • Tides {10.4 9.8	*our*
22	Th.	THANKSGIVING DAY • Explorer La Salle born, 1643 • Pirate Blackbeard died, 1718	*turkey*
23	Fr.	St. Clement • FULL BEAVER ○ • Lake Merced water level dropped 30', Calif., 1852	*isn't*
24	Sa.	Artist Henri de Toulouse-Lautrec born, 1864 • Pianist Scott Joplin born, 1868	*jerky.*
25	**G**	**27th S. af. P.** • ☾ RIDES HIGH • ♆ STAT. • {10.2 11.6	*Quirky:*
26	M.	☾ AT PERIG. • ☌♃☉ • First major football game played indoors, Chicago Coliseum, Ill., 1896	*mild,*
27	Tu.	☾ AT ☊ • ☌☿♃ • ☿ IN INF. ☌ • Blizzard with lightning struck parts of S.Dak., 1983	*wild,*
28	W.	North Pacific Canning Co. formed, B.C., 1888 • {9.9 10.9	*wet,*
29	Th.	Maj. Henry Hitchcock, Sherman's March, Ga., 1864: *Weather so warm I could not wear any cape after 10 A.M.*	*and*
30	Fr.	St. Andrew • *A heavy November snow will last until April.*	*murky.*

Farmer's Calendar

In late autumn, after most of the leaves have fallen, the forest suddenly becomes transparent. The contours of the land leap out in 3-D, exposing all kinds of subtleties. Many of them are small, bashful, the kind of sights that require us to look down instead of up.

For example, just before Thanksgiving, I noticed for the first time some spectacular maple leaves in colors—rose, bright yellow, hunter's orange—that had long since left the canopy above me. They were big leaves, 6 inches or more across, but they were growing on stems less than 18 inches tall.

Why do these tiny trees put forth such unusually large and brilliant leaves? Perhaps it's because now the sunlight streams down to the forest floor unhindered, so these "mini-maples" can suck up energy with their outsized solar collectors.

Once I noticed the first, the second, the third, I saw them everywhere. They fluttered, but there was no breeze. They looked like cops doing that palm-down hand-waggle that means, "You're not going fast enough for me to stop you, but you're going too fast."

The semaphore of the leaves has a similar message: "Slow down. You're going too fast to see me."

DECEMBER

SKY WATCH: Venus excels as a morning star, now at greatest brilliancy at a gorgeous, shadow-casting magnitude –4.9. High at predawn twilight, it's below the Moon on the 3rd. Mercury also begins a good morning apparition, below the Moon on the 5th. On the 6th, Jupiter takes its turn dangling below the crescent Moon. The Geminid meteors should be excellent on the 13th, after the Moon sets at around 10:00 P.M. Zero-magnitude Mars stands above the Moon on the 14th, with both about half-way up the southern sky at nightfall. Jupiter and Mercury hang out together most of the month and are quite close on the 21st, some 10 degrees high, 40 minutes before sunrise. Winter begins with the solstice on the 21st at 5:23 P.M.

| ● NEW MOON | 7th day 2:20 A.M. | ○ FULL MOON | 22nd day 12:49 P.M. |
| ◑ FIRST QUARTER | 15th day 6:49 A.M. | ◐ LAST QUARTER | 29th day 4:34 A.M. |

All times are given in Eastern Standard Time.

GET THESE PAGES WITH TIMES SET TO YOUR ZIP CODE AT ALMANAC.COM/ACCESS.

DAY OF YEAR	DAY OF MONTH	DAY OF WEEK	☀ RISES H.M.	RISE KEY	☀ SETS H.M.	SET KEY	LENGTH OF DAY H.M.	SUN FAST M.	SUN DECLINATION ° ′	HIGH TIDE TIMES BOSTON		☾ RISES H.M.	RISE KEY	☾ SETS H.M.	SET KEY	☾ ASTRON. PLACE	☾ AGE
335	1	Sa.	6:54	E	4:13	A	9 19	27	21 s. 51	5¾	6¼	12:30	D	1:29	D	VIR	24
336	2	**G**	6:55	E	4:12	A	9 17	26	22 s. 00	6¾	7¼	1:38	D	1:58	C	VIR	25
337	3	M.	6:56	E	4:12	A	9 16	26	22 s. 09	7¾	8¼	2:46	E	2:27	C	VIR	26
338	4	Tu.	6:57	E	4:12	A	9 15	25	22 s. 17	8¾	9¼	3:52	E	2:57	C	VIR	27
339	5	W.	6:58	E	4:12	A	9 14	25	22 s. 24	9½	10	4:58	E	3:30	B	LIB	28
340	6	Th.	6:59	E	4:12	A	9 13	25	22 s. 32	10¼	10¾	6:02	E	4:06	B	SCO	29
341	7	Fr.	7:00	E	4:12	A	9 12	24	22 s. 38	11	11½	7:03	E	4:47	B	OPH	0
342	8	Sa.	7:01	E	4:12	A	9 11	24	22 s. 45	11½	—	8:00	E	5:32	B	SAG	1
343	9	**G**	7:01	E	4:12	A	9 11	23	22 s. 51	12¼	12¼	8:53	E	6:22	B	SAG	2
344	10	M.	7:02	E	4:12	A	9 10	23	22 s. 56	1	1	9:39	E	7:16	B	SAG	3
345	11	Tu.	7:03	E	4:12	A	9 09	22	23 s. 01	1½	1¾	10:19	E	8:12	B	CAP	4
346	12	W.	7:04	E	4:12	A	9 08	22	23 s. 06	2¼	2½	10:55	E	9:10	C	CAP	5
347	13	Th.	7:05	E	4:12	A	9 07	22	23 s. 10	3	3¼	11:26	E	10:09	C	AQU	6
348	14	Fr.	7:06	E	4:12	A	9 06	21	23 s. 13	3¾	4	11:55	D	11:08	C	AQU	7
349	15	Sa.	7:06	E	4:12	A	9 06	21	23 s. 17	4¾	5	12:21	D	—	-	AQU	8
350	16	**G**	7:07	E	4:13	A	9 06	20	23 s. 19	5½	5¾	12:47	D	12:08	D	PSC	9
351	17	M.	7:08	E	4:13	A	9 05	20	23 s. 21	6¼	6¾	1:14	C	1:09	D	CET	10
352	18	Tu.	7:08	E	4:13	A	9 05	19	23 s. 23	7¼	7½	1:43	C	2:13	E	PSC	11
353	19	W.	7:09	E	4:14	A	9 05	19	23 s. 24	8	8½	2:15	B	3:19	E	CET	12
354	20	Th.	7:09	E	4:14	A	9 05	18	23 s. 25	8¾	9¼	2:52	B	4:28	E	TAU	13
355	21	Fr.	7:10	E	4:15	A	9 05	18	23 s. 26	9½	10¼	3:36	B	5:38	E	TAU	14
356	22	Sa.	7:10	E	4:15	A	9 05	17	23 s. 25	10¼	11	4:30	B	6:48	E	TAU	15
357	23	**G**	7:11	E	4:16	A	9 05	17	23 s. 25	11¼	11¾	5:32	B	7:54	E	GEM	16
358	24	M.	7:11	E	4:16	A	9 05	16	23 s. 24	12	—	6:41	B	8:52	E	GEM	17
359	25	Tu.	7:12	E	4:17	A	9 05	16	23 s. 22	12¾	12¾	7:54	C	9:42	E	CAN	18
360	26	W.	7:12	E	4:18	A	9 06	15	23 s. 20	1½	1¾	9:08	C	10:25	E	LEO	19
361	27	Th.	7:12	E	4:18	A	9 06	15	23 s. 18	2½	2¾	10:20	D	11:01	D	LEO	20
362	28	Fr.	7:13	E	4:19	A	9 06	14	23 s. 15	3½	3¾	11:30	D	11:33	D	LEO	21
363	29	Sa.	7:13	E	4:20	A	9 07	14	23 s. 11	4¼	4¾	—	-	12:03	C	VIR	22
364	30	**G**	7:13	E	4:21	A	9 08	13	23 s. 08	5½	5¾	12:38	D	12:32	C	VIR	23
365	31	M.	7:13	E	4:21	A	9 08	13	23 s. 03	6½	7	1:44	E	1:01	C	VIR	24

To use this page, see p. 116; for Key Letters, see p. 238. LIGHT = A.M. **BOLD = P.M.**

CALENDAR

THE TWELFTH MONTH · 2018

DECEMBER

DECEMBER HATH 31 DAYS

Come give the holly a song;
For it helps to drive stern winter away.
–Eliza Cook

DAY OF MONTH	DAY OF WEEK	DATES, FEASTS, FASTS, ASPECTS, TIDE HEIGHTS, AND WEATHER	
1	Sa.	♀ AT GR. ILLUM. EXTENT • –25.6°F, Fort Saskatchewan, Alta., 1990	*Shopping*
2	G	**1st S. of Advent** • Chanukah begins at sundown • ☾ ON EQ.	*rush*
3	M.	☌♀☾ • Ill. admitted to Union as 21st state, 1818 • Tides {10.4 9.8	*slowed*
4	Tu.	Naturalist Stuart Criddle died, 1877 • Tides {10.6 9.8	*by*
5	W.	☌☿☾ • Canada's first electric car debuted, Toronto, Ont., 1893 • Tides {10.8 9.8	*slush;*
6	Th.	St. Nicholas • ☌♃☾ • ☿ STAT. • 5" snow, Savannah, Ga., 1740	*we'll*
7	Fr.	St. Ambrose • **NAT'L PEARL HARBOR REMEMBRANCE DAY** • NEW ● • ☌♂♆	*have*
8	Sa.	Winterberry fruits especially showy now. • {10.7 —	*to mush!*
9	G	**2nd S. of Advent** • ☾ RUNS LOW • ☌♄☾ • ☌♇☾ • {9.4 10.5	*A*
10	M.	St. Eulalia • ☾ AT ☋ • *One ounce of discretion is worth a pound of wit.* • {9.2 10.2	*snow*
11	Tu.	Astronomer Annie Jump Cannon born, 1863 • *Dec. 11–12:* Ice storm hit Northeast, 2008 • {9.0 9.9	*event*
12	W.	**Our Lady of Guadalupe** • ☾ AT APO. • U.S. diplomat Joel Roberts Poinsett died, 1851	*may*
13	Th.	St. Lucia • Wilson first U.S. president to visit Europe while in office, 1918 • {8.7 9.3	*leave*
14	Fr.	Halcyon Days begin. • ☌♂☾ • ☌♆☾ • "Diplogen" suggested for isotope name, 1933	*us*
15	Sa.	☿ GR. ELONG. (21° WEST) • Architect Alexandre Gustave Eiffel born, 1832 • Tides {8.7 8.8	*wan,*
16	G	**3rd S. of Advent** • ☾ ON EQ. • Boston Tea Party occurred, 1773	*spent.*
17	M.	☌♅☾ • *When the snow falls dry, it means to lie; But flakes light and soft bring rain oft.* • {9.1 8.7	*Arctic*
18	Tu.	Beware the Pogonip. • Actress Zsa Zsa Gabor died, 2016	*blast*
19	W.	Ember Day • *Intelsat III F-2* communications satellite launched, 1968 • {10.0 9.2	*is*
20	Th.	Industrialist Harvey S. Firestone born, 1868 • {10.5 9.5	*quickly*
21	Fr.	St. Thomas • Ember Day • **WINTER SOLSTICE** • ☌☿♃ • {11.0 9.8	*past,*
22	Sa.	Ember Day • **FULL COLD** ○ • Writer Beatrix Potter died, 1943	*so*
23	G	**4th S. of Advent** • ☾ RIDES HIGH • Van Gogh cut off most of left ear, 1888	*Santa's*
24	M.	☾ AT ☊ • ☾ AT PERIG. • Pepper, a Bolivian gray titi monkey, born at Philadelphia Zoo, Pa., 2012	*not*
25	Tu.	**Christmas** • G. Washington's troops crossed Delaware R., Am. Revolution, 1776	*despondent.*
26	W.	St. Stephen • **BOXING DAY (CANADA)** • **FIRST DAY OF KWANZAA** • {10.4 11.6	*Snowy*
27	Th.	St. John • Ill diarist, N.Y., 1864: *I don't see no need of being sick now that school is out. Darn it!*	*and shivery*
28	Fr.	Holy Innocents • First sudden-death overtime game in NFL, Baltimore Colts vs. N.Y. Giants, 1958	*for*
29	Sa.	☾ ON EQ. • Lake Washington Floating Bridge construction began, Seattle, Wash., 1938	*infant*
30	G	**1st S. af. Ch.** • *Good to begin well, better to end well.* • Tides {10.1 9.5	*'19's*
31	M.	St. Sylvester • Helium-filled sun shade patented, 1991	*delivery!*

Farmer's Calendar

Those of us who lived through the Great New England Ice Storm of December 11–12, 2008, still have posttraumatic stress disorder. The storm lasted 2 days, but the power was out for more than a week at our house. Now, when ice is predicted, we check our water supplies, our batteries, our candles. We sleep with a flashlight; we unplug the computers. We lie awake listening for the chatter of sleet on the windows or, God forbid, the rifle shots of branches breaking or the chandelier-fall crash of a treetop.

But in many ways this was the most joyous holiday season ever. People checked on their neighbors. The General Store contributed 200 turkey dinners to a supper at the elementary school so that people could enjoy a hot meal and some company. One couple went ahead with a church wedding, lit by candles. Bundled up like fur trappers, they left little puffs of fog when they said their vows.

We're just not quite ready to go through it all again. The worst part was going a week without a shower. Come to think of it: No, it was hauling water up from the creek in buckets. Actually: No, it was using up half a winter's firewood in a fortnight!

This ice storm followed the last big one by 12 years. We're about due for another.

JANUARY

SKY WATCH: The year begins with a predawn string of pearls: Some 40 minutes before sunrise on the 1st, the Moon, Venus, Jupiter, and Mercury hover from upper right to lower left, low in the eastern sky. Venus is now at its brightest of the year. The alignment on the 2nd finds the Moon between Venus and Jupiter. On the 3rd, the Moon is to the left of Jupiter. Through January, Venus sinks lower at first light but Jupiter is higher; their opposing motions cause them to meet from the 20th to the 26th. At nightfall all month, Mars in Pisces is due south at a bright magnitude 0. A total lunar eclipse on the 20th, visible from the entire United States and Canada, begins at 10:34 P.M., with totality starting at 11:41 P.M.

● **NEW MOON**   5th day   8:28 P.M.   ○ **FULL MOON**   21st day 12:16 A.M.
◑ **FIRST QUARTER** 14th day   1:46 A.M.   ◐ **LAST QUARTER** 27th day   4:10 P.M.

All times are given in Eastern Standard Time.

GET THESE PAGES WITH TIMES SET TO YOUR ZIP CODE AT ALMANAC.COM/ACCESS.

DAY OF YEAR	DAY OF MONTH	DAY OF WEEK	☼ RISES H. M.	RISE KEY	☼ SETS H. M.	SET KEY	LENGTH OF DAY H. M.	SUN FAST M.	SUN DECLINATION ° '	HIGH TIDE TIMES BOSTON		☾ RISES H. M.	RISE KEY	☾ SETS H. M.	SET KEY	☾ ASTRON. PLACE	☾ AGE
1	1	Tu.	7:13	E	4:22	A	9 09	12	22 s. 58	7¼	8	2:49	E	1:32	B	LIB	25
2	2	W.	7:13	E	4:23	A	9 10	12	22 s. 53	8¼	9	3:53	E	2:07	B	LIB	26
3	3	Th.	7:13	E	4:24	A	9 11	11	22 s. 47	9	9¾	4:54	E	2:45	B	OPH	27
4	4	Fr.	7:13	E	4:25	A	9 12	11	22 s. 41	10	10½	5:53	E	3:28	B	OPH	28
5	5	Sa.	7:13	E	4:26	A	9 13	10	22 s. 35	10½	11¼	6:47	E	4:16	B	SAG	0
6	6	F	7:13	E	4:27	A	9 14	10	22 s. 28	11¼	11¾	7:35	E	5:08	B	SAG	1
7	7	M.	7:13	E	4:28	A	9 15	10	22 s. 20	12	—	8:18	E	6:04	B	CAP	2
8	8	Tu.	7:13	E	4:29	A	9 16	9	22 s. 12	12½	12½	8:55	E	7:01	B	CAP	3
9	9	W.	7:13	E	4:30	A	9 17	9	22 s. 04	1¼	1¼	9:28	E	7:59	C	CAP	4
10	10	Th.	7:13	E	4:31	A	9 18	8	21 s. 55	1¾	2	9:57	E	8:58	C	AQU	5
11	11	Fr.	7:12	E	4:32	A	9 20	8	21 s. 46	2½	2½	10:24	D	9:57	D	AQU	6
12	12	Sa.	7:12	E	4:33	A	9 21	7	21 s. 36	3¼	3½	10:50	D	10:56	D	PSC	7
13	13	F	7:12	E	4:34	A	9 22	7	21 s. 26	4	4¼	11:15	C	11:57	D	CET	8
14	14	M.	7:11	E	4:36	A	9 25	7	21 s. 15	4¾	5	11:42	C	—	-	PSC	9
15	15	Tu.	7:11	E	4:37	A	9 26	6	21 s. 04	5½	6	12:11	C	1:00	E	CET	10
16	16	W.	7:10	E	4:38	A	9 28	6	20 s. 53	6½	7	12:45	B	2:06	E	ARI	11
17	17	Th.	7:10	E	4:39	A	9 29	6	20 s. 41	7¼	8	1:24	B	3:14	E	TAU	12
18	18	Fr.	7:09	E	4:40	B	9 31	5	20 s. 29	8¼	9	2:12	B	4:23	E	TAU	13
19	19	Sa.	7:09	E	4:41	B	9 32	5	20 s. 17	9	9¾	3:09	B	5:30	E	ORI	14
20	20	F	7:08	E	4:43	B	9 35	5	20 s. 04	10	10¾	4:15	B	6:33	E	GEM	15
21	21	M.	7:07	E	4:44	B	9 37	5	19 s. 51	10¾	11½	5:28	C	7:29	E	CAN	16
22	22	Tu.	7:07	E	4:45	B	9 38	4	19 s. 37	11¾	—	6:45	C	8:17	E	CAN	17
23	23	W.	7:06	E	4:46	B	9 40	4	19 s. 23	12½	12¾	8:01	C	8:57	E	LEO	18
24	24	Th.	7:05	E	4:48	B	9 43	4	19 s. 09	1¼	1½	9:15	D	9:32	D	LEO	19
25	25	Fr.	7:04	E	4:49	B	9 45	4	18 s. 54	2	2½	10:26	D	10:04	D	VIR	20
26	26	Sa.	7:04	E	4:50	B	9 46	3	18 s. 39	3	3½	11:35	E	10:34	C	VIR	21
27	27	F	7:03	E	4:52	B	9 49	3	18 s. 24	4	4½	—	-	11:04	C	VIR	22
28	28	M.	7:02	E	4:53	B	9 51	3	18 s. 08	5	5½	12:41	E	11:35	B	LIB	23
29	29	Tu.	7:01	E	4:54	B	9 53	3	17 s. 52	6	6½	1:46	E	12:08	B	LIB	24
30	30	W.	7:00	E	4:55	B	9 55	2	17 s. 36	7	7½	2:48	E	12:45	B	OPH	25
31	31	Th.	6:59	E	4:57	B	9 58	2	17 s. 19	7¾	8½	3:47	E	1:26	B	OPH	26

   To use this page, see p. 116; for Key Letters, see p. 238. LIGHT = A.M. BOLD = P.M.   2019

Ring on, ring yet more gladly, merry bells,
Peal the new lord of days glad welcoming.
–Augusta Webster

DAY OF MONTH	DAY OF WEEK	DATES, FEASTS, FASTS, ASPECTS, TIDE HEIGHTS, AND WEATHER	
1	Tu.	Holy Name • NEW YEAR'S DAY • ☌♀☾ • First U.S. electronic hwy. toll collection, Okla., 1991	*Grab*
2	W.	☌♄☉ • *A still tongue makes a wise head.* • Tides {10.2 / 9.1	*a*
3	Th.	☌♃☾ • ⊕ AT PERIHELION • Alaska became 49th state, 1959 • {10.3 / 9.1	*sled*
4	Fr.	St. Elizabeth Ann Seton • ☌☿☾ • Ctrl-Alt-Delete computer code author David Bradley born, 1949	*and*
5	Sa.	Twelfth Night • NEW ● • ECLIPSE ☉ • ☾ RUNS LOW • ☌♄☾ • ♀ GR. ELONG. (47° WEST)	
6	F	Epiphany • ☾ AT ☋ • ☌♇☾ • ♅ STAT. • {10.3 / 9.0	*head for*
7	M.	Distaff Day • Plough Monday • *Surveyor VII* spacecraft launched, 1968 • {10.2 / —	*the*
8	Tu.	☾ AT APO. • Physicist Stephen Hawking born, 1942 • Tides {9.0 / 10.1	*hills!*
9	W.	UN headquarters opened in N.Y.C., 1951 • {9.0 / 9.9	*Chillier:*
10	Th.	☌♆☾ • U.S. Army first to bounce radar signals off Moon (Project Diana), Wall, N.J., 1946	*Swill*
11	Fr.	☌♇☉ • Canadian prime minister Jean Chrétien born, 1934 • Tides {8.8 / 9.3	*your*
12	Sa.	☌♂☾ • *A thousand probabilities do not make one truth.* • Tides {8.8 / 9.0	*cocoa*
13	F	1st S. af. Ep. • ☾ ON EQ. • ☌☿♄ • Tides {8.8 / 8.7	*before*
14	M.	☌♅☾ • First nonstop trans-Canada flight completed, 1949 • Tides {8.9 / 8.5	*it*
15	Tu.	Great Molasses Flood, Boston, Mass., 1919 • Writer André Alexis born, 1957 • {9.2 / 8.5	*spills!*
16	W.	–40°F, Coggon, Iowa, 2009 • Tides {9.5 / 8.6	*Rain*
17	Th.	U.S. statesman Benjamin Franklin born, 1706 • 6.7 earthquake, Northridge, Calif., 1994	*pelting*
18	Fr.	☌☿♇ • NASA and NOAA announced that 2016 was hottest year globally on record, 2017	*down*
19	Sa.	☾ RIDES HIGH • Writer Edgar Allan Poe born, 1809 • Tides {11.0 / 9.6	*and*
20	F	2nd S. af. Ep. • ☾ AT ☊ • *20–21:* ECLIPSE ☾	*snowmen*
21	M.	**Martin Luther King Jr.'s Birthday, observed** • FULL WOLF ○ • ☾ AT PERIG. • {11.9 / 10.4	*are*
22	Tu.	St. Vincent • ☌♀♃ • *If the Sun shines on January 22, there shall be much wind.*	*melting*
23	W.	Bob Keeshan (Captain Kangaroo) died, 2004 • {10.7 / 12.0	*down!*
24	Th.	Apple's Macintosh personal computer introduced, 1984 • Tides {10.8 / 11.7	*Flakes,*
25	Fr.	Conversion of Paul • ☾ ON EQ. • January thaw traditionally begins about now.	*flurries*
26	Sa.	Sts. Timothy & Titus • Rocky Mountain National Park established, Colo., 1915	*again,*
27	F	3rd S. af. Ep. • National Recording Registry's first 50 selections announced, 2003	*bring*
28	M.	St. Thomas Aquinas • –132°F windchill, Pelly Bay, N.W.T., 1989 • {10.1 / 9.2	*out*
29	Tu.	☿ IN SUP. ☌ • Raccoons mate now. • *All covet, all lose.*	*those*
30	W.	☌♃☾ • 31-lb. 12-oz. bluefish caught, Hatteras, N.C., 1972 • Tides {9.7 / 8.6	*furries*
31	Th.	☌♀☾ • Ice hockey player Tyler Seguin born, 1992 • {9.7 / 8.5	*again.*

Farmer's Calendar

The cottages around the lake are locked, their pipes drained, shades pulled. Where just months ago kayakers floated on silky waters, now a pickup truck zooms onto the frozen lake, towing something that looks like a deluxe privy. A handful of shanties are sprinkled across the ice—a spontaneous colony of mostly quiet anglers. I find one of them crouched over his fishing hole, withdrawing his line. The monofilament is so slender, it's hard to see; it's as if he's pantomiming the act with his hands. Finally, he crooks a finger in the emerging fish's gill as he pulls out a lake trout. Its scales are emerald, mottled with iridescent, leopard-like spots. The man has just executed a magic trick, pulling this shimmering creature from the lake's bottom—a gambler's payoff in the coldest, least hospitable casino. He measures the fish against his tackle box ruler: just barely legal. He studies his treasure once more, then lets it slip back through the hole. In a swish, it is gone. The only sounds are the shushing wind, the buzzing of a gas-powered auger, and then, in odd moments, the booming ice. It's a low bass sound, *lubb-dub*—the beat of a lake-size heart.

FEBRUARY

SKY WATCH: The heavens offer a new alignment before dawn on the 1st: Low in the east, from highest to lowest, stand Jupiter, Venus, the Moon, and Saturn. On the 2nd, the order is Jupiter, Venus, Saturn, and the Moon. On the 18th and 19th, quite low at first light, Venus meets Saturn. Throughout February, just as darkness falls, bright orange Mars stands halfway up the southwestern sky. To its left, also in Pisces, Uranus dimly shines at magnitude 5.8, just visible to the naked eye in unpolluted skies early and again late in the month. It is easily identified as the only green "star" by those who sweep binoculars leftward from Mars.

● **NEW MOON** 4th day 4:04 P.M.   ○ **FULL MOON** 19th day 10:54 A.M.
◐ **FIRST QUARTER** 12th day 5:26 P.M.   ◑ **LAST QUARTER** 26th day 6:28 A.M.

All times are given in Eastern Standard Time.

GET THESE PAGES WITH TIMES SET TO YOUR ZIP CODE AT ALMANAC.COM/ACCESS.

DAY OF YEAR	DAY OF MONTH	DAY OF WEEK	☼ RISES H. M.	RISE KEY	☼ SETS H. M.	SET KEY	LENGTH OF DAY H. M.	SUN FAST M.	SUN DECLINATION ° '	HIGH TIDE TIMES BOSTON		☾ RISES H. M.	RISE KEY	☾ SETS H. M.	SET KEY	☾ ASTRON. PLACE	☾ AGE
32	1	Fr.	6:58	E	4:58	B	10 00	2	17 s. 02	8¾	9½	4:42	E	2:12	B	SAG	27
33	2	Sa.	6:57	E	4:59	B	10 02	2	16 s. 45	9½	10¼	5:32	E	3:03	B	SAG	28
34	3	**F**	6:56	E	5:01	B	10 05	2	16 s. 27	10¼	10¾	6:16	E	3:57	B	SAG	29
35	4	M.	6:55	D	5:02	B	10 07	2	16 s. 09	11	11½	6:55	E	4:54	B	CAP	0
36	5	Tu.	6:54	D	5:03	B	10 09	2	15 s. 51	11½	—	7:30	E	5:52	C	CAP	1
37	6	W.	6:52	D	5:05	B	10 13	2	15 s. 33	12	12¼	8:00	E	6:51	C	AQU	2
38	7	Th.	6:51	D	5:06	B	10 15	2	15 s. 14	12¾	12¾	8:28	D	7:49	D	AQU	3
39	8	Fr.	6:50	D	5:07	B	10 17	2	14 s. 55	1¼	1½	8:54	D	8:48	D	AQU	4
40	9	Sa.	6:49	D	5:09	B	10 20	2	14 s. 36	2	2¼	9:19	C	9:48	D	CET	5
41	10	**F**	6:48	D	5:10	B	10 22	2	14 s. 16	2½	2¾	9:45	C	10:49	E	PSC	6
42	11	M.	6:46	D	5:11	B	10 25	2	13 s. 57	3¼	3½	10:12	C	11:52	E	CET	7
43	12	Tu.	6:45	D	5:12	B	10 27	2	13 s. 37	4	4½	10:42	B	—	-	ARI	8
44	13	W.	6:44	D	5:14	B	10 30	2	13 s. 17	4¾	5½	11:18	B	12:57	E	TAU	9
45	14	Th.	6:42	D	5:15	B	10 33	2	12 s. 56	5¾	6½	11:59	B	2:03	E	TAU	10
46	15	Fr.	6:41	D	5:16	B	10 35	2	12 s. 36	6¾	7½	12:50	B	3:09	E	TAU	11
47	16	Sa.	6:40	D	5:18	B	10 38	2	12 s. 15	7¾	8½	1:50	B	4:13	E	GEM	12
48	17	**F**	6:38	D	5:19	B	10 41	2	11 s. 54	8¾	9½	2:59	B	5:11	E	GEM	13
49	18	M.	6:37	D	5:20	B	10 43	2	11 s. 33	9¾	10¼	4:14	C	6:03	E	CAN	14
50	19	Tu.	6:35	D	5:21	B	10 46	2	11 s. 12	10½	11¼	5:31	C	6:47	E	LEO	15
51	20	W.	6:34	D	5:23	B	10 49	2	10 s. 50	11½	—	6:49	D	7:25	E	LEO	16
52	21	Th.	6:32	D	5:24	B	10 52	2	10 s. 29	12	12¼	8:04	D	8:00	D	VIR	17
53	22	Fr.	6:31	D	5:25	B	10 54	2	10 s. 07	12¾	1¼	9:17	E	8:32	C	VIR	18
54	23	Sa.	6:29	D	5:26	B	10 57	3	9 s. 45	1¾	2	10:27	E	9:03	C	VIR	19
55	24	**F**	6:28	D	5:28	B	11 00	3	9 s. 23	2½	3	11:35	E	9:34	C	LIB	20
56	25	M.	6:26	D	5:29	B	11 03	3	9 s. 00	3½	4	—	-	10:08	B	LIB	21
57	26	Tu.	6:25	D	5:30	C	11 05	3	8 s. 38	4¼	5	12:40	E	10:44	B	SCO	22
58	27	W.	6:23	D	5:31	C	11 08	3	8 s. 16	5¼	6	1:41	E	11:24	B	OPH	23
59	28	Th.	6:22	D	5:33	C	11 11	3	7 s. 53	6¼	7	2:38	E	12:09	B	SAG	24

FEBRUARY

Here delicate snow-stars, out of the cloud,
Come floating downward in airy play.
–William Cullen Bryant

DAY OF MONTH	DAY OF WEEK	DATES, FEASTS, FASTS, ASPECTS, TIDE HEIGHTS, AND WEATHER	
1	Fr.	St. Brigid • ☾ runs low • –50°F, Gavilan, N.Mex., 1951 • {9.8 / 8.6	*Groundhogs*
2	Sa.	Candlemas • Groundhog Day • ☌♄☾ • ☌♇☾ • {9.9 / 8.7	*blinded,*
3	**F**	☾ at ☋ • Artist Norman Rockwell born, 1894 • Tides {10.0 / 8.9	*more*
4	M.	NEW ● • *Codex Sinaiticus* discovered, St. Catherine's Monastery, Mt. Sinai, Egypt, 1859	*winter,*
5	Tu.	St. Agatha • **Chinese New Year (Pig)** • ☾ at apo. • ☌☿☾ • {10.1 / —	*we're*
6	W.	Woodrow Wilson became first U.S. president to be buried in D.C., 1924 • Tides {9.1 / 10.1	*reminded.*
7	Th.	☌♆☾ • Manufacturer John Deere born, 1804 • *Stardust* probe launched, Cape Canaveral, Fla., 1999	
8	Fr.	Politician Thelma Chalifoux born, 1929 • Tides {9.2 / 9.7	*Whiteout, then*
9	Sa.	☾ on eq. • First train passed through Hoosac Tunnel, Mass., 1875 • Tides {9.3 / 9.5	*bright*
10	**F**	☌♂☾ • ☌♅☾ • Olympic swimmer Victor Davis born, 1964 • {9.3 / 9.2	*out!*
11	M.	First joint U.S.-Russian space shuttle mission completed, 1994 • Tides {9.3 / 8.9	*Snow*
12	Tu.	U.S. president Abraham Lincoln born, 1809 • {9.3 / 8.6	*on and*
13	W.	☌♂♅ • *Absence sharpens love; presence strengthens it.* –Thomas Fuller • {9.4 / 8.5	*offing, coats*
14	Th.	Sts. Cyril & Methodius • **Valentine's Day** • {9.6 / 8.5	*doffing.*
15	Fr.	**National Flag of Canada Day** • Astronomer Galileo Galilei born, 1564 • Social reformer Susan B. Anthony born, 1820	
16	Sa.	☾ rides high • 250-hr., 3-min., 20-sec. ice hockey marathon ended, Saiker's Acres, Alta., 2015	*Mercury*
17	**F**	**Septuagesima** • ☾ at ☊ • Winter's back breaks. • {11.0 / 9.8	*plummets,*
18	M.	**Presidents' Day** • ☌♀♄ • "Firenado" captured on video, Platte County, Mo., 2016	*more*
19	Tu.	FULL SNOW ○ • ☾ at perig. • ☌☿♆ • {11.9 / 10.8	*flurries*
20	W.	*It is wise not to seek a secret, and honest not to reveal it.* • Tides {12.1 / —	*come; it's*
21	Th.	Polaroid instant camera first demonstrated, 1947 • Tides {11.2 / 12.0	*suddenly*
22	Fr.	☾ on eq. • U.S. president George Washington born, 1732 • "Florida Purchase" treaty signed, 1819	*springlike!*
23	Sa.	☌♀♇ • 97°F, San Antonio, Tex., 1996 • Tides {11.2 / 11.0	*Who*
24	**F**	**Sexagesima** • Skunks mate now. • Tides {10.9 / 10.3	*would*
25	M.	St. Matthias[T] • 49.3" snow fell, Mt. Washington, N.H., 1969 • {10.5 / 9.6	*guess*
26	Tu.	☿ gr. elong. (18° east) • Grand Canyon National Park established, Ariz., 1919 • {10.0 / 8.9	*a*
27	W.	☌♃☾ • *When gnats dance in February, the husbandman becomes a beggar.* • {9.6 / 8.5	*thing like*
28	Th.	St. Romanus • Radio broadcaster Paul Harvey died, 2009 • Tides {9.3 / 8.3	*this?*

What's the fastest vegetable? A runner bean.

Farmer's Calendar

While snow levels fluctuate or mostly rise, our winter stores subside. The woodshed looks like a mouth of broken teeth, and the chest freezer has new cavities, too. The same goes for our livestock supplies. Our cows wait out the days gazing at snow that they can't eat covering fields that they used to graze—thank heavens for hay. Last summer we stuffed the mow with a winter's worth (one bale per cow, per day, plus extra, just in case). As I deliver flakes to the Jersey and her yearling calf, I second-guess what's left, wondering if it'll last until they're back on pasture; so much depends on winter's strength and length. Years ago, when I worked on a bigger farm, each morning I climbed into the loft, where the bales were stacked to the rafters. Summiting the steep pile, I'd pry down a dozen, clenching them by their twine. As winter days ticked by and the mountain of dried grass dwindled, the barn's walls re-emerged. One day in mid-February, by luck or barn maker's design, I saw a sign I took to mean that we'd reached the season's halfway mark: Sunlight streamed through a hole bored near the roof's peak, a vent in the shape of a valentine.

MARCH

SKY WATCH: Mercury hovers low in the west during the first few evenings of March. On the 1st, in the east just before dawn, a line of celestial objects becomes visible above Sagittarius's "Teapot" asterism (pattern of stars). From right to left, these are Jupiter, the Moon, Saturn, and Venus. On the morning of the 2nd, the thin crescent Moon passes to the right of Venus, which presents a gibbous shape through binoculars and small telescopes. Earth stands sideways to the Sun on the 20th. This is the vernal equinox, marking the start of spring, which occurs at 5:58 P.M., shortly before the Sun sets at precisely the cardinal direction of due west.

● **NEW MOON**   6th day 11:04 A.M.   ○ **FULL MOON**   20th day 9:43 P.M.
◑ **FIRST QUARTER** 14th day 6:27 A.M.   ◐ **LAST QUARTER** 28th day 12:10 A.M.

After 2:00 A.M. on March 10, Eastern Daylight Time is given.

GET THESE PAGES WITH TIMES SET TO YOUR ZIP CODE AT ALMANAC.COM/ACCESS.

DAY OF YEAR	DAY OF MONTH	DAY OF WEEK	☼ RISES H. M.	RISE KEY	☼ SETS H. M.	SET KEY	LENGTH OF DAY H. M.	SUN FAST M.	SUN DECLINATION ° '	HIGH TIDE TIMES BOSTON	☾ RISES H. M.	RISE KEY	☾ SETS H. M.	SET KEY	☾ ASTRON. PLACE	☾ AGE
60	1	Fr.	6:20	D	5:34	C	11 14	4	7 s.30	7¼ 8	3:30	E	12:58	B	SAG	25
61	2	Sa.	6:18	D	5:35	C	11 17	4	7 s.07	8¼ 9	4:16	E	1:51	B	SAG	26
62	3	F	6:17	D	5:36	C	11 19	4	6 s.44	9¼ 9¾	4:56	E	2:47	B	CAP	27
63	4	M.	6:15	D	5:37	C	11 22	4	6 s.21	10 10½	5:31	E	3:45	C	CAP	28
64	5	Tu.	6:13	D	5:39	C	11 26	4	5 s.58	10½ 11	6:03	E	4:44	C	AQU	29
65	6	W.	6:12	D	5:40	C	11 28	5	5 s.35	11¼ 11½	6:31	D	5:43	C	AQU	0
66	7	Th.	6:10	D	5:41	C	11 31	5	5 s.11	11¾ —	6:57	D	6:42	D	AQU	1
67	8	Fr.	6:08	D	5:42	C	11 34	5	4 s.48	12¼ 12½	7:23	D	7:42	D	PSC	2
68	9	Sa.	6:07	D	5:43	C	11 36	5	4 s.25	12¾ 1	7:48	C	8:43	E	CET	3
69	10	F	7:05	C	6:45	C	11 40	6	4 s.01	1¼ 2¾	9:15	C	10:45	E	PSC	4
70	11	M.	7:03	C	6:46	C	11 43	6	3 s.38	3 3½	9:44	C	11:49	E	ARI	5
71	12	Tu.	7:02	C	6:47	C	11 45	6	3 s.14	3¾ 4¼	10:17	B	—	-	TAU	6
72	13	W.	7:00	C	6:48	C	11 48	6	2 s.50	4½ 5	10:55	B	12:53	E	TAU	7
73	14	Th.	6:58	C	6:49	C	11 51	7	2 s.27	5¼ 6	11:40	B	1:58	E	TAU	8
74	15	Fr.	6:57	C	6:50	C	11 53	7	2 s.03	6¼ 7	12:34	B	3:00	E	GEM	9
75	16	Sa.	6:55	C	6:52	C	11 57	7	1 s.39	7¼ 8	1:37	B	3:59	E	GEM	10
76	17	F	6:53	C	6:53	C	12 00	8	1 s.16	8½ 9	2:47	C	4:51	E	CAN	11
77	18	M.	6:51	C	6:54	C	12 03	8	0 s.52	9½ 10	4:02	C	5:37	E	LEO	12
78	19	Tu.	6:50	C	6:55	C	12 05	8	0 s.28	10½ 11	5:19	C	6:17	D	LEO	13
79	20	W.	6:48	C	6:56	C	12 08	8	0 s.04	11¼ 11¾	6:35	D	6:53	D	LEO	14
80	21	Th.	6:46	C	6:57	C	12 11	9	0 N.18	12¼ —	7:50	D	7:26	D	VIR	15
81	22	Fr.	6:44	C	6:59	C	12 15	9	0 N.42	12¾ 1	9:04	E	7:58	C	VIR	16
82	23	Sa.	6:43	C	7:00	C	12 17	9	1 N.06	1½ 2	10:15	E	8:30	B	VIR	17
83	24	F	6:41	C	7:01	C	12 20	10	1 N.29	2¼ 2¾	11:24	E	9:03	B	LIB	18
84	25	M.	6:39	C	7:02	C	12 23	10	1 N.53	3 3½	—	-	9:39	B	LIB	19
85	26	Tu.	6:37	C	7:03	C	12 26	10	2 N.16	4 4½	12:29	E	10:19	B	OPH	20
86	27	W.	6:36	C	7:04	C	12 28	10	2 N.40	4¾ 5½	1:30	E	11:03	B	OPH	21
87	28	Th.	6:34	C	7:05	D	12 31	11	3 N.03	5¾ 6½	2:25	E	11:51	B	SAG	22
88	29	Fr.	6:32	C	7:06	D	12 34	11	3 N.27	6¾ 7½	3:13	E	12:44	B	SAG	23
89	30	Sa.	6:31	C	7:08	D	12 37	11	3 N.50	7¾ 8½	3:56	E	1:39	B	CAP	24
90	31	F	6:29	C	7:09	D	12 40	12	4 N.13	8¾ 9½	4:33	E	2:37	B	CAP	25

RUSH!
Priority Order!

RUSH!
Priority Order!

MARCH

The warring hosts of Winter and of Spring
Are hurtling o'er the plains.
–Christopher Pearse Cranch

DAY OF MONTH	DAY OF WEEK	DATES, FEASTS, FASTS, ASPECTS, TIDE HEIGHTS, AND WEATHER	
1	Fr.	St. David • ☾ RUNS LOW • ☌♄☾ • ☌♇☾ • Tides {9.3 / 8.3}	*Wintry*
2	Sa.	St. Chad • ☾ AT ☋ • ☌♀☾ • Writer Theodor Seuss Geisel born, 1904	*reentry:*
3	**F**	**Quinquagesima** • *A good life keeps off wrinkles.* • {9.5 / 8.7}	*sunny,*
4	M.	☾ AT APO. • *Voyager I* spacecraft revealed rings of Jupiter, 1979 • Playwright Horton Foote died, 2009	*but*
5	Tu.	Shrove Tuesday • St. Piran • ☿ STAT. • Tides {9.9 / 9.2}	*hard*
6	W.	**Ash Wednesday** • NEW ● • ☌♆☉ • ☌♆☾	*to*
7	Th.	St. Perpetua • ☌☿☾ • Horticulturist Luther Burbank born, 1849 • {10.0 / —}	*feel*
8	Fr.	☾ ON EQ. • Baseball player Joe DiMaggio died, 1999 • {9.6 / 10.0}	*cheery in*
9	Sa.	☌♅☾ • Hummingbirds migrate north now. • Tides {9.7 / 9.8}	*(after*
10	**F**	**1st S. in Lent** • DAYLIGHT SAVING TIME BEGINS, 2:00 A.M. • {9.8 / 9.6}	*some*
11	M.	Clean Monday • ☌♂☾ • 9.0 earthquake moved Honshu, Japan, 8' east, 2011	*rain),*
12	Tu.	*Winds that change against the Sun Are always sure to backward run.* • Tides {9.8 / 9.0}	*it's*
13	W.	Ember Day • Geomagnetic storm collapsed Hydro-Québec power grid, 1989 • {9.8 / 8.8}	*Siberian!*
14	Th.	☿ IN INF. ☌ • Physicist Albert Einstein born, 1879 • {9.8 / 8.6}	*Snowstorm*
15	Fr.	Ember Day • Beware the ides of March. • ☾ RIDES HIGH • American Legion org. founded, 1919	*enormous*
16	Sa.	Ember Day • ☾ AT ☊ • Norman Thagard first American to visit Russian space station *Mir*, 1995	*to*
17	**F**	**2nd S. in Lent** • ST. PATRICK'S DAY • {10.5 / 9.5}	*flurries*
18	M.	$500 million in artwork stolen, Isabella Stewart Gardner Museum, Boston, 1990 • {10.9 / 10.1}	*diminishing;*
19	Tu.	St. Joseph • ☾ AT PERIG. • 1,383-sq. ft. omelet made, 1994 • {11.4 / 10.7}	*south*
20	W.	VERNAL EQUINOX • FULL WORM ○ • Musician John Lennon wed Yoko Ono, 1969	*winds*
21	Th.	☾ ON EQ. • "Royals" winning name for new Kansas City baseball team, 1968 • {11.8 / —}	*will*
22	Fr.	☌☿♆ • Alaska's Mt. Redoubt volcano began series of eruptions, 2009 • {11.5 / 11.7}	*warm*
23	Sa.	NHL player Wayne Gretzky scored 802nd career goal, 1994 • Tides {11.6 / 11.3}	*us,*
24	**F**	**3rd S. in Lent** • Maser patented, 1959 • {11.4 / 10.7}	*soft*
25	M.	Annunciation • *Mar. 25–26:* 20.6" snow fell in 24 hours, Amarillo, Tex., 1934 • {11.0 / 10.1}	*rains*
26	Tu.	☌♃☾ • "Melissa" macro computer virus released, disrupting email systems worldwide, 1999	*inform*
27	W.	☿ STAT. • Chipmunks emerge from hibernation now. • Tides {9.9 / 8.8}	*us*
28	Th.	☾ RUNS LOW • Partial meltdown of Three Mile Island nuclear power station, Pa., 1979	*that*
29	Fr.	☾ AT ☋ • ☌♄☾ • ☌♇☾ • First performance of Ringling Bros. and Barnum & Bailey Circus, 1919	
30	Sa.	*A kind word is like a spring day.* • Tides {9.0 / 8.3}	*winter is*
31	**F**	**4th S. in Lent** • ☾ AT APO. • Nfld. became 10th province, 1949	*finishing.*

Farmer's Calendar

When the bird with black-and-white–flecked feathers and a poinsettia-red head swooped into our yard, I didn't need binoculars to observe it. North America's largest woodpecker, the pileated is notorious for clinging to trees and hammering with its beak, sending blonde splinters sprinkling onto the snow. Viewed up close, this avian air hammer strikes me as faintly spooky. So when this one latched on to my favorite silver maple and began its carpentry, I felt uneasy. We'd lost an ancient oak to lightning the year before, and I was averse to uninvited things alighting in our remaining trees. Pileateds can be beneficial, extracting insects and larvae lurking under the bark, even when the cavities they bore are wide and deep. Still, I wanted to preclude its excavation. Therefore, when the bird commenced to drill and a pile of bark chips began to accrue, I tried to shoo it off, hooting and waving my arms. But this only deterred it momentarily. So I opened my laptop to play a recording of its species at maximum volume. Did the digital voice express a curse or hex? Whatever it proclaimed halted the yard bird in midpeck. Then it trilled a reply, flapped off, and hasn't been back.

APRIL

SKY WATCH: Mercury is now a morning star and on the 1st participates in an alignment low in the east some 40 minutes before sunrise: Look to see, from highest to lowest, the Moon, Venus, and Mercury. On the 2nd, the Moon is below Venus, with Mercury to their left. Jupiter, brightening steadily, now appears several hours before sunrise, high enough for useful telescopic observation at dawn. Saturn is marginally high enough, too, but its rings are not as wide open as they've been in recent years. Mars, now in Taurus and fading, stands above the fat waxing crescent Moon on the 8th.

● **NEW MOON** 5th day 4:50 A.M. ○ **FULL MOON** 19th day 7:12 A.M.
◑ **FIRST QUARTER** 12th day 3:06 P.M. ◐ **LAST QUARTER** 26th day 6:18 P.M.

All times are given in Eastern Daylight Time.

GET THESE PAGES WITH TIMES SET TO YOUR ZIP CODE AT ALMANAC.COM/ACCESS.

DAY OF YEAR	DAY OF MONTH	DAY OF WEEK	☀ RISES H. M.	RISE KEY	☀ SETS H. M.	SET KEY	LENGTH OF DAY H. M.	SUN FAST M.	SUN DECLINATION ° '	HIGH TIDE TIMES BOSTON		☽ RISES H. M.	RISE KEY	☽ SETS H. M.	SET KEY	☽ ASTRON. PLACE	☽ AGE
91	1	M.	6:27	C	7:10	D	12 43	12	4 N. 37	9½	10¼	5:05	E	3:35	C	CAP	26
92	2	Tu.	6:25	C	7:11	D	12 46	12	5 N. 00	10¼	10¾	5:34	E	4:35	C	AQU	27
93	3	W.	6:24	C	7:12	D	12 48	13	5 N. 23	11	11½	6:01	D	5:34	D	AQU	28
94	4	Th.	6:22	C	7:13	D	12 51	13	5 N. 46	11¾	—	6:27	D	6:34	D	PSC	29
95	5	Fr.	6:20	C	7:14	D	12 54	13	6 N. 08	12	12¼	6:52	C	7:36	D	CET	0
96	6	Sa.	6:19	B	7:15	D	12 56	13	6 N. 31	12½	1	7:18	C	8:38	E	PSC	1
97	7	**F**	6:17	B	7:17	D	13 00	14	6 N. 54	1¼	1½	7:46	C	9:42	E	CET	2
98	8	M.	6:15	B	7:18	D	13 03	14	7 N. 16	1¾	2¼	8:18	E	10:47	E	ARI	3
99	9	Tu.	6:13	B	7:19	D	13 06	14	7 N. 39	2½	3	8:54	E	11:52	E	TAU	4
100	10	W.	6:12	B	7:20	D	13 08	14	8 N. 01	3¼	3¾	9:37	B	—	-	TAU	5
101	11	Th.	6:10	B	7:21	D	13 11	15	8 N. 23	4	4¾	10:27	B	12:55	E	GEM	6
102	12	Fr.	6:09	B	7:22	D	13 13	15	8 N. 45	5	5¾	11:26	B	1:54	E	GEM	7
103	13	Sa.	6:07	B	7:23	D	13 16	15	9 N. 07	6	6¾	12:32	B	2:47	E	CAN	8
104	14	**F**	6:05	B	7:25	D	13 20	15	9 N. 28	7	7¾	1:43	C	3:33	E	CAN	9
105	15	M.	6:04	B	7:26	D	13 22	16	9 N. 50	8	8¾	2:56	C	4:14	D	LEO	10
106	16	Tu.	6:02	B	7:27	D	13 25	16	10 N. 11	9¼	9¾	4:11	D	4:50	D	LEO	11
107	17	W.	6:00	B	7:28	D	13 28	16	10 N. 32	10¼	10¾	5:25	D	5:23	D	VIR	12
108	18	Th.	5:59	B	7:29	D	13 30	16	10 N. 53	11	11½	6:39	E	5:54	C	VIR	13
109	19	Fr.	5:57	B	7:30	D	13 33	17	11 N. 14	12	—	7:52	E	6:25	C	VIR	14
110	20	Sa.	5:56	B	7:31	D	13 35	17	11 N. 35	12¼	12¾	9:03	E	6:57	C	LIB	15
111	21	**F**	5:54	B	7:32	D	13 38	17	11 N. 55	1	1½	10:11	E	7:32	B	LIB	16
112	22	M.	5:53	B	7:34	D	13 41	17	12 N. 15	1¾	2½	11:16	E	8:10	B	OPH	17
113	23	Tu.	5:51	B	7:35	D	13 44	17	12 N. 35	2½	3¼	—	-	8:53	B	OPH	18
114	24	W.	5:50	B	7:36	D	13 46	18	12 N. 55	3½	4	12:15	E	9:41	B	SAG	19
115	25	Th.	5:48	B	7:37	D	13 49	18	13 N. 15	4¼	5	1:08	E	10:33	B	SAG	20
116	26	Fr.	5:47	B	7:38	D	13 51	18	13 N. 34	5	6	1:54	E	11:29	B	SAG	21
117	27	Sa.	5:45	B	7:39	D	13 54	18	13 N. 53	6	6¾	2:33	E	12:26	B	CAP	22
118	28	**F**	5:44	B	7:40	D	13 56	18	14 N. 12	7	7¾	3:07	E	1:25	C	CAP	23
119	29	M.	5:42	B	7:41	E	13 59	18	14 N. 31	8	8¾	3:37	E	2:24	C	AQU	24
120	30	Tu.	5:41	B	7:43	E	14 02	18	14 N. 49	9	9½	4:04	D	3:23	C	AQU	25

APRIL

The gray hills deepen in green again;
The rainbow hangs in heaven.
–Emma Lazarus

DAY OF MONTH	DAY OF WEEK	DATES, FEASTS, FASTS, ASPECTS, TIDE HEIGHTS, AND WEATHER		
1	M.	**ALL FOOLS'** • *It is a great point of wisdom to find out one's own folly.* • {9.3 8.9		Snow
2	Tu.	☌��☾ • ☌☿♅ • ☌♀☾ • ☌♆☾ • Tides {9.5 9.2		a foot
3	W.	St. Richard of Chichester • First mobile phone call made, 1973 • {9.7 9.5		thick!
4	Th.	☾ ON EQ. • *Apr. 3–4:* "Super Outbreak" of 148 tornadoes hit 13 U.S. states and Ont., 1974		How's
5	Fr.	NEW ● • Actor Charlton Heston died, 2008 • {9.8 9.9		that
6	Sa.	☌�ြ☾ • Explorer Robert Peary's party reached what was believed to be North Pole, 1909		for a
7	**F**	5th ☉. in Lent • World Health Organization established, 1948 • {10.2 9.8		trick?
8	M.	Gallaudet University founded, D.C., 1864 • Hank Aaron broke Babe Ruth's record w/ 715th home run, 1974		Promise
9	Tu.	☌♀♅ • ☌♂☾ • Names of first 7 NASA astronauts announced, 1959 • {10.3 9.5		of
10	W.	♃ STAT. • Walter Hunt rec'd patent for safety pin, 1849 • Tides {10.3 9.2		better
11	Th.	☾ RIDES HIGH • ☿ GR. ELONG. (28° WEST) • Geneva, Switz., chosen as League of Nations location, 1919		times,
12	Fr.	☾ AT ☊ • *Sour grapes can ne'er make sweet wine.* • Tides {10.1 9.0		but first
13	Sa.	U.S. president Thomas Jefferson born, 1743 • Tides {10.1 9.1		some
14	**F**	**Palm Sunday** • Noah Webster's *American Dict. of the English Language* printed, 1828		wetter
15	M.	Canadian thanksgiving day held after Prince of Wales recovered from serious illness, 1872 • {10.4 9.9		times.
16	Tu.	☾ AT PERIG. • Toronto Maple Leafs won 3rd consecutive NHL Stanley Cup, 1949		Sunshine
17	W.	Discovery of first Earth-size planet in "Habitable Zone" publicized, 2014 • Tides {11.0 11.1		enraptures
18	Th.	Maundy Thursday • ☾ ON EQ. • First U.S. public laundromat opened, Fort Worth, Tex., 1934		us,
19	Fr.	**Good Friday** • Passover begins at sundown • **FULL PINK** ○ • {— 11.3		then
20	Sa.	Daredevil Felix Baumgartner born, 1969 • Tides {11.7 11.1		showers
21	**F**	**Easter** • Half-dollar–size hail fell near Marion, S.C., 2012 • Tides {11.6 10.8		will
22	M.	Easter Monday • **EARTH DAY** • ☌�ြ☉ • {11.4 10.3		capture
23	Tu.	☌♃☾ • Guelph, Ont., incorporated as city, 1879 • Tides {11.0 9.8		us.
24	W.	☾ RUNS LOW • *The Old Farmer's Almanac* founder Robert B. Thomas born, 1766 • {10.4 9.3		Steadily
25	Th.	☾ AT ☋ • ☌♄☾ • ☌♇☾ • ♇ STAT. • Tides {9.9 8.8		Steadily
26	Fr.	*If ants their walls do frequent build, Rain will from the clouds be spilled.* • Tides {9.4 8.5		soaking
27	Sa.	Odd green light shot across night sky, experts concluded likely meteor, southern Calif., 2016 • {9.1 8.4		and
28	**F**	2nd ☉. of **Easter** • **Orthodox Easter** • ☾ AT APO.		we're
29	M.	St. George[T] • ♄ STAT. • Poplars leaf out about now. • Tides {8.9 8.7		not
30	Tu.	St. Mark[T] • ☌♆☾ • George Washington inaugurated as first U.S. president, 1789		joking.

Farmer's Calendar

Winter's true finish is anyone's guess—precisely the point of the annual contest on Joe's Pond in West Danville, Vermont. This year, I'm betting it's April 2 at 11:27 A.M. This guess cost me a buck. So if I'm correct and if the "ice-out" contraption—a pallet, a cinder block, and a flag tethered by 250 feet of nylon rope to a power source for the clock on land—if that wacky raft hunkered on the frozen pond should slump during the thaw of a warm March and begin to sink beneath the pond's waters around breakfast on April 2, and its descent strains the rope such that it finally breaks the electrical connection, stopping the clock at precisely 11:27 A.M., as the raft submerges into the newly liquefied pond, then I stand to collect half the betting cash. What's more, come July, no matter who won, everybody in the vicinity of Joe's Pond gets a prize: On the evening of Independence Day, the sky will fill with sparkles and crackles and scintillating falling stars. This fireworks display is funded with the remaining money from those hunches, those best guesses when our winter went out not with a bang, but with a gurgle.

MAY

SKY WATCH: This is a transition month. At nightfall on the 1st, Orion stands upright on the western horizon but vanishes by month's end. Mars, fading rapidly, starts this month in Taurus but zooms into Gemini by midmonth. Jupiter, in the "13th zodiac constellation," Ophiuchus, now rises well before midnight and is near the Moon on the 20th and 21st. Saturn, in Sagittarius, rises at about 1:00 A.M. on the 1st and is well placed for the rest of the short night. In the predawn east, the planetary alignments have ended; only Venus remains, hovering low to float above the waning crescent Moon on the 2nd.

● NEW MOON	4th day	6:46 P.M.	○ FULL MOON	18th day	5:11 P.M.
◐ FIRST QUARTER	11th day	9:12 P.M.	◑ LAST QUARTER	26th day	12:34 P.M.

All times are given in Eastern Daylight Time.

GET THESE PAGES WITH TIMES SET TO YOUR ZIP CODE AT ALMANAC.COM/ACCESS.

DAY OF YEAR	DAY OF MONTH	DAY OF WEEK	☼ RISES H. M.	RISE KEY	☼ SETS H. M.	SET KEY	LENGTH OF DAY H. M.	SUN FAST M.	SUN DECLINATION ° '	HIGH TIDE TIMES BOSTON		☽ RISES H. M.	RISE KEY	☽ SETS H. M.	SET KEY	☽ ASTRON. PLACE	☽ AGE
121	1	W.	5:40	B	7:44	E	14 04	19	15 N. 08	9¾	10	4:30	D	4:23	D	PSC	26
122	2	Th.	5:38	B	7:45	E	14 07	19	15 N. 26	10½	10¾	4:55	D	5:24	D	CET	27
123	3	Fr.	5:37	B	7:46	E	14 09	19	15 N. 43	11¼	11½	5:21	C	6:27	E	PSC	28
124	4	Sa.	5:36	B	7:47	E	14 11	19	16 N. 01	11¾	—	5:48	C	7:31	E	CET	0
125	5	F	5:34	B	7:48	E	14 14	19	16 N. 18	12	12½	6:18	B	8:37	E	ARI	1
126	6	M.	5:33	B	7:49	E	14 16	19	16 N. 35	12¾	1¼	6:53	B	9:44	E	TAU	2
127	7	Tu.	5:32	B	7:50	E	14 18	19	16 N. 52	1¼	2	7:34	B	10:49	E	TAU	3
128	8	W.	5:31	B	7:51	E	14 20	19	17 N. 08	2	2¾	8:23	B	11:51	E	ORI	4
129	9	Th.	5:30	B	7:52	E	14 22	19	17 N. 24	2¾	3½	9:19	B	—	-	GEM	5
130	10	Fr.	5:28	B	7:53	E	14 25	19	17 N. 40	3¾	4½	10:23	B	12:46	E	GEM	6
131	11	Sa.	5:27	B	7:55	E	14 28	19	17 N. 55	4¾	5½	11:32	C	1:34	E	CAN	7
132	12	F	5:26	B	7:56	E	14 30	19	18 N. 11	5¾	6½	12:44	C	2:15	E	LEO	8
133	13	M.	5:25	B	7:57	E	14 32	19	18 N. 25	6¾	7½	1:56	C	2:52	E	LEO	9
134	14	Tu.	5:24	B	7:58	E	14 34	19	18 N. 40	7¾	8½	3:08	D	3:24	D	VIR	10
135	15	W.	5:23	B	7:59	E	14 36	19	18 N. 54	9	9½	4:20	D	3:54	D	VIR	11
136	16	Th.	5:22	B	8:00	E	14 38	19	19 N. 08	9¾	10¼	5:32	E	4:24	C	VIR	12
137	17	Fr.	5:21	A	8:01	E	14 40	19	19 N. 22	10¾	11	6:42	E	4:55	C	VIR	13
138	18	Sa.	5:20	A	8:02	E	14 42	19	19 N. 35	11¾	—	7:52	E	5:27	B	LIB	14
139	19	F	5:19	A	8:03	E	14 44	19	19 N. 48	12	12½	8:59	E	6:03	B	SCO	15
140	20	M.	5:18	A	8:04	E	14 46	19	20 N. 01	12¾	1¼	10:02	E	6:44	B	OPH	16
141	21	Tu.	5:17	A	8:05	E	14 48	19	20 N. 13	1½	2	10:58	E	7:30	B	SAG	17
142	22	W.	5:17	A	8:06	E	14 49	19	20 N. 25	2¼	2¾	11:48	E	8:21	B	SAG	18
143	23	Th.	5:16	A	8:07	E	14 51	19	20 N. 36	3	3½	—	-	9:16	B	SAG	19
144	24	Fr.	5:15	A	8:08	E	14 53	19	20 N. 48	3¾	4½	12:31	E	10:14	B	CAP	20
145	25	Sa.	5:14	A	8:09	E	14 55	19	20 N. 58	4½	5¼	1:07	E	11:12	C	CAP	21
146	26	F	5:14	A	8:09	E	14 55	19	21 N. 09	5½	6	1:39	E	12:12	C	AQU	22
147	27	M.	5:13	A	8:10	E	14 57	19	21 N. 19	6¼	7	2:07	E	1:11	C	AQU	23
148	28	Tu.	5:12	A	8:11	E	14 59	18	21 N. 29	7¼	7¾	2:33	D	2:10	D	AQU	24
149	29	W.	5:12	A	8:12	E	15 00	18	21 N. 38	8¼	8½	2:57	D	3:10	D	CET	25
150	30	Th.	5:11	A	8:13	E	15 02	18	21 N. 47	9	9¼	3:22	C	4:12	E	CET	26
151	31	Fr.	5:11	A	8:14	E	15 03	18	21 N. 56	9¾	10	3:49	C	5:16	E	PSC	27

To use this page, see p. 116; for Key Letters, see p. 238. LIGHT = A.M. **BOLD = P.M.**

Then came fair May, the fairest maid on ground,
Decked all with dainties of her season's pride.
–**Edmund Spenser**

DAY OF MONTH	DAY OF WEEK	DATES, FEASTS, FASTS, ASPECTS, TIDE HEIGHTS, AND WEATHER	
1	W.	Sts. Philip & James • May Day • Existence of Van Allen radiation belts announced, 1958	*Wet*
2	Th.	St. Athanasius • ☾ on Eq. • ☌♀☾ • Horse *Mine That Bird* won Kentucky Derby, 2009	*as*
3	F.	☌☿☾ • ☌♅☾ • Tornado outbreak struck Okla. and Kans., 1999 • {9.6 10.2	*we*
4	Sa.	NEW ● • Royal Canadian Mint produced its last penny, 2012 • {9.8 —	*can*
5	F	**3rd S. of Easter** • Ramadan begins at sundown • *After black clouds, clear weather.*	*get,*
6	M.	State of emergency declared due to flooding, Winnipeg, Man., 1950 • Tides {10.7 9.8	*we*
7	Tu.	☌♂☾ • 9.4-inch-long, 14-lb. pearl found in giant clam, set world record, Philippines, 1934	*regret.*
8	W.	St. Julian of Norwich • ☌☿♅ • Baseball player Dom DiMaggio died, 2009 • {10.9 9.6	*Brilliant,*
9	Th.	St. Gregory of Nazianzus • ☾ rides high • ☾ at ☊ • {10.8 9.5	*but*
10	Fr.	Golden spike linked Union Pacific and Central Pacific railroads, Promontory Point, Utah, 1869	*briefly;*
11	Sa.	James Monroe first U.S. president to ride on steamboat (SS *Savannah*), 1819 • Three • {10.5 9.4	*more*
12	F	**4th S. of Easter** • Mother's Day • Chilly • {10.3 9.6	*showers,*
13	M.	☾ at perig. • Cranberries in bud now. • Saints • {10.2 9.9	*chiefly.*
14	Tu.	Entrepreneur Henry John Heinz died, 1919 • Filmmaker George Lucas born, 1944 • Tides {10.3 10.3	*No*
15	W.	☾ on Eq. • 4 bear cubs playing on backyard trampoline caught on video, Avon, Conn., 2017	*signs*
16	Th.	*Night is the mother of thought.* • Discovery of 2.6-billion-year-old water in Ont. mine announced, 2013	*of*
17	Fr.	Allan Ganz honored for 67-year career as ice-cream man, 2014 • Tides {10.5 11.4	*relief,*
18	Sa.	Vesak • Full Flower ○ • ☌♀♅ • 116°F, Death Valley, Calif., 2006 • {10.5 11.5	*we*
19	F	**5th S. of Easter** • U.S. First Lady Jacqueline Kennedy Onassis died, 1994	*report,*
20	M.	Victoria Day (Canada) • ☌♃☾ • 6" snow, Lexington, Ky., 1894 • {11.4 10.1	*to*
21	Tu.	☿ in sup. ☌ • Painter Henri Rousseau born, 1844 • {11.1 9.8	*our*
22	W.	☾ runs low • ☾ at ☋ • ☌♄☾ • ☌♇☾ • {10.7 9.5	*grief.*
23	Th.	Townsend-Purnell Plant Patent Act first in U.S. to grant patent protection to plant breeders, 1930	*Be*
24	Fr.	Britain's Queen Victoria born, 1819 • Samuel Morse sent first telegraphic message, "What hath God wrought," 1844	*of*
25	Sa.	St. Bede • First shave in space, *Apollo 10,* 1969 • Tides {9.5 8.7	*good*
26	F	**Rogation Sunday** • ☾ at apo. • Tides {9.1 8.7	
27	M.	Memorial Day, observed • ☌♆☾ • Lightning struck storm chaser in car, S.Dak., 2014	*cheer!*
28	Tu.	R. H. Macy & Co. incorporated, 1919 • Tides {8.8 9.0	*Summer*
29	W.	☾ on Eq. • *If the brain sows not corn, it plants thistles.* • Tides {8.9 9.3	*appears*
30	Th.	**Ascension** • Musician Benny Goodman born, 1909 • {9.0 9.7	*to be*
31	Fr.	Visit. of Mary • ☌♅☾ • Waterspout formed, Dollar Lake, Riverton, Wyo., 2014	*here!*

Farmer's Calendar

Sometimes I get lonesome for a moose to lumber through the back field, if only to prove that they really do exist, that these aren't mythic beasts. Maine drivers are believers and, sadly, all too familiar with humongous ungulates who come strolling out of the woods and onto the highway. Vermonters often have to hunt for an encounter, as a few of us did one spring when the leaves were still as tender as the muzzle of an *Alces alces.* We rose before dawn and piled into a car, friends on a mission to glimpse the gangly cousins of lovely deer. We drove to their favored habitat, a patch of swampy woods. As the Sun's rays broke over the hills, we pulled off by a "Moose Crossing" sign and waited like fools for our improbable quarry. When I think back now, I wonder: What were the odds of us spotting the apocryphal animal? But as luck would have it, within minutes, a shaggy specimen came stilting across the asphalt. Cell-phone cameras were still years away, so we have no photograph of the hulking bull who nonchalantly swiveled to consider our vehicle and then plodded on, leaving hoofprints the size of our amazed faces.

JUNE

SKY WATCH: The thin crescent Moon hangs to the right of Venus on the 1st, very low in the east during dawn's first light. Mercury is an evening star, not difficult to see in the west during the first half of the month. It closely meets Mars on the 18th, but both are low in evening twilight; use binoculars. Jupiter reaches opposition on the 10th and shines at magnitude –2.6, its brightest of the year, in the constellation Ophiuchus; it is joined by the full Moon on the 16th. Rising at sunset, Jupiter dominates as the night's brightest "star." Far to its right floats Antares, the supergiant alpha star of Scorpius. Far to Jupiter's left hovers bright but not dazzling Saturn, which now rises at nightfall. Summer begins with the solstice on the 21st at 11:54 A.M.

| ● NEW MOON | 3rd day | 6:02 A.M. | ○ FULL MOON | 17th day | 4:31 A.M. |
| ◐ FIRST QUARTER | 10th day | 1:59 A.M. | ◑ LAST QUARTER | 25th day | 5:46 A.M. |

All times are given in Eastern Daylight Time.

GET THESE PAGES WITH TIMES SET TO YOUR ZIP CODE AT ALMANAC.COM/ACCESS.

DAY OF YEAR	DAY OF MONTH	DAY OF WEEK	☼ RISES H.M.	RISE KEY	☼ SETS H.M.	SET KEY	LENGTH OF DAY H.M.	SUN FAST M.	SUN DECLINATION ° '	HIGH TIDE TIMES BOSTON		☾ RISES H.M.	RISE KEY	☾ SETS H.M.	SET KEY	☾ ASTRON. PLACE	☾ AGE
152	1	Sa.	5:10	A	8:14	E	15 04	18	22 N. 04	10½	10¾	4:17	B	6:22	E	ARI	28
153	2	F	5:10	A	8:15	E	15 05	18	22 N. 12	11¼	11½	4:50	B	7:29	E	TAU	29
154	3	M.	5:09	A	8:16	E	15 07	18	22 N. 20	12	—	5:29	B	8:37	E	TAU	0
155	4	Tu.	5:09	A	8:17	E	15 08	17	22 N. 27	12¼	12¾	6:16	B	9:42	E	TAU	1
156	5	W.	5:08	A	8:17	E	15 09	17	22 N. 33	1	1¾	7:10	B	10:41	E	GEM	2
157	6	Th.	5:08	A	8:18	E	15 10	17	22 N. 40	1¾	2½	8:13	B	11:33	E	GEM	3
158	7	Fr.	5:08	A	8:19	E	15 11	17	22 N. 46	2½	3¼	9:22	B	—	-	CAN	4
159	8	Sa.	5:08	A	8:19	E	15 11	17	22 N. 51	3½	4¼	10:34	C	12:17	E	LEO	5
160	9	F	5:07	A	8:20	E	15 13	16	22 N. 56	4½	5¼	11:47	C	12:55	E	LEO	6
161	10	M.	5:07	A	8:20	E	15 13	16	23 N. 01	5½	6¼	12:59	D	1:28	D	LEO	7
162	11	Tu.	5:07	A	8:21	E	15 14	16	23 N. 05	6½	7¼	2:10	D	1:58	D	VIR	8
163	12	W.	5:07	A	8:21	E	15 14	16	23 N. 09	7½	8	3:19	E	2:27	C	VIR	9
164	13	Th.	5:07	A	8:22	E	15 15	16	23 N. 13	8½	9	4:29	E	2:57	C	VIR	10
165	14	Fr.	5:07	A	8:22	E	15 15	15	23 N. 16	9½	10	5:37	E	3:27	C	LIB	11
166	15	Sa.	5:07	A	8:23	E	15 16	15	23 N. 18	10½	10¾	6:45	E	4:01	B	LIB	12
167	16	F	5:07	A	8:23	E	15 16	15	23 N. 21	11½	11½	7:49	E	4:39	B	OPH	13
168	17	M.	5:07	A	8:24	E	15 17	15	23 N. 22	12¼	—	8:48	E	5:22	B	OPH	14
169	18	Tu.	5:07	A	8:24	E	15 17	15	23 N. 24	12¼	1	9:41	E	6:11	B	SAG	15
170	19	W.	5:07	A	8:24	E	15 17	14	23 N. 25	1	1¾	10:26	E	7:04	B	SAG	16
171	20	Th.	5:07	A	8:24	E	15 17	14	23 N. 25	1¾	2½	11:06	E	8:01	B	CAP	17
172	21	Fr.	5:07	A	8:25	E	15 18	14	23 N. 26	2½	3	11:39	E	9:00	C	CAP	18
173	22	Sa.	5:08	A	8:25	E	15 17	14	23 N. 25	3¼	3¾	—	-	10:00	C	CAP	19
174	23	F	5:08	A	8:25	E	15 17	13	23 N. 25	4	4½	12:09	E	10:59	C	AQU	20
175	24	M.	5:08	A	8:25	E	15 17	13	23 N. 24	4¾	5½	12:35	D	11:58	C	AQU	21
176	25	Tu.	5:08	A	8:25	E	15 17	13	23 N. 22	5½	6¼	1:00	D	12:57	D	PSC	22
177	26	W.	5:09	A	8:25	E	15 16	13	23 N. 20	6½	7	1:24	C	1:57	D	CET	23
178	27	Th.	5:09	A	8:25	E	15 16	13	23 N. 18	7½	7¾	1:50	C	2:59	E	PSC	24
179	28	Fr.	5:10	A	8:25	E	15 15	12	23 N. 15	8¼	8½	2:17	C	4:03	E	CET	25
180	29	Sa.	5:10	A	8:25	E	15 15	12	23 N. 12	9¼	9½	2:47	B	5:10	E	ARI	26
181	30	F	5:10	A	8:25	E	15 15	12	23 N. 09	10	10¼	3:23	B	6:17	E	TAU	27

On the grass the fallen apple blossoms
Heap a pillow rosy-hued and rare.
–Elizabeth Anne Chase Akers Allen

DAY OF MONTH	DAY OF WEEK	DATES, FEASTS, FASTS, ASPECTS, TIDE HEIGHTS, AND WEATHER	
1	Sa.	☌♀☾ • 1" snow, Delta Junction, Alaska, 2015 • {9.3 / 10.4	*Hot*
2	**F**	**1st S. af. Asc.** • Grover Cleveland became first U.S. president to wed in White House, 1886	*stuff!*
3	M.	NEW ● • *Sweet discourse makes short days and nights.* • Tides {9.7 / —	*Cool*
4	Tu.	☌☿☾ • Writer Joyce Meyer born, 1943 • Tides {11.1 / 9.8	*enough*
5	W.	St. Boniface • ☾ RIDES HIGH • ☾ AT ☊ • ☌♂☾ • {11.3 / 9.9	*to*
6	Th.	Orthodox Ascension • D-Day, 1944 • *Tetris* video game released, 1984 • {11.3 / 9.9	*dampen*
7	Fr.	☾ AT PERIG. • King George VI, with Queen Elizabeth, first reigning British monarch to visit U.S., 1939	*campers.*
8	Sa.	Shavuot begins at sundown • Tornado struck National Weather Service office in Oklahoma City, 1974	*Warmer,*
9	**F**	**Whit S. • Pentecost** • Donald Duck debuted in "The Wise Little Hen," 1934	*but*
10	M.	♃ AT ☍ • "Maunder Minimum" astronomer John Eddy died, 2009 • {10.5 / 10.1	*watch*
11	Tu.	St. Barnabas • ☾ ON EQ. • Marine explorer Jacques-Yves Cousteau born, 1910 • {10.2 / 10.3	*out*
12	W.	Ember Day • Writer Anne Frank born, 1929 • {10.0 / 10.6	*for*
13	Th.	Alexander the Great died, 323 B.C. • Deadly hurricane hit Labrador, 1871 • {9.9 / 10.8	*a*
14	Fr.	St. Basil • Ember Day • FLAG DAY • Composer Henry Mancini died, 1994 • {9.9 / 11.0	*storm or*
15	Sa.	Ember Day • Charles Goodyear granted patent for process to strengthen rubber, 1844	*two!*
16	**F**	**Trinity** • Orthodox Pentecost • FATHER'S DAY • ☌♃☾ • {9.8 / 11.1	*Rainy*
17	M.	FULL STRAWBERRY ○ • 15th FIFA World Cup soccer games began, first time held in U.S., 1994	*and*
18	Tu.	☾ RUNS LOW • ☾ AT ☋ • ☌☿♂ • ☌♄☾ • {10.9 / 9.6	*cool,*
19	W.	☌♇☾ • 100°F, Billings, Mont., 1989 • Tides {10.7 / 9.4	*friend, for*
20	Th.	Danielle formed, setting record for earliest 4th tropical storm in Atlantic basin, 2016 • {10.5 / 9.3	*school's*
21	Fr.	SUMMER SOLSTICE • ♆ STAT. • First 999 emergency phone service in N. America began, Winnipeg, Man., 1959	
22	Sa.	St. Alban • 102°F, Vero Beach, Fla., 2009 • Tides {9.9 / 9.0	*end.*
23	**F**	Corpus Christi • Orthodox All Saints' • ☾ AT APO. • ☿ GR. ELONG. (25° EAST) • ☌♆☾	*Chance*
24	M.	Nativ. John the Baptist • MIDSUMMER DAY • *Rain on St. John's Day, damage to nuts.* • {9.2 / 8.9	*of*
25	Tu.	☾ ON EQ. • Five English monks saw "flaming torch" spew "fire, hot coals, and sparks" on Moon, 1178	*noisy*
26	W.	Physicist Lord Kelvin born, 1824 • St. Lawrence Seaway officially opened, 1959	*precipitation*
27	Th.	☌♅☾ • British scientist James Smithson died, leaving will that led to founding of Smithsonian Institution, 1829	*for*
28	Fr.	St. Irenaeus • Labor Day made official U.S. holiday, 1894 • Treaty of Versailles signed, WWI, 1919	*high*
29	Sa.	Sts. Peter & Paul • *If you would enjoy the fruit, pluck not the flower.* • {8.9 / 10.2	*school*
30	**F**	**3rd S. af. P.** • Canada's loonie coin entered circulation, 1987 • {9.1 / 10.6	*graduation!*

Farmer's Calendar

Far from Wall Street, our rural stock exchange thrives with unlisted commodities and functions at all hours. On Saturday, I might swap my extra laying hens for my neighbor's spare vacuum cleaner, and then on Sunday trade a box of frozen beef for pork. But every so often, a transaction occurs that at first seems an outright loss, such as on the morning when I awoke at dawn to a strange noise outside. On the single occasion that I'd neglected to electrify the turkeys' fence, a fox had feasted; telltale white feathers were strewn about like leaves. Still on the premises, the fox, seeing me, attempted to flee. Having already devoured a 10-pound fowl, the intruder toted another as it approached the electric mesh encircling the birds' yard. It botched its leap, dropped its prey, and became entangled in the fence. Instead of fury, I felt awe for its audacity and, now, for its predicament. As the fox thrashed and panted, whining slightly in its panic, I stared at its lavish tail, elegant paws, and auburn coat—I'd never seen a fox this close. Was this a swindle? I wondered, as the animal twisted and, at last, leapt free. Or a barter: two of my flock for hearing the fox's getaway huff.

SKY WATCH: On the 2nd, a total solar eclipse sweeps across central Chile and Argentina. Mercury and Mars hover just above the thin crescent Moon on the 3rd, low in dusk's western twilight. Earth is farthest from the Sun (at aphelion) on the 4th. Saturn reaches opposition on the 9th, in Sagittarius, at a bright but not brilliant magnitude 0.1; the Ringed Planet rises at sunset to the left of Sagittarius's "Teapot" asterism and is highest at about 1:00 A.M. It is next to the Moon on the 15th. Meanwhile, Jupiter remains optimally placed and is nicely up in the southeast at nightfall as the night's brightest "star." Mars is gone by month's end.

● NEW MOON	2nd day	3:16 P.M.
◑ FIRST QUARTER	9th day	6:55 A.M.
○ FULL MOON	16th day	5:38 P.M.
◐ LAST QUARTER	24th day	9:18 P.M.
● NEW MOON	31st day	11:12 P.M.

All times are given in Eastern Daylight Time.

GET THESE PAGES WITH TIMES SET TO YOUR ZIP CODE AT ALMANAC.COM/ACCESS.

DAY OF YEAR	DAY OF MONTH	DAY OF WEEK	☼ RISES H.M.	RISE KEY	☼ SETS H.M.	SET KEY	LENGTH OF DAY H.M.	SUN FAST M.	SUN DECLINATION ° ′	HIGH TIDE TIMES BOSTON		☾ RISES H.M.	RISE KEY	☾ SETS H.M.	SET KEY	☾ ASTRON. PLACE	☾ AGE
182	1	M.	5:11	A	8:25	E	15 14	12	23 N. 05	10¾	11	4:05	B	7:25	E	TAU	28
183	2	Tu.	5:12	A	8:25	E	15 13	12	23 N. 01	11¾	11¾	4:57	B	8:28	E	GEM	0
184	3	W.	5:12	A	8:25	E	15 13	11	22 N. 56	12½	—	5:58	B	9:25	E	GEM	1
185	4	Th.	5:13	A	8:24	E	15 11	11	22 N. 51	12½	1¼	7:06	B	10:13	E	CAN	2
186	5	Fr.	5:13	A	8:24	E	15 11	11	22 N. 45	1½	2¼	8:20	C	10:55	E	CAN	3
187	6	Sa.	5:14	A	8:24	E	15 10	11	22 N. 39	2¼	3	9:34	C	11:30	E	LEO	4
188	7	**F**	5:15	A	8:23	E	15 08	11	22 N. 33	3¼	4	10:48	D	—	-	LEO	5
189	8	M.	5:15	A	8:23	E	15 08	11	22 N. 26	4¼	4¾	12:01	D	12:02	D	VIR	6
190	9	Tu.	5:16	A	8:23	E	15 07	10	22 N. 19	5¼	5¾	1:11	E	12:32	C	VIR	7
191	10	W.	5:17	A	8:22	E	15 05	10	22 N. 12	6¼	6¾	2:20	E	1:01	C	VIR	8
192	11	Th.	5:17	A	8:22	E	15 05	10	22 N. 04	7¼	7¾	3:28	E	1:31	C	LIB	9
193	12	Fr.	5:18	A	8:21	E	15 03	10	21 N. 56	8¼	8¾	4:35	E	2:03	B	LIB	10
194	13	Sa.	5:19	A	8:21	E	15 02	10	21 N. 47	9¼	9½	5:39	E	2:39	B	OPH	11
195	14	**F**	5:20	A	8:20	E	15 00	10	21 N. 38	10¼	10½	6:39	E	3:19	B	OPH	12
196	15	M.	5:21	A	8:19	E	14 58	10	21 N. 29	11¼	11¼	7:34	E	4:05	B	SAG	13
197	16	Tu.	5:21	A	8:19	E	14 58	10	21 N. 19	12	—	8:22	E	4:56	B	SAG	14
198	17	W.	5:22	A	8:18	E	14 56	10	21 N. 09	12	12½	9:04	E	5:52	B	SAG	15
199	18	Th.	5:23	A	8:17	E	14 54	10	20 N. 59	12¾	1¼	9:39	E	6:50	B	CAP	16
200	19	Fr.	5:24	A	8:17	E	14 53	9	20 N. 48	1¼	2	10:10	E	7:49	C	CAP	17
201	20	Sa.	5:25	A	8:16	E	14 51	9	20 N. 37	2	2½	10:38	D	8:49	C	AQU	18
202	21	**F**	5:26	A	8:15	E	14 49	9	20 N. 25	2¾	3¼	11:03	D	9:48	C	AQU	19
203	22	M.	5:27	A	8:14	E	14 47	9	20 N. 13	3½	4	11:27	D	10:47	D	PSC	20
204	23	Tu.	5:28	A	8:13	E	14 45	9	20 N. 01	4¼	4¾	11:52	C	11:46	D	CET	21
205	24	Th.	5:29	A	8:12	E	14 43	9	19 N. 49	5	5½	—	-	12:46	E	PSC	22
206	25	Th.	5:29	A	8:11	E	14 42	9	19 N. 36	5¾	6¼	12:17	C	1:47	E	CET	23
207	26	Fr.	5:30	A	8:10	E	14 40	9	19 N. 23	6¾	7	12:45	D	2:51	E	ARI	24
208	27	Sa.	5:31	A	8:09	E	14 38	9	19 N. 09	7½	8	1:17	B	3:57	E	TAU	25
209	28	**F**	5:32	A	8:08	E	14 36	9	18 N. 55	8½	8¾	1:55	B	5:04	E	TAU	26
210	29	M.	5:33	B	8:07	E	14 34	9	18 N. 41	9½	9¾	2:42	B	6:09	E	TAU	27
211	30	Tu.	5:34	B	8:06	E	14 32	9	18 N. 27	10¼	10½	3:38	B	7:09	E	GEM	28
212	31	W.	5:35	B	8:05	E	14 30	9	18 N. 12	11¼	11½	4:43	B	8:03	E	GEM	0

CALENDAR

JULY

JULY HATH 31 DAYS

All the heat was singing,
The insect chorus hummed in undertone.
–Herman Charles Merivale

DAY OF MONTH	DAY OF WEEK	DATES, FEASTS, FASTS, ASPECTS, TIDE HEIGHTS, AND WEATHER	
1	M.	CANADA DAY • ☌♀☾ • NASA's *Cassini* spacecraft first to orbit Saturn, 2004	*Fireworks*
2	Tu.	NEW ● • ECLIPSE ☉ • ☾ RIDES HIGH • Tides {9.7 / 11.4	*fizzle*
3	W.	Dog Days begin. • ☾ AT ☊ • First cog-driven train ride up Mt. Washington, N.H., 1869 • {9.9 / —	*in*
4	Th.	INDEPENDENCE DAY • ☌☿☾ • ☌♂☾ • ⊕ AT APHELION	*foggy*
5	Fr.	☾ AT PERIG. • Football's Winnipeg Blue Bombers beat Saskatchewan Roughriders, 56-0, 1986	*drizzle.*
6	Sa.	First east-to-west Atlantic crossing by dirigible *(R34)* completed, Scotland to N.Y., 1919 • {11.6 / 10.4	*It's*
7	**F**	4th S. af. P. • ☌☿♂ • ☿ STAT. • Tides {11.4 / 10.5	*fine*
8	M.	☾ ON EQ. • *In the morning, mountains, In the evening, fountains.* • Tides {11.0 / 10.5	*on*
9	Tu.	♄ AT ☍ • 96°F, Glennallen, Alaska, 2009 • Tides {10.5 / 10.5	*the*
10	W.	Orchestra conductor Arthur Fiedler died, 1979 • "Whipped Cream King" Aaron Lapin died, 1999	*front*
11	Th.	Black-eyed Susans in bloom now. • Last slide rule manufactured in U.S., 1976 • {9.7 / 10.6	*nine.*
12	Fr.	U.S. statesman Alexander Hamilton died, 1804 • Tides {9.4 / 10.6	*Cool*
13	Sa.	☌♃☾ • Lightning strike triggered 24-hour blackout, N.Y.C., 1977 • Tides {9.3 / 10.6	*air*
14	**F**	5th S. af. P. • Bastille Day • ♇ AT ☍ • {9.2 / 10.6	*prevails*
15	M.	St. Swithin • ☾ RUNS LOW • Ice hockey player Bryan Helmer born, 1972 • {9.2 / 10.6	*on*
16	Tu.	FULL BUCK ○ • ECLIPSE ☾ • ☌♄☾ • ☌♇☾ • ☾ AT ☋	*mountain*
17	W.	Newscaster Walter Cronkite died, 2009 • *Two of a trade seldom agree.* • Tides {9.2 / —	*trails.*
18	Th.	Armadillos mate now. • First day of storm that brought flooding to Saguenay region, Que., 1996	*Picknickers*
19	Fr.	Fire began near Circus Maximus that destroyed 2/3 of Rome, Italy, A.D. 64 • Tides {10.3 / 9.2	*beware*
20	Sa.	☾ AT APO. • Sir Edmund Hillary (one of first to summit Mt. Everest) born, 1919 • {10.1 / 9.2	*of*
21	**F**	6th S. af P. • ☌♆☾ • ☿ IN INF. ☌ • {9.9 / 9.2	*cornscateous*
22	M.	St. Mary Magdalene • Cornscateous air is everywhere. • {9.6 / 9.2	*air!*
23	Tu.	☾ ON EQ. • *Tarzan,* Disney's first all-digital film, released, 1999 • {9.3 / 9.2	*Hot*
24	W.	☌☿♀ • 67-lb. 8-oz. muskellunge caught, Lac Courte Oreilles, Hayward, Wisc., 1949 • {9.0 / 9.2	*enough*
25	Th.	St. James • ☌♅☾ • 5.6 earthquake struck western Mont., 2005 • Tides {8.8 / 9.3	*to*
26	Fr.	St. Anne • First Moon rock samples analyzed, Lunar Receiving Laboratory, Houston, Tex., 1969	*melt*
27	Sa.	Northern white rhino Nabire died, leaving just 4 others on Earth, 2015 • Adult gypsy moths emerge.	*butter.*
28	**F**	7th S. af. P. • Coffee rationing in U.S. ended, WWII, 1943 • {8.8 / 10.3	*Listen*
29	M.	St. Martha • *Neither heat nor cold abides always in the sky.* • Tides {9.0 / 10.8	*to*
30	Tu.	☾ RIDES HIGH • ☌☿☾ • ☾ AT ☊ • USS *Indianapolis* sunk, WWII, 1945	*thunder's*
31	W.	St. Ignatius of Loyola • NEW ● • ☌☿☾ • ☿ STAT. • {9.8 / 11.7	*mutter.*

Farmer's Calendar

Soon a tractor will rumble up the road, its motorized growl growing louder, as its sidebar mower makes its first and only pass, lancing through roadside grasses. This annual act creates a "before" and "after." Prior to the mower's arrival, summer stretches endlessly. The timothy, switch, and orchard grasses have been rising since they first poked through the soil in April. Some mingle with the lowest branches of the maples and apples. Not for long. One pass of that tractor—the tin reaper of summer—and all that growth will cascade back to earth. Sure, its stubble will resume a skyward journey, but it won't achieve this same kind of height. Since June's summer solstice, each day's been snipped of a minute. Night will have lopped off nearly half an hour of light by the time the tractor sidles up in mid-July. Which leads me to anticipate this smooth operator who wields the roadside mower: Is he the tardy barber of spring or the first shearer of autumn? Perhaps it's the latter, for in the wake of the blades, beneath the flat top of collapsed grass, the crickets' murmur grows louder, as if they too are whetting their scythes.

AUGUST

SKY WATCH: Venus passes behind the Sun in superior conjunction on the 14th, marking its transition to an evening star for the rest of the year. It is 5 degrees from the Sun even at month's end and hopelessly lost in solar glare. Mars is lost behind the Sun, too. Jupiter and Saturn are wonderfully positioned at nightfall, in the south. Although both have far southern declinations and neither ascends more than a third of the way up the sky this year, they are both easy viewing targets all night long throughout the summer. The Moon is strikingly close to Jupiter on the 9th. The fat gibbous Moon hovers to the right of Saturn on the 11th and to its left on the 12th. These bright lunar phases will spoil the Perseid meteor showers.

◑ **FIRST QUARTER** 7th day 1:31 P.M.　　◐ **LAST QUARTER** 23rd day 10:56 A.M.
○ **FULL MOON** 15th day 8:29 A.M.　　● **NEW MOON** 30th day 6:37 A.M.

All times are given in Eastern Daylight Time.

GET THESE PAGES WITH TIMES SET TO YOUR ZIP CODE AT ALMANAC.COM/ACCESS.

DAY OF YEAR	DAY OF MONTH	DAY OF WEEK	☼ RISES H. M.	RISE KEY	☼ SETS H. M.	SET KEY	LENGTH OF DAY H. M.	SUN FAST M.	SUN DECLINATION ° '	HIGH TIDE TIMES BOSTON		☾ RISES H. M.	RISE KEY	☾ SETS H. M.	SET KEY	☾ ASTRON. PLACE	☾ AGE
213	1	Th.	5:36	B	8:04	E	14 28	9	17 N. 57	12	—	5:56	C	8:48	E	CAN	1
214	2	Fr.	5:37	B	8:03	E	14 26	10	17 N. 42	12¼	1	7:13	C	9:28	E	LEO	2
215	3	Sa.	5:38	B	8:02	E	14 24	10	17 N. 26	1¼	1¾	8:30	C	10:02	D	LEO	3
216	4	F	5:40	B	8:00	E	14 20	10	17 N. 10	2	2¾	9:46	D	10:33	D	VIR	4
217	5	M.	5:41	B	7:59	E	14 18	10	16 N. 54	3	3½	10:59	D	11:03	C	VIR	5
218	6	Tu.	5:42	B	7:58	E	14 16	10	16 N. 38	4	4½	12:11	E	11:33	C	VIR	6
219	7	W.	5:43	B	7:57	E	14 14	10	16 N. 21	5	5½	1:20	E	—	-	LIB	7
220	8	Th.	5:44	B	7:55	E	14 11	10	16 N. 04	6	6¼	2:28	E	12:05	B	LIB	8
221	9	Fr.	5:45	B	7:54	E	14 09	10	15 N. 47	7	7¼	3:33	E	12:40	B	SCO	9
222	10	Sa.	5:46	B	7:53	E	14 07	10	15 N. 29	8	8¼	4:34	E	1:18	B	OPH	10
223	11	F	5:47	B	7:51	E	14 04	11	15 N. 12	9	9¼	5:30	E	2:02	B	SAG	11
224	12	M.	5:48	B	7:50	D	14 02	11	14 N. 54	10	10¼	6:20	E	2:52	B	SAG	12
225	13	Tu.	5:49	B	7:48	D	13 59	11	14 N. 36	10¾	11	7:03	E	3:45	B	SAG	13
226	14	W.	5:50	B	7:47	D	13 57	11	14 N. 17	11½	11¾	7:40	E	4:43	B	CAP	14
227	15	Th.	5:51	B	7:46	D	13 55	11	13 N. 59	12¼	—	8:12	E	5:41	C	CAP	15
228	16	Fr.	5:52	B	7:44	D	13 52	12	13 N. 40	12¼	12¾	8:41	E	6:41	C	AQU	16
229	17	Sa.	5:53	B	7:43	D	13 50	12	13 N. 21	1	1½	9:07	D	7:40	C	AQU	17
230	18	F	5:54	B	7:41	D	13 47	12	13 N. 01	1½	2	9:31	D	8:39	D	AQU	18
231	19	M.	5:55	B	7:40	D	13 45	12	12 N. 42	2¼	2¾	9:55	C	9:38	D	CET	19
232	20	Tu.	5:56	B	7:38	D	13 42	12	12 N. 22	3	3¼	10:19	C	10:37	D	CET	20
233	21	W.	5:57	B	7:37	D	13 40	13	12 N. 02	3¾	4	10:46	C	11:37	E	PSC	21
234	22	Th.	5:58	B	7:35	D	13 37	13	11 N. 42	4½	4¾	11:15	B	12:39	E	ARI	22
235	23	Fr.	6:00	B	7:33	D	13 33	13	11 N. 22	5¼	5½	11:50	B	1:42	E	TAU	23
236	24	Sa.	6:01	B	7:32	D	13 31	13	11 N. 01	6	6½	—	-	2:47	E	TAU	24
237	25	F	6:02	B	7:30	D	13 28	14	10 N. 41	7	7¼	12:31	B	3:51	E	TAU	25
238	26	M.	6:03	B	7:29	D	13 26	14	10 N. 20	8	8¼	1:21	B	4:52	E	GEM	26
239	27	Tu.	6:04	B	7:27	D	13 23	14	9 N. 59	9	9¼	2:21	C	5:48	E	GEM	27
240	28	W.	6:05	B	7:25	D	13 20	14	9 N. 38	10	10¼	3:29	C	6:37	E	CAN	28
241	29	Th.	6:06	B	7:24	D	13 18	15	9 N. 17	10¾	11	4:45	C	7:20	E	LEO	29
242	30	Fr.	6:07	B	7:22	D	13 15	15	8 N. 55	11¾	—	6:03	C	7:57	D	LEO	0
243	31	Sa.	6:08	B	7:20	D	13 12	15	8 N. 34	12	12½	7:21	D	8:30	D	LEO	1

AUGUST

Then waxed the heavens black,
Until the lightning leapt from cloud to cloud.
–**William Morris**

DAY OF MONTH	DAY OF WEEK	DATES, FEASTS, FASTS, ASPECTS, TIDE HEIGHTS, AND WEATHER	
1	Th.	Lammas Day • ☌♂☾ • Writer Herman Melville born, 1819 • Tides {10.3 / —}	*These*
2	F.	☾ AT PERIG. • Viking ship replica *Gaia* arrived at L'Anse aux Meadows, Nfld., 1991 • {11.9 / 10.6}	*are*
3	Sa.	115°F, Fort Smith, Ark., 2011 • Tides {12.0 / 10.9}	*the*
4	**F**	**8th S. af. P.** • U.S. president Barack Obama born, 1961 • Tides {11.9 / 11.0}	*climes*
5	M.	**Civic Holiday (Canada)** • ☾ ON EQ. • *A good neighbor is a precious thing.* • {11.5 / 11.0}	*that*
6	Tu.	Transfiguration • Sonic boom broke windows in Kelowna, B.C., 1969 • {11.0 / 10.9}	*fry*
7	W.	Gray squirrels have second litters now. • Low temperature of 40°F, Valentine, Nebr., 1989 • {10.3 / 10.7}	*men's*
8	Th.	St. Dominic • Tornado touched down in Brooklyn, N.Y., 2007 • Tides {9.8 / 10.5}	*soles.*
9	Fr.	☌♃☾ • ☿ GR. ELONG. (19° WEST) • Smokey Bear chosen fire prevention symbol, 1944	*Sweltering!*
10	Sa.	St. Lawrence • Coldest temp. on Earth at time: –135.8°F, East Antarctic Plateau, Antarctica, 2010	*Perseid*
11	**F**	**9th S. af. P.** • Dog Days end. • ♃ STAT. • Tides {8.9 / 10.1}	*meteors*
12	M.	☾ RUNS LOW • ☾ AT ☋ • ☌♄☾ • ☌♇☾ • ⛢ STAT. • {8.9 / 10.2}	*streak*
13	Tu.	Samuel Leeds Allen granted patent for Flexible Flyer sled, 1889 • Chef Julia Child died, 2004	*the*
14	W.	♀ IN SUP. ☌ • *A good nut year, a good corn year.* • Tides {9.1 / 10.2}	*sky*
15	Th.	Assumption • FULL STURGEON ○ • 1,224-lb. cupcake set world record, 2009	*with*
16	Fr.	Ragweed in bloom. • Element 110 named "darmstadtium," 2003 • Tides {10.2 / 9.3}	*fiery*
17	Sa.	Cat Nights commence. • ☾ AT APO. • ☌♆☾ • {10.2 / 9.4}	*letters.*
18	**F**	**10th S. af. P.** • Woodstock Festival ended, Bethel, N.Y., 1969 • {10.0 / 9.4}	*It's*
19	M.	☾ ON EQ. • Gymnast Carly Patterson won women's all-around Olympic gold medal, 2004 • {9.8 / 9.5}	*turning*
20	Tu.	Parade of 83 tow trucks set world record, Wenatchee, Wash., 2004 • Tides {9.6 / 9.5}	*cool*
21	W.	☌⛢☾ • Singer Kenny Rogers born, 1938 • Tides {9.3 / 9.5}	*enough*
22	Th.	1¼" hail, Castle Rock, Colo., 2007 • Tides {9.0 / 9.5}	*for*
23	Fr.	2-lb. blue lobster caught off Pine Point, Scarborough, Maine, 2014 • *Every shoe fits not every foot.*	*sweaters.*
24	Sa.	St. Bartholomew • ☌♀♂ • White House set on fire (War of 1812), D.C., 1814	*Summer's*
25	**F**	**11th S. af. P.** • Hurricane Harvey made landfall, Corpus Christi, Tex., 2017	*buglers*
26	M.	☾ RIDES HIGH • ☾ AT ☊ • Starch process that led to puffed grain cereals patented, 1902	*blow*
27	Tu.	Largest trade at time in NBA, 11 players, 3 teams, 1999 • Tides {9.2 / 10.8}	*their*
28	W.	St. Augustine of Hippo • Hummingbirds migrate south. • Tides {9.7 / 11.3}	*last*
29	Th.	St. John the Baptist • ☌☿☾ • Astronaut Chris Hadfield born, 1959 • {10.2 / 11.8}	*call;*
30	Fr.	First of Muharram begins at sundown • NEW ● • ☾ AT PERIG. • ☌♀☾ • ☌♂☾	*enter*
31	Sa.	Comet Howard-Koomur-Michels collided with Sun, 1979 • Tides {12.0 / 12.2}	*fall.*

Farmer's Calendar

I follow tiny hand-painted signs, each depicting a blueberry, from the paved straightaway of Wild Branch Road onto a dirt road winding through Collinsville. Day, lovers of the small blue fruit travel this route to arrive at Arnold Brown's gravel drive, sign the guest log, grab a bucket, and traipse into a field teeming with hundreds of mature berry bushes. Last year was a light one, as only 15,000 pounds of berries were gleaned. The year before, pickers hauled out 10 tons! I find, as usual, that Brown's hillside is abuzz with people; their voices carry easily. I overhear snippets of heart-to-heart conversations, as well as an excited child discovering a "big one!" But none of us could be gathering these sweet surprises if not for an overeager man with a tractor mower. Back in the 1990s, Arnold had just planted this hillside with 7,500 Christmas tree saplings. All was proceeding according to plan until the man hired to cut the east field did Arnold a misinformed favor. He thought: "Arnold would probably like me to mow this field. He just forgot to ask." So, here we are with our buckets, gossiping across the bushes, harvesting Plan B.

SKY WATCH: The September Moon offers both an easy spectacle and a difficult challenge. The easy part is a series of conjunctions with brilliant Jupiter and bright Saturn at nightfall. The Moon floats to the right of Jupiter on the 5th, left of Jupiter on the 6th, right of Saturn on the 7th, and left of Saturn on the 8th. The visually challenging portion of the program occurs on the 29th, when the thin crescent Moon, very low in the west soon after sunset, forms a triangle with Mercury to its lower left and bright returning Venus to its lower right. Autumn begins with the equinox on the 23rd at 3:50 A.M.

◗ FIRST QUARTER	5th day	11:10 P.M.
○ FULL MOON	14th day	12:33 A.M.
◑ LAST QUARTER	21st day	10:41 P.M.
● NEW MOON	28th day	2:26 P.M.

All times are given in Eastern Daylight Time.

GET THESE PAGES WITH TIMES SET TO YOUR ZIP CODE AT ALMANAC.COM/ACCESS.

DAY OF YEAR	DAY OF MONTH	DAY OF WEEK	☼ RISES H. M.	RISE KEY	☼ SETS H. M.	SET KEY	LENGTH OF DAY H. M.	SUN FAST M.	SUN DECLINATION ° ′	HIGH TIDE TIMES BOSTON		☽ RISES H. M.	RISE KEY	☽ SETS H. M.	SET KEY	☽ ASTRON. PLACE	☽ AGE
244	1	F	6:09	B	7:19	D	13 10	16	8 N. 12	1	1½	8:38	D	9:01	C	VIR	2
245	2	M.	6:10	B	7:17	D	13 07	16	7 N. 50	1¾	2¼	9:53	E	9:32	C	VIR	3
246	3	Tu.	6:11	C	7:15	D	13 04	16	7 N. 28	2¾	3	11:06	E	10:04	C	VIR	4
247	4	W.	6:12	C	7:14	D	13 02	17	7 N. 06	3½	4	12:17	E	10:39	B	LIB	5
248	5	Th.	6:13	C	7:12	D	12 59	17	6 N. 44	4½	5	1:25	E	11:17	B	LIB	6
249	6	Fr.	6:14	C	7:10	D	12 56	17	6 N. 21	5½	6	2:28	E	—	B	OPH	7
250	7	Sa.	6:15	C	7:08	D	12 53	18	5 N. 59	6½	7	12:00	E	3:26	-	SAG	8
251	8	F	6:16	C	7:07	D	12 51	18	5 N. 36	7¾	8	4:18	E	12:48	B	SAG	9
252	9	M.	6:17	C	7:05	D	12 48	18	5 N. 14	8¾	9	5:03	E	1:40	B	SAG	10
253	10	Tu.	6:19	C	7:03	D	12 44	19	4 N. 51	9½	9¾	5:42	E	2:36	B	CAP	11
254	11	W.	6:20	C	7:01	D	12 41	19	4 N. 28	10½	10½	6:15	E	3:35	B	CAP	12
255	12	Th.	6:21	C	7:00	C	12 39	20	4 N. 06	11	11¼	6:44	E	4:34	C	AQU	13
256	13	Fr.	6:22	C	6:58	C	12 36	20	3 N. 43	11¾	—	7:11	D	5:33	C	AQU	14
257	14	Sa.	6:23	C	6:56	C	12 33	20	3 N. 20	12	12¼	7:35	D	6:32	D	AQU	15
258	15	F	6:24	C	6:54	C	12 30	21	2 N. 57	12½	1	7:59	C	7:31	D	PSC	16
259	16	M.	6:25	C	6:53	C	12 28	21	2 N. 33	1¼	1½	8:23	C	8:31	D	CET	17
260	17	Tu.	6:26	C	6:51	C	12 25	21	2 N. 10	1¾	2	8:49	C	9:31	E	PSC	18
261	18	W.	6:27	C	6:49	C	12 22	22	1 N. 47	2½	2¾	9:17	B	10:32	E	CET	19
262	19	Th.	6:28	C	6:47	C	12 19	22	1 N. 24	3¼	3¼	9:49	B	11:34	E	TAU	20
263	20	Fr.	6:29	C	6:45	C	12 16	22	1 N. 01	4	4	10:26	B	12:37	E	TAU	21
264	21	Sa.	6:30	C	6:44	C	12 14	23	0 N. 37	4¾	5	11:11	B	1:40	E	TAU	22
265	22	F	6:31	C	6:42	C	12 11	23	0 N. 14	5½	5¾	—	-	2:41	E	GEM	23
266	23	M.	6:32	C	6:40	C	12 08	23	0 s. 08	6½	6¾	12:05	B	3:37	E	GEM	24
267	24	Tu.	6:33	C	6:38	C	12 05	24	0 s. 32	7½	8	1:08	B	4:27	E	CAN	25
268	25	W.	6:34	C	6:37	C	12 03	24	0 s. 55	8½	9	2:18	C	5:11	E	CAN	26
269	26	Th.	6:35	C	6:35	C	12 00	24	1 s. 19	9½	9¾	3:34	C	5:50	E	LEO	27
270	27	Fr.	6:37	C	6:33	C	11 56	25	1 s. 42	10½	10¾	4:51	D	6:24	D	LEO	28
271	28	Sa.	6:38	C	6:31	C	11 53	25	2 s. 05	11¼	11¾	6:09	D	6:56	D	VIR	0
272	29	F	6:39	C	6:30	C	11 51	25	2 s. 29	12¼	—	7:27	D	7:28	C	VIR	1
273	30	M.	6:40	C	6:28	C	11 48	26	2 s. 52	12½	1	8:43	E	8:00	C	VIR	2

THE NINTH MONTH · 2019

SEPTEMBER

SEPTEMBER HATH 30 DAYS

The sheaves flew fast and thick
From fork to fork, to feed the growing rick.
–**Charles Tennyson Turner**

DAY OF MONTH	DAY OF WEEK	DATES, FEASTS, FASTS, ASPECTS, TIDE HEIGHTS, AND WEATHER	
1	**F**	**12th S. af. P.** • ☾ ON EQ. • Sundance Fire intensified, Idaho, 1967	*Children*
2	M.	LABOR DAY • ☌♂☉ • Evacuation began for 2.8 million people, Hurricane Frances, Fla., 2004	*board*
3	Tu.	☌☿♂ • ☿ IN SUP. ☌ • *When the fog falls, fair weather follows.* • {11.4 / 11.4	*buses*
4	W.	A 127-lb. cabbage won prize at Alaska State Fair, 2009 • Tides {10.8 / 11.1	*in*
5	Th.	102°F, Portland, Oreg., 1944 • Missionary Saint Teresa of Calcutta died, 1997 • {10.1 / 10.6	*yellow*
6	F.	☌♃☾ • Basketball player John Wall born, 1990 • Tides {9.5 / 10.2	*slickers;*
7	Sa.	First Canadian Official Languages Act went into effect, 1969 • Tides {9.0 / 9.9	*orchards*
8	**F**	**13th S. af. P.** • ☾ RUNS LOW • ☾ AT ☋ • ☌♄☾ • ☌♇☾	*are*
9	M.	Continental Congress declared "United States of America" name of new nation, 1776 • {8.7 / 9.7	*filled*
10	Tu.	♆ AT ☍ • Cranberry bog harvest begins, Cape Cod, Mass. • Tides {8.8 / 9.8	*with*
11	W.	PATRIOT DAY • *Queen Elizabeth 2* ocean liner struck by approx. 90-ft.-high rogue wave, 1995	*pickers.*
12	Th.	*Pride often borrows the cloak of humility.* • Tides {9.2 / 10.0	*Rain*
13	Fr.	☾ AT APO. • ☌☿♀ • ☌♆☾ • Writer Roald Dahl born, 1916 • {9.4 / 10.1	*gives*
14	Sa.	Holy Cross • FULL HARVEST ○ • World Series canceled due to strike, 1994 • {9.6 / —	*way*
15	**F**	**14th S. af. P.** • ☾ ON EQ. • First successful portable MP3 player debuted, 1998	*to*
16	M.	Physicist/educator Ursula Franklin born, 1921 • {9.9 / 9.8	*northern*
17	Tu.	☌♅☾ • First powered flight of X-15 rocket plane, 1959 • Tides {9.8 / 9.8	*gales*
18	W.	Ember Day • ♄ STAT. • Cosmonaut Arnaldo Tamayo Méndez first Latin American in space, 1980	*as*
19	Th.	International Talk Like a Pirate Day • Astronomer Jean Baptiste Joseph Delambre born, 1749 • {9.3 / 9.8	*they*
20	Fr.	Ember Day • Navigator Ferdinand Magellan left Sanlúcar de Barrameda, Spain, for Spice Islands, 1519	*fill*
21	Sa.	St. Matthew • Ember Day • N.Y. Jets' Steve O'Neal's 98-yd. punt longest in NFL history, 1969	*their*
22	**F**	**15th S. af. P.** • ☾ RIDES HIGH • Mime Marcel Marceau died, 2007 • {8.7 / 9.8	*pails*
23	M.	Harvest Home • AUTUMNAL EQUINOX • ☾ AT ☊ • Tides {8.7 / 10.0	*with*
24	Tu.	*When a friend asketh, there is no tomorrow.* • {9.0 / 10.4	*autumn's*
25	W.	Woodchucks hibernate now. • Tides {9.5 / 10.8	*riches*
26	Th.	Nurseryman Johnny "Appleseed" Chapman born, 1774 • {10.1 / 11.3	*and*
27	Fr.	St. Vincent de Paul • ☾ AT PERIG. • ☌♂☾ • Tides {10.7 / 11.6	*showers*
28	Sa.	NEW ● • 437 people dressed as Superman set world record, Calgary, Alta., 2011	*swell*
29	**F**	**16th S. af. P.** • Rosh Hashanah begins at sundown • ☾ ON EQ. • ☌☿☾ • ☌♀☾	*the*
30	M.	St. Michael[T] • U.S. Navy's first nuclear sub, USS *Nautilus*, commissioned, 1954 • {11.8 / 11.9	*ditches.*

Farmer's Calendar

"A cold pocket" sounds like something a snowman might have. Meteorologically, I live where chilly-heavy air will linger on a breezeless night. Hence, one evening sooner than most, I'll wake to find the pocket's white lint—our first deep frost—lining each blade of grass, crystallizing flower petals, glazing pumpkins' platter-like leaves. Denizens of Zone 5, we expect our first brush with frost to arrive anytime after the second week of September. I can try to avert damage to tender plants by casting blankets across the basil and tomatoes, by swaddling the fragile cuffs of morning glories in hopes of seeing one more bloom, but no amount of bedding will cushion the sharpening truth: Our growing season is over. Soon we'll have the kind of frigid night that fringes all of our vegetation in a hoary ice. Certain plants' cells can't withstand this drastic temperature change. When the rising Sun warms a morning glory's frozen leaves, its cell walls will break, irreparably. Eventually, the frostbitten garden will be blanketed with flakes. By then, we won't be able to discern any difference between the snowman's pocket and his voluminous white coat.

OCTOBER

SKY WATCH: Returning Venus, barely brightening and climbing, may be glimpsed very low in the west in evening twilight. When will you first spot it? Mercury is down there, too, this month and, although less brilliant, is higher up and may be easier to see. Mars, at an unimpressive magnitude 1.8, starts to rise ahead of the morning Sun, but it's still subdued in solar glare. This leaves Jupiter and Saturn to strut unchallenged in the southern sky nearly all night long, although both start to set before dawn. Green Uranus comes into opposition on the 28th; in Pisces at magnitude 5.7, the seventh planet from the Sun is dimly visible to the naked eye away from city lights.

◑ **FIRST QUARTER** 5th day 12:47 P.M.   ◐ **LAST QUARTER** 21st day 8:39 A.M.
○ **FULL MOON** 13th day 5:08 P.M.   ● **NEW MOON** 27th day 11:38 P.M.

All times are given in Eastern Daylight Time.

GET THESE PAGES WITH TIMES SET TO YOUR ZIP CODE AT ALMANAC.COM/ACCESS.

DAY OF YEAR	DAY OF MONTH	DAY OF WEEK	☼ RISES H. M.	RISE KEY	☼ SETS H. M.	SET KEY	LENGTH OF DAY H. M.	SUN FAST M.	SUN DECLINATION ° '	HIGH TIDE TIMES BOSTON		☽ RISES H. M.	RISE KEY	☽ SETS H. M.	SET KEY	ASTRON. PLACE	☽ AGE
274	1	Tu.	6:41	C	**6:26**	C	11 45	26	3 s. 15	1½	**1¾**	9:57	E	**8:34**	B	LIB	3
275	2	W.	6:42	C	**6:24**	C	11 42	26	3 s. 38	2¼	**2¾**	11:09	E	**9:11**	B	LIB	4
276	3	Th.	6:43	C	**6:23**	C	11 40	27	4 s. 02	3¼	**3½**	**12:17**	E	**9:54**	B	OPH	5
277	4	Fr.	6:44	D	**6:21**	C	11 37	27	4 s. 25	4¼	**4½**	**1:19**	E	**10:41**	B	OPH	6
278	5	Sa.	6:45	D	**6:19**	C	11 34	27	4 s. 48	5¼	**5½**	**2:14**	E	**11:33**	B	SAG	7
279	6	**F**	6:46	D	**6:18**	C	11 32	28	5 s. 11	6¼	**6½**	**3:02**	E	—	-	SAG	8
280	7	M.	6:48	D	**6:16**	C	11 28	28	5 s. 34	7¼	**7½**	**3:43**	E	12:29	B	CAP	9
281	8	Tu.	6:49	D	**6:14**	C	11 25	28	5 s. 57	8¼	**8½**	**4:18**	E	1:27	B	CAP	10
282	9	W.	6:50	D	**6:12**	C	11 22	29	6 s. 20	9	**9¼**	**4:48**	E	2:26	C	CAP	11
283	10	Th.	6:51	D	**6:11**	C	11 20	29	6 s. 42	9¾	**10**	**5:15**	D	3:26	C	AQU	12
284	11	Fr.	6:52	D	**6:09**	C	11 17	29	7 s. 05	10½	**10¾**	**5:40**	D	4:25	C	AQU	13
285	12	Sa.	6:53	D	**6:07**	C	11 14	29	7 s. 28	11¼	**11½**	**6:04**	D	5:24	D	PSC	14
286	13	**F**	6:54	D	**6:06**	B	11 12	30	7 s. 50	11¾	—	**6:27**	C	6:24	D	CET	15
287	14	M.	6:56	D	**6:04**	B	11 08	30	8 s. 12	12	**12¼**	**6:52**	C	7:24	E	PSC	16
288	15	Tu.	6:57	D	**6:03**	B	11 06	30	8 s. 35	12¾	**1**	**7:19**	C	8:25	E	CET	17
289	16	W.	6:58	D	**6:01**	B	11 03	30	8 s. 57	1¼	**1½**	**7:50**	B	9:28	E	ARI	18
290	17	Th.	6:59	D	**5:59**	B	11 00	30	9 s. 19	2	**2¼**	**8:25**	B	10:31	E	TAU	19
291	18	Fr.	7:00	D	**5:58**	B	10 58	31	9 s. 40	2¾	**2¾**	**9:08**	B	11:35	E	TAU	20
292	19	Sa.	7:01	D	**5:56**	B	10 55	31	10 s. 02	3½	**3½**	**9:58**	B	**12:36**	E	TAU	21
293	20	**F**	7:03	D	**5:55**	B	10 52	31	10 s. 24	4¼	**4½**	**10:56**	B	**1:32**	E	GEM	22
294	21	M.	7:04	D	**5:53**	B	10 49	31	10 s. 45	5¼	**5½**	—	-	**2:23**	E	GEM	23
295	22	Tu.	7:05	D	**5:52**	B	10 47	31	11 s. 06	6¼	**6½**	12:02	B	**3:08**	E	CAN	24
296	23	W.	7:06	D	**5:50**	B	10 44	31	11 s. 27	7¼	**7½**	1:13	C	**3:47**	E	LEO	25
297	24	Th.	7:07	D	**5:49**	B	10 42	32	11 s. 48	8¼	**8½**	2:27	C	**4:21**	D	LEO	26
298	25	Fr.	7:09	D	**5:47**	B	10 38	32	12 s. 09	9¼	**9½**	3:43	D	**4:53**	D	LEO	27
299	26	Sa.	7:10	D	**5:46**	B	10 36	32	12 s. 30	10	**10½**	4:59	D	**5:23**	C	VIR	28
300	27	**F**	7:11	D	**5:45**	B	10 34	32	12 s. 50	11	**11½**	6:15	E	**5:54**	C	VIR	0
301	28	M.	7:12	D	**5:43**	B	10 31	32	13 s. 10	11¾	—	7:31	E	**6:27**	B	VIR	1
302	29	Tu.	7:13	D	**5:42**	B	10 29	32	13 s. 30	12¼	**12½**	8:45	E	**7:03**	B	LIB	2
303	30	W.	7:15	D	**5:40**	B	10 25	32	13 s. 50	1¼	**1¼**	9:57	E	**7:44**	B	SCO	3
304	31	Th.	7:16	D	**5:39**	B	10 23	32	14 s. 09	2	**2¼**	11:05	E	**8:30**	B	OPH	4

The small red maple leaves, keen-scented, mute,
Here fleck the stream, to grape-dark purple hushed.
–Bliss Carman

DAY OF MONTH	DAY OF WEEK	DATES, FEASTS, FASTS, ASPECTS, TIDE HEIGHTS, AND WEATHER	
1	Tu.	U.S. president Jimmy Carter born, 1924 • Water polo player/coach Rosanna Tomiuk born, 1984 • {11.5 / 11.8	*Under*
2	W.	♇ STAT. • Watch for banded woolly bear caterpillars now. • Tides {11.0 / 11.5	*clouds*
3	Th.	☌♃☾ • F4 tornado struck Windsor Locks, Conn., 1979 • Tides {10.4 / 11.0	*leaden,*
4	Fr.	St. Francis of Assisi • Astronaut Gordon Cooper died, 2004 • {9.8 / 10.5	*swamp*
5	Sa.	☾ RUNS LOW • ☾ AT ☋ • ☌♄☾ • First space shuttle launch w/oceanographer, 1984	*maples*
6	F	17th S. af. P. • ☌♇☾ • *It is the tone that makes the music.* • {8.8 / 9.5	*redden.*
7	M.	Adrienne Clarkson became 26th governor-general of Canada, 1999 • Tides {8.6 / 9.4	*Bright*
8	Tu.	Yom Kippur begins at sundown • California wildfires began in wine country, 2017 • {8.7 / 9.3	*skies*
9	W.	Hailstorms hit Mont., damaging crops, 1944 • Tides {8.8 / 9.5	*are*
10	Th.	☾ AT APO. • ☌♆☾ • Asteroid Cruithne (quasi-satellite of Earth) discovered, 1986	*pluses*
11	Fr.	Little brown bats hibernate now. • *Honor the tree that gives you shelter.* • Tides {9.4 / 9.7	*for*
12	Sa.	Navy Cross recipient Doris Miller born, 1919 • {9.7 / 9.8	*foliage*
13	F	18th S. af. P. • Sukkoth begins at sundown • FULL HUNTER'S ○ • ☾ ON EQ.	*buses,*
14	M.	COLUMBUS DAY, OBSERVED • INDIGENOUS PEOPLES' DAY • THANKSGIVING DAY (CANADA) • ☌⛢☾	
15	Tu.	Edison Electric Light Co. established, N.Y.C., 1878 • Tides {9.8 / 10.2	*and early*
16	W.	7.1 earthquake near Hector Mine, Mojave Desert, Calif., 1999 • Tides {9.7 / 10.2	*snow*
17	Th.	St. Ignatius of Antioch • Frank Giannino completed run across U.S. (46 days, 8 hrs., 36 mins.), 1980	*thrills*
18	Fr.	St. Luke • Canadian prime minister Pierre Trudeau born, 1919 • St. Luke's little summer. • {9.3 / 10.1	*in*
19	Sa.	First object ('Oumuamua) from another solar system detected in ours, 2017 • {9.0 / 10.0	*the*
20	F	19th S. af. P. • ☾ RIDES HIGH • ☾ AT ☊ • ☿ GR. ELONG. (25° EAST)	*northern*
21	M.	*Better to give the wool than the sheep.* • Tides {8.8 / 10.0	*hills. But*
22	Tu.	Writer Jean-Paul Sartre rejected Nobel Prize for Literature, 1964 • Tides {9.0 / 10.1	*the*
23	W.	St. James of Jerusalem • Football coach John Heisman born, 1869 • {9.3 / 10.3	*old-timers*
24	Th.	Actor Richard Burton bought $1.1 million, 69-carat Cartier diamond ring for wife Elizabeth Taylor, 1969	*sneer,*
25	Fr.	Timber rattlesnakes move to winter dens. • Tides {10.5 / 10.9	*"You*
26	Sa.	☾ ON EQ. • ☾ AT PERIG. • ☌♂☾ • Ballet conductor George Crum born, 1926	*shoulda*
27	F	20th S. af. P. • NEW ● • 32-lb. bull trout caught, Lake Pend Oreille, Idaho, 1949	
28	M.	Sts. Simon & Jude • ⛢ AT ☍ • Cyclone 05B became Cat. 5, Indian Ocean, 1999	*seen*
29	Tu.	☌☿☾ • ☌♀☾ • First commencement of first U.S. coeducational college (Oberlin), 1834 • {11.2 / 12.0	*it*
30	W.	☌☿♀ • Patent granted to Daniel Cooper for "workman's time recorder," 1894 • {10.9 / 11.8	*last*
31	Th.	All Hallows' Eve • Reformation Day • ☌♃☾ • ☿ STAT. • {10.5 / 11.4	*year."*

Farmer's Calendar

Every fall, I bucket up some apples and haul them over to Dave's garage to make cider on his hand-cranked press. Whether he likes it or not, I've appointed my unassuming neighbor—a careful homesteader who's tended his forest and fields for nearly 40 years—my godfather in sustainability and simple living. I am perpetually on his doorstep with questions about how to make better sauerkraut or to ascertain how frequently he mulches his trees. He brushes off my studious worship as if I were a fly pesking a loaf of his wood-fired oven-baked bread. Now Dave helps me to fit the crank on the press and I begin turning. Soon the hopper full of apple mash is forced to become juice. At first the cider trickles out, but soon it gushes and fills the collecting pot to the brim. Then we swap in a new pot, until all's been squeezed from this batch of apples. Before unscrewing the press and emptying the sack of tawny mush called pomace, before we reset the press and begin the whole process again, we each fill a cup and drink a toast: to a good crop of apples, to the revolving seasons, and to my neighbor's sustaining sweetness.

CALENDAR

SKY WATCH: Mercury transits the Sun's face on the 11th, starting at 7:37 A.M. and continuing for over 5 hours. All of the United States (except Alaska) and Canada can see at least part of it (a "solar telescope" is required). From the 1st to the 14th, low in the predawn east, returning orange Mars meets Virgo's blue star, Spica. During the month's second half, bright Mercury appears below Mars. On the 24th, the crescent Moon hovers to the left of Mars, with Mercury below. On the 25th, a predawn lineup has blue Spica highest, above orange Mars, then orange Mercury, and finally the Moon, lowest. In the west after sunset, Venus and Jupiter hover side-by-side on the 23rd and 24th but quite low in twilight. The Moon floats just above brilliant Venus on the 28th.

◐ **FIRST QUARTER** 4th day 5:23 A.M.   ◑ **LAST QUARTER** 19th day 4:11 P.M.
○ **FULL MOON** 12th day 8:34 A.M.   ● **NEW MOON** 26th day 10:06 A.M.

After 2:00 A.M. on November 3, Eastern Standard Time is given.

GET THESE PAGES WITH TIMES SET TO YOUR ZIP CODE AT ALMANAC.COM/ACCESS.

DAY OF YEAR	DAY OF MONTH	DAY OF WEEK	☼ RISES H. M.	RISE KEY	☼ SETS H. M.	SET KEY	LENGTH OF DAY H. M.	SUN FAST M.	SUN DECLINATION ° '	HIGH TIDE TIMES BOSTON	☾ RISES H. M.	RISE KEY	☾ SETS H. M.	SET KEY	☾ ASTRON. PLACE	☾ AGE
305	1	Fr.	7:17	D	**5:38**	B	10 21	32	14 s. 29	2¾ 3	12:05	E	9:21	B	SAG	5
306	2	Sa.	7:18	D	**5:37**	B	10 19	32	14 s. 48	3¾ 4	12:57	E	10:17	B	SAG	6
307	3	F	6:20	D	**4:35**	B	10 15	32	15 s. 07	3¾ 3¾	12:42	E	10:16	B	SAG	7
308	4	M.	6:21	D	**4:34**	B	10 13	32	15 s. 25	4½ 4¾	1:19	E	11:16	B	CAP	8
309	5	Tu.	6:22	E	**4:33**	B	10 11	32	15 s. 43	5½ 5¾	1:51	E	—	-	CAP	9
310	6	W.	6:23	E	**4:32**	B	10 09	32	16 s. 01	6½ 6¾	2:19	E	12:16	C	AQU	10
311	7	Th.	6:25	E	**4:31**	B	10 06	32	16 s. 19	7½ 7¾	2:44	D	1:15	C	AQU	11
312	8	Fr.	6:26	E	**4:29**	B	10 03	32	16 s. 37	8¼ 8½	3:08	D	2:15	D	PSC	12
313	9	Sa.	6:27	E	**4:28**	B	10 01	32	16 s. 54	9 9¼	3:31	C	3:14	D	CET	13
314	10	F	6:28	E	**4:27**	B	9 59	32	17 s. 11	9½ 10	3:56	C	4:14	D	PSC	14
315	11	M.	6:30	E	**4:26**	B	9 56	32	17 s. 28	10¼ 10½	4:22	C	5:16	E	CET	15
316	12	Tu.	6:31	E	**4:25**	B	9 54	32	17 s. 44	10¾ 11¼	4:51	B	6:19	E	ARI	16
317	13	W.	6:32	E	**4:24**	B	9 52	32	18 s. 00	11½ —	5:25	B	7:23	E	TAU	17
318	14	Th.	6:33	E	**4:23**	B	9 50	31	18 s. 16	12 12	6:05	B	8:28	E	TAU	18
319	15	Fr.	6:35	E	**4:22**	B	9 47	31	18 s. 31	12½ 12¾	6:53	B	9:31	E	TAU	19
320	16	Sa.	6:36	E	**4:22**	B	9 46	31	18 s. 46	1¼ 1½	7:49	B	10:30	E	GEM	20
321	17	F	6:37	E	**4:21**	B	9 44	31	19 s. 01	2¼ 2¼	8:53	B	11:22	E	GEM	21
322	18	M.	6:38	E	**4:20**	B	9 42	31	19 s. 15	3 3¼	10:02	B	12:08	E	CAN	22
323	19	Tu.	6:40	E	**4:19**	B	9 39	30	19 s. 29	4 4¼	11:13	C	12:48	E	LEO	23
324	20	W.	6:41	E	**4:18**	B	9 37	30	19 s. 43	5 5¼	—	-	1:23	E	LEO	24
325	21	Th.	6:42	E	**4:18**	B	9 36	30	19 s. 56	6 6¼	12:26	E	1:54	D	LEO	25
326	22	Fr.	6:43	E	**4:17**	B	9 34	30	20 s. 09	7 7¼	1:39	D	2:23	D	VIR	26
327	23	Sa.	6:44	E	**4:16**	B	9 32	29	20 s. 22	7¾ 8¼	2:53	D	2:52	C	VIR	27
328	24	F	6:46	E	**4:16**	A	9 30	29	20 s. 34	8¾ 9¼	4:07	E	3:23	C	VIR	28
329	25	M.	6:47	E	**4:15**	A	9 28	29	20 s. 46	9½ 10¼	5:20	E	3:56	B	LIB	29
330	26	Tu.	6:48	E	**4:15**	A	9 27	28	20 s. 58	10½ 11	6:34	E	4:34	B	LIB	0
331	27	W.	6:49	E	**4:14**	A	9 25	28	21 s. 09	11¼ 11¾	7:44	E	5:18	B	OPH	1
332	28	Th.	6:50	E	**4:14**	A	9 24	28	21 s. 19	12 —	8:49	E	6:07	B	SAG	2
333	29	Fr.	6:51	E	**4:13**	A	9 22	27	21 s. 30	12¾ 12¾	9:47	E	7:02	B	SAG	3
334	30	Sa.	6:52	E	**4:13**	A	9 21	27	21 s. 40	1½ 1½	10:36	E	8:01	B	SAG	4

NOVEMBER

Chill winds sweep down the mountain way,
The skies are leaden-like and gray.
–**James Berry Bensel**

DAY OF MONTH	DAY OF WEEK	DATES, FEASTS, FASTS, ASPECTS, TIDE HEIGHTS, AND WEATHER	
1	Fr.	All Saints' • ☾ RUNS LOW • ☾ AT ☋ • U.S. First Lady Mamie Eisenhower died, 1979	*An*
2	Sa.	All Souls' • Sadie Hawkins Day • ☌♄☾ • ☌♇☾ • Tides { 9.5 / 10.2	*echo*
3	**F**	**21st S. af. P.** • **DAYLIGHT SAVING TIME ENDS, 2:00 A.M.** • Tides { 9.0 / 9.7	*of*
4	M.	Manufacturer Benjamin F. Goodrich born, 1841 • { 8.7 / 9.3	*summer,*
5	Tu.	**ELECTION DAY** • GPS system patented, 1996 • { 8.6 / 9.0	*before*
6	W.	☌♆☾ • Posthumous Victoria Cross recipient James Robertson died, 1917 • { 8.6 / 9.0	*rain's*
7	Th.	☾ AT APO. • U.S. president FDR re-elected for 4th term, 1944 • { 8.9 / 9.1	*drummer*
8	Fr.	Mont. statehood (Dakotas, Nov. 2; Wash., Nov. 11), 1889 • Tides { 9.2 / 9.2	*sends*
9	Sa.	☾ ON EQ. • First documented Canadian gridiron football game played, Univ. of Toronto, Ont., 1861	*the*
10	**F**	**22nd S. af. P.** • ☌♅☾ • TV's *Sesame Street* debuted, 1969	*last*
11	M.	St. Martin of Tours • **VETERANS DAY** • ☿ IN INF. ☌ • ☿ TRANSIT OVER ☉ • { 10.1 / 9.5	*leaves*
12	Tu.	Indian Summer • **FULL BEAVER** ○ • Voters OK'd creation of Nunavut territory, 1992 • { 10.3 / 9.5	*fleeing.*
13	W.	*Set trees poor, and they will grow rich; set them rich, and they will grow poor.* • Tides { 10.5 / 9.5	*Rain*
14	Th.	Just after launch, *Apollo 12* struck twice by lightning, 1969 • Tides { 10.6 / —	*turns*
15	Fr.	Judge Joseph Wapner born, 1919 • Tides { 9.4 / 10.6	*to*
16	Sa.	☾ RIDES HIGH • ☾ AT ☊ • Meteor fireball turned night into day, Finland, 2017 • { 9.3 / 10.5	*snow*
17	**F**	**23rd S. af. P.** • 1800s champagne sampled from Baltic Sea shipwreck, 2010 • { 9.2 / 10.4	*and*
18	M.	St. Hilda of Whitby • *November take flail, Let ships no more sail.* • { 9.1 / 10.3	*thoughts*
19	Tu.	David L. Pickens granted patent for "registered pedigree stuffed animals," 2002 • { 9.2 / 10.1	*turn*
20	W.	☿ STAT. • Tucson Municipal Flying Field, Ariz., first municipal airport in U.S., 1919 • { 9.3 / 10.0	*to*
21	Th.	N.C. statehood, 1789 • Dusting of snow, central Fla., 2006 • Tides { 9.7 / 10.1	*skiing.*
22	Fr.	☾ ON EQ. • Humane Society of the United States founded, 1954 • Writer George Eliot born, 1819	*Turkey's*
23	Sa.	St. Clement • ☾ AT PERIG. • Thespis first actor on record in Greek drama, 534 B.C. • { 10.7 / 10.4	*been*
24	**F**	**24th S. af. P.** • ☌☿☾ • ☌♀♃ • ☌♂☾ • Tides { 11.2 / 10.5	*fixed;*
25	M.	U.S. chess champion John Donaldson wed Soviet champion Elena Akhmilovskaya, 1988	*precipitation's*
26	Tu.	NEW ● • 1.5" rain fell in 1 minute, setting world record, Barot, Guadeloupe, 1970 • { 11.7 / 10.5	*mixed.*
27	W.	♆ STAT. • *Better some of a pudding than none of a pie.* • Tides { 11.7 / 10.3	*So*
28	Th.	**THANKSGIVING DAY** • ☾ AT ☋ • ☌♀☾ • ☌♃☾ • ☿ GR. ELONG. (20° WEST)	*are*
29	Fr.	☾ RUNS LOW • ☌♄☾ • ☌♇☾ • First governor-general of Canada, Sir Charles Stanley, died, 1894	*our*
30	Sa.	St. Andrew • Discovery of 215 fossilized pterosaur eggs in Gobi Desert, China, announced, 2017	*feelings.*

Farmer's Calendar

The rungs had rattled my mind for months, as I wondered what I might see from the silo's cusp. One night shy of the full Moon, I climbed up. During the growing season, a homesteader is devoted to the ground: trundling hoses, sinking fence posts, dumping manure, stooping to tend everything. And then, suddenly, there is nothing left to weed or harvest and her focus can drift upward. Twice I'd queried the neighbors for permission to scale their tower of corn silage and twice they'd declined. So, what happened next might just be a lie. At dusk, I crept to the silo with a friend who boosted me to the ladder's bottom rung. From there, I scrambled up to where the view was generous, expansive. At height, the three nearby farmhouses appeared as diminutive as butter pats. The neighbors' dairy barn seemed no bigger than a mailbox amid the shorn cornfield with its plaid of tractor ruts. As the neighbors' lights snapped out, my friend waited gamely by the ladder's start. Maybe I was the highest living thing in our valley? Just then a Canada goose squawked, correcting me, as it soared over the silo toward the Milky Way.

DECEMBER

SKY WATCH: The year ends with a planetary whimper. All of the superior planets are on the far side of the Sun, near their dimmest magnitudes and further diminished by solar glare. Several farewell conjunctions provide compensation. On the 1st, low in the west at evening twilight, float Jupiter (highest), Venus, Saturn, and the crescent Moon. Venus meets Saturn on the 10th and 11th. Meanwhile, Mars rises a bit higher as a predawn morning star, but it's still low and shines at a mere magnitude 2. The Geminid meteors on the 13th are spoiled by a nearly full Moon parked in Gemini that very night. Winter begins with the solstice on the 21st at 11:19 P.M.

◑ **FIRST QUARTER** 4th day 1:58 A.M. ◐ **LAST QUARTER** 18th day 11:57 P.M.
○ **FULL MOON** 12th day 12:12 A.M. ● **NEW MOON** 26th day 12:13 A.M.

All times are given in Eastern Standard Time.

GET THESE PAGES WITH TIMES SET TO YOUR ZIP CODE AT ALMANAC.COM/ACCESS.

DAY OF YEAR	DAY OF MONTH	DAY OF WEEK	☼ RISES H.M.	RISE KEY	☼ SETS H.M.	SET KEY	LENGTH OF DAY H.M.	SUN FAST M.	SUN DECLINATION ° '	HIGH TIDE TIMES BOSTON		☾ RISES H.M.	RISE KEY	☾ SETS H.M.	SET KEY	☾ ASTRON. PLACE	☾ AGE
335	1	**F**	6:53	E	**4:13**	A	9 20	27	21 s. 49	2¼	2½	11:17	E	**9:02**	B	CAP	5
336	2	M.	6:54	E	**4:12**	A	9 18	26	21 s. 58	3	3¼	11:52	E	**10:03**	C	CAP	6
337	3	Tu.	6:55	E	**4:12**	A	9 17	26	22 s. 07	4	4¼	**12:21**	E	**11:03**	C	AQU	7
338	4	W.	6:57	E	**4:12**	A	9 15	26	22 s. 15	4¾	5	**12:47**	D	—	–	AQU	8
339	5	Th.	6:58	E	**4:12**	A	9 14	25	22 s. 23	5¾	6	**1:11**	D	12:03	C	AQU	9
340	6	Fr.	6:58	E	**4:12**	A	9 14	25	22 s. 30	6½	7	**1:35**	C	1:02	D	CET	10
341	7	Sa.	6:59	E	**4:12**	A	9 13	24	22 s. 37	7½	7¾	**1:58**	C	2:01	D	CET	11
342	8	**F**	7:00	E	**4:11**	A	9 11	24	22 s. 43	8¼	8½	**2:23**	C	3:02	E	PSC	12
343	9	M.	7:01	E	**4:11**	A	9 10	23	22 s. 49	8¾	9¼	**2:51**	B	4:04	E	ARI	13
344	10	Tu.	7:02	E	**4:12**	A	9 10	23	22 s. 55	9½	10	**3:23**	B	5:09	E	TAU	14
345	11	W.	7:03	E	**4:12**	A	9 09	23	23 s. 00	10¼	10¾	**4:01**	B	6:14	E	TAU	15
346	12	Th.	7:04	E	**4:12**	A	9 08	22	23 s. 05	11	11½	**4:47**	B	7:19	E	TAU	16
347	13	Fr.	7:05	E	**4:12**	A	9 07	22	23 s. 09	11½	—	**5:41**	B	8:22	E	GEM	17
348	14	Sa.	7:05	E	**4:12**	A	9 07	21	23 s. 13	12¼	12¼	**6:44**	B	9:18	E	GEM	18
349	15	**F**	7:06	E	**4:12**	A	9 06	21	23 s. 16	1	1¼	**7:52**	B	10:08	E	CAN	19
350	16	M.	7:07	E	**4:13**	A	9 06	20	23 s. 19	1¾	2	**9:04**	C	10:50	E	CAN	20
351	17	Tu.	7:07	E	**4:13**	A	9 06	20	23 s. 21	2¾	3	**10:17**	C	11:26	E	LEO	21
352	18	W.	7:08	E	**4:13**	A	9 05	19	23 s. 23	3½	4	**11:29**	D	11:58	E	LEO	22
353	19	Th.	7:09	E	**4:14**	A	9 05	19	23 s. 24	4½	5	—	–	12:27	D	VIR	23
354	20	Fr.	7:09	E	**4:14**	A	9 05	18	23 s. 25	5½	6	12:41	D	12:55	C	VIR	24
355	21	Sa.	7:10	E	**4:15**	A	9 05	18	23 s. 26	6½	7	1:52	E	1:24	C	VIR	25
356	22	**F**	7:10	E	**4:15**	A	9 05	17	23 s. 26	7½	8	3:04	E	1:55	B	LIB	26
357	23	M.	7:11	E	**4:16**	A	9 05	17	23 s. 25	8½	9	4:15	E	2:30	B	LIB	27
358	24	Tu.	7:11	E	**4:16**	A	9 05	16	23 s. 24	9¼	10	5:26	E	3:10	B	SCO	28
359	25	W.	7:12	E	**4:17**	A	9 05	16	23 s. 23	10¼	10¾	6:32	E	3:56	B	OPH	29
360	26	Th.	7:12	E	**4:17**	A	9 05	15	23 s. 21	11	11½	7:33	E	4:48	B	SAG	0
361	27	Fr.	7:12	E	**4:18**	A	9 06	15	23 s. 18	11¾	—	8:27	E	5:46	B	SAG	1
362	28	Sa.	7:13	E	**4:19**	A	9 06	14	23 s. 16	12¼	12½	9:12	E	6:47	C	CAP	2
363	29	**F**	7:13	E	**4:20**	A	9 07	14	23 s. 12	1	1¼	9:50	E	7:48	C	CAP	3
364	30	M.	7:13	E	**4:20**	A	9 07	13	23 s. 09	1¾	2	10:22	E	8:50	C	CAP	4
365	31	Tu.	7:13	E	**4:21**	A	9 08	13	23 s. 04	2½	2¾	10:49	E	9:50	C	AQU	5

To use this page, see p. 116; for Key Letters, see p. 238. LIGHT = A.M. BOLD = P.M.

CALENDAR

DECEMBER

Send the ruddy firelight higher;
Draw your easy chair up nigher.
–Ina Donna Coolbrith

DAY OF MONTH	DAY OF WEEK	DATES, FEASTS, FASTS, ASPECTS, TIDE HEIGHTS, AND WEATHER	
1	**F**	**1st S. of Advent** • Winnie (bear Pooh named after) donated to London Zoo, 1919	*Deck*
2	M.	St. Viviana • First T. Eaton Co. Santa Claus parade, Toronto, Ont., 1905 • Tides {8.9 / 9.6	*the*
3	Tu.	*Pioneer 11* Jupiter flyby, 1974 • 68°F, Portland, Maine, 2009 • Tides {8.7 / 9.2	*halls;*
4	W.	☾ at apo. • ☌♆☾ • French statesman Armand-Jean du Plessis (Cardinal de Richelieu) died, 1642	*hit*
5	Th.	Pusuke, a Shiba Inu mix and world's oldest dog at time (26 yrs., 8 mos.), died, 2011 • Tides {8.6 / 8.7	*the*
6	Fr.	St. Nicholas • ☾ on Eq. • Kitty Hambleton reached 512.71 mph land speed, 1976	*malls;*
7	Sa.	St. Ambrose • Nat'l Pearl Harbor Remembrance Day • Tides {9.1 / 8.7	*scan*
8	**F**	**2nd S. of Advent** • ☌♅☾ • Astronaut John Glenn died, 2016 • {9.4 / 8.8	*the*
9	M.	Quebec adopted new coat of arms, 1939 • Tides {9.8 / 9.0	*Web*
10	Tu.	St. Eulalia • ☌♀♄ • *All doors open to courtesy.* –Thomas Fuller • {10.1 / 9.2	*with*
11	W.	United Nations International Children's Emergency Fund (UNICEF) established, 1946 • {10.4 / 9.3	*passion!*
12	Th.	**Our Lady of Guadalupe** • **Full Cold** ○ • Paul Martin became Canada's 21st prime minister, 2003	*These*
13	Fr.	St. Lucia • ☾ rides high • ☾ at ☊ • ☌♀♇ • Tides {10.9 / —	*mild*
14	Sa.	Halcyon Days begin. • Ala. statehood, 1819 • Millau Viaduct opened, France, 2004	*days*
15	**F**	**3rd S. of Advent** • *Dec. 14–15:* Windstorm caused flooding/ power outages, Wash./Oreg., 2006	*are*
16	M.	9,000th episode of *All My Children* aired, 2004 • Tides {9.6 / 10.8	*flashin' by—*
17	Tu.	Project Blue Book (UFO investigations) terminated, 1969 • {9.6 / 10.6	*Snowstorm's*
18	W.	Ember Day • ☾ at perig. • Freezing rain caused 170 auto accidents, Memphis, Tenn., 1989	*crashin'*
19	Th.	Beware the Pogonip. • *A snow year, a rich year.* • {9.8 / 10.0	*Santa's*
20	Fr.	Ember Day • ☾ on Eq. • Calif. angler caught 230-lb. Nile perch, Lake Nasser, Egypt, 2000 • {10.0 / 9.8	*party!*
21	Sa.	St. Thomas • Ember Day • **Winter Solstice** • Tides {10.3 / 9.7	*May*
22	**F**	**4th S. of Advent** • Chanukah begins at sundown • ☌♂☾ • {10.6 / 9.7	*your*
23	M.	Entrepreneur Madam C. J. Walker born, 1867 • –50°F, Williston, N.Dak., 1983 • Tides {10.9 / 9.7	*Yule*
24	Tu.	Clement Moore's "A Visit From St. Nicholas" likely written, 1822 • Tides {11.1 / 9.8	*be filled*
25	W.	**Christmas** • ☌☿☾ • *Be merry and wise.* • Tides {11.2 / 9.8	*with*
26	Th.	**Boxing Day (Canada)** • **1st day of Kwanzaa** • **New** ● • **Eclipse** ☉ • ☾ runs low • ☾ at ☋ • ☌♃☾	
27	Fr.	St. John • ☌♃☉ • ☌♄☾ • ☌♇☾ • ALH 84001 Mars meteorite found, Antarctica, 1984	*plenty*
28	Sa.	Holy Innocents • ☌♀☾ • 2nd U.S. chewing gum patent went to William Semple, 1869 • {9.6 / 10.7	*and*
29	**F**	**1st S. af. Ch.** • American Meteorological Society founded, 1919 • {9.4 / 10.4	*likewise*
30	M.	Social reformer Amelia Bloomer died, 1894 • Tides {9.2 / 10.0	*your*
31	Tu.	St. Sylvester • ☌♆☾ • *Plan your life at New Year's eve, your day at dawn.* • {9.0 / 9.6	*2020!*

Farmer's Calendar

"Can you tell the difference between a balsam and a Fraser?" Steve Moffatt grills his tree hauler, Seth Johnson, a young farmer. "Yep," replies Seth, who grows beans and wheat, raises beef and horses, and moonlights as a trucker when his growing season stalls. Together they load the culmination of Steve's decade of labor—planting, fertilizing, weeding, grooming, harvesting, and baling. Now Seth climbs onto his trailer and begins driving in the bed stakes that will gird this precious cargo. Then Steve hands over the first of 500 eight-foot balsams and Fraser firs. Seth lays them in like shingles, butts and tips sheltering each other, protecting each tree's topmost branch. In the cold, it can snap like glass, and a tree without a tip, as both driver and grower know, is useless. The cold air fills with a balsam perfume as the Christmas tree layers accrue. Finally, Seth stretches his cables and cinches the load. He climbs into his cab, equipped with his CB radio, Thermos, and Santa hat. As Seth's truck eases onto Wild Branch Road, Steve watches the results of his labor—the forest he began 10 years ago—glide off in a diesel sleigh.

CALENDAR

HOLIDAYS AND OBSERVANCES

2019 HOLIDAYS
FEDERAL HOLIDAYS ARE LISTED IN BOLD.

JAN. 1: New Year's Day

JAN. 21: Martin Luther King Jr.'s Birthday, observed

FEB. 2: Groundhog Day

FEB. 12: Abraham Lincoln's Birthday

FEB. 14: Valentine's Day

FEB. 15: Susan B. Anthony's Birthday *(Fla.)*

FEB. 18: Presidents' Day

FEB. 22: George Washington's Birthday

MAR. 2: Texas Independence Day

MAR. 5: Mardi Gras *(Baldwin & Mobile counties, Ala.; La.)*
Town Meeting Day *(Vt.)*

MAR. 8: International Women's Day

MAR. 17: St. Patrick's Day
Evacuation Day *(Suffolk Co., Mass.)*

MAR. 25: Seward's Day *(Alaska)*

MAR. 31: César Chávez Day

APR. 2: Pascua Florida Day

APR. 15: Patriots Day *(Maine, Mass.)*

APR. 21: San Jacinto Day *(Tex.)*

APR. 22: Earth Day

APR. 26: National Arbor Day

MAY 5: Cinco de Mayo

MAY 8: Truman Day *(Mo.)*

MAY 12: Mother's Day

MAY 18: Armed Forces Day

MAY 20: Victoria Day *(Canada)*

MAY 22: National Maritime Day

MAY 27: Memorial Day, observed

JUNE 5: World Environment Day

JUNE 11: King Kamehameha I Day *(Hawaii)*

JUNE 14: Flag Day

JUNE 16: Father's Day

JUNE 17: Bunker Hill Day *(Suffolk Co., Mass.)*

JUNE 19: Emancipation Day *(Tex.)*

JUNE 20: West Virginia Day

JULY 1: Canada Day

JULY 4: Independence Day

JULY 24: Pioneer Day *(Utah)*

JULY 27: National Day of the Cowboy

AUG. 1: Colorado Day

AUG. 5: Civic Holiday *(parts of Canada)*

AUG. 16: Bennington Battle Day *(Vt.)*

AUG. 19: National Aviation Day

AUG. 26: Women's Equality Day

SEPT. 2: Labor Day

SEPT. 8: Grandparents Day

SEPT. 9: Admission Day *(Calif.)*

SEPT. 11: Patriot Day

SEPT. 17: Constitution Day

SEPT. 21: International Day of Peace

OCT. 7: Child Health Day

OCT. 9: Leif Eriksson Day

OCT. 14: Columbus Day, observed
Indigenous Peoples' Day *(parts of U.S.)*
Thanksgiving Day *(Canada)*

OCT. 18: Alaska Day

OCT. 24: United Nations Day

OCT. 25: Nevada Day

OCT. 31: Halloween

NOV. 4: Will Rogers Day *(Okla.)*

NOV. 5: Election Day

NOV. 11: Veterans Day
Remembrance Day *(Canada)*

(continued)

Prepare Your Garden the EASY WAY!

HUGE TILLER SALE!
Starting at just $199⁹⁹

Walk-Behind

Tow-Behind   PTO

NEW Top-of-the-Line DR® ROTOTILLER!

DUAL ROTATING TINES on our NEW top end walk-behind model let you choose forward rotation for cultivating or counter-rotation for deep soil tilling or sod busting.

ONE-HAND OPERATION! Self-propulsion lets you walk to one side while you easily steer with one hand, leaving no footprints in the freshly tilled bed!

8 TILLER MODELS! No matter how big or small the job, we've got one for you!

19029A © 2018

DRrototiller.com

All New DR® CHIPPERS
Larger Capacity, Lower Prices!

LOWEST PRICES EVER!
Starting at just $699⁹⁹
PTO MODELS TOO!

- **Chip big branches** up to 5.75" thick!
- **Self-feeding** models available. No more force-feeding!
- **Powerful engines** spin big flywheels (up to 62 lbs.), generating massive chipping force!
- **Models that shred** yard and garden waste as well as CHIP branches.

19029B © 2018

DRchipper.com

America's ORIGINAL
Walk-Behind Brush Mower!

USA ENGINEERED & BUILT*

*Assembled in the USA using domestic and foreign parts.

The DR® Field & Brush Mower just got even better—

FASTER. Up to 20 HP and 34"-wide cut for faster mowing!

EASIER. New power steering for turn-on-a-dime ease!

LOWER PRICES. Reduced by up to $500!

NEW CHOICES: including PTO and tow-behind models for tractors and ATVs.

Now Starting at $1499⁹⁹

19029C © 2018

DRfieldbrush.com

FREE SHIPPING
6 MONTH TRIAL
SOME LIMITATIONS APPLY
Call or go online for details.

Call for a FREE DVD and Catalog!
Includes product specifications and factory-direct offers.
TOLL FREE 800-731-0493

PROFESSIONAL POWER
DR
DONE RIGHT

NOV. 19: Discovery of Puerto Rico Day	DEC. 15: Bill of Rights Day
NOV. 28: Thanksgiving Day	DEC. 17: Wright Brothers Day
NOV. 29: Acadian Day *(La.)*	**DEC. 25: Christmas Day**
DEC. 7: National Pearl Harbor Remembrance Day	DEC. 26: Boxing Day *(Canada)* First day of Kwanzaa

Movable Religious Observances

FEB. 17: Septuagesima Sunday	MAY 30: Ascension Day
MAR. 5: Shrove Tuesday	JUNE 9: Whitsunday–Pentecost
MAR. 6: Ash Wednesday	JUNE 16: Trinity Sunday
APR. 14: Palm Sunday	JUNE 23: Corpus Christi
APR. 19: Good Friday Passover begins at sundown	SEPT. 29: Rosh Hashanah begins at sundown
APR. 21: Easter	OCT. 8: Yom Kippur begins at sundown
APR. 28: Orthodox Easter	DEC. 1: First Sunday of Advent
MAY 5: Ramadan begins at sundown	DEC. 22: Chanukah begins at sundown
MAY 26: Rogation Sunday	

–Beth Krommes

CHRONOLOGICAL CYCLES

Dominical Letter **F**

Epact **24**

Golden Number (Lunar Cycle) **6**

Roman Indiction **12**

Solar Cycle **12**

Year of Julian Period **6732**

ERAS

ERA	YEAR	BEGINS
Byzantine	7528	September 14
Jewish (A.M.)*	5780	September 29
Chinese (Lunar) [Year of the Pig]	4717	February 5
Roman (A.U.C.)	2772	January 14
Nabonassar	2768	April 19
Japanese	2679	January 1
Grecian (Seleucidae)	2331	September 14 (or October 14)
Indian (Saka)	1941	March 22
Diocletian	1736	September 12
Islamic (Hegira)* [FCNA date]	1441	August 30

*Year begins at sundown.

CALENDAR

Break Free from Neuropathy with a New Supportive Care Cream

A patented relief cream stands to help millions of Americans crippled from the side effects of neuropathy by increasing sensation and blood flow wherever it's applied

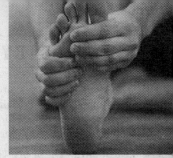

Raymond Wilson
The Associated Heath Press

AHP — A recent breakthrough stands to help millions of Americans plagued by burning, tingling and numb legs and feet.

But this time it comes in the form of a cream, not a pill, suggesting the medical community may have been going about the problem all wrong.

The breakthrough, called *Diabasens*, is a new relief cream developed for managing the relentless discomfort caused by neuropathy.

When applied directly to the legs and feet, it causes arteries and blood vessels to expand, increasing the flow of warm, nutrient rich blood to damaged tissue.

However, what's most remarkable about the cream...and what makes it so brilliant...is that it contains one of the only natural substances known to activate a special sensory pathway right below the surface of the skin.

This pathway is called TRPA1 and it controls the sensitivity of nerves. In laymen terms, it determines whether you feel pins and needles or soothing relief.

Studies show that symptoms of neuropathy arise when the nerves in your legs deteriorate and blood flow is lost to the areas which surround them.

As the nerves begins to die, sensation is lost. This lack of sensation is what causes the feelings of burning, tingling and numbness.

This is why the makers of *Diabasens* say their cream has performed so well in a recent clinical use survey trial: it increases sensation and blood flow where ever its applied.

No Pills or Prescriptions

Until now, many doctors have failed to consider a topical cream as an effective way to manage neuropathy. *Diabasens* is proving it may be the only way going forward.

"Most of today's treatment methods have focused on minimizing discomfort instead of attacking its underlining cause. That's why millions of adults are still in excruciating pain every single day, and are constantly dealing with side effects" explains Dr. Esber, the creator of *Diabasens*.

"*Diabasens* is different. Since the most commonly reported symptoms — burning, tingling and numb legs and feet — are caused by lack of sensation of the nerves, we've designed the formula increase their sensitivity.

And since these nerves are located right below the skin, we've chosen to formulate it as a cream. This allows for the ingredients to get to them faster and without any drug like side effects" he adds.

Study Finds Restoring Sensation the Key To Relief

With the conclusion of their latest human clinical use survey trial, Dr. Esber and his team are now offering *Diabasens* nationwide. And regardless of the market, its sales are exploding.

Men and women from all over the country are eager to get their hands on the new cream and, according to the results initial users reported, they should be.

Diabasens is shown to provide relief from:

- Burning
- Swelling
- Tingling
- Heaviness
- Numbness
- Cold extremities

In the trial above, as compared to baseline, participants taking *Diabasens* saw a staggering 51% increase sensitivity in just one week. This resulted in significant relief from burning, tingling and nubmness throughout their legs.

Many participants taking *Diabasens*

Topical Cream Offers Sufferers a Safer, More Effective Avenue of Relief: Diabasens increases sensation and blood flow wherever its applied. It's now being used to relieve painful legs and feet.

described feeling much more balanced and comfortable throughout the day. They also noticed that after applying, there was a pleasant warming sensation that was remarkably soothing.

Targets Nerve Damage Right Below the Skins Surface

Diabasens is a topical cream that is to be applied to your legs and feet twice a day for the first two weeks then once a day after. It does not require a prescription.

Studies show that neuropathy is caused when the peripheral nerves break down and blood is unable to circulate into your legs and feet.

As these nerves deteriorate, sensation is lost. This is why you may not feel hot or cold and your legs and feet may burn, tingle and go numb.

Additionally, without proper blood flow, tissues and cells in these areas start to die, causing unbearable pain.

An ingredient called cinnamaldehyde in *Diabasens* is one of the only compounds in existence that can activate TRPA1, a special sensory pathway that runs through your entire body.

According to research, activating this pathway (which can only be done with a cream) increases the sensitivity of nerves, relieving feelings of tingling and numbness in your legs and feet.

Supporting ingredients boost blood flow, supplying the nerves with the nutrients they need for increased sensation.

How to Get *Diabasens*

In order to get the word out about *Diabasens*, the company is offering special introductory discounts to all who call. Discounts will automatically be applied to all callers, but don't wait. This offer may not last forever. **Call toll-free: 1-800-516-6923.**

GLOSSARY OF ALMANAC ODDITIES

Many readers have expressed puzzlement over the rather obscure entries that appear on our **Right-Hand Calendar Pages, 121–147.** These "oddities" have long been fixtures in the Almanac, and we are pleased to provide some definitions. Once explained, they may not seem so odd after all!

-Beth Krommes

EMBER DAYS: These are the Wednesdays, Fridays, and Saturdays that occur in succession following (1) the First Sunday in Lent; (2) Whitsunday–Pentecost; (3) the Feast of the Holy Cross, September 14; and (4) the Feast of St. Lucia, December 13. The word *ember* is perhaps a corruption of the Latin *quatuor tempora,* "four times." The four periods are observed by some Christian denominations for prayer, fasting, and the ordination of clergy.

Folklore has it that the weather on each of the 3 days foretells the weather for the next 3 months; that is, in September, the first Ember Day, Wednesday, forecasts the weather for October; Friday predicts November; and Saturday foretells December.

DISTAFF DAY (JANUARY 7): This was the day after Epiphany, when women were expected to return to their spinning following the Christmas holiday. A distaff is the staff that women used for holding the flax or wool in spinning. (Hence the term "distaff" refers to women's work or the maternal side of the family.)

PLOUGH MONDAY (JANUARY): Traditionally, the first Monday after Epiphany was called Plough Monday because it was the day when men returned to their plough, or daily work, following the Christmas holiday. (Every few years, Plough Monday and Distaff Day fall on the same day.) It was customary at this time for farm laborers to draw a plough through the village, soliciting money for a "plough light,"

which was kept burning in the parish church all year. This traditional verse captures the spirit of it:

> *Yule is come and Yule is gone,*
> *and we have feasted well;*
> *so Jack must to his flail again*
> *and Jenny to her wheel.*

THREE CHILLY SAINTS (MAY): Mamertus, Pancras, and Gervais were three early Christian saints whose feast days, on May 11, 12, and 13, respectively, are traditionally cold; thus they have come to be known as the Three Chilly Saints. An old French saying translates to "St. Mamertus, St. Pancras, and St. Gervais do not pass without a frost."

MIDSUMMER DAY (JUNE 24): To the farmer, this day is the midpoint of the growing season, halfway between planting and harvest. The Anglican Church considered it a "Quarter Day," one of the four major divisions of the liturgical year. It also marks the feast day of St. John the Baptist. (Midsummer Eve is an occasion for festivity and celebrates fertility.)

CORNSCATEOUS AIR (JULY): First used by early almanac makers, this term signifies warm, damp air. Although it signals ideal climatic conditions for growing corn, warm, damp air poses

One Simple Trick to Reversing Memory Loss

World's Leading Brain Expert and Winner of the Prestigious Kennedy Award, Unveils Exciting News For the Scattered, Unfocused and Forgetful

BY STEVEN WUZUBIA
HEALTH CORRESPONDENT;

Clearwater, Florida: Dr. Meir Shinitzky, Ph.D., is a former visiting professor at Duke University, recipient of the prestigious J.F. Kennedy Prize and author of more than 200 international scientific papers on human body cells. But now he's come up with what the medical world considers his greatest accomplishment — A vital compound. so powerful, it's reported to repair... even regrow damaged brain cells. In layman's terms — Bring back your memory power. And leave you feeling more focused and clear-headed than you have in years!

In his last speaking engagment, Dr. Shinitsky explains this phenomenon in simple terms; "Science has shown when your brain nutrient levels drop, you can start to experience memory problems and overall mental fatigue. Your ability to concentrate and stay focused becomes compromised. And gradually, a "mental fog" sets in. It can damage every aspect of your life". Not only do brain cells die but they become dysfunctional as if they begin to fade away as we age. This affects our ability to have mental clarity and focus and impacts our ability to remember things that were easy for us to do in our 20's and 30's.

Scientists think the biggest cause of brain deterioration in older people is the decreased functioning of membranes and molecules that surround the brain cells. These really are the transmitters that connect the tissues or the brain cells to one another that help us with our sharp memory, clear thinking and mental focus, even our powers to reason well. "When we are in our 20's" according to Dr. Shinitzky "our body produces key substances like phosphatidylserine and phosphatidic acid"... unfortunately they are believed to be critical essential nutrients that just fade away with age, much like our memories often do leading to further mental deterioration.

As we get older it becomes more frustrating as there is little comfort when you forget names... misplace your keys...or just feel "a little confused". And even though your foggy memory gets laughed off as just another "senior moment," it's not very funny when it keeps happening to you.

The Missing Link is Found and Tested

It's hard to pronounce that's for sure, but it certainly appears from the astounding clinical research that this one vital nutrient phosphatidylserine (PS) can really make a huge difference in our mental wellness. 17 different double blind studies with placebo controlled groups have been involved in the clinical research of PS with patients between the ages of 55-80 years of age. Periodically the researchers gave these patients memory and cognitive tests and the results were simply amazing:

1) PS patients outperformed placebo patients in All 5 Tests - 100% Success Rate

2) After only 45 days there was a measurable improvement in mental function

3) After 90 days, there was an impressive and amazing improvement in mental function

The group taking phosphatidylserine, not only enjoyed sharper memory, but listen to this... they were also more upbeat and remarkably more happy. In contrast, the moods of the individuals who took the placebo (starch pill), remained unaffected....no mental or mood improvement at all.

Vital Nutrient Reverses "Scatter Brain"

This incredible PS nutrient feeds your brain the vital nutrient it needs to stay healthy... PS now has the attention of some of the world's most prominent brain experts. It has been written up and published in leading science and medical journals and its findings have electrified the International scientific community.

Dr. Meir Shinitzky, Ph.D. a former visiting professor at Duke University and a recipient of the prestigious J.F. Kennedy Prize

Earth-Shaking Science

Published, clinical reports show replenishing your body's natural supply of Phosphatidylserine, not only helps sharpen your memory and concentration — but also helps "perk you up" and put you in a better mood. PS as it turns out also helps to reduce everyday stress and elevate your mood by lowering your body's production of the hormone cortisol. When cortisol levels are too high for too long you experience fatigue, bad moods and weakness. This drug-free brain-boosting formula enters your bloodstream fast (in as little as thirty minutes).

Officially Reviewed by the U.S. Food and Drug Administration: PS is the ONLY Health Supplement that has a "Qualified Health Claim for both Cognitive Dysfunction and Dementia".

Special Opportunity For Our Readers

We've made arrangements with the distributor of this proprietary blend of PS, which combines with several other proven special brain boosting natural ingredients to give you the mental clarity and memory gain that you need, to give you a Risk-Free trial supply. This is a special "Readers Only Discount". This trial is 100% risk-free.

It's a terrific deal. If Lipogen PS Plus doesn't help you think better, remember more... and improve your mind, clarity and mood — you won't pay a penny! (Except S&H).

So don't wait. Now you can join the thousands of people who think better, remember more — and enjoy clear, "fog-free" memory. Think of it as making a "wake-up call" to your brain. **CALL NOW TOLL FREE 1-800-609-3558.**

a danger to those affected by asthma and other respiratory problems.

DOG DAYS (JULY 3–AUGUST 11): These 40 days are traditionally the year's hottest and unhealthiest. They once coincided with the year's heliacal (at sunrise) rising of the Dog Star, Sirius. Ancient folks thought that the "combined heat" of Sirius and the Sun caused summer's swelter.

LAMMAS DAY (AUGUST 1): Derived from the Old English *hlaf maesse,* meaning "loaf mass," Lammas Day marked the beginning of the harvest. Traditionally, loaves of bread were baked from the first-ripened grain and brought to the churches to be consecrated. In Scotland, Lammastide fairs became famous as the time when trial marriages could be made. These marriages could end after a year with no strings attached.

CAT NIGHTS COMMENCE (AUGUST 17): This term harks back to the days when people believed in witches. An Irish legend says that a witch could turn into a cat and regain herself eight times, but on the ninth time (August 17), she couldn't change back and thus began her final life permanently as a cat. Hence the saying "A cat has nine lives."

HARVEST HOME (SEPTEMBER): In Britain and other parts of Europe, this marked the conclusion of the harvest and a period of festivals for feasting and thanksgiving. It was also a time to hold elections, pay workers, and collect rents. These festivals usually took place around the autumnal equinox. Certain groups in the United States, e.g., the Pennsylvania Dutch, have kept the tradition alive.

ST. LUKE'S LITTLE SUMMER (OCTOBER): This is a period of warm weather that occurs on or near St. Luke's feast day (October 18) and is sometimes called Indian summer.

INDIAN SUMMER (NOVEMBER): A period of warm weather following a cold spell or a hard frost, Indian summer can occur between St. Martin's Day (November 11) and November 20. Although there are differing dates for its occurrence, for more than 225 years the Almanac has adhered to the saying "If All Saints' (November 1) brings out winter, St. Martin's brings out Indian summer." The term may have come from early Native Americans, some of whom believed that the condition was caused by a warm wind sent from the court of their southwestern god, Cautantowwit.

HALCYON DAYS (DECEMBER): This period of about 2 weeks of calm weather often follows the blustery winds at autumn's end. Ancient Greeks and Romans experienced this weather at around the time of the winter solstice, when the halcyon, or kingfisher, was thought to brood in a nest floating on the sea. The bird was said to have charmed the wind and waves so that waters were especially calm at this time.

BEWARE THE POGONIP (DECEMBER): The word *pogonip* refers to frozen fog and was coined by Native Americans to describe the frozen fogs of fine ice needles that occur in the mountain valleys of the western United States and Canada. According to tradition, breathing the fog is injurious to the lungs. ∎

–Beth Krommes

OH, AND THE NIGHT, THE NIGHT,
WHEN THE WIND FULL OF COSMIC SPACE
GNAWS AT OUR FACES.
–from "The First Elegy" by Rainer Maria Rilke,
Czech writer (1875–1926)

A midlevel solar flare,
as seen in the bright flash
on December 16, 2014

THE DAY THE SUN
EXPLODED

BY BOB BERMAN

YES, IT COULD HAPPEN AGAIN!

In the mid–19th century, the scientific community was puzzled and fascinated by sunspots—dark marks on the solar surface that came and went in roughly 11-year cycles. None of these experts had any idea what they were, how they moved across the Sun, or if they affected Earth. One of them, 33-year-old British astronomer Richard Carrington, was obsessed by solar activity. Through his 4-inch refracting telescope, he observed the spots on every clear day.

The days leading into September 1859 had seen unusually intense solar storms, and scientists were abuzz. Suddenly, at 11:18 A.M. on September 1,

A FLARE'S FULL EFFECTS

A very strong solar storm creates high-energy electromagnetic waves and extreme X- and ultraviolet rays that travel toward Earth at light speed. These ionize, or break apart, atoms in our atmosphere. Such solar violence often then unleashes a radiation storm that is a potential danger to airline passengers and an extreme (even lethal) hazard to astronauts. This energy could travel to ground level, where it would zap everything with radiation. A solar explosion also causes a geomagnetic storm. This could cause electric grid collapses and power blackouts; send currents of hundreds of amps along railroads, wires, and oil and gas pipelines; damage transformers; destroy radio communications; knock out satellites; and disrupt the GPS system.

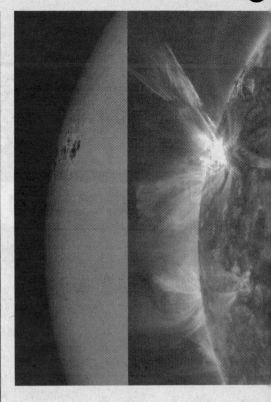

Carrington was rewarded for his diligence: To his amazement, a large sunspot cluster near the top of the Sun grew strangely dazzling. Despite a protective eye filter, he could barely watch. The flare became so luminous that it doubled the brightness of the Sun. He knew that this was no optical illusion, and his observation was soon confirmed by another British observer, Richard Hodgson.

Carrington was the first known witness to a solar flare, a violent—and as yet unmatched—solar phenomenon of the sort that makes solar researchers nervous even now, 160 years later.

As Carrington and Hodgson watched the flare, instruments at England's King's (Kew)

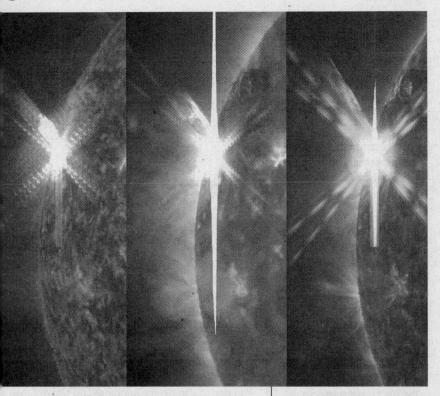

Observatory recorded a disturbance in Earth's magnetic field. Would this be the long-sought evidence that events on the Sun affect our planet?

The answer arrived that night.

Brilliant auroras in vivid deep reds (not the ordinary green hues) lit up the skies around the globe, even over regions as far south as the Caribbean. These twisted displays alarmed millions of people who had never seen or imagined that the heavens could possibly contort in this way. So bright were these illuminations over the U.S. West that some people assumed that day had dawned—so they got up and made breakfast. In New York City, gawkers crowded rooftops and sidewalks.

The light shows were breathtaking, but other effects were literally shocking. Supercharged by

NASA's Solar Dynamics Observatory captured these images of a significant solar flare on May 5, 2015. Each image shows a different wavelength of extreme ultraviolet light that highlights a different temperature of material on the Sun. By comparing different images, scientists can better understand the movement of solar matter and energy during a flare.

OUR SOLAR SENTRIES

Currently, an armada of specialized satellites keeps watch on the Sun:

• The Geostationary Operational Environmental Satellite (GOES) system stares at the Sun and Earth simultaneously from Earth orbit.

• The Solar and Heliospheric Observatory (SOHO) uses a coronagraph to observe solar flares and coronal mass ejections (CMEs)–large expulsions of magnetic field and plasma–and usually provides 2 to 4 days' warning.

• The Deep Space Climate Observatory (DSCOVR) is parked at Lagrangian Point L1 (where the Sun's gravity balances that of Earth) and measures the density and magnetic polarity of the solar wind heading to Earth; it gives 15- to 60-minute warnings.

• The Solar TErrestrial RElations Observatory (STEREO) duo observes flares, CMEs, and solar wind streams and can peer behind the Sun to see coming storms.

• The Solar Dynamic Observatory (SDO) monitors the Sun's magnetism, flares, surface pulses, and extreme UV, transmitting high-def images on 10 wavelengths.

solar emissions, the current-carrying telegraph wires that crisscrossed the United States and Europe started sizzling and popping, emitting showering sparks. For 5 minutes, the impossibly high current traveled into populated areas. Sparking equipment shocked telegraph operators, who leaped from their seats. Some did not move fast enough and were found unconscious on the floor.

A decade passed before any astronomer saw another flare, but it would be over a half-century before the world again felt the effects.

The second worst geomagnetic storm in recorded history began at 7:04 A.M. on May 13, 1921. According to *The New York Times,* all of the signal and switching mechanisms of the New York Central Railroad were knocked out of operation. A fire raged in the control tower at New York City's 57th Street and Park Avenue, while flames in the Central New England Railroad station destroyed that entire building. Telegraph operations throughout the country came to a standstill due to damaged equipment and blown fuses.

Another flare occurred on March 13, 1989. At 2:44 A.M., Sun-induced surges began wreaking havoc on Quebec's electrical power grid, and within a minute, the province and its 6 million people were in darkness. And cold. Over a half-million Quebecois depended on electricity for heat. In Montreal, the Metro came to a halt, and, with airport radar out of service, planes at the city's main airport were grounded. Meanwhile, as U.S. electric grids experienced shutdowns and voltage swings at major substations, the country managed—just barely—to avoid cascading blackouts.

The next solar storm occurred from October 19 through November 7, 2003. While it was a solar burp compared with the Carrington event, the National Oceanographic and Atmospheric

Administration (NOAA) reported the second fastest known journey of solar material to Earth; it arrived in half the normal 3 to 4 days' travel time. The storm's effects ranged from a blackout in northern Europe to rerouted airlines (to avoid high radiation levels) and damaged spacecraft—notably, the loss of the $640 million ADEOS-II satellite, which was on a mission to study climate change.

Coronal mass ejections (CMEs) are thought to be triggered by the destabilization of a series of magnetic loops (below) known as a flux rope.

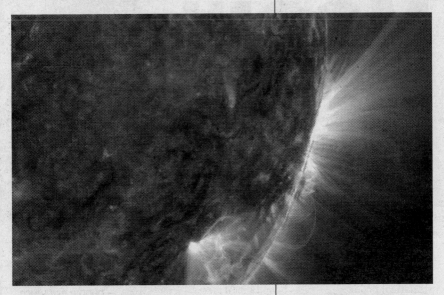

As advances in technology accelerate, so does the scale of damage that a solar flare could inflict. In May 2008, a team of space weather experts estimated that a "low-frequency/high-consequence event" would produce damage of $1 trillion to $2 trillion during the first year and that recovery would take 4 to 10 years. However, we can now see the threat as it's happening (see "Our Solar Sentries"), and the potential exists to issue warnings.

Maybe the next "big one" won't happen for another century. Let's hope that it doesn't happen at all. ∎

LISTEN UP!
Be astounded! Explore the "Astonishing Universe," Bob Berman and Jim Metzger's podcast, at Almanac.com/Podcast.

Bob Berman is the Almanac's astronomy editor.

MUST BE A
FULL
MOON!

by Tim Clark

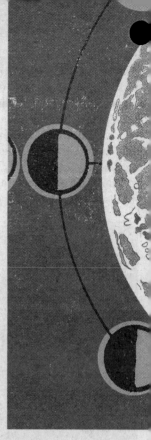

Doctors, nurses, EMTs, police officers, and elementary school teachers generally agree that full Moons will bring crazier behavior. They are not dissuaded from this belief by the complete absence of statistical proof.

Hundreds of studies have failed to turn up evidence of "the lunar effect," as some call it. Those few studies that seem to show a connection are usually disproved by attempts to confirm them. Or other studies contradict them.

For example, one study says that more animal bites (from cats, rats, dogs, horses) occur at the full Moon—but another says that there's no increase in dog bites. One shows an increase in crime, but others find no increase in arrests, calls for police assistance, prison assaults, batteries, homicides, or acting out in mental hospitals. In fact, admissions for psychosis are lowest during the full Moon, and psychiatric emergency room visits decline. Calls to suicide prevention hotlines peak at the new Moon.

Yet 43 percent of health care professionals believe in the lunar effect, as do 81 percent of mental health care specialists. What's going on?

One explanation might be what psychologists call "confirmation bias"—people are more likely to notice things that confirm a preexisting belief. So you're working in an emergency room, and something weird happens on the full Moon, and your older and wiser colleagues nod and say, "Must be a full Moon." That's what they heard from their elders when they were new at the job, too. (Psychologists

81 PERCENT of mental health care specialists believe in the lunar effect.

also have a name for that: "communal reinforcement.")

But if something weird happens at a different phase of the lunar cycle, nobody says, "Must be the first quarter Moon!" And when nothing unusual happens on the full Moon, nobody says anything.

What do we call widespread beliefs that are unsupported by fact? Folklore. Maria Leach, editor of the *Funk & Wagnalls* *Standard Dictionary of Folklore, Mythology, and Legend* (Harper & Row, 1984), defined it as "the inextinguishable hope that all that is wrong in the world can somehow be put right."

So, how does a belief that strange things happen on the full Moon help us to feel safer? The full Moon occurs only once every 29.5 days; this means that the other 4 weeks of the lunar month should be less dangerous and unpredictable.

Therefore, this folk belief suggests that our fears about everything from increased bleeding to werewolves should be limited to only the 13 actual full Moon days that occur each year.

Come to think of it, maybe that's why the number 13 worries people! ■

Tim Clark studied folklore at Harvard University.

THE BEES' LIFE IS LIKE A MAGIC WELL:
THE MORE YOU DRAW FROM IT, THE MORE IT FILLS WITH WATER.
–*Karl von Frisch, Austrian ethologist (1886–1982)*

TELLING THE BEES
A SWARM OF FACTS, FOLKLORE, AND TRADITIONS

BY TIM CLARK

For thousands of years, human beings have shared a special bond with bees. Bees are not truly domesticated; their relationship with humans is an equal partnership. In Central Europe, beekeepers gave their bees written contracts, promising to provide shelter and care in return for wax and honey.

The orderliness and industry of honeybees and their loyalty to their queen are a timeless metaphor. In ancient Egypt, the hieroglyph that represented a king was a bee. When Napoleon Bonaparte made himself emperor, he wore a sumptuous gown decorated with golden bees. Even today, a beehive adorns the state flag of Utah, along with the motto "Industry." Indeed, the bee has given its name to occasions of collective labor, such as a sewing bee.

Bees were symbolic of wisdom and morality. Muslims believe that the bee is the only animal that left the Garden of Eden unchanged and the only ani-mal that goes to heaven. The Germans believed that bees were created by God to provide wax for church candles, and the Bretons said that they were the transformed tears of Christ. In India, the three Hindu gods Indra, Krishna, and Vishnu were called "the nectar-born," and Kama, a love goddess, had a bowstring made of bees.

The Greeks and Romans thought that bees sucked their young out of flowers. In fact, queen bees are impregnated by drones in the so-called "mating flight," far from the hive. But no one understood this until the late 19th century. Until then, bees represented chastity and were a symbol of Artemis, the Greek goddess of virginity. Beekeepers had to abstain from sex during certain ritual periods, and young women would parade their sweethearts before the hives, believing that bees would sting a faithless lover. Valentine is not only the patron saint of lovers, but of beekeepers as well.

In Greek mythology, two daughters of the king of Crete, Melissa and Amalthea, protected the infant Zeus, and the grateful god turned them into bees. Greeks also believed that if a bee landed on a baby's lips, the child would grow up to be an eloquent speaker. The philosopher Plato, the dramatist Sophocles, and the historian Xenophon were said to have received the gift, and each was nicknamed "The Athenian Bee."

A vast collection of folklore relates to bees. A bee flying into a house means that a stranger is coming. If the bee flies in and out of the house, it's good luck, but it mustn't be shooed out, and if the bee dies in the house, bad luck will follow. If a swarm comes to your home without your knowledge, disaster will follow. The Roman general Scipio once canceled an attack because a swarm landed in his camp.

Bees can even predict the weather, it is said. Unusually large stores of honey in the fall mean a hard winter is coming.

Some of the most interesting folklore about bees involves human–bee communication. Bees were said to hum hymns on Christmas Eve, and beekeepers sang to their bees to prevent them from swarming. Swearing or quarreling in front of bees was strictly forbidden, lest they become upset and leave.

It was thought that the public exchange of money for bees was offensive to them, so barter was the preferred method of acquiring a swarm. If money must be used, the buyer should leave it on a stone in an agreed-upon place for the seller to collect later, and the exchange should never take place on a Friday.

The most touching custom was to tell the bees of any significant events in the beekeeper's life. Bees were often invited to weddings, for example, and in Brittany and parts of England, betrothals were announced to the bees. The new couple would introduce themselves to the gaily-decorated hives, and pieces of wedding cake would be left there as gifts for the bees.

It was critical to tell the bees of a death in the beekeeper's family. Many tales have been told of colonies leaving the farm or dying off if they were not told, especially when the beekeeper himself or herself died. A family member (some stories specify the youngest child or the oldest female relation) had to gently knock on the hive and announce, "The Master is dead." Then she or he would beg the bees not to leave the farm. Often the hives were decorated with black crepe for the funeral.

John Greenleaf Whittier's 1858 poem "Telling the Bees" relates such a story, and in 1906, Rudyard Kipling's "The Bee-Boy's Song" gave the bees themselves a voice:

Bees! Bees! Hark to your bees!
Hide from your neighbors as much as
*   you please,*
But all that has happened, to us you
*   must tell,*
Or else we will give you no honey to sell!

An ancient custom of no modern consequence? Perhaps. But following the death of England's King George VI in 1952, thousands of British beekeepers rushed outside to tell the bees. ∎

The Northern Mockingbird:
Nature's Great Crooner

BY PHILLIP HOOSE

Samuel A. Grimes, pioneering bird photographer and recorder of birdsongs, never forgot the first time he heard a mockingbird sing. "I was 5 years old," he told National Wildlife Federation interviewer Doug Harbrecht in 1992, "sitting on the porch of my family home in Kentucky, and this bird was in a tree just a few feet away, singing so clear and so close. It amazed me."

When he reached his 70s, Grimes decided that it was time to pay tribute to his favorite vocalist. He lugged a primitive tape recorder back and forth across the country, collecting 45 hours of mockingbird song onto 2 miles of tape. The result was "The Vocally Versatile Mockingbird," a 1979 release of the golden songs of *Mimus polyglottos,* the northern mockingbird's Latin name, which translates to "many-tongued mimic."

As Grimes knew, the northern mockingbird is one of the truly great singers in the animal kingdom. Parrots can be taught to mimic, but only in captivity. The mockingbird sings its famous song of varied, repeated phrases all day during nesting season (and often all night as well). The mocker begins learning songs in early youth and adds as many as 200 tunes throughout its life. Many are imitations of other birds' songs. While other songbirds sing from leafy hideouts, mockingbirds belt out their playlists from wires, towers, cactus tops, telephone poles, and rooftops. They dive-bomb cats, dogs, and even humans that stray too close to their nests.

Mockingbirds imitate human sounds, too, notably laughter, as well as inanimate objects, including sirens, musical instruments, rusty gates, cell phones, doorbells, and the whirrs, dings, and clangs of almost any home appliance. During his tape-recording odyssey, Grimes came across one mockingbird near Miami that expertly imitated an alarm clock, awakening nearby residents every morning. A Pennsylvania woman wrote of a mockingbird that picked up the sound of her telephone: "A lot of times, we would run inside to answer the phone and realize that it was that crazy bird!"

How many songs can a mockingbird sing? Author and

The northern mockingbird is one of the truly great singers in the animal kingdom.

birdsong expert Donald Kroodsma recorded the songs of one Florida mockingbird—probably a bachelor crooning for a mate—that sang all night long. In one stretch, it sang an amazing 465 songs in 26 minutes' time, and 93 of the songs were different from one another.

Mockingbirds nearly vanished from parts of the U.S. East Coast.

What is the advantage of knowing and performing hundreds of songs? Ask any rock star.

Research shows that as a male mockingbird expands his playlist, he becomes increasingly attractive to females. A great set list, which takes years to amass, shows that the singer is a good catch. In essence, the veteran crooner proclaims, "I've been around. We both know that life is tough in the wild. But I'm a survivor. I've already established a territory with plenty of food. Why not throw in with me? You could do worse." (A great concert sometimes triggers the female's reproductive system. Female mockers sing, too, but not during breeding season.)

Mockingbirds were captured and sold as caged pets like parakeets from the late 1700s to the early 1900s. The best singers sold for as much as $50. So many mockingbirds were snatched and caged that the birds nearly vanished from parts of the U.S. East Coast. The mockingbird's population has rebuilt steadily since receiving protection under the Migratory Bird Treaty Act of 1918.

Mockers have maintained their population and expanded their range by learning to coexist with humans and eating a varied diet of insects and cultivated fruit. Mockingbirds often run after insects on open lawns, sprinting a few steps and then stopping suddenly to lift up their wings and flash white patches downward, which startles insect prey to the surface. Some mockingbirds migrate south in the winter, but usually not far. Most adjust their diets, accept the hardship, and tough it out, occasionally erupting into song on bright, warm winter days. *(continued)*

A mockingbird, defending its territory, chases off the much larger osprey from its perch.

How Well Do You Know the Mockingbird?

• Mockingbirds have impressed and fascinated humans for centuries. A tribe of Algonquins called the mockingbird *cencontlatolly,* or "400 tongues." The Biloxi Native Americans believed that the bird "mocked one's words," while the Choctaws referred to it as the bird "that speaks a foreign tongue."

• In 1772, Thomas Jefferson bought a mockingbird from a slave of his father-in-law, John Wayles. Won over by the bird's intelligence and charm, Jefferson bought three more mockingbirds and took his favorite, named Dick, with him to the White House in 1801. (Dick is commonly believed to have been the first pet to live there.) According to Jefferson's friend and early American historian Margaret Bayard Smith, Jefferson routinely kept Dick's cage door open. The presidential mockingbird spent its days whizzing around Jefferson's study, perching on one object or another to "regale him with its sweetest notes." Dick sat on Jefferson's shoulder while he worked and sometimes took its food from Jefferson's lips. At naptime, Dick would hop up the stairs behind Jefferson and then perch on a couch and sing him to sleep. "How he loved the bird," Smith observed. Jefferson wrote of the mocker: "Learn all the children to venerate it as a superior being in the form of a bird, or as a being which will haunt them if any harm is done to itself or its eggs."

• Mockingbirds have inspired songs, lullabies, paintings, poetry, and literature. In 1827, celebrated

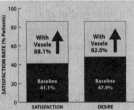

bird artist John James Audubon portrayed the mockingbird through a treetop battle scene that aroused great controversy. In the image, a rattlesnake, fangs bared, has slithered up a tree to invade a mockingbird's nest as four birds mount a defense. The painting was blasted by naturalists who asserted that rattlesnakes couldn't climb trees. Audubon huffed that he drew the birds just as he had observed them in the wild.

- The immortal lullaby "Hush, Little Baby," "Hush, Little Baby."

- "Listen to the Mockingbird" (1855) was one of the most popular songs of all time, telling the story of a young man who dreams of his dead sweetheart as a mockingbird sings over her grave. Through the years, its sheet music has sold more than 20 million copies. Union soldiers marched to it during the Civil War, and Abraham Lincoln proclaimed it "as sincere as the laughter of a little girl at play."

- Mockingbirds have continued to enchant and inspire. Slim Whitman's

- The most famous portrait, and the best case for the mockingbird, comes from a literary classic. "Mockingbirds don't do one thing but make music for us to enjoy," says Miss Maudie Atkinson famously in Harper Lee's classic, *To Kill a Mockingbird*. "They don't eat up people's gardens, don't nest in corncribs, they don't do one thing but sing their hearts out."

- *Mama's Going to Buy You a Mockingbird* (1984) is a famous book by renowned Canadian children's

Mockingbirds have inspired songs, lullabies, paintings, poetry, and literature.

whose author is unknown, was probably written during the years when mockingbirds were sold as caged birds. It begins with a famous proposition: "Hush, little baby, don't say a word, / Papa's gonna buy you a mockingbird." Inez and Charlie Foxx, James Taylor, Carly Simon, and Eminem are among the many recording artists who have made their own versions of

waltz "Mockingbird Hill" rocketed to the top of the pop music charts in 1951.

- "The Mocking Bird" (1952) was the first single recorded by famed Canadian singing group The Four Lads.

- Mockers are even present in the dystopian future. The Mockingjay—admittedly a hybrid—is the proud symbol of rebellion worn by Katniss Everdeen in *The Hunger Games*.

author Jean Little (b. 1932) that poignantly touches on death and dying, love, family, friendship, and hope. ◼

Phillip Hoose is a graduate of the Yale School of Forestry and Environmental Sciences and was a staff member of The Nature Conservancy for 37 years. He is the author of 12 books, including National Book Award–winning *Claudette Colvin: Twice Toward Justice* (Farrar, Straus, and Giroux, 2009).

NEW PROSTATE PILL HELPS RELIEVE SYMPTOMS WITHOUT DRUGS OR SURGERY

Combats all-night bathroom urges and embarrassment... *Yet most doctors don't even know about it!*

By Health Writer, Peter Metler

Thanks to a brand new discovery made from a rare prostate relief plant; thousands of men across America are taking their lives back from "prostate hell". This remarkable new natural supplement helps you:

- **MINIMIZE** constant urges to urinate
- **END** embarrassing sexual "let-downs"
- **SUPPORT** a strong, healthy urine flow
- **GET** a restful night of uninterrupted sleep
- **STOP** false alarms, dribbles
- **ENJOY** a truly empty bladder

More men than ever before are dealing with prostate problems that range from annoying to downright EMBARRASSING! But now, research has discovered a new solution so remarkable that helps alleviate symptoms associated with an enlarged prostate (sexual failure, lost sleep, bladder discomfort and urgent runs to the bathroom). Like nothing before!

Yet 9 out of 10 doctors don't know about it! Here's why: Due to strict managed health care constrictions, many MD's are struggling to keep their practices afloat. "Unfortunately, there's no money in prescribing natural products. They aren't nearly as profitable," says a confidential source. Instead, doctors rely on toxic drugs that help, but could leave you sexually "powerless" (or a lot worse)!

On a CNN Special, Medical Correspondent Dr. Steve Salvatore shocked America by quoting a statistic from the prestigious Journal of American Medical Association that stated, "... about 60% of men who go under the knife for a prostatectomy are left UNABLE to perform sexually!"

PROSTATE PROBLEM SOLVED!

But now you can now beat the odds. And enjoy better sleep, a powerful urine stream and a long and healthy love life. The secret? You need to load your diet with essential Phyto-Nutrients, (traditionally found in certain fruits, vegetables and grains).

The problem is, most Phyto-Nutrients never get into your bloodstream. They're destroyed

HERE ARE 6 WARNING SIGNS YOU BETTER NOT IGNORE

- ✓ Waking up 2 to 6 times a night to urinate
- ✓ A constant feeling that you have to "go"... but can't
- ✓ A burning sensation when you do go
- ✓ A weak urine stream
- ✓ A feeling that your bladder is never completely empty
- ✓ Embarrassing sputtering, dripping & staining

by today's food preparation methods (cooking, long storage times and food additives).

YEARS OF RESEARCH

Thankfully, a small company (Wellness Logix™) out of Maine, is on a mission to change that. They've created a product that arms men who suffer with prostate inflammation with new hope. And it's fast becoming the #1 Prostate formula in America.

Prostate IQ™ gives men the super-concentrated dose of Phyto-Nutrients they need to beat prostate symptoms. "You just can't get them from your regular diet" say Daniel. It's taken a long time to understand how to capture the prostate relieving power of this amazing botanical. But their hard work paid off. *Prostate IQ*™ is different than any other prostate supplement on the market...

DON'T BE FOOLED BY CHEAP FORMULATIONS!

Many hope you won't notice, but a lot of prostate supplements fall embarrassingly short with their dosages. The formulas may be okay, but they won't do a darn thing for you unless you take 10 or more tablets a day. *Prostate IQ*™ contains a whopping 300mg of this special "Smart Prostate Plant". So it's loaded with Phyto-Nutrients. Plus, it gets inside your bloodstream faster and stays inside for maximum results!

TRY IT RISK-FREE

SPECIAL OPPORTUNITY

Get a risk-free trial supply of *Prostate IQ*™ today - just for asking. But you must act now, supplies are limited!

Call Now, Toll-Free at:

1-800-380-0925

THESE STATEMENTS HAVE NOT BEEN EVALUATED BY THE FDA. THESE PRODUCTS ARE NOT INTENDED TO DIAGNOSE, TREAT, CURE OR PREVENT ANY DISEASE. OFFER NOT AVAILABLE TO RESIDENTS OF IOWA

The Pros
AND CONS
of Backyard
LIVESTOCK

BY JACK SAVAGE

WHO AMONG US DOESN'T ASPIRE TO SELF-sufficiency? Equipped with only a little land and less knowledge, we think about getting some chickens for the backyard. And as long as we're feeding the chickens, why not raise a pig? Or a goat? Maybe even a cow? How about a horse?

The desire for healthy, affordable food and a connection to animals has driven a backyard livestock boom. Knowing the pros and cons of common farm animals can help you to make a good choice—or send you to the nearest market, happy to empty your wallet.

CHICKENS

THE domestic chicken can be traced back some 10,000 years. Today, the world has three times as many chickens as human beings, but you may not recognize all of them: In suburbs where they are prohibited by zoning, people have been known to put their chickens in dog costumes.

PROS

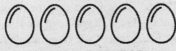

EGGS, OF COURSE.

IF you get one of the smaller (little) breeds, you will know before everyone else when the sky is falling.

FRESH meat. Yes, this means slaughtering the chicken.

EFFICIENCY. You can keep a few chickens in far less space than a goat or pig or cow. And on average it takes only 2 pounds of feed to produce 1 pound of chicken meat.

CONS

IF you become a true chicken person, you will spend all your time talking about chickens. Occasionally, you will cluck.

PREDATORS. Foxes, coyotes, and weasels love chickens. For dinner. Keeping your brood safe can be a challenge.

NO MATTER HOW HARD YOU TRY, YOU CAN NOT MILK A CHICKEN.

(continued)

HORSES are majestic, intelligent herd animals that like open space, so make sure that you have enough of it to keep your horse content. Note that you'll be feeding your horse, but the horse will not be feeding you. At least not nutritionally. Spiritually, however, the connection to a horse can be strong and meaningful.

PROS

YOU can ride a horse. Saddling up a chicken is generally frowned upon and your boots drag.

WITH A HORSE AND A COW, YOU CAN BE A COWBOY.

PEOPLE stop by, and from them you will learn a great lesson: that the best kind of horse is the one your friend owns.

CONS

HORSES are large (on average, 1,000-plus pounds), powerful, and genetically predisposed to believe that the grass is greener on the other side of the fence. If you keep a horse, then "fixing fence" will be your hobby.

IF you are not in sync with your horse or are not an experienced rider, your horse will have final say over who rides whom.

CHECK-WRITING won't stop with the hay guy, the vet, or the tack shop staff. You'll be a regular at the truck-and-trailer dealership and the permit office for that barn or run-in shed.

 HORSES

GOATS

GOATS are highly social—curious, interactive, and smart. You can read to a goat, and it will listen, especially if it's a doe. Goats are ruminants, which means that a chamber in their stomach called the rumen ferments the plant-based food that they eat. (Contrary to legend, they do not eat tin cans.) Rumination involves the goat chewing its cud, which is regurgitated food.

PROS

BABY goats are hilarious. They love to hop on top of sheep and adult goats.

YOU can halter a goat for handling and showing. They'll go where you want, if you convince them that it was their idea.

GOATS CAN PROVIDE YOU WITH MOHAIR, MILK, CHEESE, AND MEAT.

CONS

TO make that homegrown Greek salad with feta cheese, you may need goat's milk. Which means you'll need to breed the goat. Once she's lactating, you'll need to milk her. And keep milking her.

IF you have an intact boy goat, or billy, you will know it. So will your downwind neighbors. And everyone you meet at the store if you wear your barn clothes. Billy thinks that this is awesome and, occasionally, so does the nanny goat.

GOATS' feet usually have to be trimmed, and sometimes the horns, too. Good luck! *(continued)*

LET'S acknowledge that pigs are the most delicious of livestock. Plus, they are cute when they're young and not as filthy as their reputation suggests, and they put on weight fast.

 # PIGS

PROS

BACON. HAM. SAUSAGE. PORK ROAST. DID WE MENTION BACON?

YOU can raise a pig in a year, then send it off to the freezer. If the experience was a good one, you can start over.

WHEN your backyard pig escapes (and it will), you get to watch the local constabulary try to catch it. Capture that on video, and it'll go viral.

PORK fat is rendered into lard. For traditional (if short-lived) cooks, lard makes almost everything better.

CONS

PIGS can have two litters a year. If you're not careful, you can find yourself overrun.

PIGS grow fast, get big (depending on the breed), and can be destructive. Did you want your backyard excavated?

PIGS sunburn easily, and they never remember to put on sunscreen. They'll need shade.

BUTCHERING a pig is serious business. Rashers and ribs don't come vacuum-packed inside the pig.

PREMIUM MEAT

COWS

HAVING a cow makes you feel like a real farmer. And, as any elephant farmer will tell you, cows are a lot easier to handle and clean up after than elephants. Cows, too, like goats, are ruminants and thus are prone to ruminating about questions such as "What kind of cow is God?" and "Why would He allow a hamburger to be called a 'Happy Meal'?" Cows don't often come up with answers. But you might.

PROS

MILK. Unadulterated milk for you, your family, and your neighbors. And cheese.

THE answer to the question, Where's the beef?

IF you don't mind "harvesting" the manure, you can sell it. (You'll make more that way than selling the milk.)

CONS

BEFORE you get a dairy cow, talk to a dairy farmer. It won't be difficult, as they won't be on vacation. He or she will tell you how to make a small fortune (from a large one).

GET to know your large-animal veterinarian, if you can find one. Give him or her all your money. You will understand immediately what it takes to keep a cow healthy.

CONVERTING your backyard into a barnyard can make you feel like you have the working farm you've always wanted. But it's more responsibility, not less, and your animals will let you know when you're late with their dinner. You're going to love it! ■

Jack Savage is a former editor of *New Hampshire Profiles* and was a founder of the New Hampshire Writers' Project.

TAKE TWO
COCKER SPANIELS
AND CALL ME IN
THE MORNING

WHY A DOG MAY BE
THE BEST MEDICINE

BY SUSAN PEERY

PETTING, SCRATCHING, AND CUDDLING A DOG COULD BE AS SOOTHING TO THE MIND AND HEART AS DEEP MEDITATION AND ALMOST AS GOOD FOR THE SOUL AS PRAYER.

–Dean Koontz, American writer (b. 1945)

There are a lot of reasons why you might not want to live with a dog: muddy pawprints on your couch, tumbling tumbleweeds of dog hair on the floor, dog breath in your face. But what if you knew that the dirt, the hair, the very breath of the dog would improve your health?

Scientists have taken an intense interest recently in the gut microbiome—yours and your dog's. The gut microbiome refers to the billions of bacteria, viruses, and other tiny microorganisms that inhabit our innards. A few may be associated with disease, but most are needed to help us ward off infections and malfunctions. Although there is still much to be learned, researchers are certain of one thing: The more diversity in the microbiome, the better.

The discussion started in 1989, when epidemiologist David Strachan at the University of London introduced a theory called the "hygiene hypothesis." Dr. Strachan reasoned that the large increase in allergies and other autoimmune disorders in developed countries during the past century may have been an unintended consequence of cleaner environments, less contact with the great outdoors, and thereby decreased exposure to a variety of microorganisms—especially very early in life, when a baby's immune system is still developing. Had we become too clean? Too scrubbed and disinfected?

As other researchers jumped in, studying the development of the immune system and its relationship to the gut microbiome, studies began to show that exposure to a little dirt, especially in early childhood, can be beneficial and may even help to ward off disease.

This is where dogs come wagging into the picture, along with their ubiquitous fur and saliva. Researchers have documented a lower incidence of asthma among children who grew up with dogs. Scientists suspect that because people and dogs have coexisted for millennia, there's been a lot of trading of human and canine microbiomes, with mutual dependence and evolution. "All of the people alive today probably had ancestors who lived in tribes that hunted with dogs," says Dr. Jack Gilbert, director of the Microbiome Center at the University of Chicago.

Although research into the details of this transference between dogs and humans is still in the early stages, some

scientists think that the family pet, with its diverse microbiome, can convey benefits even beyond biodiversity and a reduced likelihood of allergies.

At the University of Alberta in Edmonton, Dr. Anita Kozyrskyj, a pediatric epidemiologist and leading researcher on gut microbes, thinks that pets—especially dogs—also might lower the risk of obesity. Dr. Kozyrskyj and her team have identified two different bacteria, *Ruminococcus* and *Oscillospira,* that have been linked to reduced risk of childhood allergies and obesity, respectively, and are doubly abundant in the gut microbiome of small babies who live in households with pets. The researchers are partway into a long-term investigation (the Canadian Healthy Infant Longitudinal Development, or CHILD, cohort study) to try to pinpoint what is going on.

It may be that it is mostly small children who benefit from a wet kiss from a furry friend, although studies now in the works may show a broader benefit. Or perhaps drug companies will develop a "dog pill" that will introduce those special doggy microbes without the telltale pawprints on the couch. But will a pill keep you warm on a three-dog night? Cue the cocker spaniels! Bring on the beagles!

**DOGS ARE NOT OUR WHOLE LIFE,
BUT THEY MAKE OUR LIVES WHOLE.**
–Roger A. Caras, American photographer and writer (1928–2001)

HOW TO KEEP ROVER
(AND HIS MICROBIOME) HEALTHY

BEFORE YOU CALL THE VET, KEEP CALM AND TRY A HOME
REMEDY FOR SOME COMMON CANINE CHALLENGES.

• For doggy breath: You can remove tartar (a source of bad breath) from your dog's teeth with a washcloth dipped in pet—not human!—toothpaste. Feed your dog something dry and crunchy (kibble, hard dog biscuits) every day to help scour off the tartar. Some dogs enjoy eating raw carrots and even parsley, both of which help to freshen the breath.

• For upset stomach: As long as your dog has no other alarming symptoms, withhold food and water for 12 hours, then try offering one or two ice cubes. Proceed with caution: Offer a bland diet of cooked white rice; plain skinless, boneless chicken; and plain yogurt in small amounts for 2 to 3 days, until your dog is holding down its food.

• For diarrhea: As long as the stools do not contain blood or worms and the dog has a decent appetite, make small meals of cooked white rice or potatoes and a small amount of nongreasy meat. Your dog should get better in 2 to 3 days.

• For when your dog rolls in turkey poop or something even more disgusting: Using a hose, spray off as much as you can. Then reach for a bottle of Nature's Miracle spray and rub it into the dog's coat with an old towel. Rinse and repeat. Nature's Miracle has enzymes that neutralize organic odors.

• For when your dog has been sprayed by a skunk: Forget dousing with tomato juice (it just makes a huge mess). Instead, stir together 1 quart hydrogen peroxide, ¼ cup baking soda, and 1 teaspoon dishwashing liquid. Wear rubber gloves and lather this mixture into the dog's fur (keep out of its eyes). Rinse with water. Use the tomato juice to make yourself a well-deserved Bloody Mary.

• For fleas: A daily supplement of brewer's yeast may deter the little critters.

• For ticks: Given the spread of ticks and rise of Lyme disease, which can cripple a dog, this might be one time to get your vet's best advice. New chewable tick medications last up to 3 months per dose. For maximum protection, check your dog (and humans!) nightly during the height of tick season, usually spring and fall. ■

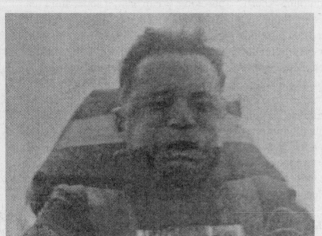

The Fastest Man's Last

... AND HOW IT LED TO

BY TIM CLARK

Bruises. Cracked ribs. Broken wrists. Bleeding blisters caused by high-speed sand abrasion. Concussions. Retinal hemorrhages and temporary blindness. The injuries suffered by John Paul Stapp in the late 1940s and early '50s sound like those from a series of high-speed, head-on auto crashes.

Which, in a way, they were. In the interest of science—specifically to study the effects of extreme deceleration on the human body—Stapp strapped himself into rocket-propelled sleds and rode the flame-belching vehicles down a railroad track at speeds of hundreds of miles per hour into braking devices that slammed him to a dead stop in less

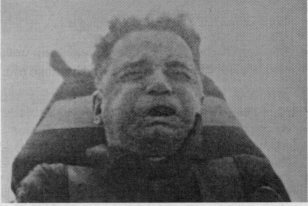

Death-Defying Ride

SEAT BELTS IN CARS

than 2 seconds. He did this 29 times!

The most extreme such experiment, which took place 65 years ago, was the equivalent of a car hitting a brick wall at 120 miles per hour.

Stapp was born in 1910 in Brazil, the son of two Baptist missionaries. A U.S. Army Air Corps flight surgeon during World War II, he took an immediate

Above: John Stapp strapped in a sled seat during high G-force acceleration and deceleration testing. Stapp reached 632 miles per hour in 5 seconds before being brought back to rest in just over a second with a force of over 40 Gs. Despite initial blindness and collapsed lungs, he quickly recovered, proving that it was possible to survive ejection from a supersonic aircraft.

Of the *Sonic Wind* ride, Stapp once remarked,
"I felt like a fly on the nose of a bullet."

interest in the challenge of keeping pilots alive while flying at (and parachuting from) extreme altitudes. This commitment ultimately led him to Holloman Air Force Base in New Mexico, in 1953, to test the limits of how much deceleration a human body could stand.

At this time, the generally accepted deceleration limit was 18 Gs, or 18 times the force of gravity at sea level. Stopping at that speed, some experts believed, would break all of the bones in a human body. By comparison, a passenger in a car making an emergency stop feels 2 Gs. (Normal life is 1 G.) Some amusement parks have rides that subject thrill-seekers to 4.5 Gs. Fighter pilots and astronauts train on centrifuges that press them into their seats at up to 15 Gs.

John Stapp on board the Sonic Wind

Stapp believed that humans could withstand far more Gs. He proved it on his record-setting "Big Run" of December 10, 1954, when he mounted a rocket sled named *Sonic Wind* and, in 5 seconds, accelerated from zero to 632 mph—close to the speed of sound and literally faster than a .45 caliber bullet. Then a series of water brakes decelerated him back to zero in 1.4 seconds, delivering a 46.2 G wallop. Of the *Sonic Wind* ride, Stapp once remarked, "I felt like a fly on the nose of a bullet."

The event set a world land-speed record, making 44-year-old Stapp the Fastest Man on Earth—and one in great discomfort.

His eyes filled with blood and he experienced pain that he compared to having teeth extracted without anesthesia, yet he insisted on walking away from the sled. He was able to stagger a few steps, with assistance, before accepting a stretcher ride. Blind at first, he was able to see shapes after 4 hours and could identify friends and colleagues the next day.

The eye doctor who cared for him at that time reported, "One might possibly expect, after 29 experiments, brain damage such as is found in a 'punch drunk' pugilist. The contrary is the case, as anyone can testify after a few minutes' conversation with Colonel Stapp." In fact, a day later he was talking excitedly about trying for a 1,000-mph run.

It would never happen. His Air Force

superiors made it clear that Stapp was far too valuable a public relations bonanza to be risked. His next run was into the history books.

A painting of his helmeted head atop *Sonic Wind* appeared on the cover of *Time* magazine in September 1955. He was lured to Hollywood to be on the popular TV show *This Is Your Life.* He won medals from the Air Force and various civilian groups.

Decades later, he would be inducted into both the Aviation and Space Halls of Fame. In 1991, he received the National Medal of Technology. There was even a feature film about him called *On the Threshold of Space,* which Stapp described to a friend as "perhaps the worst movie ever made."

F. Scott Fitzgerald once wrote, "There are no second acts in American lives." Stapp's second act was less famous than his first, but it was far more significant.

Cover of Time *magazine, 1955*

I n the course of his studies of aircraft safety, Stapp had discovered that the Air Force was losing more trained pilots to auto accidents than plane crashes. Only days after the "Big Run," he had received a letter from an engineer studying the design of seat belts, which were not at that time required in American cars. The contact resulted in the first Automotive Crash Research Field Demonstration and Conference, a gathering of military, civilian, and academic authorities, along with representatives from all of the major automakers, at Holloman AFB in 1955. The annual conference continues to this day, now known as the Stapp Car Crash Conference. It has inspired innovations such as three-point seat belts and air bags, saving millions of lives. When President Lyndon Johnson signed the 1966 law requiring automobile seat belts, Stapp was standing at his shoulder.

Stapp continued his research until he retired from the Air Force in 1970. He continued to work to improve the safety of automobiles until his death at age 89.

Think of John Stapp the next time you buckle up. ∎

The Stapp Car Crash Conference has inspired innovations such as three-point seat belts and air bags, saving millions of lives.

IN 1969, THE NEW YORK METS TURNED
THE SPORTS WORLD UPSIDE DOWN BY
WINNING THE WORLD SERIES.

By Charles P. Pierce

BASEBALL'S
AMAZIN'

MOST ___ SEASON!

THE LAST MIRACLE I DID WAS THE
1969 METS. BEFORE THAT, I THINK YOU
HAVE TO GO BACK TO THE RED SEA.
–God, played by George Burns in the film Oh, God!

THE METS HAD BUILT A SUBSTANTIAL CADRE OF TALENTED YOUNG PITCHERS.

For a number of reasons, almost nobody saw the New York Mets coming. First of all, they were the New York Mets, subject of a hilarious book by Jimmy Breslin called *Can't Anybody Here Play This Game?* The answer, for the entire previous history of the franchise (7 years), largely was no. In the first 4 years of its existence, the team lost a total of 452 games. In 1968, the Mets clearly had improved. They'd lost only 89 games. Things were looking up, but only because the franchise still was flat on its back.

But there was something stirring behind all those losses. The Mets had built a substantial cadre of talented young pitchers, including Tom Seaver, Jerry Koosman, Gary Gentry, and a young flamethrower from Texas named Nolan Ryan. (Two of them—Seaver, who would go on to win 311 games, and the lordly Ryan, winner of 324— would be elected to the Baseball Hall of Fame.)

As the '69 season began, the Mets struggled, as had become their custom. For the first time that season, the two leagues had been split up into two divisions and, in the National League East, the Mets found themselves trailing a powerful Chicago Cubs team. Even when the Mets won 11 games in a row, hardly anyone noticed, and, by mid-August, they were 9½ games behind the Cubs. At which point, the world turned upside down.

The Mets won 38 of their last 49 games. Seaver and Koosman became unhittable. Once, as the Mets

Photo: Associated Press

OPPOSITE: 1969 New York Mets team photo. ABOVE: Pitcher Nolan Ryan and catcher Jerry Grote rush toward each other after the Mets won the National League pennant with their win over the Atlanta Braves.

swept a doubleheader in Pittsburgh, Koosman and Don Cardwell won 1–0 victories in which each of them knocked in the only run. In another game, 19 Mets struck out, and the team won anyway. As the perennial doormat turned into The Amazin' Mets—or, simply, The Amazin's—the Cubs fell apart in the way that the Cubs historically had

had wont to do, and the Mets went into the first-ever National League playoff series, three out of five games against Henry Aaron and the Atlanta Braves.

The Braves were favored, but because everything was now upside down, the Mets ended up winning—and they did so not on the basis of the recognized strength of their young pitching staff, but because, suddenly, some of the more obscure members on their roster turned into hitting fools. The

Mets took the first game, 9–5, and the barrage continued through the next two contests, in which they scored 11 and 7 runs, respectively. Ryan clinched the pennant with seven innings of magnificent relief pitching in the third game. In *A Magic Summer,* his account of the 1969 season, Stanley Cohen quotes Henry Aaron, who had played his last postseason game, as saying, "They really are amazing."

In the World Series, the Mets faced the favored Baltimore Orioles, winners of

RYAN CLINCHED THE PENNANT WITH SEVEN INNINGS OF MAGNIFICENT RELIEF.

109 games during the regular season, in which they had finished 19 games ahead of the second-place Detroit Tigers. Baltimore had then swept the Minnesota Twins in the American League championship series.

In the first game of the best-of-seven Series, the Orioles batted Seaver around and won, 4–1. Despite the loss, the Mets came out of the first game convinced that they could play with Baltimore. Seaver, speaking to Donald Honig for Honig's history of the first 25 years of the New York franchise, recalled, "I swear, we came into the clubhouse more confident than when we had left it. Somebody yelled out, 'Dammit, we can beat these guys!' And we believed it." What Seaver didn't know was how this was going to come about.

For the rest of the Series, the Mets' young pitchers dominated the Orioles, holding them to five runs in the next four games. But the real magic came in the outfield. In game three, outfielder Tommie Agee saved a 5–0 shutout with two spectacular catches, including running down

IT WAS OCTOBER 16, 1969, WHEN THE MIRACLE METS WERE CROWNED THE WORLD

one drive at the 400-foot mark. In the next game, while Seaver was squeezing out a 2–1 win by pitching all 10 innings of the game, another outfielder, Ron Swoboda—who never had been compared to brilliant defender Roberto Clemente (or to Tommie Agee, for that matter)—saved the game with a ninth-inning, flat-out, diving catch on a sinking line

CHAMPS OF BASEBALL.

drive by Oriole All-Star third baseman Brooks Robinson.

In the fifth game, Baltimore seemed to be staving off elimination by jumping out to a 3–0 lead through five innings.

In the sixth inning, however, the upside-down world asserted itself for the last time. First, Jerry Koosman hit Baltimore's Frank Robinson with a pitch, but home plate umpire Lou DiMuro ruled that the ball had hit Robinson's bat first. Then, in the bottom of the frame, Oriole pitcher Dave McNally bounced a pitch at the feet of New York's Cleon Jones. The ball rebounded into the Mets dugout. New York manager Gil Hodges showed the ball to DiMuro, pointing out a smear of shoe polish on the ball that proved that Jones had been hit by the pitch. This sent Jones to first base, whence he scored on a homer by Donn Clendenon, the eventual Series Most Valuable Player. New York tied the game on the only

LEFT: Fans engulf the field at Shea Stadium after the Mets beat the Orioles to win the World Series. ABOVE: The front page of the New York *Daily News*, October 17, 1969

home run that shortstop Al Weis ever hit at Shea Stadium, and they won it by scoring two runs in the eighth inning, helped immeasurably by the Orioles' commission of two errors on the same play.

It was October 16, 1969—almost 3 months to the day from when men first walked on the Moon—and the planet was once more in awe as the Miracle Mets were crowned world champions of baseball. ∎

Charles P. Pierce is a veteran journalist, recipient of several national awards, and author of three books.

How to Make Sausage at Home

BY SUSAN PEERY

H ome sausage-making is enjoying a revival. It's as easy as making meat loaf, and anyone can do it with minimal equipment. If you don't want to stuff your sausage mixture into casings, you can make patties or rolls. Either way, once you learn the basics of making fresh sausage, you can personalize these recipes and create your own.

THE EQUIPMENT

- Meat grinder or heavy-duty food processor with coarse and fine grinding disks
- For links, a sausage stuffer or funnel attachment for pushing the mixture into casings
- Natural or other casings (available from sausage-supply houses, meatpacking companies, ethnic groceries, or butchers)

THE STEPS

1. Rinse, flush out, and soak natural casings (if using) in water for 30 minutes.

2. Cut meat and fat into 1-inch cubes. Freeze for 30 minutes to make it easier to grind.

3. Grind meat and fat together, using the proper disk (see individual recipes, page 198).

4. Add seasonings and other ingredients, knead by hand, and grind the entire mixture a second time.

5. Fry a small portion, taste, and adjust the seasonings if necessary.

6. To stuff the casings: Gather the casing over the end of the funnel. Tie a knot in the free end. Feed the mixture through the funnel, gently pushing it into the casing and filling it evenly.

7. Inspect your sausage and prick any air bubbles with a pin.

8. Begin at the tied end: Twist off the links, twisting two or three times every 3 inches or at the desired length. Cut links apart with a sharp knife.

9. Cover and refrigerate the sausage for at least 2 hours, or as directed, to meld the flavors and firm the texture. Use within 3 days, or freeze.

10. Panfry, poach, roast, or grill until golden, to an internal temperature of 160°F on a meat thermometer.   *(continued)*

Adapted from *Home Sausage Making* (Storey Publishing, 2003), by Susan Mahnke Peery and Charles G. Reavis; used with permission.

> **Everything has an
> end, except a sausage,
> which has two.**
> –Danish proverb

CONSIDERING CURING?

Cured sausages (such as pepperoni and
salami) require the addition of sodium
nitrite or nitrate, which must be handled
with caution. If you attempt one of these,
use a commercial premixed cure at the
levels recommended.

PORK

Luganega

These are a delicious companion to tomato sauces or risotto.

4 feet medium hog casing
3½ pounds lean pork butt
½ pound pork fat
1½ teaspoons kosher or coarse salt
1 teaspoon grated lemon zest
1 teaspoon grated orange zest
1 teaspoon freshly ground black pepper
1 teaspoon ground coriander
½ teaspoon ground nutmeg
2 cloves garlic, minced
½ cup dry vermouth
1 cup freshly grated Parmesan cheese

Prepare casing, then meat and fat (steps 1, 2). Grind, using the fine disk (step 3). Separately, combine remaining ingredients, except cheese. Mix well. Add meat and cheese and knead by hand. Stuff casing, twisting off 8-inch links (steps 6, 7, 8). Proceed with steps 9 and 10.

Makes 4 pounds.

Pork and Apple Sausage

Moist, savory, and sweetened with reduced apple cider

2½ feet medium hog casing
2¾ pounds lean pork butt or shoulder
¼ pound pork fat
1 cup apple cider
1 tablespoon olive oil
2 small leeks, cleaned and chopped (white part only)
1 tart apple, peeled, cored, and chopped
2 tablespoons chopped fresh parsley
2 tablespoons chopped fresh rosemary leaves
1 tablespoon kosher or coarse salt

1 teaspoon grated lemon zest
½ teaspoon freshly ground black pepper

Prepare casing, then meat and fat (steps 1, 2). Separately, simmer cider, uncovered, until it is reduced to ¼ cup syrupy liquid. Set aside. Heat oil in a skillet. Cook leeks and apple over moderate heat for 3 to 5 minutes, or until apple is golden. Grind meat and fat, using the fine disk (step 3). Transfer to a bowl and add remaining ingredients. Mix to combine. Freeze for 30 minutes.

Grind mixture again. Combine meat mixture with leeks, apples, and cider. Knead by hand. Stuff casing, twisting off 4-inch links (steps 6, 7, 8). Proceed with steps 9 and 10.

Makes 3 pounds.

BEEF

Garlic-Mustard Beef Sausage

For best flavor, grill or roast.

4 feet medium hog casing
2 pounds blade-cut boneless chuck with 25 percent fat
5 cloves garlic, minced
1 tablespoon yellow mustard seed
1 tablespoon minced fresh rosemary leaves
1 tablespoon Dijon-style mustard
2 teaspoons kosher or coarse salt
1 teaspoon freshly ground black pepper
1 teaspoon sugar
½ teaspoon crushed red pepper flakes (optional)

Prepare casing, then meat and fat (steps 1, 2). Combine meat, fat, garlic, mustard seed, and rosemary. Grind mixture, using the coarse disk (step 3). Transfer to a bowl, add remaining ingredients, and knead by hand. Stuff the casing, twisting off 4-inch links (steps 6, 7, 8). Proceed with steps 9 and 10.

Makes 2 pounds.

LAMB
Lamb, Ginger, and Fruit Sausage

Crystallized ginger and dried apricots add bite and texture.

4 feet sheep or small hog casing
2½ pounds lean lamb
½ pound lamb fat
2 tablespoons lemon juice or white wine
2 tablespoons finely chopped dried apricots
1 tablespoon finely chopped crystallized ginger
1 tablespoon kosher or coarse salt
1 teaspoon freshly ground black pepper

Prepare casing, then meat and fat (steps 1, 2). Transfer to a bowl, add remaining ingredients, and knead by hand. Freeze for 30 minutes.

Grind mixture, using the fine disk (step 3). Stuff casing, twisting off 3-inch links (steps 6, 7, 8). Proceed with steps 9 and 10.

Makes 3 pounds.

POULTRY
Chicken Sausage With Chardonnay and Apples

Delicious as an entrée or sliced and served warm with cheese and crackers

2 feet small hog or sheep casing
2 pounds boneless chicken thighs with skin
1 tart apple, peeled, cored, and chopped
¼ cup Chardonnay
2 tablespoons minced onion
2 teaspoons kosher or coarse salt
1 teaspoon ground ginger
½ teaspoon freshly ground black pepper

Prepare casing (step 1). Grind chicken and skin, using the fine disk (step 3). Transfer to a bowl, add remaining ingredients, and knead by hand. Grind mixture again. Stuff casing, twisting off 3-inch links (steps 6, 7, 8). Proceed with steps 9 and 10.

Makes 2 pounds.

Southwestern Turkey Sausage

Perfect in a fajita or black bean stew. Wear rubber gloves to handle the chiles and roast them to intensify their rich flavor.

3 feet medium hog casing
3 pounds turkey meat with skin, cut into cubes
¼ cup chopped fresh cilantro
1 Anaheim chile, roasted, seeded, and chopped
1 jalapeño chile, roasted, seeded, and chopped
2 tablespoons red-wine vinegar
2 tablespoons chili powder
1 tablespoon kosher or coarse salt
1 tablespoon lime juice
2 teaspoons minced garlic
2 teaspoons ground cumin
1 teaspoon freshly ground black pepper

Prepare casing (step 1). Grind meat, using the coarse disk (step 3). Transfer to a bowl, add remaining ingredients, mix to blend. Chill for 1 hour.

Grind mixture again. Stuff casing, twisting off 4-inch links (steps 6, 7, 8). Proceed with steps 9 and 10.

Makes 3 pounds. ■

Pickling continued from page 54

Crispy Pickled Asparagus

Test your spears: Snap one in half. If it breaks cleanly without any strings, it is fresh and will stay crispy when pickled.

5 pounds asparagus, washed
5 large cloves garlic
5 small hot peppers
2½ cups distilled white vinegar
⅓ cup pickling salt
1 teaspoon dill seed

1. Trim asparagus stems so that spears fit into jars with about ½-inch of headspace (area under the jar lid). Put a garlic clove and hot pepper into each jar. Tightly pack asparagus in jars, with tips up.

2. In a pot, combine vinegar, salt, dill seed, and 2½ cups of water. Bring to a boil. Pour hot liquid over spears, leaving ½-inch of headspace. Seal and process in a boiling-water bath for 10 minutes. Set aside to cool, then store in a dark place. For best flavor, wait 3 to 5 days before eating.

Makes five 12-ounce jars.

Variation: Instead of hot peppers, use 1 teaspoon mustard seed in each jar.

Serving suggestion: Wrap thin slices of ham (e.g., prosciutto) around pickled asparagus spears.

Swedish Pickled Beets

Beet colors range from deep red to yellow and orange—so mix them up.

2 cups cooked, peeled, and sliced beets
½ cup distilled white vinegar
½ cup sugar
1 teaspoon pickling salt
1 teaspoon caraway seed

1. Place beets in a glass bowl.

2. In a pot, combine vinegar, sugar, salt, caraway seed, and ½ cup of water. Bring to a boil. Reduce heat and simmer for about 5 minutes to dissolve sugar.

3. Pour hot vinegar mixture over the beets, cover, and chill for at least 2 hours before serving. Eat beets within a couple of weeks.

Makes 4 to 6 servings.

Variation: Instead of caraway seed, use a cinnamon stick, broken into pieces; a couple of whole cloves; and a few whole allspice buds.

Serving suggestion: Add chopped pickled beets and feta cheese to a mixed greens salad.

Pickled Corn Relish

The freshest kernels should be full and milky. Check by puncturing one with your finger.

12 ears sweet corn
2 onions, finely chopped
2 green peppers, seeded and finely chopped
1 red pepper, seeded and finely chopped

1 cup finely chopped green cabbage
2 cups distilled white vinegar
1 cup sugar
2 tablespoons pickling salt
1½ tablespoons ground mustard
¼ teaspoon freshly ground black pepper

1. Cut corn kernels from cobs but do not scrape them. Transfer kernels to a pot and add remaining ingredients. Simmer over low heat for 15 minutes, stirring occasionally. Pour into sterilized jars, leaving ½-inch of headspace. Seal and process in a boiling-water bath for 15 minutes. Set aside to cool, then store in a dark place.

Makes about five ½-pint jars.

Variation: Instead of 1 cup cabbage, use 1 cup finely chopped tomatoes.

Serving suggestion: Fold corn relish into a cheese omelet or use on hamburgers and hot dogs.

Kosher-Style Dill Pickles

Cucumber pickles may shrivel after processing but will later plump in the sealed jars.

1 small bunch fresh dill or 1 teaspoon dried dill
2 cloves garlic, blanched and sliced
1 tablespoon mustard seed
30 to 36 pickling cucumbers (3 to 4 inches long), washed
3 cups distilled white vinegar
6 tablespoons pickling salt

1. In each sterilized jar, place a layer of dill, 1 clove of garlic, and ½ tablespoon of mustard seed. Pack cucumbers into each jar until half-full, add more dill, and fill with remaining cucumbers.

2. In a pot, combine vinegar, salt, and 3 cups of water and bring to a boil. Pour hot liquid over cucumbers, leaving ½-inch of headspace. Seal and process in a boiling-water bath for 15 minutes.

Makes two 1-quart jars.

Variation: Instead of mustard seed, use ½ tablespoon coriander seed or black peppercorns.

Serving suggestion: Add dill pickle chips to grilled cheese sandwiches or chop and add to pasta salad.

Recipe Contest continued from page 60

Chunky Orange Salsa
for Orange-Glazed Grilled Chicken

1 cup coarsely chopped Granny Smith apple
1 cup coarsely chopped mandarin orange
½ cup coarsely chopped red onion
½ cup coarsely chopped green bell pepper
½ cup coarsely chopped Roma tomato
1 tablespoon finely chopped jalapeño (optional)
¼ teaspoon finely chopped cilantro
juice of 1 lime

1. In a bowl, combine apples, oranges, onions, peppers, tomatoes, jalapeños (if using), and cilantro. Add lime juice and stir to incorporate.

Makes 4 servings.

–Andrea Winget, Minden, Louisiana ■

HOW WE PREDICT THE WEATHER

We derive our weather forecasts from a secret formula that was devised by the founder of this Almanac, Robert B. Thomas, in 1792. Thomas believed that weather on Earth was influenced by sunspots, which are magnetic storms on the surface of the Sun.

Over the years, we have refined and enhanced this formula with state-of-the-art technology and modern scientific calculations. We employ three scientific disciplines to make our long-range predictions: solar science, the study of sunspots and other solar activity; climatology, the study of prevailing weather patterns; and meteorology, the study of the atmosphere. We predict weather trends and events by comparing solar patterns and historical weather conditions with current solar activity.

Our forecasts emphasize temperature and precipitation deviations from averages, or normals. These are based on 30-year statistical averages prepared by government meteorological agencies and updated every 10 years. The most-recent tabulations span the period 1981 through 2010.

The borders of the 16 weather regions of the contiguous states (page 205) are based primarily on climatology and the movement of weather systems. For example, while the average weather in Richmond, Virginia, and Boston, Massachusetts, is very different (although both are in Region 2), both areas tend to be affected by the same storms and high-pressure centers and have weather deviations from normal that are similar.

We believe that nothing in the universe happens haphazardly, that there is a cause-and-effect pattern to all phenomena. However, although neither we nor any other forecasters have as yet gained sufficient insight into the mysteries of the universe to predict the weather with total accuracy, our results are almost always very close to our traditional claim of 80%.

WEATHER

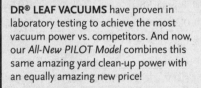

HOW ACCURATE WAS OUR FORECAST LAST WINTER?

Our overall accuracy rate in forecasting the direction of temperature change from normal in the 2017–18 winter, as shown in the table below, was 83%, which is slightly above our historical average of 80%. Temperatures in the Deep South, Desert Southwest, and Pacific Southwest were warmer than we forecast. Most other regions had a February warm enough to offset cold temperatures in other winter months, making our overall forecast of above-normal temperatures correct.

Our forecast for the change in precipitation from last winter was correct in 72% of the regions. We were correct in most regions, but our forecast missed the direction of change in the Southeast, Ohio Valley, Heartland, High Plains, and Desert Southwest.

We correctly forecast the departure of snowfall from normal in most of the country, although not everywhere. We were correct in forecasting snowfall in much of the Great Lakes area, but the snowbelts of New York State received more snow than we forecast. While we forecast above-normal snowfall in much of New England, the above-normal snowfall area extended through all of New England and southward through New Jersey. We also correctly forecast above-normal snowfall in parts of the Tennessee Valley and Deep South but did not get the orientation exactly right or have it extending eastward enough. And while we were correct that parts of the area from the Intermountain region to the Heartland and northern Texas would have above-normal snowfall, the area we forecast for this was much larger than what actually occurred. Finally, we were correct that snowfall in Alaska would be below normal in the central portion of the state and above normal in the northern and most of the southern portions, but we were wrong in our forecast for above-normal snowfall in the Panhandle.

The table below shows how the actual average temperature differed from our forecast for November through March for one city in each region. On average, the actual winter temperatures differed from our forecasts by 1.09 degrees.

REGION/ CITY	Nov.-Mar. Temp Variations From Normal (degrees)		REGION/ CITY	Nov.-Mar. Temp Variations From Normal (degrees)	
	PREDICTED	ACTUAL		PREDICTED	ACTUAL
1. Concord, NH	0.8	0.7	10. Topeka, KS	0.2	0.5
2. Washington, DC	1.4	0.5	11. Oklahoma City, OK	–1.6	–0.7
3. Hagerstown, MD	1.1	1.2	12. Cheyenne, WY	1.2	2.0
4. Savannah, GA	0.6	1.7	13. Boise, ID	–1.6	–2.7
5. Miami, FL	1.0	1.6	14. Las Vegas, NV	–2.8	3.4
6. Milwaukee, WI	2.2	0.6	15. Eureka, CA	–0.2	–0.3
7. Louisville, KY	1.7	0.2	16. San Francisco, CA	–0.8	1.8
8. Little Rock, AR	–0.2	0.6	17. Kodiak, AK	3.4	3.3
9. Green Bay, WI	2.4	0.5	18. Lihue, HI	–0.4	–0.8

WEATHER REGIONS

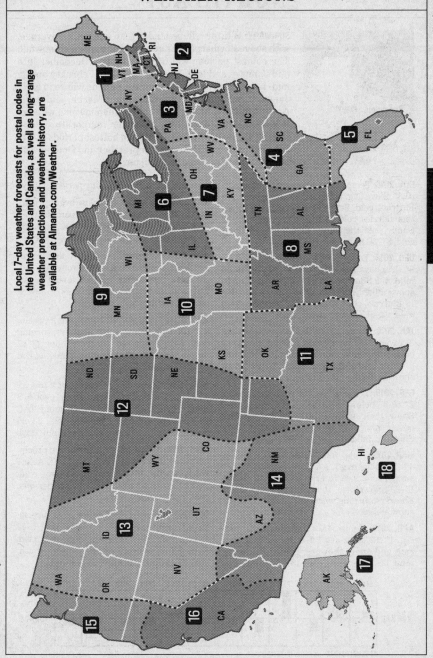

Local 7-day weather forecasts for postal codes in the United States and Canada, as well as long-range weather predictions and weather history, are available at Almanac.com/Weather.

WEATHER

NORTHEAST

SUMMARY: Winter will be milder than normal, on average, with above-normal precipitation and near-normal snowfall. The coldest periods will occur from late December into mid-January and late January into early February and in mid- to late February. The snowiest periods will be in early January, early to mid-February, mid-March, and early April. **April** and **May** will be rainier than normal, with below-normal temperatures. **Summer** temperatures and rainfall will be near normal, with the hottest periods in late July and early to mid-August. **September** and **October** will be slightly cooler and drier than normal.

NOV. 2018: Temp. 40° (1° above avg.); precip. 3" (0.5" above avg. north, 1.5" below south). 1–5 Flurries, cold. 6–14 Snow north, rain south, then flurries, cold. 15–18 Showers, mild. 19–23 Sunny, cold, then rainy, mild. 24–26 Flurries, cold. 27–30 Rain, then sunny, mild.

DEC. 2018: Temp. 30° (2° above avg.); precip. 6" (3" above avg.). 1–3 Rainy periods, quite mild. 4–9 Snowy periods, cold. 10–12 Rain to snow; mild, then cold. 13–15 Rainy, mild. 16–18 Flurries, cold. 19–23 Rainy periods, quite mild. 24–31 Snow showers, cold.

JAN. 2019: Temp. 21° (2° below avg.); precip. 3" (avg.). 1–4 Snowy, cold. 5–7 Flurries, very cold. 8–13 Snow showers, cold. 14–24 Rainy periods, turning very mild. 25–31 Snow showers, cold.

FEB. 2019: Temp. 27° (4° above avg.); precip. 2" (0.5" below avg.). 1–5 Sunny, cold. 6–9 Snow, then sunny, cold. 10–14 Snowy periods, turning mild. 15–20 Flurries, cold. 21–28 Showers, mild.

MAR. 2019: Temp. 32° (2° below avg.); precip. 4" (1" above avg.). 1–8 Snow showers, then sunny, cold. 9–12 Rain to snow, then colder. 13–22 Snowstorm, then flurries, cold. 23–29 Showers, turning warm. 30–31 Rain and wet snow, chilly.

APR. 2019: Temp. 45° (1° below avg.); precip. 4" (1" above avg.). 1–6 Snowstorm, then rain and snow showers; cold. 7–11 Sunny, mild. 12–17 Showers, cool. 18–23 Sunny, then

showers, warm. 24–30 Rainy periods, chilly.

MAY 2019: Temp. 54° (1° below avg.); precip. 3" (0.5" below avg.). 1–7 Rainy periods, cool. 8–10 Sunny, warm. 11–14 Showers, cool. 15–24 Rainy periods, cool. 25–31 Sunny, warm.

JUNE 2019: Temp. 67° (2° above avg.); precip. 4" (0.5" above avg.). 1–2 Sunny, hot. 3–6 Showers, turning cool. 7–15 A few t-storms, warm. 16–21 Showers, cool. 22–30 A few t-storms, warm.

JULY 2019: Temp. 69° (1° below avg.); precip. 3.5" (0.5" below avg.). 1–5 Showers, turning cool. 6–12 Scattered t-storms, cool. 13–17 Sunny, cool. 18–26 A few t-storms, warm. 27–31 T-storms, hot.

AUG. 2019: Temp. 65° (1° below avg.); precip. 4" (avg.). 1–4 T-storms, then sunny, cool. 5–9 Sunny, hot. 10–15 T-storms, then sunny, hot. 16–22 A few t-storms, turning cool. 23–26 Sunny, cool. 27–31 T-storms, then sunny, cool.

SEPT. 2019: Temp. 58° (1° below avg.); precip. 4" (avg.). 1–6 Showers, warm. 7–12 A few showers, cool. 13–18 Rain, then sunny, cold. 19–22 Showers, mild. 23–27 Rainy periods, cool. 28–30 Sunny, warm.

OCT. 2019: Temp. 47° (1° below avg.); precip. 2.5" (1" below avg.). 1–7 Showers, cool. 8–13 Sunny, chilly. 14–17 Showers, then sunny, cold. 18–21 Snow showers north, showers south; cold. 22–25 Rainy, mild. 26–31 Showers.

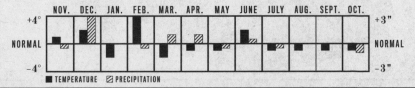

ATLANTIC CORRIDOR

SUMMARY: Winter temperatures will be much above normal, on average, with the coldest periods in early to mid-December, early and late January, and early February. Precipitation will be slightly above normal, with below-normal snowfall. The snowiest periods will occur in early December, late January, and mid-February. **April** and **May** will be slightly warmer and drier than normal. **Summer** will be rainier and cooler than normal, with the hottest periods in late June, early July, and early to mid-August. **September** and **October** will be warmer and drier than normal.

WEATHER

NOV. 2018: Temp. 51° (4° above avg.); precip. 1.5" (2" below avg.). 1–5 Rain, then sunny, cold. 6–9 Sunny, warm. 10–14 Showers, cool. 15–22 A few showers, mild. 23–26 Sunny, cool. 27–30 Showers, mild.

DEC. 2018: Temp. 40° (1° above avg.); precip. 6" (3" above avg.). 1–3 Rainy, mild. 4–7 Snow, then sunny, cold. 8–12 Rain to snow, then sunny, cold. 13–18 Rain to snow, then sunny, cold. 19–25 Rainy periods, mild. 26–31 Periods of rain and snow north, rain south.

JAN. 2019: Temp. 38° (avg. north, 6° above south); precip. 3.5" (avg.). 1–7 Snow north, rain south, then sunny, cold. 8–13 Snow showers, cold north; sunny, mild south. 14–24 Rainy periods, quite mild. 25–31 Rain to snow, then snow showers, cold.

FEB. 2019: Temp. 38° (4° above avg.); precip. 2" (1" below avg.). 1–8 Sunny, cold. 9–11 Snowy periods north, rain south. 12–16 Rainy, mild. 17–20 Snow, then sunny, cold. 21–28 Showers, quite mild.

MAR. 2019: Temp. 45° (1° above avg.); precip. 5" (1" above avg.). 1–8 Rain, then sunny, cool. 9–14 Rain, heavy at times. 15–21 Sunny, cool. 22–31 Rainy periods, turning warm.

APR. 2019: Temp. 53° (1° above avg.); precip. 3" (0.5" below avg.). 1–6 Rain, then sunny, cool. 7–13 Rain, then sunny, cool. 14–20 Showers, cool. 21–23 Sunny, warm. 24–30 Showers, cool.

MAY 2019: Temp. 62° (avg.); precip. 3" (avg.). 1–10 Scattered t-storms, turning hot. 11–15 Sunny, cool. 16–26 Scattered t-storms, cool. 27–31 Sunny.

JUNE 2019: Temp. 70° (1° below avg.); precip. 3" (0.5" below avg.). 1–8 Sunny; warm, then cool. 9–14 T-storms north, sunny south; warm. 15–24 Showers, cool. 25–30 Sunny, warm.

JULY 2019: Temp. 75° (1° below avg.); precip. 3" (1" below avg.). 1–6 Sunny; hot, then cool. 7–20 Scattered t-storms, cool. 21–25 Sunny, warm. 26–31 Scattered t-storms, warm.

AUG. 2019: Temp. 74° (avg.); precip. 7" (3" above avg.). 1–6 Sunny, cool. 7–15 Isolated t-storms, warm. 16–20 Sunny, cool. 21–31 T-storms, cool.

SEPT. 2019: Temp. 66° (1° below avg.); precip. 2.5" (1" below avg.). 1–5 Sunny, warm. 6–14 Scattered t-storms, mild. 15–21 Sunny, warm. 22–30 Rain, then sunny, cool.

OCT. 2019: Temp. 58° (2° above avg.): precip. 2.5" (1" below avg.). 1–5 Sunny, mild. 6–17 Heavy rain, then sunny, cool. 18–23 Showers, then sunny, warm. 24–31 Showers north, sunny south; mild.

SUMMARY: Winter will be warmer than normal, with above-normal precipitation and near- to below-normal snowfall. The coldest periods will be in mid- and late December, early and late January, and early and mid-February. The snowiest periods will be in mid-December, early January, and early February. **April** and **May** will be cooler and drier than normal. **Summer** will be cooler than normal, with the hottest periods in early and late June, early July, and early August. Rainfall will be below normal in the north and above normal in the south. **September** and **October** will be drier than normal, with near-normal temperatures.

NOV. 2018: Temp. 47° (3° above avg.); precip. 2.5" (1" below avg.). 1–5 Flurries, cold. 6–10 Showers, mild. 11–13 Sunny, cool. 14–21 Rainy periods, turning warm. 22–27 Sunny, mild. 28–30 Rain, then cold.

DEC. 2018: Temp. 35° (1° below avg.); precip. 5" (2" above avg.). 1–7 Rain, then flurries and sprinkles. 8–12 Snow, then sunny, cold. 13–17 Heavy rain to snow, then sunny, cold. 18–23 Rainy periods, mild. 24–27 Snowy periods north, rain south. 28–31 Flurries, cold.

JAN. 2019: Temp. 35° (2° above avg. north, 8° above south); precip. 3.5" (0.5" above avg.). 1–4 Snow north, rain south. 5–9 Sunny; cold, then mild. 10–12 Snow showers, cold north; sunny, mild south. 13–21 Rainy periods, mild. 22–25 Sunny, mild. 26–31 Snow north, rain south, then flurries, cold.

FEB. 2019: Temp. 33° (3° above avg.); precip. 1.5" (1" below avg.). 1–4 Snowy periods, cold. 5–6 Showers, mild. 7–11 Flurries, cold. 12–15 Rainy periods, mild. 16–20 Flurries cold. 21–28 Showers, turning warm.

MAR. 2019: Temp. 38° (2° below avg.); precip. 5" (2" above avg.). 1–8 Rain, then sunny, cold. 9–14 Rainy periods, cool. 15–21 Sunny, cool. 22–27 Snow north, rain south, then showers, warm. 28–31 T-storms, then sunny, cool.

APR. 2019: Temp. 49° (1° below avg.); precip. 1.5" (1" below avg.). 1–5 Rain and snow, then sunny, cool. 6–11 Showers, then sunny, cool.

12–19 Showers, cool. 20–22 Sunny, warm. 23–30 Showers, cool.

MAY 2019: Temp. 60° (avg.); precip. 3" (1" below avg.). 1–5 Showers, turning mild. 6–9 Sunny, warm. 10–14 T-storms, then sunny, cool. 15–17 Showers, warm. 18–31 Scattered t-storms, cool.

JUNE 2019: Temp. 66° (1° below avg.); precip. 3" (1" below avg.). 1–3 Sunny, hot. 4–12 Showers, then sunny, cool. 13–23 Sunny, warm, then a few t-storms, cool. 24–27 Sunny, hot. 28–30 Showers.

JULY 2019: Temp. 71° (2° below avg.); precip. 4" (1.5" below avg. north, 2" above south). 1–3 Sunny, hot. 4–6 T-storms, then sunny, cool. 7–10 T-storms, then sunny, cool. 11–15 T-storms, then sunny, cool. 16–31 A few t-storms, warm.

AUG. 2019: Temp. 70° (1° below avg.); precip. 5.5" (2" above avg.). 1–10 Scattered t-storms, warm. 11–17 Sunny, cool. 18–25 A few t-storms, warm. 26–31 T-storms, cool.

SEPT. 2019: Temp. 62° (2° below avg.); precip. 2.5" (1" below avg.). 1–4 Sunny north, t-storms south; warm. 5–10 T-storms, then sunny, cool. 11–19 T-storms, then sunny, cool. 20–22 T-storms, warm. 23–30 Sunny, cool.

OCT. 2019: Temp. 55° (2° above avg.); precip. 1" (2" below avg.). 1–7 Sunny, turning warm. 8–15 Rain, then flurries, cold. 16–22 Sunny, mild. 23–29 Showers, warm. 30–31 Sunny.

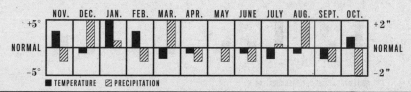

WEATHER

SUMMARY: Winter will be much warmer and slightly drier than normal, with below-normal snowfall. The coldest periods will be in mid-December, mid- and late January and mid- to late February. The best chances for snow will be in early to mid-December and mid-March. **April** and **May** will be warmer and rainier than normal. **Summer** will be cooler and rainier than normal, with the hottest periods in mid- to late May, early and late July, and mid-August. **September** and **October** will be drier than normal, with near-normal temperatures.

NOV. 2018: Temp. 59° (4° above avg.); precip. 2" (1" below avg.). 1–5 Rain, then sunny, cold. 6–8 Sunny, mild. 9–11 Showers, cool. 12–21 A few showers, warm. 22–25 Sunny, warm. 26–30 Showers, warm, then sunny, cool.

DEC. 2018: Temp. 49° (2° above avg.); precip. 5.5" (2" above avg.). 1–5 Rain, then sunny, cold. 6–9 Rainy, cool. 10–12 Rain and snow, then sunny, cold. 13–16 Rain, then sunny, cold. 17–31 Rainy periods, mild.

JAN. 2019: Temp. 50° (7° above avg.); precip. 3.5" (1" below avg.). 1–4 Showers, warm. 5–7 Sunny, cold. 8–13 Sunny, warm. 14–26 Rainy periods, warm. 27–29 Sunny, cold. 30–31 Rainy, mild.

FEB. 2019: Temp. 49° (3° above avg.); precip. 3" (1" below avg.). 1–4 Rain, then sunny, cold. 5–8 Sun, then rain; mild. 9–15 Rainy periods; cool, then mild. 16–21 Sunny, turning cold. 22–28 Sunny, warm.

MAR. 2019: Temp. 58° (3° above avg.); precip. 4.5" (avg.). 1–3 Sunny, warm. 4–11 Rain, then sunny, cool. 12–17 Rainy periods; warm, then cool. 18–21 Snow north, rain south, then sunny, cool. 22–27 Rain, then sunny, warm. 28–31 Rain, then sunny, cool.

APR. 2019: Temp. 63° (avg.); precip. 2" (1" below avg.). 1–4 Rain, then sunny, cool. 5–8 T-storms, warm. 9–14 Sunny, cool. 15–19 Showers, then sunny, cool. 20–24 Sunny, warm. 25–30 Rainy periods, turning cool.

MAY 2019: Temp. 72° (1° above avg.); precip. 6.5" (3" above avg.). 1–5 Rain and heavy t-storms. 6–11 Sunny, turning warm. 12–18 A few t-storms, warm. 19–25 Scattered t-storms, turning hot. 26–31 Sunny, north, t-storms south; cool.

JUNE 2019: Temp. 76° (2° below avg.); precip. 5" (0.5" above avg.). 1–9 Scattered t-storms, turning cool. 10–12 Sunny, cool. 13–15 Sunny, warm. 16–22 Rain, some heavy; cool. 23–25 Sunny, warm. 26–30 T-storms, cool.

JULY 2019: Temp. 80° (2° below avg.); precip. 5.5" (1" above avg.). 1–4 Sunny, warm. 5–9 T-storms, then sunny, cool. 10–17 Scattered t-storms, cool. 18–31 A few t-storms, warm.

AUG. 2019: Temp. 79° (1° below avg.); precip. 6" (1" above avg.). 1–3 T-storms, humid. 4–9 Scattered t-storms, cool. 10–24 Sunny inland, t-storms coast; turning hot. 25–31 T-storms, turning cool.

SEPT. 2019: Temp. 72° (2° below avg.); precip. 1.5" (3" below avg.). 1–5 Sunny, turning warm. 6–13 Scattered t-storms, cool. 14–19 T-storms, then sunny, cool. 20–21 Sunny, warm. 22–30 T-storms, then sunny, chilly.

OCT. 2019: Temp. 66° (2° above avg.); precip. 2" (2" below avg.). 1–7 Sunny, turning warm. 8–11 Rainy, mild. 12–16 Sunny, cold. 17–28 Sunny, turning warm. 29–31 Rain, then cool.

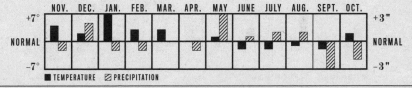

FLORIDA

Jacksonville

Orlando

Tampa

Miami

SUMMARY: Winter will be milder and drier than normal, with the coldest temperatures in early and mid-December and early and mid-February. **April** and **May** will be a bit hotter and rainier than normal. **Summer** will be slightly cooler as well as rainier than normal, with the hottest periods in mid-June, mid-July, and mid- to late August. Watch for tropical storm threats in mid- to late June, early to mid- and mid- to late September, and early October. Overall, **September** and **October** will be warmer and drier than normal.

NOV. 2018: Temp. 72° (3° above avg.); precip. 0.5" (2" below avg.). 1–6 Showers, then sunny, cool. 7–10 Sunny, warm. 11–20 Isolated showers, warm. 21–25 T-storms, then sunny, cool. 26–30 Showers, cool.

DEC. 2018: Temp. 63° (avg.); precip. 3.5" (1" above avg.). 1–5 Rain, then sunny, cold. 6–9 Showers, mild. 10–12 Sunny, cold. 13–16 Showers, then sunny, cold. 17–24 Showers, then sunny, warm. 25–31 Scattered showers, warm.

JAN. 2019: Temp. 66° (6° above avg.); precip. 1.5" (1" below avg.). 1–4 Sunny, warm. 5–8 Showers, mild. 9–27 Isolated showers, warm. 28–31 Showers, mild.

FEB. 2019: Temp. 61° (avg.); precip. 0.5" (2" below avg.). 1–6 Sunny, cool. 7–15 Scattered showers, mild. 16–20 Sunny, chilly. 21–28 Sunny, turning warm.

MAR. 2019: Temp. 70° (3° above avg.); precip. 3" (avg.). 1–4 Sunny, warm. 5–12 Scattered t-storms, cool. 13–22 Scattered t-storms north; sunny, warm south. 23–27 Sunny, warm. 28–31 T-storms, then sunny, cool.

APR. 2019: Temp. 71° (avg.); precip. 1.5" (1" below avg.). 1–4 Sunny, cool. 5–10 Scattered t-storms, warm. 11–13 Sunny, cool. 14–22 T-storms, then sunny, cool. 23–30 Scattered t-storms, warm.

MAY 2019: Temp. 78° (1° above avg.); precip. 6" (2" above avg.). 1–3 Sunny, warm. 4–19 Scattered t-storms, warm. 20–24 Sunny, warm. 25–31 T-storms, some heavy.

JUNE 2019: Temp. 81° (1° below avg.); precip. 5.5" (1" below avg.). 1–9 Several t-storms, warm. 10–13 Sunny, cool. 14–16 T-storms, hot. 17–21 Tropical storm threat. 22–30 A few t-storms, cool.

JULY 2019: Temp. 82° (1° below avg.); precip. 9.5" (3" above avg.). 1–12 Sunny north, t-storms south; warm. 13–18 Scattered t-storms, warm. 19–31 Daily t-storms, seasonable.

AUG. 2019: Temp. 83° (1° above avg.); precip. 9.5" (2" above avg.). 1–5 A few t-storms, humid. 6–16 Daily t-storms, some heavy; warm. 17–27 A few t-storms, hot. 28–31 Heavy t-storms, cool.

SEPT. 2019: Temp. 81° (1° above avg.); precip. 4.5" (1" below avg.). 1–5 T-storms, warm. 6–9 Tropical storm threat. 10–17 T-storms, humid. 18–22 Tropical storm threat. 23–27 Sunny, cool north; showers south. 28–30 Sunny, cool.

OCT. 2019: Temp. 75° (avg.); precip. 2" (2" below avg.). 1–4 Tropical storm threat. 5–18 Sunny, turning cool. 19–31 Scattered showers, warm.

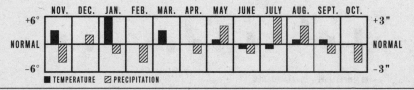

SUMMARY: Winter will be warmer and rainier than normal, with near-normal snowfall. The coldest periods will be in mid- and late December, early and late January, and early February. The snowiest periods will be in early December, early and late January, early February, and mid-March. **April** and **May** will be slightly warmer than normal, with near-normal precipitation. **Summer** will be cooler and slightly drier than normal. The hottest periods will be in late May, late June, early July, and mid-August. **September** and **October** will be drier than normal, with near-normal temperatures.

NOV. 2018: Temp. 47° (6° above avg.); precip. 3" (0.5" above avg.). 1–3 Snow showers, cold. 4–7 Sunny, warm. 8–13 Periods of rain and snow east, showers west. 14–23 Rainy periods, mild. 24–25 Sunny, cool. 26–28 Rainy, mild. 29–30 Flurries.

DEC. 2018: Temp. 29° (3° below avg.); precip. 3.5" (0.5" above avg.). 1–14 Snowy periods, cold. 15–17 Flurries, cold. 18–22 Rainy periods, mild. 23–31 Snow showers, cold.

JAN. 2019: Temp. 33° (6° above avg.); precip. 3.5" (avg. east, 2" above west). 1–6 Lake snows, cold. 7–10 Flurries east; sunny, mild west. 11–24 Rainy periods, mild. 25–31 Snowy periods, cold.

FEB. 2019: Temp. 32° (5° above avg.); precip. 2.5" (0.5" above avg.). 1–4 Lake snows, cold. 5–11 Rain and snow showers east, sprinkles west. 12–15 Rainy, mild. 16–19 Snow showers, cold. 20–28 Rainy periods, mild.

MAR. 2019: Temp. 36° (2° below avg.); precip. 4" (1" above avg.). 1–2 Rainy, mild. 3–7 Sunny, cold. 8–18 Snowy periods, cold. 19–24 Rain and snow showers, cool. 25–28 Showers, warm. 29–31 Rain to snow.

APR. 2019: Temp. 50° (2° above avg.); precip. 2.5" (1" below avg.). 1–7 Snow, then showers, turning warm. 8–15 A few showers; cool, then warm. 16–19 Showers, then sunny, cool. 20–23 T-storms, warm. 24–30 Showers, cool.

MAY 2019: Temp. 57° (1° below avg.); precip. 4.5" (1" above avg.). 1–5 Showers, cool. 6–8 Sunny, warm. 9–13 T-storms, then sunny, cool. 14–20 T-storms, then sunny, cool. 21–31 T-storms, then sunny, turning hot.

JUNE 2019: Temp. 65° (1° below avg.); precip. 3.5" (avg.). 1–6 Scattered t-storms, turning cool. 7–15 Showers, cool. 16–20 Sunny, cool. 21–27 Scattered t-storms, turning hot. 28–30 Sunny.

JULY 2019: Temp. 69.5° (1° below avg.); precip. 3" (0.5" below avg.). 1–3 Sunny, hot. 4–12 Isolated t-storms, warm. 13–18 Scattered t-storms, cool. 19–31 A few t-storms, warm.

AUG. 2019: Temp. 68° (1° below avg.); precip. 3.5" (0.5" below avg.). 1–10 Scattered t-storms, warm. 11–16 Sunny, hot. 17–24 Scattered t-storms, warm. 25–31 T-storms, then sunny, cool.

SEPT. 2019: Temp. 60° (2° below avg.); precip. 3.5" (1" below avg.). 1–4 Sunny, warm. 5–9 T-storms, then sunny, cool. 10–13 Rainy, mild. 14–17 Sunny, cold. 18–22 Showers, warm. 23–27 Sunny, cool. 28–30 Showers.

OCT. 2019: Temp. 54° (2° above avg.); precip. 2" (0.5" below avg.). 1–3 Sunny, cool. 4–9 Showers, mild. 10–14 Flurries, cold. 15–25 A few showers, turning warm. 26–31 Showers, cool.

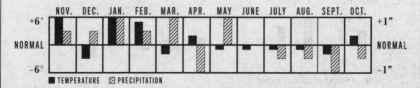

OHIO VALLEY

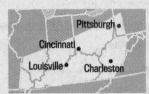

WEATHER

SUMMARY: Winter will be warmer than normal, with above-normal precipitation and below-normal snowfall. The coldest periods will be in mid- and late December, late January, and early February. The snowiest periods will be in early and mid-December and early February. **April** and **May** will be warmer than normal, with near-normal rainfall. **Summer** will be cooler and rainier than normal, with the hottest periods in late June, early and mid-July, and mid-August. **September** and **October** will be slightly drier than normal, with near-normal temperatures.

NOV. 2018: Temp. 50° (4° above avg.); precip. 4" (0.5" below avg. east, 2" above west). 1–4 Rain to snow, cold. 5–7 Sunny, turning warm. 8–16 Scattered showers, mild. 17–20 Rainy, mild. 21–26 Sunny; cool, then mild. 27–30 Rain, then flurries, cold.

DEC. 2018: Temp. 35° (2° below avg.); precip. 3" (avg.). 1–5 Snow, then sunny, cold. 6–12 Rain to snow, then flurries, cold. 13–15 Rain to snow. 16–22 Rainy periods, mild. 23–31 Snow showers, cold.

JAN. 2019: Temp. 40° (7° above avg.); precip. 4" (1" above avg.). 1–6 Snow north, rain south, then flurries, cold. 7–10 Sunny, mild. 11–16 Rainy, quite mild. 17–26 Showers, mild. 27–29 Snow showers, cold. 30–31 Rainy, mild.

FEB. 2019: Temp. 39° (5° above avg.); precip. 2" (1" below avg.). 1–4 Snowy periods, cold. 5–11 Sunny, mild. 12–15 Rainy, mild. 16–20 Snow showers, cold. 21–28 Rainy periods, quite mild.

MAR. 2019: Temp. 45° (avg.); precip. 5.5" (1.5" above avg.). 1–7 Rain to snow, then sunny, cold. 8–18 Rain and snow showers, chilly. 19–22 Sunny, mild. 23–28 Rainy periods, turning warm. 29–31 Rain and wet snow.

APR. 2019: Temp. 55° (avg.); precip. 2.5" (1" below avg.). 1–4 Rain and snow, then sunny, cool. 5–7 Showers, warm. 8–12 Sunny, cool. 13–18 T-storms, then sunny, cool. 19–22 Sunny, warm. 23–30 A few showers, cool.

MAY 2019: Temp. 65° (2° above avg.); precip. 4.5" (1" above avg.). 1–5 Rainy periods, cool. 6–9 Sunny, warm. 10–14 T-storms, then sunny, warm. 15–21 T-storms, then sunny, cool. 22–31 T-storms, then sunny, cool.

JUNE 2019: Temp. 71° (1° below avg.); precip. 5.5" (1.5" above avg.). 1–7 T-storms, then sunny, cool. 8–11 Showers, cool. 12–16 A few t-storms, warm. 17–23 Showers, cool. 24–30 Scattered t-storms, warm.

JULY 2019: Temp. 74° (1° below avg.); precip. 3" (1" below avg.). 1–2 Sunny, hot. 3–6 T-storms, then sunny, cool. 7–12 T-storms, then sunny, warm. 13–20 Isolated t-storms, warm. 21–26 T-storms, then sunny, warm. 27–31 T-storms, then sunny, cool.

AUG. 2019: Temp. 73° (avg.); precip. 6" (2" above avg.). 1–11 Scattered t-storms, warm. 12–17 Sunny, hot. 18–25 T-storms, warm. 26–31 Rain, then sunny, cool.

SEPT. 2019: Temp. 64° (3° below avg.); precip. 2" (1" below avg.). 1–4 Sunny, warm. 5–9 Showers, then sunny, cool. 10–13 T-storms, cool. 14–19 Sunny, chilly. 20–22 Rainy, warm. 23–30 Sunny, cool.

OCT. 2019: Temp. 60° (3° above avg.); precip. 2.5" (avg.). 1–7 Sunny, turning warm. 8–15 Rain, then sunny, cold. 16–22 Showers, then sunny, warm. 23–28 A few t-storms, warm. 29–31 Sunny, cool.

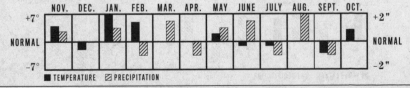

DEEP SOUTH

SUMMARY: Winter will be warmer than normal, on average, with the coldest periods in late November, the first half of December, early January, and early February. Rainfall will be above normal in the north and near normal in the south, with the best chance for snowfall in mid- and late December across the north. **April** and **May** will be warmer and rainier than normal. **Summer** will be cooler and rainier than normal, with the hottest periods in mid-June, mid-July, and early August. Watch for a hurricane threat in early September. Overall, **September** and **October** will be slightly cooler and drier than normal.

NOV. 2018: Temp. 60° (5° above avg.); precip. 6.5" (3" above avg. north, avg. south). 1–5 Rain, then sunny, cold. 6–7 Sunny, warm. 8–10 T-storms, then sunny, cool. 11–20 Scattered t-storms, some heavy; warm. 21–25 Sunny; cool, then warm. 26–30 T-storms, then sunny, cold.

DEC. 2018: Temp. 46° (2° below avg.); precip. 4" (1" below avg.). 1–6 Sunny; cold, then mild. 7–11 Showers, then sunny, cold. 12–15 Rain to snow, then sunny, cold. 16–19 Rainy, mild. 20–22 Sunny, cool. 23–27 Rain to snow north, rain south. 28–31 Showers, mild.

JAN. 2019: Temp. 52° (7° above avg.); precip. 9" (4" above avg.). 1–3 Rainy, mild. 4–6 Sunny, cold. 7–15 Showers, warm. 16–21 Rainy, mild. 22–24 Sunny, mild. 25–31 Rainy periods, turning cooler.

FEB. 2019: Temp. 50° (3° above avg.); precip. 3" (2" below avg.). 1–4 Sunny, cold. 5–14 Rainy periods, mild. 15–20 Sunny, cold. 21–28 Showers north, sunny south; mild.

MAR. 2019: Temp. 60° (4° above avg.); precip. 5" (1" below avg.). 1–3 Sunny, warm. 4–7 T-storms, then sunny, cool. 8–19 A few t-storms; warm, then cool. 20–24 Sunny, turning warm. 25–31 T-storms, then sunny, cool.

APR. 2019: Temp. 63° (avg.); precip. 5.5" (1" above avg.). 1–4 T-storms, then sunny, cool. 5–9 Rainy periods. 10–13 Sunny, nice. 14–22 T-storms, then sunny, warm. 23–27 T-storms

north, sunny south. 28–30 T-storms, cool.

MAY 2019: Temp. 73° (2° above avg.); precip. 8" (3" above avg.). 1–6 T-storms, then sunny, cool. 7–18 Scattered t-storms, warm. 19–23 Sunny, warm. 24–27 T-storms, then sunny, warm. 28–31 A few t-storms, warm.

JUNE 2019: Temp. 76° (2° below avg.); precip. 3" (2" below avg.). 1–10 Scattered t-storms, turning cool. 11–15 Sunny, turning hot. 16–23 T-storms, then sunny, cool. 24–30 Scattered t-storms, warm.

JULY 2019: Temp. 80° (1° below avg.); precip. 5.5" (1" above avg.). 1–6 Scattered t-storms, warm. 7–15 A few t-storms, turning hot. 16–22 Scattered t-storms, warm. 23–26 Sunny, cool. 27–31 T-storms, then sunny, cool.

AUG. 2019: Temp. 79° (1° below avg.); precip. 7.5" (3" above avg.). 1–10 Scattered t-storms, warm. 11–18 Sunny, warm. 19–26 Scattered t-storms, warm. 27–31 Showers, cool.

SEPT. 2019: Temp. 74° (2° below avg.); precip. 4.5" (avg.). 1–4 Hurricane threat. 5–12 Isolated t-storms, warm. 13–17 T-storms, then sunny, cool. 18–30 Rain, then sunny, chilly.

OCT. 2019: Temp. 66° (1° above avg.); precip. 2.5" (0.5" below avg.). 1–6 Sunny, turning warm. 7–16 Rain, then sunny, cool. 17–26 Scattered t-storms, turning, warm. 27–31 T-storms, then sunny, cool.

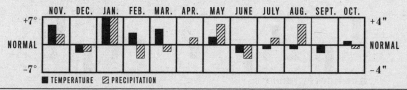

UPPER MIDWEST

SUMMARY: Winter will be slightly milder and drier than normal, with snowfall near to below normal. The coldest periods will be in early to mid-December, from late December into January, and from late January into February. The snowiest periods will be in mid- and late November, early and mid-December, and early and late March. **April** and **May** will be slightly cooler and rainier than normal. **Summer** will be slightly cooler than normal, with the hottest periods in late June, late July, and early to mid-August. Rainfall will be above normal in the east and below normal in the west. **September** and **October** will be slightly rainier than normal, with near-normal temperatures.

NOV. 2018: Temp. 33° (4° above avg.); precip. 2" (avg.). 1–3 Snow showers, cold. 4–11 Sunny, mild. 12–26 Snow, then sunny, mild. 27–30 Snow, then flurries, cold.

DEC. 2018: Temp. 12° (4° below avg.); precip. 1" (avg.). 1–2 Sunny, mild. 3–7 Snowy periods, cold. 8–14 Snow showers, very cold. 15–21 Snowy periods, mild. 22–31 Sunny, very cold.

JAN. 2019: Temp. 15° (2° above avg.); precip. 0.5" (0.5" below avg.). 1–6 Snow showers, very cold. 7–12 Snow, then sunny, mild. 13–22 Snow showers, mild. 23–31 Snow showers, cold.

FEB. 2019: Temp. 15° (3° above avg.); precip. 0.5" (0.5" below avg.). 1–3 Flurries, cold. 4–8 Snowy periods, cold. 9–14 Flurries east, sunny, mild. 15–18 Snow squalls east, sunny west; cold. 19–21 Sunny, mild. 22–28 Showers, mild.

MAR. 2019: Temp. 24° (4° below avg.); precip. 1" (0.5" below avg.). 1–5 Sunny, mild. 6–19 Snow, then flurries, very cold. 20–28 Snowy periods, cold. 29–31 Sunny, cool.

APR. 2019: Temp. 43° (1° above avg.); precip. 2" (avg.). 1–6 Sunny, then showers, mild. 7–12 Sunny, cool. 13–17 Rain, then sunny, cool. 18–25 Sunny, mild east; rain, then sunny, cool west. 26–30 Showers, cool.

MAY 2019: Temp. 53° (2° below avg.); precip. 4"

(1" above avg.). 1–8 Rainy periods, cool. 9–13 Sunny, turning warm. 14–20 T-storms, then sunny, cool. 21–26 Showers, cool. 27–31 Scattered t-storms, warm.

JUNE 2019: Temp. 63° (avg.); precip. 4" (2" above avg. east, 2" below west). 1–10 Rainy periods, cool. 11–21 Sunny, turning warm. 22–27 Scattered t-storms. 28–30 Sunny, hot.

JULY 2019: Temp. 69° (1° above avg.); precip. 4.5" (1" above avg.). 1–7 Scattered t-storms, warm. 8–17 A few t-storms, warm. 18–24 Sunny, cool. 25–31 Rain, then sunny, mild.

AUG. 2019: Temp. 64° (2° below avg.); precip. 2.5" (1" below avg.). 1–7 T-storms, then sunny, cool. 8–13 Scattered t-storms, turning hot. 14–24 Isolated t-storms, cool. 25–31 Sunny, cool.

SEPT. 2019: Temp. 54° (4° below avg.); precip. 4" (1" above avg.). 1–5 A few t-storms, cool. 6–12 Showers, cool east; sunny, warm west. 13–17 Showers, chilly. 18–20 Sunny, warm. 21–25 Rain to snow, then sunny, cold. 26–30 Rain and snow showers.

OCT. 2019: Temp. 51° (4° above avg.); precip. 2" (0.5" below avg.). 1–3 Sunny, mild. 4–7 Rain, then sunny, cold. 8–15 Rain and snow showers east, sunny west; cool. 16–21 Sunny, turning warm. 22–24 Rainy, mild. 25–31 Snow showers, cold.

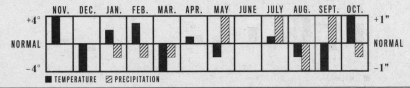

SUMMARY: Winter will be milder than normal, with above-normal precipitation. The coldest periods will be in mid- and late December and early January. Snowfall will be below normal in the north and above normal in central and southern areas, with the snowiest periods in late November, mid-December, early January, and mid-March. **April** and **May** will be warmer and rainier than normal. **Summer** will be cooler than normal, with the hottest periods in late June and the first half of July. Rainfall will be below normal in the north and above normal in the south. **September** and **October** will bring near-normal temperatures and precipitation.

WEATHER

NOV. 2018: Temp. 48° (5° above avg.); precip. 4.5" (2" above avg.). 1–6 Sunny; cold, then warm. 7–20 Rainy periods mild. 21–25 Sunny, turning warm. 26–30 Heavy rain to snow, then sunny, cold.

DEC. 2018: Temp. 27° (5° below avg.); precip. 1.5" (avg.). 1–4 Snow showers, cold. 5–11 Rain to snow, then flurries, cold. 12–15 Snowstorm, then sunny, frigid. 16–18 Rainy, mild. 19–22 Rain and snow showers. 23–31 Snowstorm, then flurries, frigid.

JAN. 2019: Temp. 34° (5° above avg.); precip. 1.5" (0.5" above avg.). 1–6 Snowy periods, cold. 7–11 Sunny, turning warm. 12–21 Rainy periods, mild. 22–24 Sunny, mild. 25–31 Snow showers, cold north; rain to snow south.

FEB. 2019: Temp. 38° (7° above avg.); precip. 1.5" (avg.). 1–6 Flurries, then sunny, mild. 7–13 Rain arriving, mild. 14–18 Rain to snow, then sunny, cold. 19–24 Sunny, turning warm. 25–28 Showers, mild.

MAR. 2019: Temp. 43° (1° below avg.); precip. 3" (0.5" above avg.). 1–4 Rainy periods, mild. 5–14 Rain and snow showers, cool. 15–17 Snowy, cold. 18–20 Sunny, mild. 21–26 Rain, then sunny, warm. 27–31 Rain, then sunny, cool.

APR. 2019: Temp. 56° (2° above avg.); precip. 4" (2" above avg. north, 1" below south). 1–6 Rainy periods, mild. 7–17 Showers, then sunny, cool. 18–22 Scattered t-storms, warm. 23–30 Rainy periods, cool.

MAY 2019: Temp. 65° (1° above avg.); precip. 6.5" (2" above avg.). 1–8 Rainy periods, cool. 9–15 A few t-storms, warm. 16–27 Rainy periods, then sunny, cool. 28–31 T-storms, warm.

JUNE 2019: Temp. 70° (2° below avg.); precip. 4.5" (avg.). 1–7 T-storms, cool. 8–11 Sunny, cool. 12–15 T-storms, warm. 16–22 Sunny, cool. 23–27 Scattered t-storms, hot. 28–30 Sunny, warm.

JULY 2019: Temp. 76° (1° below avg.); precip. 2" (2" below avg.). 1–6 Sunny, hot. 7–15 Scattered t-storms, hot. 16–27 A few t-storms, cool. 28–31 Sunny, cool.

AUG. 2019: Temp. 72° (3° below avg.); precip. 4.5" (1" below avg. north, 3" above south). 1–10 Scattered t-storms, warm. 11–17 Sunny, warm. 18–26 Rainy periods, cool. 27–31 Sunny, cool.

SEPT. 2019: Temp. 64° (3° below avg.); precip. 2.5" (1" below avg.). 1–7 Rainy periods, cool. 8–12 Sunny, warm. 13–26 Isolated t-storms, cool. 27–30 Showers, cool.

OCT. 2019: Temp. 59° (3° above avg.); precip. 4" (1" above avg.). 1–3 Sunny, cool. 4–13 Rain, then sunny, cool. 14–18 Sunny, warm. 19–26 Rainy periods, mild. 27–31 Rainy, cool.

SUMMARY: Winter will be milder and drier than normal, with below-normal snowfall. The coldest periods will be in late December, late January, and mid-February, with the best chances for snow in mid- and late December, early January, and mid-February. **April** and **May** will be warmer and slightly rainier than normal. **Summer** will be cooler and rainier than normal, with the hottest periods in mid-June and early and mid-July. Watch for a tropical storm threat in mid- to late August and a hurricane threat in early September. Otherwise, **September** and **October** will be slightly cooler and rainier than normal.

NOV. 2018: Temp. 63° (6° above avg.); precip. 2.5" (0.5" below avg.). 1–4 Rain, then sunny, cool. 5–8 Sunny, warm. 9–15 Rain, then sunny, warm. 16–25 Rain, then sunny, mild. 26–30 Rain, then sunny, cool.

DEC. 2018: Temp. 51° (2° below avg.); precip. 1.5" (1" below avg.). 1–3 Sunny, cool. 4–11 Rain, then sunny, mild. 12–16 Rain, snow north, then sunny, mild. 17–20 Showers, cool. 21–23 Sunny, mild. 24–31 Rain to snow, then sunny, cold north, showers south.

JAN. 2019: Temp. 56° (6° above avg.); precip. 1.5" (0.5" below avg.). 1–5 Snow showers north; rainy, mild south. 6–10 Sunny, turning warm. 11–16 Rainy periods, mild. 17–20 Sunny north, rainy south; mild. 21–26 Sunny, mild. 27–31 Rain, then sunny, cold.

FEB. 2019: Temp. 56° (6° above avg.); precip. 1" (1" below avg.). 1–6 Sunny, turning warm. 7–13 Rainy periods, mild. 14–19 Rain to snow, then sunny, cold. 20–28 Sunny, turning warm.

MAR. 2019: Temp. 63° (4° above avg.); precip. 1.5" (1" below avg.). 1–9 Rain, then sunny, cooler. 10–13 Sunny, warm. 14–19 Rain, then sunny, cool. 20–26 Sunny, warm. 27–31 T-storms, then sunny, cool.

APR. 2019: Temp. 68° (2° above avg.); precip. 4" (1" above avg.). 1–9 Rainy periods, cool. 10–21 Rain, then sunny, warm. 22–24 Rainy, cool north; sunny, warm south. 25–30 Sunny

north, scattered t-storms south.

MAY 2019: Temp. 76° (3° above avg.); precip. 4.5" (0.5" below avg.). 1–12 Isolated t-storms, very warm. 13–22 A few t-storms north, sunny south; hot. 23–31 Scattered t-storms; cool north, warm south.

JUNE 2019: Temp. 77° (2° below avg.); precip. 3" (1" below avg.). 1–4 T-storms, warm. 5–10 Scattered t-storms, cool. 11–14 Sunny, hot. 15–22 Sunny, warm. 23–30 Scattered t-storms, warm.

JULY 2019: Temp. 79° (2° below avg.); precip. 5" (2" above avg.). 1–3 Sunny, hot. 4–10 Sunny, hot north; a few t-storms, warm south. 11–18 Sunny, hot. 19–31 Scattered t-storms north, sunny south; turning cool.

AUG. 2019: Temp. 78° (3° below avg.); precip. 4.5" (2" above avg.). 1–7 A few t-storms, cool north; sunny, hot south. 8–14 Sunny, warm. 15–19 Scattered t-storms, cool. 20–25 Tropical storm threat. 26–31 Sunny, cool.

SEPT. 2019: Temp. 73° (3° below avg.); precip. 3.5" (avg.). 1–2 Sunny, cool. 3–6 Hurricane threat. 7–18 Rainy periods; cool north, warm south. 19–25 Sunny, cool. 26–30 Showers, cool.

OCT. 2019: Temp. 69° (2° above avg.); precip. 6" (2" above avg.). 1–5 Sunny, warm. 6–10 Rain, then sunny, cool. 11–22 A few t-storms, warm. 23–27 Heavy t-storms, warm. 28–31 Showers, cool.

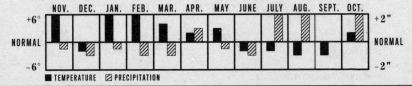

HIGH PLAINS

SUMMARY: Winter will be warmer than normal, with slightly below-normal precipitation. The coldest periods will be in late November, mid- and late December, early and late January, and mid-February. Snowfall will be below normal in the east and above normal in the west, with the snowiest periods in mid- and late December, late January, and late March. **April** and **May** will be warmer and slightly rainier than normal. **Summer** will be hotter and drier than normal, with the hottest periods in mid- and late June, mid-July, and early to mid-August. **September** and **October** will have near-normal temperatures and precipitation.

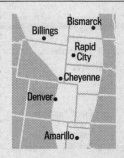

NOV. 2018: Temp. 40° (4° above avg.); precip. 0.5" (0.5" below avg.). 1–2 Flurries, cold. 3–9 Sunny, warm. 10–13 Rain to snow, then sunny, cold. 14–24 Sunny, turning mild. 25–30 Snow showers, then sunny, cold.

DEC. 2018: Temp. 28° (3° below avg.); precip. 1" (0.5" above avg.). 1–4 Sunny, mild. 5–9 Snowy, cold north; sunny, mild south. 10–13 Snowy periods, cold. 14–20 Rain and snow showers, mild. 21–31 Snowy periods, frigid.

JAN. 2019: Temp. 30° (2° above avg.); precip. 0.5" (avg.). 1–4 Snow showers, frigid. 5–12 Sunny, turning warm. 13–22 Snow, then flurries, mild. 23–31 Snowy periods, turning cold.

FEB. 2019: Temp. 36° (8° above avg.); precip. 0.5" (avg.). 1–12 A few showers and flurries, mild. 13–17 Flurries, cold. 18–23 Sunny, mild. 24–28 Snow showers north, sunny south.

MAR. 2019: Temp. 38° (1° below avg.); precip. 0.5" (0.5" below avg.). 1–5 Showers, then sunny, mild. 6–16 Rain and snow showers, turning cold. 17–24 Flurries north; sunny, warm south. 25–31 Snow, then sunny, cool.

APR. 2019: Temp. 52° (4° above avg.); precip. 2.5" (0.5" above avg.). 1–6 Rain and snow north, sunny south; cool. 7–11 Sunny, warm. 12–19 A few showers, warm. 20–24 Showers, cool. 25–30 Sunny, turning warm.

MAY 2019: Temp. 56° (2° below avg.); precip. 2.5" (avg.). 1–14 Rainy periods, quite cool north; sunny, hot south. 15–20 Scattered t-storms, warm. 21–24 Rainy, cool north; sunny, hot south. 25–31 Rainy periods, cool.

JUNE 2019: Temp. 70° (3° above avg.); precip. 1.5" (1" below avg.). 1–4 Showers, cool. 5–13 Scattered showers, turning hot. 14–24 Sunny, turning hot. 25–30 Showers, then sunny, hot.

JULY 2019: Temp. 75° (3° above avg.); precip. 1" (1" below avg.) 1–5 T-storms, warm. 6–18 Isolated t-storms, hot. 19–31 A few showers, turning cool.

AUG. 2019: Temp. 68° (3° below avg.); precip. 2.5" (0.5" above avg.). 1–7 A few t-storms, cool. 8–12 Sunny, turning hot. 13–20 Scattered t-storms; cool, then warm. 21–27 Showers, cool. 28–31 Sunny, cool.

SEPT. 2019: Temp. 58° (3° below avg.); precip. 1" (0.5" below avg.). 1–6 A few showers, chilly. 7–11 Sunny, warm. 12–18 Sunny north; rainy, cool south. 19–24 Rain, then sunny, cold. 25–30 Rain and snow showers.

OCT. 2019: Temp. 52° (3° above avg.); precip. 1.5" (0.5" above avg.). 1–3 Sunny, mild. 4–7 Showers, cool. 8–14 Sunny, mild. 15–22 Sunny, mild north; showers south. 23–25 Rain to snow. 26–31 Sunny, turning mild.

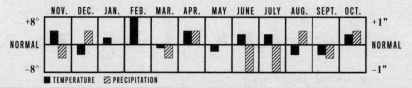

INTERMOUNTAIN

Spokane
Pendleton
Boise
Reno
Salt Lake City
Grand Junction
Flagstaff

SUMMARY: Winter temperatures and precipitation will be above normal, on average, with the coldest periods in late December, early January, and early February. Snowfall will be above normal in the north and below normal in the south, with the snowiest periods in late November, late December, early and late January, mid- to late February, and early March. **April** and **May** will have temperatures below normal in the north and above normal in the south and will be slightly drier than normal. **Summer** will be hotter and slightly drier than normal, with the hottest periods in mid- and late June and mid- to late July. **September** and **October** will be warmer than normal, with near-normal precipitation.

NOV. 2018: Temp. 43° (3° above avg.); precip. 2.5" (1" above avg.). 1–9 Rainy north, sunny south; mild. 10–15 Rain and snow, cold. 16–20 Showers, cool. 21–24 Rainy, mild. 25–30 Rain and snow north; snow, then sunny south.

DEC. 2018: Temp. 34° (1° above avg.); precip. 2" (0.5" above avg.). 1–3 Sunny, mild. 4–14 Rainy north, sunny south; mild. 15–22 Rain and snow north, sunny south; mild. 23–31 Snow showers, frigid north; snowy periods, cold south.

JAN. 2019: Temp. 33.5° (4° above avg. north, 1° below south); precip. 1.5" (1" above avg. north, 0.5" below south). 1–4 Flurries, frigid north; snowstorm south. 5–9 Rainy north, sunny south; mild. 10–22 Rain and snow showers; mild north, turning cold south. 23–27 Snowstorm, then sunny, mild north; sunny, cold south. 28–31 Sunny, mild north; snowstorm central; sunny, cold south.

FEB. 2019: Temp. 35° (1° above avg.); precip. 1.5" (avg.). 1–5 Sunny, cold. 6–15 Periods of rain and snow, cold. 16–19 Sunny, mild. 20–24 Snowstorm north, sunny south. 25–28 Rain and snow showers, cold.

MAR. 2019: Temp. 45.5° (avg. north, 5° above south); precip. 2" (0.5" above avg.). 1–3 Sunny, mild north, snow south. 4–11 Rain and snow showers north; sunny, warm south. 12–16 Sunny north, showers south. 17–23 Showers north; sunny, mild south. 24–29 Rainy north; rain and snow showers south. 30–31 Sunny.

APR. 2019: Temp. 51° (2° above avg.); precip. 0.5" (0.5" below avg.). 1–6 Rain and snow show-ers, chilly. 7–10 Sunny, cool. 11–22 A few showers, warm. 23–30 Sunny; cool, then warm.

MAY 2019: Temp. 57.5° (3° below avg. north, 4° above south); precip. 0.5" (0.5" below avg.). 1–10 Showers, cold north; sunny, warm south. 11–17 Isolated showers; cool north, warm south. 18–31 Scattered t-storms, cool north; sunny, warm south.

JUNE 2019: Temp. 71° (5° above avg.); precip. 0.3" (0.2" below avg.). 1–12 Sunny, warm. 13–17 T-storms, hot. 18–22 T-storms; cool north, hot south. 23–30 Sunny; cool, then hot.

JULY 2019: Temp. 74° (1° above avg.); precip. 1" (0.5" above avg.). 1–3 Showers, cool. 4–7 Sunny; cool north, warm south. 8–17 A couple of t-storms, warm. 18–25 Sunny north, a couple of t-storms south; hot. 26–31 Scattered t-storms, turning cool.

AUG. 2019: Temp. 73° (1° below avg. north, 3° above south); precip. 0.5" (0.5" below avg.). 1–11 Sunny, cool. 12–14 T-storms north, sunny south; cool. 15–24 Sunny, warm. 25–31 Sunny, cool north; t-storms, warm south.

SEPT. 2019: Temp. 62° (avg.); precip. 0.5" (0.5" below avg.). 1–5 Showers, cool north; sunny, hot south. 6–9 Sunny, cool. 10–18 Sunny, warm north; scattered t-storms, cool south. 19–24 Isolated t-storms, warm. 25–30 Sunny, chilly.

OCT. 2019: Temp. 53° (2° above avg.); precip. 1.5" (0.5" above avg.). 1–5 A few showers, cool. 6–13 Sunny, warm. 14–19 Sunny north, show-ers south; warm. 20–23 Showers north, snow-storm south. 24–31 Rainy periods, cool.

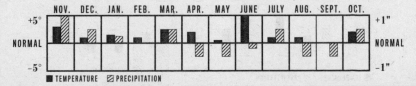

	NOV.	DEC.	JAN.	FEB.	MAR.	APR.	MAY	JUNE	JULY	AUG.	SEPT.	OCT.	

+5° / +1"
NORMAL / NORMAL
−5° / −1"

■ TEMPERATURE ☑ PRECIPITATION

DESERT SOUTHWEST

SUMMARY: Winter will be colder than normal, with above-normal precipitation. The coldest periods will be in mid- and late December, early and late January, and mid-February. Snowfall will be below normal in the east and above normal in other places that receive snow, with the snowiest periods in late December, early January, and mid-February. **April** and **May** will be warmer

Las Vegas · Albuquerque · Phoenix · Tucson · El Paso

and slightly drier than normal. **Summer** will be slightly hotter than normal in most of the region, with slightly below-normal rainfall. The hottest periods will occur in much of June, mid-July, and early to mid-August. **September** and **October** will be rainier than normal, with near- or below-normal temperatures.

NOV. 2018: Temp. 54° (2° below avg.); precip. 1" (avg.). 1–9 Sunny; warm, then cool. 10–20 Scattered t-storms, cool. 21–30 A few rain and snow showers east, sunny west; cool.

DEC. 2018: Temp. 46° (2° below avg.); precip. 1" (0.5" above avg.). 1–10 Sunny, warm. 11–20 Scattered showers and flurries, cold. 21–24 Sunny; warm east, cool west. 25–31 Periods of rain and snow, cold.

JAN. 2019: Temp. 47° (1° below avg.); precip. 0.3" (0.2" below avg.). 1–4 Rain and snow showers, cold. 5–9 Sunny, warmer. 10–14 Scattered showers, warm. 15–23 Isolated showers and flurries, cool. 24–31 Sunny, cold.

FEB. 2019: Temp. 50° (1° below avg.); precip. 0.3" (0.2" below avg.). 1–5 Sunny, turning mild. 6–11 Showers, then sunny, cool. 12–19 Rain to snow, then sunny, cold. 20–22 Sunny, mild. 23–28 Showers, then sunny, cool.

MAR. 2019: Temp. 61° (3° above avg.); precip. 1" (0.5" above avg.). 1–5 Rain, then sunny, cool. 6–10 Sunny, warm. 11–20 Rain, then sunny, cool east; sunny, warm west. 21–24 Sunny, warm. 25–31 Showers, then sunny, cool.

APR. 2019: Temp. 66° (1° above avg.); precip. 0.5" (avg.). 1–8 Sunny, cool. 9–14 Sunny; warm, then cool. 15–22 Sunny, warm. 23–30 T-storms, then sunny, warm.

MAY 2019: Temp. 77° (3° above avg.); precip. 0.3" (0.2" below avg.). 1–8 Sunny, hot. 9–14 T-storms, then sunny, cool. 15–22 Isolated t-storms, turning hot. 23–31 Sunny, warm.

JUNE 2019: Temp. 87° (4° above avg.); precip. 0.5" (avg.). 1–9 Isolated t-storms; cool, then hot. 10–14 Sunny, hot. 15–23 Scattered t-storms east, sunny west; hot. 24–30 Scattered t-storms, warm.

JULY 2019: Temp. 85° (2° below avg.); precip. 2" (0.5" above avg.). 1–5 T-storms east, sunny west; warm. 6–16 A few t-storms, warm. 17–21 Sunny, hot. 22–31 A few t-storms, cool.

AUG. 2019: Temp. 84.5° (2° below avg. east, 1° above west); precip. 0.5" (1" below avg.). 1–11 Isolated t-storms, warm. 12–22 Scattered t-storms; cool east, hot west. 23–31 Sunny, cool east; isolated t-storms, hot west.

SEPT. 2019: Temp. 78° (3° below avg. east, 1° above west); precip. 2" (2" above avg. east, avg. west). 1–5 Sunny, hot. 6–8 Sunny, cool. 9–17 Rain and t-storms, cool east; sunny, warm west. 18–24 Sunny; cool east, warm west. 25–30 Scattered showers, warm.

OCT. 2019: Temp. 67° (1° below avg.); precip. 2" (1" above avg.). 1–5 A few showers, warm. 6–12 Sunny; cool east, warm west. 13–18 T-storms east; sunny, warm west. 19–26 Showers, cool. 27–31 Sunny, cool.

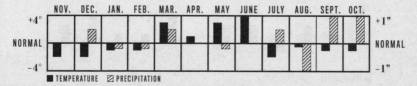

■ TEMPERATURE ▨ PRECIPITATION

WEATHER

PACIFIC NORTHWEST

SUMMARY: Winter will be warmer and much rainier than normal, with below-normal snowfall. The coldest periods will occur in early and late December, early January, and mid- and late February, with the snowiest periods in early January and mid-February. **April** and **May** will be warmer and drier than normal. **Summer** will be warmer and drier than normal, with the hottest temperatures in mid- to late July and early and mid-August. **September** and **October** will be warmer and slightly drier than normal.

NOV. 2018: Temp. 49° (2° above avg.); precip. 11.5" (5" above avg.). 1–5 Rainy, mild. 6–9 Heavy rain, cool. 10–11 Sunny, cool. 12–19 Rainy periods, cool. 20–30 Rainy, mild.

DEC. 2018: Temp. 44° (1° above avg.); precip. 8.5" (2" above avg.). 1–2 Sunny, cold. 3–10 Rain, some heavy; mild. 11–18 Rainy, mild. 19–23 Showers, mild. 24–31 Sunny, very cold.

JAN. 2019: Temp. 45° (2° above avg.); precip. 10" (4" above avg.). 1–2 Sunny, cold. 3–5 Snow to rain. 6–9 Stormy, heavy rain. 10–14 Rainy periods, turning cool. 15–22 Rainy periods, mild. 23–27 Heavy rain. 28–31 Sunny, cool.

FEB. 2019: Temp. 43° (1° below avg.); precip. 7" (2" above avg.). 1–4 Sunny, cool. 5–13 Rainy periods, mild. 14–16 Rain and snow, cold. 17–26 Rainy periods, cool. 27–28 Flurries, cold.

MAR. 2019: Temp. 49° (2° above avg.); precip. 7" (3" above avg.). 1–9 Rainy periods, mild. 10–17 Sunny, mild. 18–24 Rainy, mild. 25–31 Showers, mild.

APR. 2019: Temp. 52° (2° above avg.); precip. 2" (1" below avg.). 1–4 Showers, cool. 5–10 Sunny, warm. 11–20 Rainy periods, cool. 21–23 Sunny, warm. 24–30 Showers north, sunny south; warm.

MAY 2019: Temp. 55° (avg.); precip. 1.5" (0.5" below avg.). 1–11 Rainy periods, cool. 12–18 Showers, turning warm. 19–21 Sunny, cool. 22–26 Rain, then sunny, warm. 27–31 Rainy, turning cool.

JUNE 2019: Temp. 63° (3° above avg.); precip. 1" (0.5" below avg.). 1–14 Sunny, very warm. 15–20 Showers, cool. 21–25 Sunny; hot, then cool. 26–30 Showers, cool.

JULY 2019: Temp. 66° (1° above avg.); precip. 1" (0.5" above avg.). 1–4 Showers, cool. 5–7 Sunny, turning warm. 8–11 Rainy periods, cool. 12–21 Sunny, turning hot. 22–27 T-storms, then sunny, hot. 28–31 Sunny, cool.

AUG. 2019: Temp. 67° (1° above avg.); precip. 0.5" (0.5" below avg.). 1–3 Sunny, hot. 4–15 Isolated t-storms, cool. 16–21 Sunny, hot. 22–26 Scattered t-storms; cool, then hot. 27–31 A couple of showers, warm.

SEPT. 2019: Temp. 64° (3° above avg.); precip. 0.5" (1" below avg.). 1–5 Showers, then sunny, cool. 6–18 Sunny, turning hot. 19–27 Scattered showers, cool. 28–30 Sunny, cool.

OCT. 2019: Temp. 56° (2° above avg.); precip. 3" (avg.). 1–3 Showers, warm. 4–11 Sunny, mild. 12–17 Showers, then sunny, cool. 18–23 Rainy periods, mild. 24–31 Rainy periods; cool, then mild.

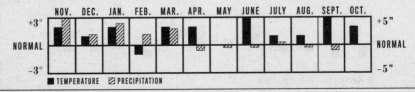

PACIFIC SOUTHWEST

SUMMARY: Winter temperatures will be near or cooler than normal, with rainfall above normal in the north and slightly below normal in the south. The coldest periods will occur in late December, mid-January, and early February. Mountain snows will be near normal, with the stormiest periods in late November, late December, and early January. **April** and **May** will be cooler and drier than normal. **Summer** will be warmer than normal, with near-normal rainfall. The hottest periods will be in mid- to late June, mid-July, and late August. **September** and **October** will see temperatures above normal in the northeast and below normal in the southwest. Rainfall will be slightly above normal.

NOV. 2018: Temp. 57° (1° below avg.); precip. 4.5" (3" above avg.). 1–6 Rainy north, sunny south; cool. 7–8 Sunny, cool. 9–17 Rainy periods, cool. 18–21 Showers, cool. 22–24 Rain, heavy north. 25–30 Sunny, cool.

DEC. 2018: Temp. 55° (0.5° below avg. coast, 2° above inland); precip. 1" (1" below avg.). 1–3 Sunny; cool north, warm south. 4–10 Rainy periods north, sunny south; mild. 11–18 A few showers, mild. 19–23 Rain north, sprinkles south; mild. 24–31 Rain, some heavy; chilly.

JAN. 2019: Temp. 54° (avg.); precip. 4" (3.5" above avg. north, 1.5" below south). 1–3 Rainy periods, cool. 4–11 Rainy periods north, sunny south; mild. 12–13 Showers. 14–23 Sunny, cool. 24–31 Rain, then sunny, mild.

FEB. 2019: Temp. 54° (1° below avg.); precip. 3.5" (2" above avg. north, 1" below south). 1–4 Sunny, cool. 5–12 Rainy periods, cool. 13–20 Showers, cool north; sunny, warm south. 21–28 Rainy periods, cool.

MAR. 2019: Temp. 57° (avg.); precip. 2.5" (avg.). 1–4 Rainy periods, cool. 5–17 Sunny, seasonable. 18–25 Rainy periods, mild. 26–31 Showers, cool north; sunny, warm south.

APR. 2019: Temp. 59° (1° below avg.); precip. 0.5" (0.5" below avg.). 1–4 Rain, then sunny, cool. 5–10 Sunny, cool. 11–19 Showers north, sunny south; cool. 20–30 A few sprinkles, cool.

MAY 2019: Temp. 62.5° (1° below avg.); precip. 0.4" (0.1" below avg.). 1–5 Sunny, hot inland; A.M. sprinkles, P.M. sun coast. 6–14 Sunny north, A.M. sprinkles south; cool. 15–20 Sunny;

hot north, cool south. 21–31 Isolated showers, cool coast; sunny, turning hot inland.

JUNE 2019: Temp. 69° (1° above avg.); precip. 0.1" (avg.). 1–7 Sunny, hot inland; A.M. sprinkles, P.M. sun coast. 8–11 Showers north, sunny south. 12–17 Sunny, turning hot inland; A.M. clouds, P.M. sun coast. 18–22 Sunny, turning hot. 23–30 Sunny, cool.

JULY 2019: Temp. 73° (2° above avg.); precip. 0" (avg.). 1–7 A.M. clouds, P.M. sun; cool. 8–14 Sunny; cool north, hot south. 15–19 Sunny, turning hot. 20–26 Isolated showers, warm. 27–31 Sunny, warm.

AUG. 2019: Temp. 70° (1° below avg.); precip. 0.1" (avg.). 1–6 Sunny, seasonable. 7–13 Sunny, cool. 14–19 Sunny, hot inland; A.M. clouds, P.M. sun coast. 20–25 Sunny inland, A.M. clouds coast. 26–31 Sunny; turning hot inland, warm coast.

SEPT. 2019: Temp. 70.5° (2° above avg. coast, 1° below inland); precip. 0.5" (0.5" above avg. north, avg. south). 1–4 Sunny; hot north, warm south. 5–10 Sunny, cool. 11–20 Sunny, hot inland; A.M. sprinkles, P.M. sun coast. 21–23 Sunny; turning hot north, warm south. 24–30 Scattered showers, cool.

OCT. 2019: Temp. 65° (1° above avg. north, 1° below south); precip. 1.5" (2" above avg. north, 0.5" below south). 1–4 Sunny, cool. 5–11 Sunny, turning warm. 12–19 Sunny, warm north; A.M. sprinkles, P.M. sun south. 20–25 Rainy periods, cool. 26–31 Sunny, cool.

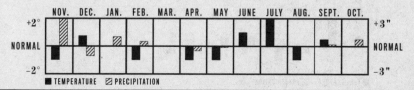

ALASKA

WEATHER

SUMMARY: Winter temperatures will be milder than normal, with the coldest periods in mid-January and early February. Precipitation will be above normal N (see key below) and below normal S, while snowfall will be near to below normal. The snowiest periods will be in early to mid-November and mid- to late December. **April** and **May** will be warmer than normal, with slightly above-normal precipitation. **Summer** will be slightly warmer and drier than normal, with the hottest periods in mid- to late July and early August. **September** and **October** temperatures will be colder than normal N and milder C and S. There will be near-normal precipitation and snowfall, with the snowiest periods in early to mid-October C and early October E and W.

KEY: north (N), central (C), south (S), east (E), west (W), elsewhere (EW).

NOV. 2018: Temp. 10° N, 44° S (8° above avg. N, 2° below S); precip. 0.4" N, 5" S (avg.). 1–3 Snowy, mild. 4–9 Flurries, mild N; sunny, cold S. 10–14 Sunny N, snowy periods S; cold. 15–18 Snowy periods, mild. 19–22 Snowy periods, mild N; sunny, cold S. 23–30 Flurries, mild N; snowy periods, cold S.

DEC. 2018: Temp. 1° N, 39° S (8° above avg.); precip. 1.2" N, 3" S (1" above avg. N, 2" below S). 1–4 Snow showers, mild. 5–10 Flurries, cold. 11–17 Snow showers, cold. 18–25 Snowy, mild. 26–31 Snow showers, turning cold.

JAN. 2019: Temp. –14° N, 27° S (2° below avg.); precip. 0.2" N, 5" S (avg.). 1–7 Snow showers; mild N and C, cold S. 8–20 Snow showers, cold. 21–25 Flurries, mild N; clear, cold C and S. 26–31 Flurries, cold N; snowy periods, mild C and S.

FEB. 2019: Temp. –18° N, 27° S (4° below avg.); precip. 0.2" N, 4" S (avg.). 1–11 Flurries, cold. 12–15 Snow showers, mild. 16–20 Clear, mild N+C; Snow showers, cold S. 21–28 Snow showers, cold.

MAR. 2019: Temp. –2° N, 37° S (3° above avg.); precip. 0.2" N, 4.7" S (0.3" below avg.). 1–3 Flurries, cold. 4–8 Clear; mild N, cold S. 9–13 Snow showers, turning mild. 14–20 Flurries north, rain and snow showers C and S; mild. 21–31 Flurries, cold N; showers, mild S.

APR. 2019: Temp. 5° N, 44° S (3° above avg.); precip. 0.7" N, 3" S (avg.). 1–14 Flurries, cold N; showers, then sunny, mild S. 15–22 Snow showers, then sunny, mild. 23–27 Sunny N, showers S; mild. 28–30 Flurries N, sunny S; mild.

MAY 2019: Temp. 21° N, 47° EW (avg.); precip. 1.1" N, 3.5" S (0.5" above avg.). 1–10 Flurries N, rain and snow showers C, showers S: mild. 11–19 Sunny, mild. 20–31 Snowy periods N, showers C+S; cool.

JUNE 2019: Temp. 32° N, 52° EW (2° below avg.); precip. 0.2" N, 2.5" S (0.5" below avg.). 1–6 A few showers, cool. 7–10 Sunny, cool. 11–18 A few showers, cool. 19–30 Showers, cool N; sunny, warm S.

JULY 2019: Temp. 43° N, 58° EW (1° above avg.); precip. 0.7" N, 3.5" S (0.5" below avg.). 1–11 Showers; cool, then warm. 12–22 Sunny, then rainy, mild N and C; showers, then sunny, cool S. 23–31 Scattered showers, warm.

AUG. 2019: Temp. 42° N, 58° EW (2° above avg.); precip. 1.2" N, 5" S (avg.). 1–13 A few showers, mild. 14–16 Sunny, cool. 17–22 Sunny, warm N; rainy periods, cool S. 23–31 A few showers, warm.

SEPT. 2019: Temp. 33° N, 55° EW (1° above avg.); precip. 0.1" N, 6" S (1" below avg.). 1–9 A few showers; cool N, warm C, mild S. 10–19 Rainy periods, mild. 20–26 Rain and snow showers N and C, sunny S; turning cold. 27–30 Snow showers.

OCT. 2019: Temp. 9° N, 48° S (3° below avg. N, 5° above S); precip. 1.5" N, 8" S (1" above avg.). 1–4 Rain and snow showers. 5–9 Flurries, cold N; snowy periods C; rainy periods, mild S. 10–23 Flurries, cold N; Snow, then sunny C; rainy periods, mild S. 24–25 Sunny, mild. 26–31 Snow showers, turning cold N and C; rain, then sunny, mild S.

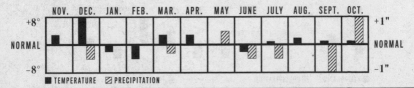

	NOV.	DEC.	JAN.	FEB.	MAR.	APR.	MAY	JUNE	JULY	AUG.	SEPT.	OCT.	
+8°													+1"
NORMAL													NORMAL
–8°													–1"

■ TEMPERATURE ▧ PRECIPITATION

HAWAII

WEATHER

SUMMARY: Winter temperatures will be above normal, on average, with the coolest periods in early to mid-December, mid-February, and early March. Rainfall will be above normal E (see key below) and below normal W, with the stormiest periods in mid- to late November and early February. **April** and **May** will be warmer than normal, with rainfall above normal E and below normal W. **Summer** temperatures will be slightly cooler than normal, on average, with above-normal rainfall. The warmest periods will be in late June, late July, and early August. **September** and **October** will see temperatures above normal E and below normal W and be slightly rainier than normal.

KEY: east (E), central (C), west (W). Note: Temperature and precipitation are based substantially upon topography. The detailed forecast focuses on the Honolulu–Waikiki area and provides general trends elsewhere.

NOV. 2018: Temp. 77° (1° above avg. E, 2° below W); precip. 3.5" (6" above avg. E, 4" below W). 1–6 A few showers, cool. 7–20 Scattered showers, warm. 21–25 Rain and t-storms. 26–30 Sunny, cool.

DEC. 2018: Temp. 75.5° (2° above avg. E, 1° below W); precip. 4.3" (1" above avg.). 1–3 Rainy periods, cool. 4–8 A few showers, warm. 9–15 Sunny, cool. 16–21 A few showers, warm. 22–31 Rainy periods, warm.

JAN. 2019: Temp. 75° (2° above avg.); precip. 2.5" (avg.). 1–4 Showers, warm. 5–14 Sunny E, a few showers C and W; warm. 15–20 Rainy periods, warm. 21–25 Sunny, warm E; rainy periods C and W. 26–31 Showers, warm.

FEB. 2019: Temp. 74° (1° above avg.); precip. 2" (4" above avg. E, 4" below W). 1–11 Rain and t-storms E, a few showers C and W; warm. 12–14 Sunny, cool. 15–28 Rain and t-storms E, scattered showers C and W; warm.

MAR. 2019: Temp. 75° (1° above avg.); precip. 1" (2" below avg. E and W, 1" above C). 1–3 Sunny, cool. 4–13 Showers and heavy t-storms E, scattered t-storms C and W; cool. 14–20 A few showers; warm E, cool C and W. 21–27 Sunny, warm. 28–31 Showers, warm.

APR. 2019: Temp. 76.5° (1° above avg.); precip. 2.7" (7" above E, 3" below W). 1–10 Showers, warm. 11–15 Showers and heavy t-storms, warm. 16–30 Daily showers, seasonable.

MAY 2019: Temp. 77.5° (0.5° above avg.); precip. 1.7" (1" above avg.). 1–12 Rainy periods, cool E and W; showers, warm C. 13–17 Showers E and W, sunny C; warm. 18–31 A few showers, warm.

JUNE 2019: Temp. 79.5° (avg.); precip. 1.4" (1" above avg.). 1–5 A few showers, warm. 6–11 Showers E and W, sunny C; warm. 12–22 Sunny; warm, then cooler. 23–30 Showers E and W, sunny C; warm.

JULY 2019: Temp. 80° (1° below avg.); precip. 0.5" (avg.). 1–11 Showers and t-storms E and W, daily showers C; warm. 12–15 Sunny, cool. 16–31 Showers and a few heavier t-storms E, daily showers C and W; warm.

AUG. 2019: Temp. 80.5° (1° below avg.); precip. 1.1" (0.5" above avg.). 1–7 Rainy periods E and W, sprinkles C; warm. 8–18 Showers and heavier t-storms E, sunny C and W; warm. 19–21 Sunny, cool. 22–31 A few showers, warm.

SEPT. 2019: Temp. 81.5° (2° above avg. E, 2° below W); precip. 1.3" (0.5" above avg.). 1–5 Showers, warm. 6–15 Sunny E, a few showers C and W; hot. 16–23 A few showers, hot. 24–30 Scattered t-storms, cooler.

OCT. 2019: Temp. 80° (avg.); precip. 2" (avg.). 1–7 Showers E and W, isolated showers C; cool. 8–12 Rainy periods, warm. 13–19 Daily showers E, a few showers C and W; warm. 20–25 Scattered t-storms, warm. 26–31 Daily showers, cool.

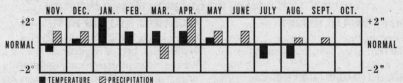

SECRETS OF THE ZODIAC

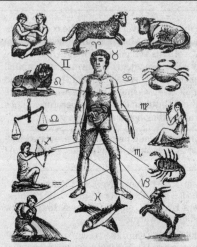

The Man of the Signs

Ancient astrologers believed that each astrological sign influenced a specific part of the body. The first sign of the zodiac—Aries—was attributed to the head, with the rest of the signs moving down the body, ending with Pisces at the feet.

♈ Aries, head	ARI	*Mar. 21–Apr. 20*
♉ Taurus, neck	TAU	*Apr. 21–May 20*
♊ Gemini, arms	GEM	*May 21–June 20*
♋ Cancer, breast	CAN	*June 21–July 22*
♌ Leo, heart	LEO	*July 23–Aug. 22*
♍ Virgo, belly	VIR	*Aug. 23–Sept. 22*
♎ Libra, reins	LIB	*Sept. 23–Oct. 22*
♏ Scorpio, secrets	SCO	*Oct. 23–Nov. 22*
♐ Sagittarius, thighs	SAG	*Nov. 23–Dec. 21*
♑ Capricorn, knees	CAP	*Dec. 22–Jan. 19*
♒ Aquarius, legs	AQU	*Jan. 20–Feb. 19*
♓ Pisces, feet	PSC	*Feb. 20–Mar. 20*

ASTROLOGY VS. ASTRONOMY

Astrology is a tool we use to plan events according to the placements of the Sun, the Moon, and the planets in the 12 signs of the zodiac. In astrology, the planetary movements do not cause events; rather, they explain the path, or "flow," that events tend to follow. *The Moon's astrological place is given on the next page.* **Astronomy** is the study of the actual placement of the known planets and constellations. The Moon's astronomical place is given in the **Left-Hand Calendar Pages, 120–146.** (*The placement of the planets in the signs of the zodiac is not the same astrologically and astronomically. See page 85.*)

The dates in the **Best Days** table, **pages 226–227,** are based on the astrological passage of the Moon.

WHEN MERCURY IS RETROGRADE

Sometimes the other planets appear to be traveling backward through the zodiac; this is an illusion. We call this illusion *retrograde motion.*

Mercury's retrograde periods can cause our plans to go awry. However, intuition is high during these periods and coincidences can be extraordinary.

When Mercury is retrograde, remain flexible, allow extra time for travel, and avoid signing contracts. Review projects and plans but wait until Mercury is direct again to make final decisions.

In 2019, Mercury will be retrograde during **March 5–28, July 7–August 2,** and **October 31–November 20.**

—Celeste Longacre

GARDENING BY THE MOON'S SIGN

USE CHART ON NEXT PAGE TO FIND THE BEST DATES FOR THE FOLLOWING GARDEN TASKS . . .

PLANT, TRANSPLANT, AND GRAFT: Cancer, Scorpio, Pisces, or Taurus
HARVEST: Aries, Leo, Sagittarius, Gemini, or Aquarius
BUILD/FIX FENCES OR GARDEN BEDS: Capricorn

CONTROL INSECT PESTS, PLOW, AND WEED: Aries, Gemini, Leo, Sagittarius, or Aquarius
PRUNE: Aries, Leo, or Sagittarius. During a waxing Moon, pruning encourages growth; during a waning Moon, it discourages it.

SETTING EGGS BY THE MOON'S SIGN

Chicks take about 21 days to hatch. Those born under a waxing Moon in Cancer, Scorpio, or Pisces are healthier and mature faster. To ensure that chicks are born during these times, "set eggs" (place eggs in an incubator or under a hen) 21 days before the desired hatching dates.

EXAMPLE:
The Moon is new on April 5 and full on April 19. Between these dates, the Moon is in the sign of Cancer on April 11 and 12, and in Scorpio on April 19. To have chicks born on April 11, count back 21 days; set eggs on March 21.

Below are the best days to set eggs in 2019, using only the fruitful dates
between the new and full Moons, and counting back 21 days:

JAN.: 16, 17, 25, 26	**APR.:** 17, 18, 26, 27	**JULY:** 16–18	**OCT.:** 7, 8, 16, 17
FEB.: 13, 14, 22, 23	**MAY:** 14–16, 23, 24	**AUG.:** 13, 14, 22–24	**NOV.:** 12, 13
MAR.: 21, 22, 29	**JUNE:** 11, 12, 19, 20	**SEPT.:** 9, 10, 18-20	**DEC.:** 9–11, 19, 20

The Moon's Astrological Place, 2018–19

	NOV.	DEC.	JAN.	FEB.	MAR.	APR.	MAY	JUNE	JULY	AUG.	SEPT.	OCT.	NOV.	DEC.
1	LEO	LIB	SCO	CAP	CAP	PSC	ARI	TAU	GEM	LEO	LIB	SCO	CAP	AQU
2	VIR	LIB	SAG	CAP	CAP	PSC	ARI	GEM	CAN	VIR	LIB	SAG	CAP	AQU
3	VIR	LIB	SAG	AQU	AQU	PSC	ARI	GEM	CAN	VIR	SCO	SAG	AQU	PSC
4	LIB	SCO	SAG	AQU	AQU	ARI	TAU	CAN	LEO	LIB	SCO	CAP	AQU	PSC
5	LIB	SCO	CAP	AQU	PSC	ARI	TAU	CAN	LEO	LIB	SAG	CAP	AQU	ARI
6	SCO	SAG	CAP	PSC	PSC	TAU	GEM	CAN	VIR	SCO	SAG	CAP	PSC	ARI
7	SCO	SAG	AQU	PSC	PSC	TAU	GEM	LEO	VIR	SCO	CAP	AQU	PSC	ARI
8	SCO	CAP	AQU	ARI	ARI	TAU	CAN	LEO	LIB	SCO	CAP	AQU	ARI	TAU
9	SAG	CAP	AQU	ARI	ARI	GEM	CAN	VIR	LIB	SAG	CAP	PSC	ARI	TAU
10	SAG	CAP	PSC	ARI	TAU	GEM	LEO	VIR	SCO	SAG	AQU	PSC	ARI	GEM
11	CAP	AQU	PSC	TAU	TAU	CAN	LEO	LIB	SCO	CAP	AQU	PSC	TAU	GEM
12	CAP	AQU	ARI	TAU	GEM	CAN	VIR	LIB	SAG	CAP	PSC	ARI	TAU	GEM
13	AQU	PSC	ARI	GEM	GEM	LEO	VIR	SCO	SAG	AQU	PSC	ARI	GEM	CAN
14	AQU	PSC	ARI	GEM	GEM	LEO	VIR	SCO	SAG	AQU	PSC	TAU	GEM	CAN
15	AQU	PSC	TAU	CAN	CAN	VIR	LIB	SAG	CAP	AQU	ARI	TAU	CAN	LEO
16	PSC	ARI	TAU	CAN	CAN	VIR	LIB	SAG	PSC	ARI	TAU	CAN	LEO
17	PSC	ARI	GEM	LEO	LEO	LIB	SCO	CAP	AQU	PSC	TAU	GEM	CAN	VIR
18	ARI	TAU	GEM	LEO	LEO	LIB	SCO	CAP	AQU	ARI	TAU	GEM	LEO	VIR
19	ARI	TAU	CAN	VIR	VIR	SCO	SAG	CAP	AQU	ARI	TAU	CAN	LEO	LIB
20	ARI	GEM	CAN	VIR	VIR	SCO	SAG	AQU	PSC	ARI	GEM	CAN	VIR	LIB
21	TAU	GEM	LEO	LIB	LIB	SAG	CAP	AQU	PSC	TAU	GEM	LEO	VIR	SCO
22	TAU	CAN	LEO	LIB	LIB	SAG	CAP	PSC	ARI	TAU	CAN	LEO	LIB	SCO
23	GEM	CAN	VIR	SCO	SCO	SAG	AQU	PSC	ARI	GEM	CAN	LEO	LIB	SAG
24	GEM	CAN	VIR	SCO	SCO	CAP	AQU	PSC	ARI	GEM	LEO	VIR	SCO	SAG
25	CAN	LEO	LIB	SCO	SAG	CAP	AQU	ARI	TAU	GEM	LEO	VIR	SCO	SAG
26	CAN	LEO	LIB	SAG	SAG	AQU	PSC	ARI	TAU	CAN	VIR	LIB	SAG	CAP
27	LEO	VIR	SCO	SAG	CAP	AQU	PSC	TAU	GEM	CAN	VIR	LIB	SAG	CAP
28	LEO	VIR	SCO	CAP	CAP	AQU	PSC	TAU	GEM	LEO	LIB	SCO	CAP	AQU
29	VIR	LIB	SAG	—	CAP	PSC	ARI	TAU	CAN	LEO	LIB	SCO	CAP	AQU
30	VIR	LIB	SAG	—	AQU	PSC	ARI	GEM	CAN	VIR	SCO	SAG	CAP	PSC
31	—	SCO	SAG	—	AQU	—	TAU	—	LEO	VIR	—	SAG	—	PSC

BEST DAYS FOR 2019

This chart is based on the Moon's sign and shows the best days each
month for certain activities. –*Celeste Longacre*

	JAN.	FEB.	MAR.	APR.	MAY	JUNE	JULY	AUG.	SEPT.	OCT.	NOV.	DEC.
Quit smoking	24	20, 25	24, 29	20, 24	27, 31	1, 24, 29	21, 26	17, 22	18, 27	16, 25	21, 25	18, 22
Bake	19, 20	15, 16	15, 16	11, 12	8, 9	4–6	2, 3, 29, 30	26, 27	22, 23	19, 20	15–17	13, 14
Brew	1, 27, 28	23–25	23, 24	19, 20	17, 18	13, 14	10, 11	6–8	3, 4, 30	1, 28, 29	24, 25	21, 22
Dry fruit/vegetables/meat	3, 4, 29–31	26, 27	25, 26	21–23	1–3, 29, 30	25, 26	22–24	18–20	24, 25	22, 23	18, 19	15, 16
Make jams/jellies	10, 11	6, 7	5–7	1–3, 29, 30	26–28	22–24	20, 21	16, 17	12–14	9–11	6, 7	3, 4, 30, 31
Can, pickle, or make sauerkraut	1, 27, 28	23–25	5, 23, 24	1–3, 29, 30	26–28	22–24	20, 21	16, 17	22, 23	19, 20	15–17	21, 22
Begin diet to lose weight	24	20, 25	24, 29	20, 24	27, 31	1, 24, 29	21, 26	17, 22	18, 27	16, 25	21, 25	18, 22
Begin diet to gain weight	11, 16	7, 12	7, 11, 20	7, 11	5, 18	10, 14	7, 11	3, 8	4, 8	1, 11	7, 30	9, 31
Cut hair to encourage growth	10, 11, 15, 16	11, 12	10, 11	17, 18	5, 15, 16	11, 12	8, 9	4, 5	1, 2, 29	9–11	6, 7	3, 4
Cut hair to discourage growth	25, 26	21, 22	5, 22	1–3, 29, 30	26–28	22–24	20, 21	21, 22	17–19	26	22, 23	19, 20
Perm hair	7–9	3–5	3, 4, 30, 31	26–28	23–25	20, 21	17–19	13–15	10, 11	7, 8	3–5	1, 2, 28, 29
Color hair	15, 16	11, 12	10, 11	6–8	4, 5	1, 27–29	25, 26	21, 22	17–19	14–16	11, 12	8, 9
Straighten hair	2–4, 29–31	26, 27	25, 26	21–23	19, 20	15, 16	12–14	9, 10	5, 6	2, 3, 30, 31	26, 27	23–25
Have dental care	23, 24	19, 20	19, 20	15, 16	12–14	9, 10	6, 7	2, 3, 30, 31	26, 27	24, 25	20, 21	17, 18
Start projects	7	5	7	6	5	4	3	2	29	29	27	27
End projects	4	3	5	4	3	2	1	29	27	26	25	25
Demolish	1, 27, 28	23–25	23, 24	19, 20	17, 18	13, 14	10, 11	6–8	3, 4, 30	1, 28, 29	24, 25	21, 22
Lay shingles	21, 22	17, 18	17, 18	13, 14	10, 11	7, 8	4, 5	1, 28, 29	24, 25	21–23	18, 19	15, 16
Paint	15, 16, 25, 26	11, 12	21, 22	6–8	4, 5	11, 12	25, 26	21, 22	17–19	14–16	11, 12	8, 9
Wash windows	12–14	8–10	8, 9	4, 5	2, 3, 29, 30	25, 26	22–24	18–20	15, 16	12, 13	8–10	5–7
Wash floors	10, 11	6, 7	5–7	1–3, 29, 30	26–28	22–24	20, 21	16, 17	12–14	9–11	6, 7	3, 4, 30, 31
Go camping	2–4, 29–31	26, 27	25, 26	21–23	19, 20	15, 16	12–14	9, 10	5, 6	2, 3	26, 27	23–25

	JAN.	FEB.	MAR.	APR.	MAY	JUNE	JULY	AUG.	SEPT.	OCT.	NOV.	DEC.
Travel for pleasure	21, 22	17, 18	17, 18	13, 14	10, 11	7, 8	4, 5	1, 28, 29	24, 25	22, 23	18, 19	15, 16
Get married	25, 26	21, 22	21, 22	17, 18	15, 16	11, 12	8, 9	4, 5	1, 2, 28, 29	26, 27	22, 23	19, 20
Ask for a loan	24, 28	24, 28	23, 24	20, 29, 30	23–25	20, 21	23–25	21, 22	17, 18	14–16	24, 25	21, 22
Buy a home	16, 20	12, 16	10, 11	6–8	5, 17	13, 14	10, 11	6–8	3, 4	1, 29	11, 29, 30	8, 9
Move (house/household)	17, 18	13, 14	12–14	9, 10	6, 7	2, 3	1, 27, 28	23–25	20, 21	17, 18	13, 14	10–12
Advertise to sell	15, 16	11, 12	10, 11	6–8	5, 17	13, 14	10, 11	6–8	3, 4	1, 28, 29	11	8, 9
Mow to promote growth	12–14	8–10	8, 9	5	17	13, 14	10, 11	6–8	3, 4	12	8–10	6, 7
Mow to slow growth	27, 28	23–25	23, 24	4	29, 30	25, 26	22, 23	19, 20	15, 16	19, 20	24, 25	21, 22
Plant aboveground crops	10, 11, 19, 20	15, 16	15, 16	11, 12	8, 9	5, 6, 13, 14	10, 11	7, 8	3, 4, 30	1, 9, 10	6, 7	3, 4
Plant belowground crops	1, 27, 28	23–25	5, 23, 24	1–3, 29, 30	26–28	22, 23	20, 21	17, 26, 27	22, 23	19, 20	15–17	21, 22
Destroy pests and weeds	12–14	8–10	8, 9	4, 5	1–3, 29, 30	25, 26	22–24	18–20	15, 16	12, 13	8–10	5–7
Graft or pollinate	19, 20	15, 16	15, 16	11, 12	8, 9	4–6	2, 3, 29, 30	26, 27	22, 23	19, 20	15–17	13, 14
Prune to encourage growth	12–14	8–10	8, 9	13, 14	10, 11	7, 8	4, 5	9, 10	5, 6	2, 3	8–10	5–7
Prune to discourage growth	2–4, 29–31	26, 27	25, 26	22, 23	1–3, 29, 30	25, 26	22–24	18–20	15, 16	21, 22	18, 19	15, 16
Pick fruit	23, 24	19, 20	19, 20	15, 16	12–14	9, 10	6, 7	2, 3, 30, 31	26, 27	24, 25	20, 21	17, 18
Harvest above-ground crops	15, 16	11, 12	10, 11	6–8	4, 5, 12–14	9, 10	6, 7	2, 3	7–9	4–6	1, 2, 29, 30	8, 9
Harvest below-ground crops	23, 24	1, 2, 28	27, 28	24, 25	21, 22, 31	1, 27–29	25, 26	21, 22	17, 18	14–16	20, 21	17, 18
Cut hay	12–14	8–10	8, 9	4, 5	1–3, 29, 30	25, 26	22–24	18–20	15, 16	12, 13	8–10	5–7
Begin logging	5, 6	1, 2, 28	1, 2, 27–29	24, 25	21, 22	17–19	15, 16	11, 12	7–9	4–6	1, 2, 28–30	26, 27
Set posts or pour concrete	5, 6	1, 2, 28	1, 2, 27–29	24, 25	21, 22	17–19	15, 16	11, 12	7–9	4–6	1, 2, 28–30	26, 27
Purchase animals	19, 20	15, 16	15, 16	11, 12	8, 9	4–6	2, 3, 29, 30	26, 27	22, 23	19, 20	15–17	13, 14
Breed animals	1, 27, 28	23–25	23, 24	19, 20	17, 18	13, 14	10, 11	6–8	3, 4, 30	1, 28, 29	24, 25	21, 22
Wean animals or children	24	20, 25	24, 29	20, 24	27, 31	1, 24, 29	21, 26	17, 22	18, 27	16, 25	21, 25	18, 22
Castrate animals	7–9	3–5	3, 4, 30, 31	26, 27	23–25	20, 21	17–19	13–15	10, 11	7, 8	3–5	28, 29
Slaughter livestock	1, 27, 28	23–25	23, 24	19, 20	17, 18	13, 14	10, 11	6–8	3, 4, 30	1, 28, 29	24, 25	21, 22

BEST FISHING DAYS AND TIMES

The best times to fish are when the fish are naturally most active. The Sun, Moon, tides, and weather all influence fish activity. For example, fish tend to feed more at sunrise and sunset, and also during a full Moon (when tides are higher than average). However, most of us go fishing simply when we can get the time off. But there are best times, according to fishing lore:

■ One hour before and one hour after high tides, and one hour before and one hour after low tides. The times of high tides for Boston are given on **pages 120–146**; also see **pages 236–237**. (Inland, the times for high tides correspond with the times when the Moon is due south. Low tides are halfway between high tides.)

GET HIGH AND LOW TIDE TIMES NEAREST TO YOUR LOCATION AT ALMANAC.COM/TIDES.

■ During the "morning rise" (after sunup for a spell) and the "evening rise" (just before sundown and the hour or so after).

■ During the rise and set of the Moon.

■ When the barometer is steady or on the rise. (But even during stormy periods, the fish aren't going to give up feeding. The clever angler will find just the right bait.)

■ When there is a hatch of flies—caddis flies or mayflies, commonly.

■ When the breeze is from a westerly quarter, rather than from the north or east.

■ When the water is still or slightly rippled, rather than during a wind.

THE BEST FISHING DAYS FOR 2019, WHEN THE MOON IS BETWEEN NEW AND FULL

January 5–21
February 4–19
March 6–20
April 5–19
May 4–18
June 3–17
July 2–16, 31
August 1–15, 30, 31
September 1–14, 28–30
October 1–13, 27–31
November 1–12, 26–30
December 1–12, 26–31

Dates based on Eastern Time.

HOW TO ESTIMATE THE WEIGHT OF A FISH

Measure the fish from the tip of its nose to the tip of its tail. Then measure its girth at the thickest portion of its midsection.

The weight of a fat-bodied fish (bass, salmon) =
(length x girth x girth)/800

SALMON

The weight of a slender fish (trout, northern pike) =
(length x girth x girth)/900

TROUT

EXAMPLE: If a trout is 20 inches long and has a 12-inch girth, its estimated weight is
(20 x 12 x 12)/900 =
2,880/900 = 3.2 pounds

CATFISH

GESTATION AND MATING TABLES

	PROPER AGE OR WEIGHT FOR FIRST MATING	PERIOD OF FERTILITY (YRS.)	NUMBER OF FEMALES FOR ONE MALE	PERIOD OF GESTATION (DAYS) AVERAGE	RANGE
CATTLE: Cow	15–18 mos.[1]	10–14		283	279–290[2] 262–300[3]
Bull	1 yr., well matured	10–12	50[4] / thousands[5]		
GOAT: Doe	10 mos. or 85–90 lbs.	6		150	145–155
Buck	well matured	5	30		
HORSE: Mare	3 yrs.	10–12		336	310–370
Stallion	3 yrs.	12–15	40–45[4] / record 252[5]		
PIG: Sow	5–6 mos. or 250 lbs.	6		115	110–120
Boar	250–300 lbs.	6	50[6] / 35–40[7]		
RABBIT: Doe	6 mos.	5–6		31	30–32
Buck	6 mos.	5–6	30		
SHEEP: Ewe	1 yr. or 90 lbs.	6		147 / 151[8]	142–154
Ram	12–14 mos., well matured	7	50–75[6] / 35–40[7]		
CAT: Queen	12 mos.	6		63	60–68
Tom	12 mos.	6	6–8		
DOG: Bitch	16–18 mos.	8		63	58–67
Male	12–16 mos.	8	8–10		

[1]Holstein and beef: 750 lbs.; Jersey: 500 lbs. [2]Beef; 8–10 days shorter for Angus. [3]Dairy. [4]Natural. [5]Artificial. [6]Hand-mated. [7]Pasture. [8]For fine wool breeds.

INCUBATION PERIOD OF POULTRY (DAYS)

Chicken	21
Duck	26–32
Goose	30–34
Guinea	26–28
Turkey	28

AVERAGE LIFE SPAN OF ANIMALS IN CAPTIVITY (YEARS)

Cat (domestic)	14	Goose (domestic)	20
Chicken (domestic)	8	Horse	22
Dog (domestic)	13	Pig	12
Duck (domestic)	10	Rabbit	6
Goat (domestic)	14	Turkey (domestic)	10

	ESTRAL/ESTROUS CYCLE (INCLUDING HEAT PERIOD) AVERAGE	RANGE	LENGTH OF ESTRUS (HEAT) AVERAGE	RANGE	USUAL TIME OF OVULATION	WHEN CYCLE RECURS IF NOT BRED
Cow	21 days	18–24 days	18 hours	10–24 hours	10–12 hours after end of estrus	21 days
Doe goat	21 days	18–24 days	2–3 days	1–4 days	Near end of estrus	21 days
Mare	21 days	10–37 days	5–6 days	2–11 days	24–48 hours before end of estrus	21 days
Sow	21 days	18–24 days	2–3 days	1–5 days	30–36 hours after start of estrus	21 days
Ewe	16½ days	14–19 days	30 hours	24–32 hours	12–24 hours before end of estrus	16½ days
Queen cat		15–21 days	3–4 days, if mated	9–10 days, in absence of male	24–56 hours after coitus	Pseudo-pregnancy
Bitch	24 days	16–30 days	7 days	5–9 days	1–3 days after first acceptance	Pseudo-pregnancy

PLANTING BY THE MOON'S PHASE

ACCORDING TO THIS AGE-OLD PRACTICE, CYCLES OF THE MOON AFFECT PLANT GROWTH.

Plant annual flowers and vegetables that bear crops above ground during the light, or waxing, of the Moon: from the day the Moon is new to the day it is full.

Plant flowering bulbs, biennial and perennial flowers, and vegetables that bear crops below ground during the dark, or waning, of the Moon: from the day after it is full to the day before it is new again.

The Planting Dates columns give the safe periods for planting in areas that receive frost. (See **page 232** for frost dates in your area.) The Moon Favorable columns give the best planting days within the Planting Dates based on the Moon's phases for 2019. (See **pages 120–146** for the exact days of the new and full Moons.)

The dates listed in this table are meant as general guidelines only. For seed-sowing dates based on frost dates in your local area, go to **Almanac.com/PlantingTable.**

Aboveground crops are marked *.
(E) means early; (L) means late.

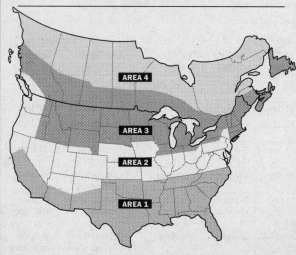

* Barley	
* Beans	(E)
	(L)
Beets	(E)
	(L)
* Broccoli plants	(E)
	(L)
* Brussels sprouts	
* Cabbage plants	
Carrots	(E)
	(L)
* Cauliflower plants	(E)
	(L)
* Celery plants	(E)
	(L)
* Collards	(E)
	(L)
* Corn, sweet	(E)
	(L)
* Cucumbers	
* Eggplant plants	
* Endive	(E)
	(L)
* Kale	(E)
	(L)
Leek plants	
* Lettuce	
* Muskmelons	
* Okra	
Onion sets	
* Parsley	
Parsnips	
* Peas	(E)
	(L)
* Pepper plants	
Potatoes	
* Pumpkins	
Radishes	(E)
	(L)
* Spinach	(E)
	(L)
* Squashes	
Sweet potatoes	
* Swiss chard	
* Tomato plants	
Turnips	(E)
	(L)
* Watermelons	
* Wheat, spring	
* Wheat, winter	

AREA 4
AREA 3
AREA 2
AREA 1

15-3/7	2/15-19, 3/6-7	3/15-4/7	3/15-20, 4/5-7	5/15-6/21	5/15-18, 6/3-17	6/1-30	6/3-17
15-4/7	3/15-20, 4/5-7	4/15-30	4/15-19	5/7-6/21	5/7-18, 6/3-17	5/30-6/15	6/3-15
7-31	8/7-15, 8/30-31	7/1-21	7/2-16	6/15-7/15	6/15-17, 7/2-15	—	—
7-28	2/20-28	3/15-4/3	3/21-4/3	5/1-15	5/1-3	5/25-6/10	5/25-6/2
1-30	9/15-27	8/15-31	8/16-29	7/15-8/15	7/17-30	6/15-7/8	6/18-7/1
15-3/15	2/15-19, 3/6-15	3/7-31	3/7-20	5/15-31	5/15-18	6/1-25	6/3-17
7-30	9/7-14, 9/28-30	8/1-20	8/1-15	6/15-7/7	6/15-17, 7/2-7	—	—
11-3/20	2/11-19, 3/6-20	3/7-4/15	3/7-20, 4/5-15	5/15-31	5/15-18	6/1-25	6/3-17
11-3/20	2/11-19, 3/6-20	3/7-4/15	3/7-20, 4/5-15	5/15-31	5/15-18	6/1-25	6/3-17
15-3/7	2/20-3/5	3/7-31	3/21-31	5/15-31	5/19-31	5/25-6/10	5/25-6/2
8-9/7	8/16-29	7/7-31	7/17-30	6/15-7/21	6/18-7/1, 7/17-21	6/15-7/8	6/18-7/1
15-3/7	2/15-19, 3/6-7	3/15-4/7	3/15-20, 4/5-7	5/15-31	5/15-18	6/1-25	6/3-17
7-31	8/7-15, 8/30-31	7/1-8/7	7/2-16, 7/31-8/7	6/15-7/21	6/15-17, 7/2-16	—	—
15-28	2/15-19	3/7-31	3/7-20	5/15-6/30	5/15-18, 6/3-17	6/1-30	6/3-17
15-30	9/28-30	8/15-9/7	8/15, 8/30-9/7	7/15-8/15	7/15-16, 7/31-8/15	—	—
11-3/20	2/11-19, 3/6-20	3/7-4/7	3/7-20, 4/5-7	5/15-31	5/15-18	6/1-25	6/3-17
7-30	9/7-14, 9/28-30	8/15-31	8/15, 8/30-31	7/1-8/7	7/2-16, 7/31-8/7	—	—
15-31	3/15-20	4/1-17	4/5-17	5/10-6/15	5/10-18, 6/3-15	5/30-6/20	6/3-17
7-31	8/7-15, 8/30-31	7/7-21	7/7-16	6/15-30	6/15-17	—	—
7-4/15	3/7-20, 4/5-15	4/7-5/15	4/7-19, 5/4-15	5/7-6/20	5/7-18, 6/3-17	5/30-6/15	6/3-15
7-4/15	3/7-20, 4/5-15	4/7-5/15	4/7-19, 5/4-15	6/1-30	6/3-17	6/15-30	6/15-17
15-3/20	2/15-19, 3/6-20	4/7-5/15	4/7-19, 5/4-15	5/15-31	5/15-18	6/1-25	6/3-17
15-9/7	8/15, 8/30-9/7	7/15-8/15	7/15-16, 7/31-8/15	6/7-30	6/7-17	—	—
11-3/20	2/11-19, 3/6-20	3/7-4/7	3/7-20, 4/5-7	5/15-31	5/15-18	6/1-15	6/3-15
7-30	9/7-14, 9/28-30	8/15-31	8/15, 8/30-31	7/1-8/7	7/2-16, 7/31-8/7	6/25-7/15	7/2-15
15-4/15	2/20-3/5, 3/21-4/4	3/7-4/7	3/21-4/4	5/15-31	5/19-31	6/1-25	6/1-2, 6/18-25
15-3/7	2/15-19, 3/6-7	3/1-31	3/6-20	5/15-6/30	5/15-18, 6/3-17	6/1-30	6/3-17
15-4/7	3/15-20, 4/5-7	4/15-5/7	4/15-19, 5/4-7	5/15-6/30	5/15-18, 6/3-17	6/1-30	6/3-17
15-6/1	4/15-19, 5/4-18	5/25-6/15	6/3-15	6/15-7/10	6/15-17, 7/2-10	6/25-7/7	7/2-7
1-28	2/1-3, 2/20-28	3/1-31	3/1-5, 3/21-31	5/15-6/7	5/19-6/2	6/1-25	6/1-2, 6/18-25
20-3/15	3/6-15	3/1-31	3/6-20	5/15-31	5/15-18	6/1-15	6/3-15
15-2/4	1/22-2/3	3/7-31	3/21-31	4/1-30	4/1-4, 4/20-30	5/10-31	5/19-31
15-2/7	1/15-21, 2/4-7	3/7-31	3/7-20	4/15-5/7	4/15-19, 5/4-7	5/15-31	5/15-18
15-30	9/28-30	8/7-31	8/7-15, 8/30-31	7/15-31	7/15-16, 7/31	7/10-28	7/10-16
1-20	3/6-20	4/1-30	4/5-19	5/15-6/30	5/15-18, 6/3-17	6/1-30	6/3-17
10-28	2/20-28	4/1-30	4/1-4, 4/20-30	5/1-31	5/1-3, 5/19-31	6/1-25	6/1-2, 6/18-25
7-20	3/7-20	4/23-5/15	5/4-15	5/15-31	5/15-18	6/1-30	6/3-17
21-3/1	1/22-2/3, 2/20-3/1	3/7-31	3/21-31	4/15-30	4/20-30	5/15-6/5	5/19-6/2
/1-21	10/14-21	9/7-30	9/15-27	8/15-31	8/16-29	7/10-31	7/17-30
7-3/15	2/7-19, 3/6-15	3/15-4/20	3/15-20, 4/5-19	5/15-31	5/15-18	6/1-25	6/3-17
/1-21	10/1-13	8/1-9/15	8/1-15, 8/30-9/14	7/17-9/7	7/31-8/15, 8/30-9/7	7/20-8/5	7/31-8/5
15-4/15	3/15-20, 4/5-15	4/15-30	4/15-19	5/15-6/15	5/15-18, 6/3-15	6/1-30	6/3-17
23-4/6	3/23-4/4	4/21-5/9	4/21-5/3	5/15-6/15	5/19-6/2	6/1-30	6/1-2, 6/18-30
7-3/15	2/7-19, 3/6-15	3/15-4/15	3/15-20, 4/5-15	5/1-31	5/4-18	5/15-31	5/15-18
7-20	3/7-20	4/7-30	4/7-19	5/15-31	5/15-18	6/1-15	6/3-15
20-2/15	1/22-2/3	3/15-31	3/21-31	4/7-30	4/20-30	5/10-31	5/19-31
1-10/15	9/15-27, 10/14-15	8/1-20	8/16-20	7/1-8/15	7/1, 7/17-30	—	—
15-4/7	3/15-20, 4/5-7	4/15-5/7	4/15-19, 5/4-7	5/15-6/30	5/15-18, 6/3-17	6/1-30	6/3-17
15-28	2/15-19	3/1-20	3/6-20	4/7-30	4/7-19	5/15-6/10	5/15-18, 6/3-10
/15-12/7	10/27-11/12, 11/26-12/7	9/15-10/20	9/28-10/13	8/11-9/15	8/11-15, 8/30-9/14	8/5-30	8/5-15, 8/30

FROSTS AND GROWING SEASONS

Dates given are normal averages for a light freeze; local weather and topography may cause considerable variations. The possibility of frost occurring after the spring dates and before the fall dates is 30 percent. The classification of freeze temperatures is usually based on their effect on plants. **Light freeze:** 29° to 32°F—tender plants killed. **Moderate freeze:** 25° to 28°F—widely destructive to most plants. **Severe freeze:** 24°F and colder—heavy damage to most plants. –dates courtesy of National Centers for Environmental Information

STATE	CITY	GROWING SEASON (DAYS)	LAST SPRING FROST	FIRST FALL FROST	STATE	CITY	GROWING SEASON (DAYS)	LAST SPRING FROST	FIRST FALL FROST
AK	Juneau	142	May 8	Sept. 28	ND	Bismarck	122	May 19	Sept. 19
AL	Mobile	267	Mar. 6	Nov. 29	NE	Omaha	160	Apr. 27	Oct. 5
AR	Pine Bluff	226	Mar. 26	Nov. 8	NE	North Platte	146	May 6	Sept. 30
AZ	Phoenix	340	Jan. 20	Dec. 27	NH	Concord	127	May 19	Sept. 24
AZ	Tucson	271	Mar. 3	Nov. 30	NJ	Newark	209	Apr. 8	Nov. 4
CA	Eureka	222	Apr. 6	Nov. 15	NM	Carlsbad	209	Apr. 5	Nov. 1
CA	Sacramento	263	Mar. 1	Nov. 20	NM	Los Alamos	146	May 10	Oct. 4
CA	San Francisco	*	*	*	NV	Las Vegas	300	Feb. 6	Dec. 4
CO	Denver	145	May 7	Sept. 30	NY	Albany	153	May 4	Oct. 5
CT	Hartford	159	May 1	Oct. 8	NY	Syracuse	156	May 4	Oct. 8
DE	Wilmington	194	Apr. 14	Oct. 26	OH	Akron	165	May 2	Oct. 15
FL	Orlando	331	Jan. 31	Dec. 29	OH	Cincinnati	175	Apr. 23	Oct. 16
FL	Tallahassee	224	Mar. 29	Nov. 9	OK	Lawton	211	Apr. 3	Nov. 1
GA	Athens	214	Apr. 3	Nov. 4	OK	Tulsa	210	Apr. 4	Nov. 1
GA	Savannah	249	Mar. 15	Nov. 20	OR	Pendleton	152	May 2	Oct. 2
IA	Atlantic	136	May 8	Sept. 22	OR	Portland	226	Mar. 25	Nov. 7
IA	Cedar Rapids	157	Apr. 30	Oct. 5	PA	Franklin	156	May 10	Oct. 14
ID	Boise	152	May 7	Oct. 7	PA	Williamsport	162	May 3	Oct. 13
IL	Chicago	186	Apr. 18	Oct. 22	RI	Kingston	142	May 12	Oct. 2
IL	Springfield	168	Apr. 23	Oct. 9	SC	Charleston	247	Mar. 17	Nov. 20
IN	Indianapolis	171	Apr. 25	Oct. 14	SC	Columbia	235	Mar. 23	Nov. 14
IN	South Bend	162	May 3	Oct. 13	SD	Rapid City	128	May 17	Sept. 23
KS	Topeka	173	Apr. 22	Oct. 13	TN	Memphis	225	Mar. 27	Nov. 8
KY	Lexington	183	Apr. 20	Oct. 21	TN	Nashville	198	Apr. 12	Oct. 28
LA	Monroe	234	Mar. 17	Nov. 7	TX	Amarillo	179	Apr. 21	Oct. 18
LA	New Orleans	309	Feb. 9	Dec. 16	TX	Denton	227	Mar. 27	Nov. 10
MA	Worcester	167	Apr. 28	Oct. 13	TX	San Antonio	257	Mar. 10	Nov. 23
MD	Baltimore	187	Apr. 18	Oct. 23	UT	Cedar City	122	May 28	Sept. 28
ME	Portland	152	May 5	Oct. 5	UT	Spanish Fork	158	May 4	Oct. 10
MI	Lansing	147	May 9	Oct. 4	VA	Norfolk	234	Mar. 28	Nov. 18
MI	Marquette	155	May 11	Oct. 14	VA	Richmond	202	Apr. 10	Oct. 30
MN	Duluth	119	May 25	Sept. 22	VT	Burlington	145	May 10	Oct. 3
MN	Willmar	146	May 5	Sept. 29	WA	Seattle	239	Mar. 18	Nov. 13
MO	Jefferson City	189	Apr. 14	Oct. 21	WA	Spokane	148	May 6	Oct. 2
MS	Columbia	234	Mar. 20	Nov. 10	WI	Green Bay	140	May 11	Sept. 29
MS	Tupelo	211	Apr. 3	Nov. 1	WI	Sparta	138	May 12	Sept. 28
MT	Fort Peck	129	May 15	Sept. 22	WV	Parkersburg	179	Apr. 23	Oct. 20
MT	Helena	123	May 19	Sept. 20	WY	Casper	107	May 31	Sept. 16
NC	Fayetteville	208	Apr. 8	Nov. 3	*Frosts do not occur every year.				

HOW TO ROTATE CROPS

Crop rotation is the practice of planting annual vegetables with their botanical families. Each vegetable family rotates together; it is not necessary to grow every family or every plant in each family. The benefits of rotating crops include fewer pests and soil-borne diseases, improved soil nutrition, and better soil structure. Failure to rotate vegetable crops eventually results in plants that fail to thrive and decreased harvest.

Here's how crop rotation works: In a single-crop plot, legumes (pea family) are planted in year 1, nightshade plants (tomatoes, etc.) in year 2, and gourds in year 3. In year 4, the cycle begins again. Alternatively, these three crops could be planted in three separate plots in year 1 and moved to the next plot in ensuing years. Additional families can be added. A simple plot plan keeps track of what goes where.

PLANT FAMILIES AND MEMBERS

Plants in the same family are genetically related and thus share similar characteristics (e.g., leaf appearance, tendrils for climbing).

CARROT, aka PARSLEY (Apiaceae, aka Umbelliferae): caraway, carrot*, celeriac, celery, chervil, coriander, dill, fennel, lovage, parsley, parsnip

GOOSEFOOT, aka CHARD (Chenopodiaceae): beet*, orach, quinoa, spinach, Swiss chard

GOURD, aka SQUASH (Cucurbitaceae): cucumber, gourd, melon, pumpkin, squash (summer and winter), watermelon

GRASS (Poaceae, aka Gramineae): sweet corn

MALLOW (Malvaceae): okra

MINT (Lamiaceae, aka Labiatae): anise hyssop, basil, Chinese artichoke, lavender, mint, oregano, rosemary, sage, savory (summer and winter), sweet marjoram, thyme

MORNING GLORY (Convolvulaceae): sweet potato

MUSTARD (Brassicaceae, aka Cruciferae): arugula, bok choy, broccoli, brussels sprouts, cabbage, cauliflower, collard, kale, kohlrabi, komatsuna, mizuna, mustard greens, radish*, rutabaga, turnip, watercress

NIGHTSHADE (Solanaceae): eggplant, pepper, potato, tomatillo, tomato

ONION (Alliaceae*): chives, garlic, leek, onion, shallot

PEA (Fabaceae, aka Leguminosae): bush, kidney, lima, pole, and soy beans; lentil; pea; peanut

SUNFLOWER (Asteraceae, aka Compositae): artichoke (globe and Jerusalem), calendula, chamomile, endive, escarole, lettuce, radicchio, salsify, sunflower, tarragon

These can be planted among any family.

TABLE OF MEASURES

LINEAR

1 hand = 4 inches
1 link = 7.92 inches
1 span = 9 inches
1 foot = 12 inches
1 yard = 3 feet
1 rod = 5½ yards
1 mile = 320 rods = 1,760 yards = 5,280 feet
1 international nautical mile = 6,076.1155 feet
1 knot = 1 nautical mile per hour
1 fathom = 2 yards = 6 feet
1 furlong = ⅛ mile = 660 feet = 220 yards
1 league = 3 miles = 24 furlongs
1 chain = 100 links = 22 yards

SQUARE

1 square foot = 144 square inches
1 square yard = 9 square feet
1 square rod = 30½ square yards = 272½ square feet = 625 square links
1 square chain = 16 square rods
1 acre = 10 square chains = 160 square rods = 43,560 square feet
1 square mile = 640 acres = 102,400 square rods

CUBIC

1 cubic foot = 1,728 cubic inches
1 cubic yard = 27 cubic feet
1 cord = 128 cubic feet
1 U.S. liquid gallon = 4 quarts = 231 cubic inches
1 imperial gallon = 1.20 U.S. gallons = 0.16 cubic foot
1 board foot = 144 cubic inches

DRY

2 pints = 1 quart
4 quarts = 1 gallon
2 gallons = 1 peck
4 pecks = 1 bushel

LIQUID

4 gills = 1 pint
63 gallons = 1 hogshead
2 hogsheads = 1 pipe or butt
2 pipes = 1 tun

KITCHEN

3 teaspoons = 1 tablespoon
16 tablespoons = 1 cup
1 cup = 8 ounces
2 cups = 1 pint
2 pints = 1 quart
4 quarts = 1 gallon

AVOIRDUPOIS
(for general use)

1 ounce = 16 drams
1 pound = 16 ounces
1 short hundredweight = 100 pounds
1 ton = 2,000 pounds
1 long ton = 2,240 pounds

APOTHECARIES'
(for pharmaceutical use)

1 scruple = 20 grains
1 dram = 3 scruples
1 ounce = 8 drams
1 pound = 12 ounces

METRIC CONVERSIONS

LINEAR

1 inch = 2.54 centimeters
1 centimeter = 0.39 inch
1 meter = 39.37 inches
1 yard = 0.914 meter
1 mile = 1.61 kilometers
1 kilometer = 0.62 mile

SQUARE

1 square inch = 6.45 square centimeters
1 square yard = 0.84 square meter
1 square mile = 2.59 square kilometers

1 square kilometer = 0.386 square mile
1 acre = 0.40 hectare
1 hectare = 2.47 acres

CUBIC

1 cubic yard = 0.76 cubic meter
1 cubic meter = 1.31 cubic yards

HOUSEHOLD

½ teaspoon = 2 mL
1 teaspoon = 5 mL
1 tablespoon = 15 mL
¼ cup = 60 mL

⅓ cup = 75 mL
½ cup = 125 mL
⅔ cup = 150 mL
¾ cup = 175 mL
1 cup = 250 mL
1 liter = 1.057 U.S. liquid quarts
1 U.S. liquid quart = 0.946 liter
1 U.S. liquid gallon = 3.78 liters
1 gram = 0.035 ounce
1 ounce = 28.349 grams
1 kilogram = 2.2 pounds
1 pound = 0.45 kilogram

TO CONVERT CELSIUS AND FAHRENHEIT: °C = (°F - 32)/1.8; °F = (°C × 1.8) + 32

TIDAL GLOSSARY

APOGEAN TIDE: A monthly tide of decreased range that occurs when the Moon is at apogee (farthest from Earth).

CURRENT: Generally, a horizontal movement of water. Currents may be classified as tidal and nontidal. Tidal currents are caused by gravitational interactions between the Sun, Moon, and Earth and are part of the same general movement of the sea that is manifested in the vertical rise and fall, called tide. Nontidal currents include the permanent currents in the general circulatory systems of the sea as well as temporary currents arising from more pronounced meteorological variability.

DIURNAL TIDE: A tide with one high water and one low water in a tidal day of approximately 24 hours.

MEAN LOWER LOW WATER: The arithmetic mean of the lesser of a daily pair of low waters, observed over a specific 19-year cycle called the National Tidal Datum Epoch.

NEAP TIDE: A tide of decreased range that occurs twice a month, when the Moon is in quadrature (during its first and last quarters, when the Sun and the Moon are at right angles to each other relative to Earth).

PERIGEAN TIDE: A monthly tide of increased range that occurs when the Moon is at perigee (closest to Earth).

RED TIDE: Toxic algal blooms caused by several genera of dinoflagellates that usually turn the sea red or brown. These pose a serious threat to marine life and may be harmful to humans.

RIP CURRENT: A potentially dangerous, narrow, intense, surf-zone current flowing outward from shore.

SEMIDIURNAL TIDE: A tide with one high water and one low water every half-day. East Coast tides, for example, are semidiurnal, with two highs and two lows during a tidal day of approximately 24 hours.

SLACK WATER (SLACK): The state of a tidal current when its speed is near zero, especially the moment when a reversing current changes direction and its speed is zero.

SPRING TIDE: A tide of increased range that occurs at times of syzygy each month. Named not for the season of spring but from the German *springen* ("to leap up"), a spring tide also brings a lower low water.

STORM SURGE: The local change in the elevation of the ocean along a shore due to a storm, measured by subtracting the astronomic tidal elevation from the total elevation. It typically has a duration of a few hours and is potentially catastrophic, especially on low-lying coasts with gently sloping offshore topography.

SYZYGY: The nearly straight-line configuration that occurs twice a month, when the Sun and the Moon are in conjunction (on the same side of Earth, at the new Moon) and when they are in opposition (on opposite sides of Earth, at the full Moon). In both cases, the gravitational effects of the Sun and the Moon reinforce each other, and tidal range is increased.

TIDAL BORE: A tide-induced wave that propagates up a relatively shallow and sloping estuary or river with a steep wave front.

TSUNAMI: Commonly called a tidal wave, a tsunami is a series of long-period waves caused by an underwater earthquake or volcano. In open ocean, the waves are small and travel at high speed; as they near shore, some may build to more than 30 feet high, becoming a threat to life and property.

VANISHING TIDE: A mixed tide of considerable inequality in the two highs and two lows, so that the lower high (or higher low) may appear to vanish. ■

TIDE CORRECTIONS

Many factors affect tides, including the shoreline, time of the Moon's southing (crossing the meridian), and the Moon's phase. The High Tide Times column on the **Left-Hand Calendar Pages, 120–146,** lists the times of high tide at Commonwealth Pier in Boston (MA) Harbor. The heights of some of these tides, reckoned from Mean Lower Low Water, are given on the **Right-Hand Calendar Pages, 121–147.** Use the table below to calculate the approximate times and heights of high tide at the places shown. Apply the time difference to the times of high tide at Boston and the height difference to the heights at Boston. A more detailed and accurate tide calculator for the United States and Canada can be found at **Almanac.com/Tides.**

EXAMPLE:

The conversion of the times and heights of the tides at Boston to those at Cape Fear, North Carolina, is given below:

High tide at Boston	11:45 A.M.
Correction for Cape Fear	− 3 55
High tide at Cape Fear	7:50 A.M.

Tide height at Boston	11.6 ft.
Correction for Cape Fear	− 5.0 ft.
Tide height at Cape Fear	6.6 ft.

Estimations derived from this table are *not* meant to be used for navigation. *The Old Farmer's Almanac* accepts no responsibility for errors or any consequences ensuing from the use of this table.

TIDAL SITE	TIME (H. M.)	HEIGHT (FT.)	TIDAL SITE	TIME (H. M.)	HEIGHT (FT.)
CANADA			Cape Cod Canal		
Alberton, PE	*−5 45	−7.5	East Entrance	−0 01	−0.8
Charlottetown, PE	*−0 45	−3.5	West Entrance	−2 16	−5.9
Halifax, NS	−3 23	−4.5	Chatham Outer Coast	+0 30	−2.8
North Sydney, NS	−3 15	−6.5	Inside	+1 54	**0.4
Saint John, NB	+0 30	+15.0	Cohasset	+0 02	−0.07
St. John's, NL	−4 00	−6.5	Cotuit Highlands	+1 15	**0.3
Yarmouth, NS	−0 40	+3.0	Dennis Port	+1 01	**0.4
MAINE			Duxbury–Gurnet Point	+0 02	−0.3
Bar Harbor	−0 34	+0.9	Fall River	−3 03	−5.0
Belfast	−0 20	+0.4	Gloucester	−0 03	−0.8
Boothbay Harbor	−0 18	−0.8	Hingham	+0 07	0.0
Chebeague Island	−0 16	−0.6	Hull	+0 03	−0.2
Eastport	−0 28	+8.4	Hyannis Port	+1 01	**0.3
Kennebunkport	+0 04	−1.0	Magnolia–Manchester	−0 02	−0.7
Machias	−0 28	+2.8	Marblehead	−0 02	−0.4
Monhegan Island	−0 25	−0.8	Marion	−3 22	−5.4
Old Orchard	0 00	−0.8	Monument Beach	−3 08	−5.4
Portland	−0 12	−0.6	Nahant	−0 01	−0.5
Rockland	−0 28	+0.1	Nantasket	+0 04	−0.1
Stonington	−0 30	+0.1	Nantucket	+0 56	**0.3
York	−0 09	−1.0	Nauset Beach	+0 30	**0.6
NEW HAMPSHIRE			New Bedford	−3 24	−5.7
Hampton	+0 02	−1.3	Newburyport	+0 19	−1.8
Portsmouth	+0 11	−1.5	Oak Bluffs	+0 30	**0.2
Rye Beach	−0 09	−0.9	Onset–R.R. Bridge	−2 16	−5.9
MASSACHUSETTS			Plymouth	+0 05	0.0
Annisquam	−0 02	−1.1	Provincetown	+0 14	−0.4
Beverly Farms	0 00	−0.5	Revere Beach	−0 01	−0.3

TIDAL SITE	TIME (H. M.)	HEIGHT (FT.)	TIDAL SITE	TIME (H. M.)	HEIGHT (FT.)
Rockport	−0 08	−1.0	**PENNSYLVANIA**		
Salem	0 00	−0.5	Philadelphia	+2 40	−3.5
Scituate	−0 05	−0.7	**DELAWARE**		
Wareham	−3 09	−5.3	Cape Henlopen	−2 48	−5.3
Wellfleet	+0 12	+0.5	Rehoboth Beach	−3 37	−5.7
West Falmouth	−3 10	−5.4	Wilmington	+1 56	−3.8
Westport Harbor	−3 22	−6.4	**MARYLAND**		
Woods Hole			Annapolis	+6 23	−8.5
Little Harbor	−2 50	**0.2	Baltimore	+7 59	−8.3
Oceanographic			Cambridge	+5 05	−7.8
Institute	−3 07	**0.2	Havre de Grace	+11 21	−7.7
RHODE ISLAND			Point No Point	+2 28	−8.1
Bristol	−3 24	−5.3	Prince Frederick–		
Narragansett Pier	−3 42	−6.2	Plum Point	+4 25	−8.5
Newport	−3 34	−5.9	**VIRGINIA**		
Point Judith	−3 41	−6.3	Cape Charles	−2 20	−7.0
Providence	−3 20	−4.8	Hampton Roads	−2 02	−6.9
Sakonnet	−3 44	−5.6	Norfolk	−2 06	−6.6
Watch Hill	−2 50	−6.8	Virginia Beach	−4 00	−6.0
CONNECTICUT			Yorktown	−2 13	−7.0
Bridgeport	+0 01	−2.6	**NORTH CAROLINA**		
Madison	−0 22	−2.3	Cape Fear	−3 55	−5.0
New Haven	−0 11	−3.2	Cape Lookout	−4 28	−5.7
New London	−1 54	−6.7	Currituck	−4 10	−5.8
Norwalk	+0 01	−2.2	Hatteras		
Old Lyme–			Inlet	−4 03	−7.4
Highway Bridge	−0 30	−6.2	Kitty Hawk	−4 14	−6.2
Stamford	+0 01	−2.2	Ocean	−4 26	−6.0
Stonington	−2 27	−6.6	**SOUTH CAROLINA**		
NEW YORK			Charleston	−3 22	−4.3
Coney Island	−3 33	−4.9	Georgetown	−1 48	**0.36
Fire Island Light	−2 43	**0.1	Hilton Head	−3 22	−2.9
Long Beach	−3 11	−5.7	Myrtle Beach	−3 49	−4.4
Montauk Harbor	−2 19	−7.4	St. Helena–		
New York City–Battery	−2 43	−5.0	Harbor Entrance	−3 15	−3.4
Oyster Bay	+0 04	−1.8	**GEORGIA**		
Port Chester	−0 09	−2.2	Jekyll Island	−3 46	−2.9
Port Washington	−0 01	−2.1	St. Simon's Island	−2 50	−2.9
Sag Harbor	−0 55	−6.8	Savannah Beach		
Southampton–			River Entrance	−3 14	−5.5
Shinnecock Inlet	−4 20	**0.2	Tybee Light	−3 22	−2.7
Willets Point	0 00	−2.3	**FLORIDA**		
NEW JERSEY			Cape Canaveral	−3 59	−6.0
Asbury Park	−4 04	−5.3	Daytona Beach	−3 28	−5.3
Atlantic City	−3 56	−5.5	Fort Lauderdale	−2 50	−7.2
Bay Head–Sea Girt	−4 04	−5.3	Fort Pierce Inlet	−3 32	−6.9
Beach Haven	−1 43	**0.24	Jacksonville–		
Cape May	−3 28	−5.3	Railroad Bridge	−6 55	**0.1
Ocean City	−3 06	−5.9	Miami Harbor Entrance	−3 18	−7.0
Sandy Hook	−3 30	−5.0	St. Augustine	−2 55	−4.9
Seaside Park	−4 03	−5.4			

*VARIES WIDELY; ACCURATE ONLY TO WITHIN 1½ HOURS. CONSULT LOCAL TIDE TABLES FOR PRECISE TIMES AND HEIGHTS.
**WHERE THE DIFFERENCE IN THE HEIGHT COLUMN IS SO MARKED, THE HEIGHT AT BOSTON SHOULD BE MULTIPLIED BY THIS RATIO.

TIME CORRECTIONS

Astronomical data for Boston is given on **pages 104, 108–109,** and **120–146.** Use the Key Letters shown on those pages with this table to find the number of minutes that you must add to or subtract from Boston time to get the correct time for your city. (Times are approximate.) For more information on the use of Key Letters, see **How to Use This Almanac, page 116.**

GET TIMES SIMPLY AND SPECIFICALLY: Download astronomical times calculated for your zip code and presented as Left-Hand Calendar Pages at **Almanac.com/Access.**

TIME ZONES CODES represent standard time. Atlantic is –1, Eastern is 0, Central is 1, Mountain is 2, Pacific is 3, Alaska is 4, and Hawaii-Aleutian is 5.

STATE	CITY	NORTH LATITUDE °	'	WEST LONGITUDE °	'	TIME ZONE CODE	KEY LETTERS (MINUTES) A	B	C	D	E
AK	Anchorage	61	10	149	59	4	–46	+27	+71	+122	+171
AK	Cordova	60	33	145	45	4	–55	+13	+55	+103	+149
AK	Fairbanks	64	48	147	51	4	–127	+2	+61	+131	+205
AK	Juneau	58	18	134	25	4	–76	–23	+10	+49	+86
AK	Ketchikan	55	21	131	39	4	–62	–25	0	+29	+56
AK	Kodiak	57	47	152	24	4	0	+49	+82	+120	+154
AL	Birmingham	33	31	86	49	1	+30	+15	+3	–10	–20
AL	Decatur	34	36	86	59	1	+27	+14	+4	–7	–17
AL	Mobile	30	42	88	3	1	+42	+23	+8	–8	–22
AL	Montgomery	32	23	86	19	1	+31	+14	+1	–13	–25
AR	Fort Smith	35	23	94	25	1	+55	+43	+33	+22	+14
AR	Little Rock	34	45	92	17	1	+48	+35	+25	+13	+4
AR	Texarkana	33	26	94	3	1	+59	+44	+32	+18	+8
AZ	Flagstaff	35	12	111	39	2	+64	+52	+42	+31	+22
AZ	Phoenix	33	27	112	4	2	+71	+56	+44	+30	+20
AZ	Tucson	32	13	110	58	2	+70	+53	+40	+24	+12
AZ	Yuma	32	43	114	37	2	+83	+67	+54	+40	+28
CA	Bakersfield	35	23	119	1	3	+33	+21	+12	+1	–7
CA	Barstow	34	54	117	1	3	+27	+14	+4	–7	–16
CA	Fresno	36	44	119	47	3	+32	+22	+15	+6	0
CA	Los Angeles-Pasadena-Santa Monica	34	3	118	14	3	+34	+20	+9	–3	–13
CA	Palm Springs	33	49	116	32	3	+28	+13	+1	–12	–22
CA	Redding	40	35	122	24	3	+31	+27	+25	+22	+19
CA	Sacramento	38	35	121	30	3	+34	+27	+21	+15	+10
CA	San Diego	32	43	117	9	3	+33	+17	+4	–9	–21
CA	San Francisco-Oakland-San Jose	37	47	122	25	3	+40	+31	+25	+18	+12
CO	Craig	40	31	107	33	2	+32	+28	+25	+22	+20
CO	Denver-Boulder	39	44	104	59	2	+24	+19	+15	+11	+7
CO	Grand Junction	39	4	108	33	2	+40	+34	+29	+24	+20
CO	Pueblo	38	16	104	37	2	+27	+20	+14	+7	+2
CO	Trinidad	37	10	104	31	2	+30	+21	+13	+5	0
CT	Bridgeport	41	11	73	11	0	+12	+10	+8	+6	+4
CT	Hartford-New Britain	41	46	72	41	0	+8	+7	+6	+5	+4
CT	New Haven	41	18	72	56	0	+11	+8	+7	+5	+4
CT	New London	41	22	72	6	0	+7	+5	+4	+2	+1
CT	Norwalk-Stamford	41	7	73	22	0	+13	+10	+9	+7	+5
CT	Waterbury-Meriden	41	33	73	3	0	+10	+9	+7	+6	+5
DC	Washington	38	54	77	1	0	+35	+28	+23	+18	+13
DE	Wilmington	39	45	75	33	0	+26	+21	+18	+13	+10

STATE	CITY	NORTH LATITUDE °	′	WEST LONGITUDE °	′	TIME ZONE CODE	KEY LETTERS (MINUTES) A	B	C	D	E
FL	Fort Myers	26	38	81	52	0	+87	+63	+44	+21	+4
FL	Jacksonville	30	20	81	40	0	+77	+58	+43	+25	+11
FL	Miami	25	47	80	12	0	+88	+57	+37	+14	−3
FL	Orlando	28	32	81	22	0	+80	+59	+42	+22	+6
FL	Pensacola	30	25	87	13	1	+39	+20	+5	−12	−26
FL	St. Petersburg	27	46	82	39	0	+87	+65	+47	+26	+10
FL	Tallahassee	30	27	84	17	0	+87	+68	+53	+35	+22
FL	Tampa	27	57	82	27	0	+86	+64	+46	+25	+9
FL	West Palm Beach	26	43	80	3	0	+79	+55	+36	+14	−2
GA	Atlanta	33	45	84	24	0	+79	+65	+53	+40	+30
GA	Augusta	33	28	81	58	0	+70	+55	+44	+30	+19
GA	Macon	32	50	83	38	0	+79	+63	+50	+36	+24
GA	Savannah	32	5	81	6	0	+70	+54	+40	+25	+13
HI	Hilo	19	44	155	5	5	+94	+62	+37	+7	−15
HI	Honolulu	21	18	157	52	5	+102	+72	+48	+19	−1
HI	Lanai City	20	50	156	55	5	+99	+69	+44	+15	−6
HI	Lihue	21	59	159	23	5	+107	+77	+54	+26	+5
IA	Davenport	41	32	90	35	1	+20	+19	+17	+16	+15
IA	Des Moines	41	35	93	37	1	+32	+31	+30	+28	+27
IA	Dubuque	42	30	90	41	1	+17	+18	+18	+18	+18
IA	Waterloo	42	30	92	20	1	+24	+24	+24	+25	+25
ID	Boise	43	37	116	12	2	+55	+58	+60	+62	+64
ID	Lewiston	46	25	117	1	3	−12	−3	+2	+10	+17
ID	Pocatello	42	52	112	27	2	+43	+44	+45	+46	+46
IL	Cairo	37	0	89	11	1	+29	+20	+12	+4	−2
IL	Chicago-Oak Park	41	52	87	38	1	+7	+6	+6	+5	+4
IL	Danville	40	8	87	37	1	+13	+9	+6	+2	0
IL	Decatur	39	51	88	57	1	+19	+15	+11	+7	+4
IL	Peoria	40	42	89	36	1	+19	+16	+14	+11	+9
IL	Springfield	39	48	89	39	1	+22	+18	+14	+10	+6
IN	Fort Wayne	41	4	85	9	0	+60	+58	+56	+54	+52
IN	Gary	41	36	87	20	1	+7	+6	+4	+3	+2
IN	Indianapolis	39	46	86	10	0	+69	+64	+60	+56	+52
IN	Muncie	40	12	85	23	0	+64	+60	+57	+53	+50
IN	South Bend	41	41	86	15	0	+62	+61	+60	+59	+58
IN	Terre Haute	39	28	87	24	0	+74	+69	+65	+60	+56
KS	Fort Scott	37	50	94	42	1	+49	+41	+34	+27	+21
KS	Liberal	37	3	100	55	1	+76	+66	+59	+51	+44
KS	Oakley	39	8	100	51	1	+69	+63	+59	+53	+49
KS	Salina	38	50	97	37	1	+57	+51	+46	+40	+35
KS	Topeka	39	3	95	40	1	+49	+43	+38	+32	+28
KS	Wichita	37	42	97	20	1	+60	+51	+45	+37	+31
KY	Lexington-Frankfort	38	3	84	30	0	+67	+59	+53	+46	+41
KY	Louisville	38	15	85	46	0	+72	+64	+58	+52	+46
LA	Alexandria	31	18	92	27	1	+58	+40	+26	+9	−3
LA	Baton Rouge	30	27	91	11	1	+55	+36	+21	+3	−10
LA	Lake Charles	30	14	93	13	1	+64	+44	+29	+11	−2
LA	Monroe	32	30	92	7	1	+53	+37	+24	+9	−1
LA	New Orleans	29	57	90	4	1	+52	+32	+16	−1	−15
LA	Shreveport	32	31	93	45	1	+60	+44	+31	+16	+4
MA	Brockton	42	5	71	1	0	0	0	0	0	−1
MA	Fall River-New Bedford	41	42	71	9	0	+2	+1	0	0	−1
MA	Lawrence-Lowell	42	42	71	10	0	0	0	0	0	+1
MA	Pittsfield	42	27	73	15	0	+8	+8	+8	+8	+8
MA	Springfield-Holyoke	42	6	72	36	0	+6	+6	+6	+5	+5
MA	Worcester	42	16	71	48	0	+3	+2	+2	+2	+2

STATE	CITY	NORTH LATITUDE °	NORTH LATITUDE '	WEST LONGITUDE °	WEST LONGITUDE '	TIME ZONE CODE	KEY LETTERS (MINUTES) A	B	C	D	E
MD	Baltimore	39	17	76	37	0	+32	+26	+22	+17	+13
MD	Hagerstown	39	39	77	43	0	+35	+30	+26	+22	+18
MD	Salisbury	38	22	75	36	0	+31	+23	+18	+11	+6
ME	Augusta	44	19	69	46	0	−12	−8	−5	−1	0
ME	Bangor	44	48	68	46	0	−18	−13	−9	−5	−1
ME	Eastport	44	54	67	0	0	−26	−20	−16	−11	−8
ME	Ellsworth	44	33	68	25	0	−18	−14	−10	−6	−3
ME	Portland	43	40	70	15	0	−8	−5	−3	−1	0
ME	Presque Isle	46	41	68	1	0	−29	−19	−12	−4	+2
MI	Cheboygan	45	39	84	29	0	+40	+47	+53	+59	+64
MI	Detroit-Dearborn	42	20	83	3	0	+47	+47	+47	+47	+47
MI	Flint	43	1	83	41	0	+47	+49	+50	+51	+52
MI	Ironwood	46	27	90	9	1	0	+9	+15	+23	+29
MI	Jackson	42	15	84	24	0	+53	+53	+53	+52	+52
MI	Kalamazoo	42	17	85	35	0	+58	+57	+57	+57	+57
MI	Lansing	42	44	84	33	0	+52	+53	+53	+54	+54
MI	St. Joseph	42	5	86	26	0	+61	+61	+60	+60	+59
MI	Traverse City	44	46	85	38	0	+49	+54	+57	+62	+65
MN	Albert Lea	43	39	93	22	1	+24	+26	+28	+31	+33
MN	Bemidji	47	28	94	53	1	+14	+26	+34	+44	+52
MN	Duluth	46	47	92	6	1	+6	+16	+23	+31	+38
MN	Minneapolis-St. Paul	44	59	93	16	1	+18	+24	+28	+33	+37
MN	Ortonville	45	19	96	27	1	+30	+36	+40	+46	+51
MO	Jefferson City	38	34	92	10	1	+36	+29	+24	+18	+13
MO	Joplin	37	6	94	30	1	+50	+41	+33	+25	+18
MO	Kansas City	39	1	94	20	1	+44	+37	+33	+27	+23
MO	Poplar Bluff	36	46	90	24	1	+35	+25	+17	+8	+1
MO	St. Joseph	39	46	94	50	1	+43	+38	+35	+30	+27
MO	St. Louis	38	37	90	12	1	+28	+21	+16	+10	+5
MO	Springfield	37	13	93	18	1	+45	+36	+29	+20	+14
MS	Biloxi	30	24	88	53	1	+46	+27	+11	−5	−19
MS	Jackson	32	18	90	11	1	+46	+30	+17	+1	−10
MS	Meridian	32	22	88	42	1	+40	+24	+11	−4	−15
MS	Tupelo	34	16	88	34	1	+35	+21	+10	−2	−11
MT	Billings	45	47	108	30	2	+16	+23	+29	+35	+40
MT	Butte	46	1	112	32	2	+31	+39	+45	+52	+57
MT	Glasgow	48	12	106	38	2	−1	+11	+21	+32	+42
MT	Great Falls	47	30	111	17	2	+20	+31	+39	+49	+58
MT	Helena	46	36	112	2	2	+27	+36	+43	+51	+57
MT	Miles City	46	25	105	51	2	+3	+11	+18	+26	+32
NC	Asheville	35	36	82	33	0	+67	+55	+46	+35	+27
NC	Charlotte	35	14	80	51	0	+61	+49	+39	+28	+19
NC	Durham	36	0	78	55	0	+51	+40	+31	+21	+13
NC	Greensboro	36	4	79	47	0	+54	+43	+35	+25	+17
NC	Raleigh	35	47	78	38	0	+51	+39	+30	+20	+12
NC	Wilmington	34	14	77	55	0	+52	+38	+27	+15	+5
ND	Bismarck	46	48	100	47	1	+41	+50	+58	+66	+73
ND	Fargo	46	53	96	47	1	+24	+34	+42	+50	+57
ND	Grand Forks	47	55	97	3	1	+21	+33	+43	+53	+62
ND	Minot	48	14	101	18	1	+36	+50	+59	+71	+81
ND	Williston	48	9	103	37	1	+46	+59	+69	+80	+90
NE	Grand Island	40	55	98	21	1	+53	+51	+49	+46	+44
NE	Lincoln	40	49	96	41	1	+47	+44	+42	+39	+37
NE	North Platte	41	8	100	46	1	+62	+60	+58	+56	+54
NE	Omaha	41	16	95	56	1	+43	+40	+39	+37	+36
NH	Berlin	44	28	71	11	0	−7	−3	0	+3	+7
NH	Keene	42	56	72	17	0	+2	+3	+4	+5	+6

STATE	CITY	NORTH LATITUDE °	NORTH LATITUDE ′	WEST LONGITUDE °	WEST LONGITUDE ′	TIME ZONE CODE	KEY LETTERS (MINUTES) A	B	C	D	E
NH	Manchester-Concord	42	59	71	28	0	0	0	+1	+2	+3
NH	Portsmouth	43	5	70	45	0	−4	−2	−1	0	0
NJ	Atlantic City	39	22	74	26	0	+23	+17	+13	+8	+4
NJ	Camden	39	57	75	7	0	+24	+19	+16	+12	+9
NJ	Cape May	38	56	74	56	0	+26	+20	+15	+9	+5
NJ	Newark-East Orange	40	44	74	10	0	+17	+14	+12	+9	+7
NJ	Paterson	40	55	74	10	0	+17	+14	+12	+9	+7
NJ	Trenton	40	13	74	46	0	+21	+17	+14	+11	+8
NM	Albuquerque	35	5	106	39	2	+45	+32	+22	+11	+2
NM	Gallup	35	32	108	45	2	+52	+40	+31	+20	+11
NM	Las Cruces	32	19	106	47	2	+53	+36	+23	+8	−3
NM	Roswell	33	24	104	32	2	+41	+26	+14	0	−10
NM	Santa Fe	35	41	105	56	2	+40	+28	+19	+9	0
NV	Carson City-Reno	39	10	119	46	3	+25	+19	+14	+9	+5
NV	Elko	40	50	115	46	3	+3	0	−1	−3	−5
NV	Las Vegas	36	10	115	9	3	+16	+4	−3	−13	−20
NY	Albany	42	39	73	45	0	+9	+10	+10	+11	+11
NY	Binghamton	42	6	75	55	0	+20	+19	+19	+18	+18
NY	Buffalo	42	53	78	52	0	+29	+30	+30	+31	+32
NY	New York	40	45	74	0	0	+17	+14	+11	+9	+6
NY	Ogdensburg	44	42	75	30	0	+8	+13	+17	+21	+25
NY	Syracuse	43	3	76	9	0	+17	+19	+20	+21	+22
OH	Akron	41	5	81	31	0	+46	+43	+41	+39	+37
OH	Canton	40	48	81	23	0	+46	+43	+41	+38	+36
OH	Cincinnati-Hamilton	39	6	84	31	0	+64	+58	+53	+48	+44
OH	Cleveland-Lakewood	41	30	81	42	0	+45	+43	+42	+40	+39
OH	Columbus	39	57	83	1	0	+55	+51	+47	+43	+40
OH	Dayton	39	45	84	10	0	+61	+56	+52	+48	+44
OH	Toledo	41	39	83	33	0	+52	+50	+49	+48	+47
OH	Youngstown	41	6	80	39	0	+42	+40	+38	+36	+34
OK	Oklahoma City	35	28	97	31	1	+67	+55	+46	+35	+26
OK	Tulsa	36	9	95	60	1	+59	+48	+40	+30	+22
OR	Eugene	44	3	123	6	3	+21	+24	+27	+30	+33
OR	Pendleton	45	40	118	47	3	−1	+4	+10	+16	+21
OR	Portland	45	31	122	41	3	+14	+20	+25	+31	+36
OR	Salem	44	57	123	1	3	+17	+23	+27	+31	+35
PA	Allentown-Bethlehem	40	36	75	28	0	+23	+20	+17	+14	+12
PA	Erie	42	7	80	5	0	+36	+36	+35	+35	+35
PA	Harrisburg	40	16	76	53	0	+30	+26	+23	+19	+16
PA	Lancaster	40	2	76	18	0	+28	+24	+20	+17	+13
PA	Philadelphia-Chester	39	57	75	9	0	+24	+19	+16	+12	+9
PA	Pittsburgh-McKeesport	40	26	80	0	0	+42	+38	+35	+32	+29
PA	Reading	40	20	75	56	0	+26	+22	+19	+16	+13
PA	Scranton-Wilkes-Barre	41	25	75	40	0	+21	+19	+18	+16	+15
PA	York	39	58	76	43	0	+30	+26	+22	+18	+15
RI	Providence	41	50	71	25	0	+3	+2	+1	0	0
SC	Charleston	32	47	79	56	0	+64	+48	+36	+21	+10
SC	Columbia	34	0	81	2	0	+65	+51	+40	+27	+17
SC	Spartanburg	34	56	81	57	0	+66	+53	+43	+32	+23
SD	Aberdeen	45	28	98	29	1	+37	+44	+49	+54	+59
SD	Pierre	44	22	100	21	1	+49	+53	+56	+60	+63
SD	Rapid City	44	5	103	14	2	+2	+5	+8	+11	+13
SD	Sioux Falls	43	33	96	44	1	+38	+40	+42	+44	+46
TN	Chattanooga	35	3	85	19	0	+79	+67	+57	+45	+36
TN	Knoxville	35	58	83	55	0	+71	+60	+51	+41	+33
TN	Memphis	35	9	90	3	1	+38	+26	+16	+5	−3
TN	Nashville	36	10	86	47	1	+22	+11	+3	−6	−14

STATE/ PROVINCE	CITY	NORTH LATITUDE		WEST LONGITUDE		TIME ZONE CODE	KEY LETTERS (MINUTES)				
		°	′	°	′		A	B	C	D	E
TX	Amarillo	35	12	101	50	1	+85	+73	+63	+52	+43
TX	Austin	30	16	97	45	1	+82	+62	+47	+29	+15
TX	Beaumont	30	5	94	6	1	+67	+48	+32	+14	0
TX	Brownsville	25	54	97	30	1	+91	+66	+46	+23	+5
TX	Corpus Christi	27	48	97	24	1	+86	+64	+46	+25	+9
TX	Dallas-Fort Worth	32	47	96	48	1	+71	+55	+43	+28	+17
TX	El Paso	31	45	106	29	2	+53	+35	+22	+6	−6
TX	Galveston	29	18	94	48	1	+72	+52	+35	+16	+1
TX	Houston	29	45	95	22	1	+73	+53	+37	+19	+5
TX	McAllen	26	12	98	14	1	+93	+69	+49	+26	+9
TX	San Antonio	29	25	98	30	1	+87	+66	+50	+31	+16
UT	Kanab	37	3	112	32	2	+62	+53	+46	+37	+30
UT	Moab	38	35	109	33	2	+46	+39	+33	+27	+22
UT	Ogden	41	13	111	58	2	+47	+45	+43	+41	+40
UT	Salt Lake City	40	45	111	53	2	+48	+45	+43	+40	+38
UT	Vernal	40	27	109	32	2	+40	+36	+33	+30	+28
VA	Charlottesville	38	2	78	30	0	+43	+35	+29	+22	+17
VA	Danville	36	36	79	23	0	+51	+41	+33	+24	+17
VA	Norfolk	36	51	76	17	0	+38	+28	+21	+12	+5
VA	Richmond	37	32	77	26	0	+41	+32	+25	+17	+11
VA	Roanoke	37	16	79	57	0	+51	+42	+35	+27	+21
VA	Winchester	39	11	78	10	0	+38	+33	+28	+23	+19
VT	Brattleboro	42	51	72	34	0	+4	+5	+5	+6	+7
VT	Burlington	44	29	73	13	0	0	+4	+8	+12	+15
VT	Rutland	43	37	72	58	0	+2	+5	+7	+9	+11
VT	St. Johnsbury	44	25	72	1	0	−4	0	+3	+7	+10
WA	Bellingham	48	45	122	29	3	0	+13	+24	+37	+47
WA	Seattle-Tacoma-Olympia	47	37	122	20	3	+3	+15	+24	+34	+42
WA	Spokane	47	40	117	24	3	−16	−4	+4	+14	+23
WA	Walla Walla	46	4	118	20	3	−5	+2	+8	+15	+21
WI	Eau Claire	44	49	91	30	1	+12	+17	+21	+25	+29
WI	Green Bay	44	31	88	0	1	0	+3	+7	+11	+14
WI	La Crosse	43	48	91	15	1	+15	+18	+20	+22	+25
WI	Madison	43	4	89	23	1	+10	+11	+12	+14	+15
WI	Milwaukee	43	2	87	54	1	+4	+6	+7	+8	+9
WI	Oshkosh	44	1	88	33	1	+3	+6	+9	+12	+15
WI	Wausau	44	58	89	38	1	+4	+9	+13	+18	+22
WV	Charleston	38	21	81	38	0	+55	+48	+42	+35	+30
WV	Parkersburg	39	16	81	34	0	+52	+46	+42	+36	+32
WY	Casper	42	51	106	19	2	+19	+19	+20	+21	+22
WY	Cheyenne	41	8	104	49	2	+19	+16	+14	+12	+11
WY	Sheridan	44	48	106	58	2	+14	+19	+23	+27	+31
CANADA											
AB	Calgary	51	5	114	5	2	+13	+35	+50	+68	+84
AB	Edmonton	53	34	113	25	2	−3	+26	+47	+72	+93
BC	Vancouver	49	13	123	6	3	0	+15	+26	+40	+52
MB	Winnipeg	49	53	97	10	1	+12	+30	+43	+58	+71
NB	Saint John	45	16	66	3	−1	+28	+34	+39	+44	+49
NS	Halifax	44	38	63	35	−1	+21	+26	+29	+33	+37
NS	Sydney	46	10	60	10	−1	+1	+9	+15	+23	+28
ON	Ottawa	45	25	75	43	0	+6	+13	+18	+23	+28
ON	Peterborough	44	18	78	19	0	+21	+25	+28	+32	+35
ON	Thunder Bay	48	27	89	12	0	+47	+61	+71	+83	+93
ON	Toronto	43	39	79	23	0	+28	+30	+32	+35	+37
QC	Montreal	45	28	73	39	0	−1	+4	+9	+15	+20
SK	Saskatoon	52	10	106	40	1	+37	+63	+80	+101	+119

GENERAL STORE CLASSIFIEDS

CLASSIFIEDS

CLASSIFIEDS

Advertisements and statements contained herein are the sole responsibility of the persons or entities that post the advertisement, and *The Old Farmer's Almanac* does not make any warranty as to the accuracy, completeness, truthfulness, or reliability of such advertisements. *The Old Farmer's Almanac* has no liability whatsoever for any third-party claims arising in connection with such advertisements or any products or services mentioned therein.

Index to Advertisers

2018 ESSAY CONTEST WINNERS

"How Weather Changed My Life"

First Prize: $300

All my life, I've been afraid of storms, and growing up in Tornado Alley never helped any. When I was young, one year we were experiencing more storms than usual. I stayed on high alert every time clouds would cover the sky and was especially worried on this occasion because my aunt's house had been devastated by a tornado the week before.

One evening, a storm was rapidly approaching and the alarms sounded. Mom hurried us to a shelter. A little girl there was clinging to her father, and I was sat down beside her. You could hear the wind rushing something terrible outside, and I became scared. As I was about to jump into my mother's arms, a hand grabbed my wrist and went for my hand. It made me feel very calm. I looked to see whose hand I was holding, and it was the girl's. I guess she sensed how afraid I was. She made me so calm that I quickly forgot about the noises coming from outside.

To this day, that little girl still keeps me calm during troubling times. She's my wife now.

–Sidney Rippetoe,
Tahlequah, Oklahoma

Second Prize: $200

It's October 3, 1986, a Friday. I'm 16 and have my heart set on an away football game. Predictions for the day are rain and fog. Accommodating my desire despite the precipitation forecast, my mother slips her stocking feet into my faux leather loafers and we push out the door.

At 5:08 P.M., Mom angles her brown Dodge Dart onto the highway. Soon, we're driving through a liquid shroud. Even the wipers click-clacking on highest speed can't eliminate the deluge smacking the windshield between their urgent swipes.

My mother keeps her eyes focused on the yellow line. We make it to the turnoff to the school and chug up the hill to the main entrance. Mom noses the automobile in close to the portico, where tarmac meets cement, so that not a drop of rain will touch me. "This is stupid," I say, embarrassed by the coddling. I leap out, slam the door shut, and rush into the building. It is 5:28 P.M.

At 5:30 P.M., a drunk driver slams into my mother.

In Wales, they say, it rains old women and walking sticks. At 45, my mother died in the rain, never to become an old woman.

–Kathy Kehrli,
Factoryville, Pennsylvania

Third Prize: $100

One snowy February day, when my mother was pregnant with me, she went down to the creek to get some butter. Had no electricity, so they kept the milk and butter in the creek. On the way down the bank of the creek, she got to sliding and landed in the icy water. My grandmother came running and got her back to the house. My mother went into labor. When I was born, she named me Icie. All my life I've heard, "Were you born in winter?" "Was it cold when you were born?" "Icy hot!" And on and on. Then I met my husband, love of my life. He made me Icie Winter. I said, "Lord, I'll never live this one down!" He says, "We were meant to be."

–Icie Winter, Sugar Tree, Tennessee

Honorable Mention

While canoeing on Chesapeake Bay in an aluminum canoe, my friend and I saw this storm approaching from the north. Not long after realizing that we had no rubber, a bolt of lightning hit a tree on the shoreline. The tree exploded into dust. A storm with explosive lightning! My friend and I began to paddle for our lives. By the time we had paddled the mile back to the dock, there was no place to land along the way, and we were getting pretty tired. I yelled to my friend to just beach the canoe, chuck the paddles, and run! He replied that we might as well pull the canoe in with us. I said, "Okay," as we came around the dock. The canoe hit the beach, we grabbed the canoe, and just as we got to shore, a bolt of lightning split our wake coming around the dock. We were so close, we never heard thunder. Our hair was still sticking up on end an hour later when we were picked up to ride home.

–David E. Goldberg,
Junction City, Oregon

ANNOUNCING THE 2019 ESSAY CONTEST TOPIC:
KIDS SAY THE FUNNIEST THINGS

SEE CONTEST RULES ON PAGE 251.

MADDENING MIND-MANGLERS

An Apple Romance

*How many names of heirloom apple varieties can you find hidden
in the following romantic tale? Use your imagination!*

The duchess and Ben Davis went on a date. They met at the Blue Pearmain, a tea room on the bank of the Wolf River. Many people called it "Courtland" because so many people met there. There was snow in the air, so the duchess wore her yellow transparent raincoat, her stout russet boots, and her red astrakhan fur toque. Ben wore his macintosh. The duchess was very beautiful, so everyone was looking at her. One brash young fellow was heard to say that she sure was a pippin, a remark that made more than one maiden blush. One girl was heard to ask, "How can one so bald win such a Rome beauty?" Her companion replied that Ben was very wealthy.

They found a table, and Ben hung up their coats. Before he sat down, he presented the duchess with a corsage of bellflowers from his greenhouse. As he gave them to her, he told her that she was every pound sweet.

They studied the menu, and the duchess said that she would like some creamed crabmeat on toast and a peach melba. Ben said that he would have the crab and a strawberry shortcake. He asked the duchess if she would like a little porter. She declined with thanks, saying that she thought that wine saps the mind. The waitress took their order and soon returned with their food. When they had finished, the waitress came back. The duchess thanked her for her kind service and said that the food had been delicious.

The duchess's uncle, the king, disapproved of his niece's keeping company with a commoner, so he had his spies watching all the time. Just as they had finished their meal, Ben's brother Jonathan dashed in and announced that Red William, the king's northern spy, was coming at great speed astride the king's fastest steed, Pewaukee.

They left hastily by a back door. Red William entered the tea room and sighed with relief when he found that they had gone, because he had sympathy for them. He sat down at a table and ordered a piece of apple pie and a cup of coffee.

–courtesy of Bessie DesRosiers,
The Old Farmer's Almanac, *1977*

Mental Math

Using only your brain, answer the following:

1. What is the sum of 1, 2, 3, 4, 5, 6, all the way through 100?

2. Assuming that pi = 3, what is the difference between the area of a square with sides of 10 and the area of a circle with a diameter of 10?

3. 0, 1, 1, 2, 3, 5, 8, __.
What number comes next?

4. 1, 1, 2, 8, 3, 27, 4, __.
What number comes next?

5. 2, 3, 4, 5, 6, 7, 12, 9, __.
What number comes next?

6. 1, 0, 1, 2, 2, 3, 5, 7, 10, __.
What number comes next?

–courtesy of Morris Bowles, Cane Ridge, Tennessee

ANSWERS:

Apple Romance (in order of appearance): Duchess, Ben Davis, Blue Pearmain, Wolf River, Cortland ("Courtland"), Snow, Yellow Transparent, Russet, Red Astrachan (astrakhan), McIntosh (macintosh), Pippin, Maiden Blush, Baldwin, Rome Beauty, Wealthy, Bellflower, Pound Sweet, Crab, Peach, Strawberry, Porter, Winesap, Delicious, King, Jonathan, Red William, Northern Spy, Pewaukee.

Mental Math: **1.** 5,050. **2.** 25. **3.** 13 (add number plus previous number). **4.** 64 (cube every other number). **5.** 24 (keep totaling the preceding even numbers). **6.** 15 (to get the next number, add the present number to the second number back). ■

ESSAY AND RECIPE CONTEST RULES

Cash prizes (first, $300; second, $200; third, $100) will be awarded for the best essays in 200 words or less on the subject "Kids Say the Funniest Things" and the best recipes in the category "Pasta." Entries must be yours, original, and unpublished. Amateur cooks only, please. One recipe per person. All entries become the property of Yankee Publishing, which reserves all rights to the material. The deadline for entries is Friday, January 25, 2019. Enter at Almanac.com/EssayContest or at Almanac.com/RecipeContest or label "Essay Contest" or "Recipe Contest" and mail to The Old Farmer's Almanac, P.O. Box 520, Dublin, NH 03444. Include your name, mailing address, and email address. Winners will appear in *The 2020 Old Farmer's Almanac* and on Almanac.com. ■

ANECDOTES & PLEASANTRIES

A sampling from the thousands of letters, clippings, articles, and emails sent to us by Almanac readers from all over the United States and Canada during the past year.

ILLUSTRATIONS BY TIM ROBINSON

The Underwear Soil Test

A "brief" explanation of how healthy soil devours drawers.

STEP #1: Dig a hole 6 to 8 inches deep in your garden or field bed. Bury a pair of clean, 100 percent cotton, white or undyed men's underwear. (Of course, the waistband will not be 100 percent cotton.) Repeat, as desired.

STEP #2: Leave them for 2 months.

STEP #3: Remove the briefs from the soil. The amount of remaining cotton fabric indicates, roughly, the amount of earthworms, fungi, bacteria, and other microscopic organisms in the soil, or its organic quality.

If only the waistband remains, the organic quality is very high. If most of the drawers remain, the soil is lacking in biological life because it has been overused.

–courtesy of the Soil Conservation Council of Canada

IN THE NEWS

• Jason and the Cornstalks: After growing a world-record 35-foot-tall cornstalk in 2011, upstate New York's Jason Karl moved to the milder winters of Costa Rica, where his tassels now reach 45 feet above ground.

• Nashoba Brook Bakery in West Concord, Massachusetts, tried to list "Love" as an ingredient in its granola. Not so fast, said the FDA: "'Love' is not a common or usual name of an ingredient and is considered to be intervening material because it is not part of the common or usual name of the ingredient."

• In Berlin, Germany, a 16-inch, 11-pound zucchini was mistaken for an unexploded World War II bomb.

–courtesy of The Scientist, *Associated Press, Bloomberg*

The Kid's in the Mail

The early days of parcel post gave new meaning to the term "special delivery."

Need a way to get your kids to Grandma's house? Just slap on a few stamps, and off they go! Or at least that was the practice back at the beginning of the last century, when U.S. postal patrons figured out that new parcel post regulations allowed just that.

The first parcel poster child was shipped off in 1913 in Batavia, Ohio, when a young boy was sent to his grandmother's, about a mile away, for 15 cents.

As word spread about this easy and economical way to get the kids out of the house, so too did the number of children entrusted to the Post Office. Fifteen cents was the going rate if the "parcel" weighed less than 50 pounds; a 6-year-old was once sent 73 miles for just 53 cents. In reality, mailed kids were accompanied by trusted postal workers, but photographs of toddlers in mailbags and sweet-faced children who supposedly had been treated like freight eventually

called into question the whole idea.

By 1914, Postmaster General Albert Burleson had heard enough to issue an edict barring humans from the post—for all the good it did him, as 1915 then turned out to be the biggest kid-shipping year yet, with several more trips being made. Six-year-old Edna Neff, for example, set the distance record by being posted from Pensacola, Florida, to Christiansburg, Virginia. Fortunately for her, she rode the mail train for most of the 700-plus miles.

But enough was enough, and eventually the rules were enforced and the practice ended. There is no record of any kid ever having been "lost in the mail," but just in case, postal insurance was always available. In fact, Mr. and Mrs. Jesse Beauge of Glen Este, Ohio, senders of that first child back in 1913, had covered all of their bases by insuring their son for a whopping $50.

–courtesy of O. P., Ames, Iowa, from http://postalmuseumblog.si.edu

(continued)

The Almanac

Cold it was, clear and fair.
Frost was hanging in midair.
A halo held the Sun at bay.
No warmth would be reaching here
    today.

Snow was due sometime tonight,
Time to bundle up real tight.
Can't escape this winter's chill.
Guess I'll head back up the hill . . .

Close up the barn and throw some
    hay
To feed the mare and the old bay.
Then go into the house to have
    some tea
And a piece of apple pie for me.

Nothin' more that I can do
'Cept hunker down and wait for you.

I'll put more wood upon the fire,
Read a book and then retire
To our cozy little featherbed
With a woolly cap upon my head.

Spring is still so far away.
Nothin' I do, nothin' I say
Will make it come before it's due,
If what I read in the Almanac's true.

–R. V. Bartles, Meriden, New Hampshire

THREE SISTERS

Three sisters, ages 92, 94, and 96, live in a house together. One night, the 96-year-old draws a bath. She puts her foot in, pauses, and yells to the other sisters, "Was I getting into or out of the bath?"

The 94-year-old yells back, "I don't know—I'll come and see!" She starts up the stairs, pauses, and calls out, "Was I going up the stairs or down?"

The 92-year-old is sitting in the kitchen having tea and listening to her sisters. She shakes her head, raps on the table, and says, "Knock on wood, I sure hope I never get that forgetful."

Then she yells, "I'll come up and help you both as soon as I see who's at the door!"

–courtesy of L. M., Little Rock, Arkansas

You Never Know What You'll Find in Canada

- Stuart Thompson, of Charlottetown, Prince Edward Island, found a 15-inch-long piece of string in a can of crushed tomatoes in 2017.

- Also in that year, an anonymous Manitoban uncovered the 44,000-year-old fossilized jawbone of a giant beaver that would have weighed as much as a black bear.

- 1-carrot ring: In 2017, a woman near Armena, Alberta, pulled up a carrot growing through an engagement ring—which had been lost by her mother-in-law in 2004.

–courtesy of CBC.ca, gearsofbiz.com, CBC.ca

ARE YOU LOSING YOUR GRIP?

Take this simple test to find out.

QUESTION #1: What do you put in a toaster?

QUESTION #2: Say "silk" 10 times. Now spell "silk." What do cows drink?

QUESTION #3: If a red house is made from red bricks and a blue house is made from blue bricks and a pink house is made from pink bricks and a black house is made from black bricks, what is a green house made from?

QUESTION #4: *(Use of calculator not permitted, but pencil and paper are OK.)* You are driving a bus from New York City to Philadelphia. On Staten Island, 17 people get on the bus. In New Brunswick, six people get off the bus and nine people get on. In Windsor, two people get off and four get on. In Trenton, 11 people get off and 16 people get on. In Bristol, three people get off and five people get on. And in Camden, six people get off and three get on. The bus then arrives at Philadelphia Station. Without going back to review, how old is the bus driver?

–courtesy of A. B., Wilmington, Vermont, from the Internet

ANSWERS: 1. Bread. 2. Water. 3. Glass. 4. Your own age.

SCORING: 4 correct—You're holding on tight. 3 correct—Slippage! 2 correct—Uh-oh. Only 1 correct—Hanging on by your fingertips, like most people who take this quiz. None correct—Yup, you've officially lost it!

Send your contribution for *The 2020 Old Farmer's Almanac* by January 25, 2019, to "A & P," The Old Farmer's Almanac, P.O. Box 520, Dublin, NH 03444, or email it to almanac@ypi.com (subject: A & P).

A Reference Compendium

REFERENCE

PHASES OF THE MOON

New

Waxing Crescent

First Quarter

Waxing Gibbous

Full

Waning Gibbous

Last Quarter

Waning Crescent

New

W A X I N G

W A N I N G

WHEN WILL THE MOON RISE?

Use the following saying to remember the time of moonrise on a day when a Moon phase occurs. Keep in mind that the phase itself may happen earlier or later that day, depending on location.

The new Moon always rises near sunrise;

The first quarter, near noon;

The full Moon always rises near sunset;

The last quarter, near midnight.

Moonrise occurs about 50 minutes later each day.

FULL MOON NAMES

NAME	MONTH	VARIATIONS
Full Wolf Moon	JANUARY	Full Old Moon
Full Snow Moon	FEBRUARY	Full Hunger Moon
Full Worm Moon	MARCH	Full Crow Moon Full Crust Moon Full Sugar Moon Full Sap Moon
Full Pink Moon	APRIL	Full Sprouting Grass Moon Full Egg Moon Full Fish Moon
Full Flower Moon	MAY	Full Corn Planting Moon Full Milk Moon
Full Strawberry Moon	JUNE	Full Rose Moon Full Hot Moon
Full Buck Moon	JULY	Full Thunder Moon Full Hay Moon
Full Sturgeon Moon	AUGUST	Full Red Moon Full Green Corn Moon
Full Harvest Moon*	SEPTEMBER	Full Corn Moon Full Barley Moon
Full Hunter's Moon	OCTOBER	Full Travel Moon Full Dying Grass Moon
Full Beaver Moon	NOVEMBER	Full Frost Moon
Full Cold Moon	DECEMBER	Full Long Nights Moon

*The Harvest Moon is always the full Moon closest to the autumnal equinox. If the Harvest Moon occurs in October, the September full Moon is usually called the Corn Moon.

THE ORIGIN OF FULL MOON NAMES

Historically, the Native Americans who lived in the area that is now the northern and eastern United States kept track of the seasons by giving a distinctive name to each recurring full Moon. This name was applied to the entire month in which it occurred. These names, and some variations, were used by the Algonquin tribes from New England to Lake Superior.

Meanings of Full Moon Names

JANUARY'S full Moon was called the **Wolf Moon** because it appeared when wolves howled outside Native American villages.

FEBRUARY'S full Moon was called the **Snow Moon** because it was a time of heavy snow. It was also called the **Hunger Moon** because hunting was difficult and hunger often resulted.

MARCH'S full Moon was called the **Worm Moon** because, as the Sun increasingly warmed the soil, earthworms became active and their castings (excrement) began to appear.

APRIL'S full Moon was called the **Pink Moon** because it heralded the appearance of the moss pink, or wild ground phlox—one of the first spring flowers.

MAY'S full Moon was called the **Flower Moon** because blossoms were abundant everywhere at this time.

JUNE'S full Moon was called the **Strawberry Moon** because it appeared when the strawberry harvest took place.

JULY'S full Moon was called the **Buck Moon;** it arrived when a male deer's antlers were in full growth mode.

AUGUST'S full Moon was called the **Sturgeon Moon** because this large fish, which is found in the Great Lakes and Lake Champlain, was caught easily at this time.

SEPTEMBER'S full Moon was called the **Corn Moon** because this was the time to harvest corn.

The **Harvest Moon** is the full Moon that occurs closest to the autumnal equinox. It can occur in either September or October. At this time, crops such as corn, pumpkins, squash, and wild rice were ready for gathering.

OCTOBER'S full Moon was called the **Hunter's Moon** because this was the time to hunt in preparation for winter.

NOVEMBER'S full Moon was called the **Beaver Moon** because it was the time to set beaver traps, before the waters froze over.

DECEMBER'S full Moon was called the **Cold Moon.** It was also called the **Long Nights Moon** because nights at this time of year were the longest.

THE ORIGIN OF MONTH NAMES

JANUARY. For the Roman god Janus, protector of gates and doorways. Janus is depicted with two faces, one looking into the past, the other into the future.

FEBRUARY. From the Latin *februa,* "to cleanse." The Roman Februalia was a festival of purification and atonement that took place during this time of year.

MARCH. For the Roman god of war, Mars. This was the time of year to resume military campaigns that had been interrupted by winter.

APRIL. From the Latin *aperio,* "to open (bud)," because plants begin to grow now.

MAY. For the Roman goddess Maia, who oversaw the growth of plants. Also from the Latin *maiores,* "elders," who were celebrated now.

JUNE. For the Roman goddess Juno, patroness of marriage and the well-being of women. Also from the Latin *juvenis,* "young people."

JULY. To honor Roman dictator Julius Caesar (100 B.C.–44 B.C.). In 46 B.C., with the help of Sosigenes, he developed the Julian calendar.

AUGUST. To honor the first Roman emperor (and grandnephew of Julius Caesar), Augustus Caesar (63 B.C.–A.D. 14).

SEPTEMBER. From the Latin *septem,* "seven," because this was the seventh month of the early Roman calendar.

OCTOBER. From the Latin *octo,* "eight," because this was the eighth month of the early Roman calendar.

NOVEMBER. From the Latin *novem,* "nine," because this was the ninth month of the early Roman calendar.

DECEMBER. From the Latin *decem,* "ten," because this was the tenth month of the early Roman calendar.

Easter Dates (2019–22)

Christian churches that follow the Gregorian calendar celebrate Easter on the first Sunday after the paschal full Moon on or just after the vernal equinox.

YEAR	EASTER
2019	April 21
2020	April 12
2021	April 4
2022	April 17

The Julian calendar is used by some churches, including many Eastern Orthodox. The dates below are Julian calendar dates for Easter converted to Gregorian dates.

YEAR	EASTER
2019	April 28
2020	April 19
2021	May 2
2022	April 24

FRIGGATRISKAIDEKAPHOBIA TRIVIA

Here are a few facts about Friday the 13th:

In the 14 possible configurations for the annual calendar (see any perpetual calendar), the occurrence of Friday the 13th is this:

6 of 14 years have one Friday the 13th.
6 of 14 years have two Fridays the 13th.
2 of 14 years have three Fridays the 13th.

No year is without one Friday the 13th, and no year has more than three.

Months that have a Friday the 13th begin on a Sunday.

2019 has a Friday the 13th in September and December.

REFERENCE

THE ORIGIN OF DAY NAMES

The days of the week were named by ancient Romans with the Latin words for the Sun, the Moon, and the five known planets. These names have survived in European languages, but English names also reflect Anglo-Saxon and Norse influences.

ENGLISH	LATIN	FRENCH	ITALIAN	SPANISH	ANGLO-SAXON AND NORSE
SUNDAY	dies Solis (Sol's day)	dimanche	domenica	domingo	Sunnandaeg (Sun's day)
		from the Latin for "Lord's day"			
MONDAY	dies Lunae (Luna's day)	lundi	lunedì	lunes	Monandaeg (Moon's day)
TUESDAY	dies Martis (Mars's day)	mardi	martedì	martes	Tiwesdaeg (Tiw's day)
WEDNESDAY	dies Mercurii (Mercury's day)	mercredi	mercoledì	miércoles	Wodnesdaeg (Woden's day)
THURSDAY	dies Jovis (Jupiter's day)	jeudi	giovedì	jueves	Thursdaeg (Thor's day)
FRIDAY	dies Veneris (Venus's day)	vendredi	venerdì	viernes	Frigedaeg (Frigga's day)
SATURDAY	dies Saturni (Saturn's day)	samedi	sabato	sábado	Saeterndaeg (Saturn's day)
		from the Latin for "Sabbath"			

How to Find the Day of the Week for Any Given Date

To compute the day of the week for any given date as far back as the mid–18th century, proceed as follows:

Add the last two digits of the year to one-quarter of the last two digits (discard any remainder), the day of the month, and the month key from the key box below. Divide the sum by 7; the remainder is the day of the week (1 is Sunday, 2 is Monday, and so on). If there is no remainder, the day is Saturday. If you're searching for a weekday prior to 1900, add 2 to the sum before dividing; prior to 1800, add 4. The formula doesn't work for days prior to 1753. From 2000 through 2099, subtract 1 from the sum before dividing.

KEY	
JANUARY	1
LEAP YEAR	0
FEBRUARY	4
LEAP YEAR	3
MARCH	4
APRIL	0
MAY	2
JUNE	5
JULY	0
AUGUST	3
SEPTEMBER	6
OCTOBER	1
NOVEMBER	4
DECEMBER	6

Example:

THE DAYTON FLOOD WAS ON MARCH 25, 1913.

Last two digits of year:	13
One-quarter of these two digits:	3
Given day of month:	25
Key number for March:	4
Sum:	45

45 ÷ 7 = 6, with a remainder of 3. The flood took place on Tuesday, the third day of the week.

REFERENCE

ANIMAL SIGNS OF THE CHINESE ZODIAC

The animal designations of the Chinese zodiac follow a 12-year cycle and are always used in the same sequence. The Chinese year of 354 days begins 3 to 7 weeks into the western 365-day year, so the animal designation changes at that time, rather than on January 1. This year, the Chinese New Year starts on February 5.

RAT

Ambitious and sincere, you can be generous with your money. Compatible with the dragon and the monkey. Your opposite is the horse.

1924	1936	1948
1960	1972	1984
1996	2008	2020

OX OR BUFFALO

A leader, you are bright, patient, and cheerful. Compatible with the snake and the rooster. Your opposite is the sheep.

1925	1937	1949
1961	1973	1985
1997	2009	2021

TIGER

Forthright and sensitive, you possess great courage. Compatible with the horse and the dog. Your opposite is the monkey.

1926	1938	1950
1962	1974	1986
1998	2010	2022

RABBIT OR HARE

Talented and affectionate, you are a seeker of tranquility. Compatible with the sheep and the pig. Your opposite is the rooster.

1927	1939	1951
1963	1975	1987
1999	2011	2023

DRAGON

Robust and passionate, your life is filled with complexity. Compatible with the monkey and the rat. Your opposite is the dog.

1928	1940	1952
1964	1976	1988
2000	2012	2024

SNAKE

Strong-willed and intense, you display great wisdom. Compatible with the rooster and the ox. Your opposite is the pig.

1929	1941	1953
1965	1977	1989
2001	2013	2025

HORSE

Physically attractive and popular, you like the company of others. Compatible with the tiger and the dog. Your opposite is the rat.

1930	1942	1954
1966	1978	1990
2002	2014	2026

SHEEP OR GOAT

Aesthetic and stylish, you enjoy being a private person. Compatible with the pig and the rabbit. Your opposite is the ox.

1931	1943	1955
1967	1979	1991
2003	2015	2027

MONKEY

Persuasive, skillful, and intelligent, you strive to excel. Compatible with the dragon and the rat. Your opposite is the tiger.

1932	1944	1956
1968	1980	1992
2004	2016	2028

ROOSTER OR COCK

Seeking wisdom and truth, you have a pioneering spirit. Compatible with the snake and the ox. Your opposite is the rabbit.

1933	1945	1957
1969	1981	1993
2005	2017	2029

DOG

Generous and loyal, you have the ability to work well with others. Compatible with the horse and the tiger. Your opposite is the dragon.

1934	1946	1958
1970	1982	1994
2006	2018	2030

PIG OR BOAR

Gallant and noble, your friends will remain at your side. Compatible with the rabbit and the sheep. Your opposite is the snake.

1935	1947	1959
1971	1983	1995
2007	2019	2031

REFERENCE

A Table Foretelling the Weather Through All the Lunations of Each Year, or Forever

This table is the result of many years of actual observation and shows what sort of weather will probably follow the Moon's entrance into any of its quarters. For example, the table shows that the week following January 27, 2019, will be fair, because the Moon enters the last quarter on that day at 4:10 P.M. EST. (See the **Left-Hand Calendar Pages, 120–146,** for Moon phases.)

EDITOR'S NOTE: Although the data in this table is taken into consideration in the year-long process of compiling the annual long-range weather forecasts for *The Old Farmer's Almanac,* we rely far more on our projections of solar activity.

TIME OF CHANGE	SUMMER	WINTER
Midnight to 2 A.M.	Fair	Hard frost, unless wind is south or west
2 A.M. to 4 A.M.	Cold, with frequent showers	Snow and stormy
4 A.M. to 6 A.M.	Rain	Rain
6 A.M. to 8 A.M.	Wind and rain	Stormy
8 A.M. to 10 A.M.	Changeable	Cold rain if wind is west; snow, if east
10 A.M. to noon	Frequent showers	Cold with high winds
Noon to 2 P.M.	Very rainy	Snow or rain
2 P.M. to 4 P.M.	Changeable	Fair and mild
4 P.M. to 6 P.M.	Fair	Fair
6 P.M. to 10 P.M.	Fair if wind is northwest; rain if wind is south or southwest	Fair and frosty if wind is north or northeast; rain or snow if wind is south or southwest
10 P.M. to midnight	Fair	Fair and frosty

This table was created more than 180 years ago by Dr. Herschell for the Boston Courier; *it first appeared in* The Old Farmer's Almanac *in 1834.*

SAFE ICE THICKNESS*

ICE THICKNESS	PERMISSIBLE LOAD	ICE THICKNESS	PERMISSIBLE LOAD
3 inches	Single person on foot	12 inches	Heavy truck (8-ton gross)
4 inches	Group in single file	15 inches	10 tons
7½ inches	Passenger car (2-ton gross)	20 inches	25 tons
8 inches	Light truck (2½-ton gross)	30 inches	70 tons
10 inches	Medium truck (3½-ton gross)	36 inches	110 tons

*Solid, clear, blue/black pond and lake ice

The strength value of river ice is 15 percent less. Slush ice has only half the strength of blue ice.

HEAT INDEX °F (°C)

TEMP. °F (°C)	RELATIVE HUMIDITY (%)								
	40	45	50	55	60	65	70	75	80
100 (38)	109 (43)	114 (46)	118 (48)	124 (51)	129 (54)	136 (58)			
98 (37)	105 (41)	109 (43)	113 (45)	117 (47)	123 (51)	128 (53)	134 (57)		
96 (36)	101 (38)	104 (40)	108 (42)	112 (44)	116 (47)	121 (49)	126 (52)	132 (56)	
94 (34)	97 (36)	100 (38)	103 (39)	106 (41)	110 (43)	114 (46)	119 (48)	124 (51)	129 (54)
92 (33)	94 (34)	96 (36)	99 (37)	101 (38)	105 (41)	108 (42)	112 (44)	116 (47)	121 (49)
90 (32)	91 (33)	93 (34)	95 (35)	97 (36)	100 (38)	103 (39)	105 (41)	109 (43)	113 (45)
88 (31)	88 (31)	89 (32)	91 (33)	93 (34)	95 (35)	98 (37)	100 (38)	103 (39)	106 (41)
86 (30)	85 (29)	87 (31)	88 (31)	89 (32)	91 (33)	93 (34)	95 (35)	97 (36)	100 (38)
84 (29)	83 (28)	84 (29)	85 (29)	86 (30)	88 (31)	89 (32)	90 (32)	92 (33)	94 (34)
82 (28)	81 (27)	82 (28)	83 (28)	84 (29)	84 (29)	85 (29)	86 (30)	88 (31)	89 (32)
80 (27)	80 (27)	80 (27)	81 (27)	81 (27)	82 (28)	82 (28)	83 (28)	84 (29)	84 (29)

EXAMPLE: *When the temperature is 88°F (31°C) and the relative humidity is 60 percent, the heat index, or how hot it feels, is 95°F (35°C).*

THE UV INDEX FOR MEASURING ULTRAVIOLET RADIATION RISK

The U.S. National Weather Service's daily forecasts of ultraviolet levels use these numbers for various exposure levels:

UV INDEX NUMBER	EXPOSURE LEVEL	ACTIONS TO TAKE
0, 1, 2	Low	Wear UV-blocking sunglasses on bright days. In winter, reflection off snow can nearly double UV strength. If you burn easily, cover up and apply SPF 30+ sunscreen.
3, 4, 5	Moderate	Apply SPF 30+ sunscreen; wear a hat and sunglasses. Stay in shade when sun is strongest.
6, 7	High	Apply SPF 30+ sunscreen; wear a hat, sunglasses, and protective clothing; limit midday exposure.
8, 9, 10	Very High	Apply SPF 30+ sunscreen; wear a hat, sunglasses, and protective clothing; limit midday exposure. Seek shade. Unprotected skin will be damaged and can burn quickly.
11 or higher	Extreme	Apply SPF 30+ sunscreen; wear a hat, sunglasses, and protective clothing; avoid midday exposure; seek shade. Unprotected skin can burn in minutes.

85	90	95	100
135 (57)			
126 (52)	131 (55)		
117 (47)	122 (50)	127 (53)	132 (56)
110 (43)	113 (45)	117 (47)	121 (49)
102 (39)	105 (41)	108 (42)	112 (44)
96 (36)	98 (37)	100 (38)	103 (39)
90 (32)	91 (33)	93 (34)	95 (35)
85 (29)	86 (30)	86 (30)	87 (31)

What Are Cooling/Heating Degree Days?

In an attempt to measure the need for air-conditioning, each degree of a day's mean temperature that is above a base temperature, such as 65°F (U.S.) or 18°C (Canada), is considered one cooling degree day. If the daily mean temperature is 75°F, for example, that's 10 cooling degree days.

Similarly, to measure the need for heating fuel consumption, each degree of a day's mean temperature that is below 65°F (18°C) is considered one heating degree. For example, a day with a high of 60°F and low of 40°F results in a mean of 50°, or 15 degrees less than 65°. Hence, that day had 15 heating degree days.

HOW TO MEASURE HAIL

The **TORRO HAILSTORM INTENSITY SCALE** was introduced by Jonathan Webb of Oxford, England, in 1986 as a means of categorizing hailstorms. The name derives from the private and mostly British research body named the TORnado and storm Research Organisation.

INTENSITY/DESCRIPTION OF HAIL DAMAGE

H0 True hail of pea size causes no damage

H1 Leaves and flower petals are punctured and torn

H2 Leaves are stripped from trees and plants

H3 Panes of glass are broken; auto bodies are dented

H4 Some house windows are broken; small tree branches are broken off; birds are killed

H5 Many windows are smashed; small animals are injured; large tree branches are broken off

H6 Shingle roofs are breached; metal roofs are scored; wooden window frames are broken away

H7 Roofs are shattered to expose rafters; autos are seriously damaged

H8 Shingle and tile roofs are destroyed; small tree trunks are split; people are seriously injured

H9 Concrete roofs are broken; large tree trunks are split and knocked down; people are at risk of fatal injuries

H10 Brick houses are damaged; people are at risk of fatal injuries

HOW TO MEASURE WIND SPEED

The **BEAUFORT WIND FORCE SCALE** is a common way of estimating wind speed. It was developed in 1805 by Admiral Sir Francis Beaufort of the British Navy to measure wind at sea. We can also use it to measure wind on land.

Admiral Beaufort arranged the numbers 0 to 12 to indicate the strength of the wind from calm, force 0, to hurricane, force 12. Here's a scale adapted to land.

"Used Mostly at Sea but of Help to All Who Are Interested in the Weather"

BEAUFORT FORCE	DESCRIPTION	WHEN YOU SEE OR FEEL THIS EFFECT	WIND SPEED (mph)	WIND SPEED (km/h)
0	CALM	Smoke goes straight up	less than 1	less than 2
1	LIGHT AIR	Wind direction is shown by smoke drift but not by wind vane	1–3	2–5
2	LIGHT BREEZE	Wind is felt on the face; leaves rustle; wind vanes move	4–7	6–11
3	GENTLE BREEZE	Leaves and small twigs move steadily; wind extends small flags straight out	8–12	12–19
4	MODERATE BREEZE	Wind raises dust and loose paper; small branches move	13–18	20–29
5	FRESH BREEZE	Small trees sway; waves form on lakes	19–24	30–39
6	STRONG BREEZE	Large branches move; wires whistle; umbrellas are difficult to use	25–31	40–50
7	NEAR GALE	Whole trees are in motion; walking against the wind is difficult	32–38	51–61
8	GALE	Twigs break from trees; walking against the wind is very difficult	39–46	62–74
9	STRONG GALE	Buildings suffer minimal damage; roof shingles are removed	47–54	75–87
10	STORM	Trees are uprooted	55–63	88–101
11	VIOLENT STORM	Widespread damage	64–72	102–116
12	HURRICANE	Widespread destruction	73+	117+

RETIRED ATLANTIC HURRICANE NAMES

These storms have been some of the most destructive and costly.

NAME	YEAR	NAME	YEAR	NAME	YEAR	NAME	YEAR
Dennis	2005	Felix	2007	Tomas	2010	Matthew	2016
Katrina	2005	Noel	2007	Irene	2011	Otto	2016
Rita	2005	Gustav	2008	Sandy	2012	Harvey	2017
Stan	2005	Ike	2008	Ingrid	2013	Irma	2017
Wilma	2005	Paloma	2008	Erika	2015	Maria	2017
Dean	2007	Igor	2010	Joaquin	2015	Nate	2017

ATLANTIC TROPICAL (AND SUBTROPICAL) STORM NAMES FOR 2019			EASTERN NORTH-PACIFIC TROPICAL (AND SUBTROPICAL) STORM NAMES FOR 2019		
Andrea	Humberto	Olga	Alvin	Ivo	Raymond
Barry	Imelda	Pablo	Barbara	Juliette	Sonia
Chantal	Jerry	Rebekah	Cosme	Kiko	Tico
Dorian	Karen	Sebastien	Dalila	Lorena	Velma
Erin	Lorenzo	Tanya	Erick	Mario	Wallis
Fernand	Melissa	Van	Flossie	Narda	Xina
Gabrielle	Nestor	Wendy	Gil	Octave	York
			Henriette	Priscilla	Zelda

The lists above are used in rotation and recycled every 6 years,
e.g., the 2019 list will be used again in 2025.

How to Measure Hurricane Strength

The **SAFFIR-SIMPSON HURRICANE WIND SCALE** assigns a rating from 1 to 5 based on a hurricane's intensity. It is used to give an estimate of the potential property damage from a hurricane landfall. Wind speed is the determining factor in the scale, as storm surge values are highly dependent on the slope of the continental shelf in the landfall region. Wind speeds are measured at a height of 33 feet (10 meters) using a 1-minute average.

CATEGORY ONE. Average wind: 74–95 mph. Significant damage to mobile homes. Some damage to roofing and siding of well-built frame homes. Large tree branches snap and shallow-rooted trees may topple. Power outages may last a few to several days.

CATEGORY TWO. Average wind: 96–110 mph. Mobile homes may be destroyed. Major roof and siding damage to frame homes. Many shallow-rooted trees snap or topple, blocking roads. Widespread power outages could last from several days to weeks. Potable water may be scarce.

CATEGORY THREE. Average wind: 111–129 mph. Most mobile homes destroyed.

Frame homes may sustain major roof damage. Many trees snap or topple, blocking numerous roads. Electricity and water may be unavailable for several days to weeks.

CATEGORY FOUR. Average wind: 130–156 mph. Mobile homes destroyed. Frame homes severely damaged or destroyed. Windborne debris may penetrate protected windows. Most trees snap or topple. Residential areas isolated by fallen trees and power poles. Most of the area uninhabitable for weeks to months.

CATEGORY FIVE. Average wind: 157+ mph. Most homes destroyed. Nearly all windows blown out of high-rises. Most of the area uninhabitable for weeks to months.

REFERENCE

HOW TO MEASURE A TORNADO

The original **FUJITA SCALE** (or F Scale) was developed by Dr. Theodore Fujita to classify tornadoes based on wind damage. All tornadoes, and other severe local windstorms, were assigned a number according to the most intense damage caused by the storm. An enhanced F (EF) scale was implemented in the United States on February 1, 2007. The EF scale uses 3-second gust estimates based on a more detailed system for assessing damage, taking into account different building materials.

F SCALE		EF SCALE (U.S.)
F0 · 40–72 mph (64–116 km/h)	LIGHT DAMAGE	EF0 · 65–85 mph (105–137 km/h)
F1 · 73–112 mph (117–180 km/h)	MODERATE DAMAGE	EF1 · 86–110 mph (138–178 km/h)
F2 · 113–157 mph (181–253 km/h)	CONSIDERABLE DAMAGE	EF2 · 111–135 mph (179–218 km/h)
F3 · 158–207 mph (254–332 km/h)	SEVERE DAMAGE	EF3 · 136–165 mph (219–266 km/h)
F4 · 208–260 mph (333–419 km/h)	DEVASTATING DAMAGE	EF4 · 166–200 mph (267–322 km/h)
F5 · 261–318 mph (420–512 km/h)	INCREDIBLE DAMAGE	EF5 · over 200 mph (over 322 km/h)

Wind/Barometer Table

BAROMETER (REDUCED TO SEA LEVEL)	WIND DIRECTION	CHARACTER OF WEATHER INDICATED
30.00 to 30.20, and steady	WESTERLY	Fair, with slight changes in temperature, for one to two days
30.00 to 30.20, and rising rapidly	WESTERLY	Fair, followed within two days by warmer and rain
30.00 to 30.20, and falling rapidly	SOUTH TO EAST	Warmer, and rain within 24 hours
30.20 or above, and falling rapidly	SOUTH TO EAST	Warmer, and rain within 36 hours
30.20 or above, and falling rapidly	WEST TO NORTH	Cold and clear, quickly followed by warmer and rain
30.20 or above, and steady	VARIABLE	No early change
30.00 or below, and falling slowly	SOUTH TO EAST	Rain within 18 hours that will continue a day or two
30.00 or below, and falling rapidly	SOUTHEAST TO NORTHEAST	Rain, with high wind, followed within two days by clearing, colder
30.00 or below, and rising	SOUTH TO WEST	Clearing and colder within 12 hours
29.80 or below, and falling rapidly	SOUTH TO EAST	Severe storm of wind and rain imminent; in winter, snow or cold wave within 24 hours
29.80 or below, and falling rapidly	EAST TO NORTH	Severe northeast gales and heavy rain or snow, followed in winter by cold wave
29.80 or below, and rising rapidly	GOING TO WEST	Clearing and colder

NOTE: *A barometer should be adjusted to show equivalent sea-level pressure for the altitude at which it is to be used. A change of 100 feet in elevation will cause a decrease of ¹/₁₀ inch in the reading.*

WINDCHILL TABLE

As wind speed increases, your body loses heat more rapidly, making the air feel colder than it really is. The combination of cold temperature and high wind can create a cooling effect so severe that exposed flesh can freeze.

							TEMPERATURE (°F)								
Calm	**35**	**30**	**25**	**20**	**15**	**10**	**5**	**0**	**–5**	**–10**	**–15**	**–20**	**–25**	**–30**	**–35**
5	31	25	19	13	7	1	–5	–11	–16	–22	–28	–34	–40	–46	–52
10	27	21	15	9	3	–4	–10	–16	–22	–28	–35	–41	–47	–53	–59
15	25	19	13	6	0	–7	–13	–19	–26	–32	–39	–45	–51	–58	–64
20	24	17	11	4	–2	–9	–15	–22	–29	–35	–42	–48	–55	–61	–68
25	23	16	9	3	–4	–11	–17	–24	–31	–37	–44	–51	–58	–64	–71
30	22	15	8	1	–5	–12	–19	–26	–33	–39	–46	–53	–60	–67	–73
35	21	14	7	0	–7	–14	–21	–27	–34	–41	–48	–55	–62	–69	–76
40	20	13	6	–1	–8	–15	–22	–29	–36	–43	–50	–57	–64	–71	–78
45	19	12	5	–2	–9	–16	–23	–30	–37	–44	–51	–58	–65	–72	–79
50	19	12	4	–3	–10	–17	–24	–31	–38	–45	–52	–60	–67	–74	–81
55	18	11	4	–3	–11	–18	–25	–32	–39	–46	–54	–61	–68	–75	–82
60	17	10	3	–4	–11	–19	–26	–33	–40	–48	–55	–62	–69	–76	–84

WIND SPEED (mph)

FROSTBITE OCCURS IN ▨ **30 MINUTES** ▨ **10 MINUTES** ▨ **5 MINUTES**

EXAMPLE: *When the temperature is 15°F and the wind speed is 30 miles per hour, the windchill, or how cold it feels, is –5°F. For a Celsius version of this table, visit Almanac.com/WindchillCelsius.*
–courtesy of National Weather Service

HOW TO MEASURE EARTHQUAKES

In 1979, seismologists developed a measurement of earthquake size called **MOMENT MAGNITUDE**. It is more accurate than the previously used Richter scale, which is precise only for earthquakes of a certain size and at a certain distance from a seismometer. All earthquakes can now be compared on the same scale.

MAGNITUDE	DESCRIPTION	EFFECT
LESS THAN 3	MICRO	GENERALLY NOT FELT
3-3.9	MINOR	OFTEN FELT, LITTLE DAMAGE
4-4.9	LIGHT	SHAKING, SOME DAMAGE
5-5.9	MODERATE	SLIGHT TO MAJOR DAMAGE
6-6.9	STRONG	DESTRUCTIVE
7-7.9	MAJOR	SEVERE DAMAGE
8 OR MORE	GREAT	SERIOUS DAMAGE

A GARDENER'S WORST PHOBIAS

NAME OF FEAR	OBJECT FEARED
Alliumphobia	Garlic
Anthophobia	Flowers
Apiphobia	Bees
Arachnophobia	Spiders
Batonophobia	Plants
Bufonophobia	Toads
Dendrophobia	Trees
Entomophobia	Insects
Lachanophobia	Vegetables
Melissophobia	Bees
Mottephobia	Moths
Myrmecophobia	Ants
Ornithophobia	Birds
Ranidaphobia	Frogs
Rupophobia	Dirt
Scoleciphobia	Worms
Spheksophobia	Wasps

PLANTS FOR LAWNS

Choose varieties that suit your soil and your climate. All of these can withstand mowing and considerable foot traffic.

Ajuga or bugleweed (*Ajuga reptans*)
Corsican mint (*Mentha requienii*)
Dwarf cinquefoil (*Potentilla tabernaemontani*)
English pennyroyal (*Mentha pulegium*)
Green Irish moss (*Sagina subulata*)
Pearly everlasting (*Anaphalis margaritacea*)
Roman chamomile (*Chamaemelum nobile*)
Rupturewort (*Herniaria glabra*)
Speedwell (*Veronica officinalis*)
Stonecrop (*Sedum ternatum*)
Sweet violets (*Viola odorata* or *V. tricolor*)
Thyme (*Thymus serpyllum*)
White clover (*Trifolium repens*)
Wild strawberries (*Fragaria virginiana*)
Wintergreen or partridgeberry (*Mitchella repens*)

Lawn-Growing Tips

• Test your soil: The pH balance should be 7.0 or more; 6.2 to 6.7 puts your lawn at risk for fungal diseases. If the pH is too low, correct it with liming, best done in the fall.

• The best time to apply fertilizer is just before it rains.

• If you put lime and fertilizer on your lawn, spread half of it as you walk north to south, the other half as you walk east to west to cut down on missed areas.

• Any feeding of lawns in the fall should be done with a low-nitrogen, slow-acting fertilizer.

• In areas of your lawn where tree roots compete with the grass, apply some extra fertilizer to benefit both.

• Moss and sorrel in lawns usually means poor soil, poor aeration or drainage, or excessive acidity.

• Control weeds by promoting healthy lawn growth with natural fertilizers in spring and early fall.

• Raise the level of your lawn-mower blades during the hot summer days. Taller grass resists drought better than short.

• You can reduce mowing time by redesigning your lawn, reducing sharp corners and adding sweeping curves.

• During a drought, let the grass grow longer between mowings and reduce fertilizer.

• Water your lawn early in the morning or in the evening.

REFERENCE

Flowers and Herbs That Attract Butterflies

Allium	*Allium*	Mallow	*Malva*
Aster	*Aster*	Mealycup sage	*Salvia farinacea*
Bee balm	*Monarda*	Milkweed	*Asclepias*
Butterfly bush	*Buddleia*	Mint	*Mentha*
Catmint	*Nepeta*	Oregano	*Origanum vulgare*
Clove pink	*Dianthus*	Pansy	*Viola*
Cornflower	*Centaurea*	Parsley	*Petroselinum*
Creeping thyme	*Thymus serpyllum*		*crispum*
Daylily	*Hemerocallis*	Phlox	*Phlox*
Dill	*Anethum graveolens*	Privet	*Ligustrum*
False indigo	*Baptisia*	Purple coneflower	*Echinacea purpurea*
Fleabane	*Erigeron*	Rock cress	*Arabis*
Floss flower	*Ageratum*	Sea holly	*Eryngium*
Globe thistle	*Echinops*	Shasta daisy	*Chrysanthemum*
Goldenrod	*Solidago*	Snapdragon	*Antirrhinum*
Helen's flower	*Helenium*	Stonecrop	*Sedum*
Hollyhock	*Alcea*	Sweet alyssum	*Lobularia*
Honeysuckle	*Lonicera*	Sweet marjoram	*Origanum majorana*
Lavender	*Lavandula*	Sweet rocket	*Hesperis*
Lilac	*Syringa*	Tickseed	*Coreopsis*
Lupine	*Lupinus*	Verbena	*Verbena*
Lychnis	*Lychnis*	Zinnia	*Zinnia*

FLOWERS* THAT ATTRACT HUMMINGBIRDS

Beard tongue	*Penstemon*	Soapwort	*Saponaria*
Bee balm	*Monarda*	Summer phlox	*Phlox paniculata*
Butterfly bush	*Buddleia*	Trumpet honeysuckle	*Lonicera*
Catmint	*Nepeta*		*sempervirens*
Clove pink	*Dianthus*	Verbena	*Verbena*
Columbine	*Aquilegia*	Weigela	*Weigela*
Coral bells	*Heuchera*		
Daylily	*Hemerocallis*		
Desert candle	*Yucca*		
Flag iris	*Iris*		
Flowering tobacco	*Nicotiana alata*		
Foxglove	*Digitalis*		
Larkspur	*Delphinium*		
Lily	*Lilium*		
Lupine	*Lupinus*		
Petunia	*Petunia*		
Pincushion flower	*Scabiosa*		
Red-hot poker	*Kniphofia*		
Scarlet sage	*Salvia splendens*		

*NOTE: *Choose varieties in red and orange shades, if available.*

pH PREFERENCES OF TREES, SHRUBS, FLOWERS, AND VEGETABLES

An accurate soil test will indicate your soil pH and will specify the amount of lime or sulfur that is needed to bring it up or down to the appropriate level. A pH of 6.5 is just about right for most home gardens, since most plants thrive in the 6.0 to 7.0 (slightly acidic to neutral) range. Some plants (azaleas, blueberries) prefer more strongly acidic soil in the 4.0 to 6.0 range, while a few (asparagus, plums) do best in soil that is neutral to slightly alkaline. Acidic, or sour, soil (below 7.0) is counteracted by applying finely ground limestone, and alkaline, or sweet, soil (above 7.0) is treated with ground sulfur.

COMMON NAME	OPTIMUM pH RANGE	COMMON NAME	OPTIMUM pH RANGE	COMMON NAME	OPTIMUM pH RANGE
TREES AND SHRUBS		Bee balm	6.0–7.5	Snapdragon	5.5–7.0
Apple	5.0–6.5	Begonia	5.5–7.0	Sunflower	6.0–7.5
Azalea	4.5–6.0	Black-eyed Susan	5.5–7.0	Tulip	6.0–7.0
Beautybush	6.0–7.5	Bleeding heart	6.0–7.5	Zinnia	5.5–7.0
Birch	5.0–6.5	Canna	6.0–8.0		
Blackberry	5.0–6.0	Carnation	6.0–7.0	**VEGETABLES**	
Blueberry	4.0–5.0	Chrysanthemum	6.0–7.5	Asparagus	6.0–8.0
Boxwood	6.0–7.5	Clematis	5.5–7.0	Bean	6.0–7.5
Cherry, sour	6.0–7.0	Coleus	6.0–7.0	Beet	6.0–7.5
Crab apple	6.0–7.5	Coneflower, purple	5.0–7.5	Broccoli	6.0–7.0
Dogwood	5.0–7.0	Cosmos	5.0–8.0	Brussels sprout	6.0–7.5
Fir, balsam	5.0–6.0	Crocus	6.0–8.0	Cabbage	6.0–7.5
Hemlock	5.0–6.0	Daffodil	6.0–6.5	Carrot	5.5–7.0
Hydrangea, blue-flowered	4.0–5.0	Dahlia	6.0–7.5	Cauliflower	5.5–7.5
Hydrangea, pink-flowered	6.0–7.0	Daisy, Shasta	6.0–8.0	Celery	5.8–7.0
		Daylily	6.0–8.0	Chive	6.0–7.0
Juniper	5.0–6.0	Delphinium	6.0–7.5	Collard	6.5–7.5
Laurel, mountain	4.5–6.0	Foxglove	6.0–7.5	Corn	5.5–7.0
Lemon	6.0–7.5	Geranium	6.0–8.0	Cucumber	5.5–7.0
Lilac	6.0–7.5	Gladiolus	5.0–7.0	Eggplant	6.0–7.0
Maple, sugar	6.0–7.5	Hibiscus	6.0–8.0	Garlic	5.5–8.0
Oak, white	5.0–6.5	Hollyhock	6.0–8.0	Kale	6.0–7.5
Orange	6.0–7.5	Hyacinth	6.5–7.5	Leek	6.0–8.0
Peach	6.0–7.0	Iris, blue flag	5.0–7.5	Lettuce	6.0–7.0
Pear	6.0–7.5	Lily-of-the-valley	4.5–6.0	Okra	6.0–7.0
Pecan	6.4–8.0	Lupine	5.0–6.5	Onion	6.0–7.0
Plum	6.0–8.0	Marigold	5.5–7.5	Pea	6.0–7.5
Raspberry, red	5.5–7.0	Morning glory	6.0–7.5	Pepper, sweet	5.5–7.0
Rhododendron	4.5–6.0	Narcissus, trumpet	5.5–6.5	Potato	4.8–6.5
Willow	6.0–8.0	Nasturtium	5.5–7.5	Pumpkin	5.5–7.5
		Pansy	5.5–6.5	Radish	6.0–7.0
FLOWERS		Peony	6.0–7.5	Spinach	6.0–7.5
Alyssum	6.0–7.5	Petunia	6.0–7.5	Squash, crookneck	6.0–7.5
Aster, New England	6.0–8.0	Phlox, summer	6.0–8.0	Squash, Hubbard	5.5–7.0
Baby's breath	6.0–7.0	Poppy, oriental	6.0–7.5	Swiss chard	6.0–7.0
Bachelor's button	6.0–7.5	Rose, hybrid tea	5.5–7.0	Tomato	5.5–7.5
		Rose, rugosa	6.0–7.0	Watermelon	5.5–6.5

PRODUCE WEIGHTS AND MEASURES

VEGETABLES

ASPARAGUS: 1 pound = 3 cups chopped

BEANS (STRING): 1 pound = 4 cups chopped

BEETS: 1 pound (5 medium) = 2½ cups chopped

BROCCOLI: 1 pound = 6 cups chopped

CABBAGE: 1 pound = 4½ cups shredded

CARROTS: 1 pound = 3½ cups sliced or grated

CELERY: 1 pound = 4 cups chopped

CUCUMBERS: 1 pound (2 medium) = 4 cups sliced

EGGPLANT: 1 pound = 4 cups chopped = 2 cups cooked

GARLIC: 1 clove = 1 teaspoon chopped

LEEKS: 1 pound = 4 cups chopped = 2 cups cooked

MUSHROOMS: 1 pound = 5 to 6 cups sliced = 2 cups cooked

ONIONS: 1 pound = 4 cups sliced = 2 cups cooked

PARSNIPS: 1 pound = 1½ cups cooked, puréed

PEAS: 1 pound whole = 1 to 1½ cups shelled

POTATOES: 1 pound (3 medium) sliced = 2 cups mashed

PUMPKIN: 1 pound = 4 cups chopped = 2 cups cooked and drained

SPINACH: 1 pound = ¾ to 1 cup cooked

SQUASHES (SUMMER): 1 pound = 4 cups grated = 2 cups sliced and cooked

SQUASHES (WINTER): 2 pounds = 2½ cups cooked, puréed

SWEET POTATOES: 1 pound = 4 cups grated = 1 cup cooked, puréed

SWISS CHARD: 1 pound = 5 to 6 cups packed leaves = 1 to 1½ cups cooked

TOMATOES: 1 pound (3 or 4 medium) = 1½ cups seeded pulp

TURNIPS: 1 pound = 4 cups chopped = 2 cups cooked, mashed

FRUIT

APPLES: 1 pound (3 or 4 medium) = 3 cups sliced

BANANAS: 1 pound (3 or 4 medium) = 1¾ cups mashed

BERRIES: 1 quart = 3½ cups

DATES: 1 pound = 2½ cups pitted

LEMON: 1 whole = 1 to 3 tablespoons juice; 1 to 1½ teaspoons grated rind

LIME: 1 whole = 1½ to 2 tablespoons juice

ORANGE: 1 medium = 6 to 8 tablespoons juice; 2 to 3 tablespoons grated rind

PEACHES: 1 pound (4 medium) = 3 cups sliced

PEARS: 1 pound (4 medium) = 2 cups sliced

RHUBARB: 1 pound = 2 cups cooked

SOWING VEGETABLE SEEDS

SOW OR PLANT IN COOL WEATHER	Beets, broccoli, brussels sprouts, cabbage, lettuce, onions, parsley, peas, radishes, spinach, Swiss chard, turnips
SOW OR PLANT IN WARM WEATHER	Beans, carrots, corn, cucumbers, eggplant, melons, okra, peppers, squashes, tomatoes
SOW OR PLANT FOR ONE CROP PER SEASON	Corn, eggplant, leeks, melons, peppers, potatoes, spinach (New Zealand), squashes, tomatoes
RESOW FOR ADDITIONAL CROPS	Beans, beets, cabbage, carrots, kohlrabi, lettuce, radishes, rutabagas, spinach, turnips

A Beginner's Vegetable Garden

The vegetables suggested below are common, easy-to-grow crops. Make 11 rows, 10 feet long, with at least 18 inches between them. Ideally, the rows should run north and south to take full advantage of the sun. This garden, planted as suggested, can feed a family of four for one summer, with a little extra for canning and freezing or giving away.

ROW	
1	Zucchini (4 plants)
2	Tomatoes (5 plants, staked)
3	Peppers (6 plants)
4	Cabbage

ROW	
5	Bush beans
6	Lettuce
7	Beets
8	Carrots
9	Swiss chard
10	Radishes
11	Marigolds (to discourage rabbits!)

TRADITIONAL PLANTING TIMES

• Plant **CORN** when elm leaves are the size of a squirrel's ear, when oak leaves are the size of a mouse's ear, when apple blossoms begin to fall, or when the dogwoods are in full bloom.

• Plant **LETTUCE, SPINACH, PEAS,** and other cool-weather vegetables when the lilacs show their first leaves or when daffodils begin to bloom.

• Plant **TOMATOES** and **PEPPERS** when dogwoods are in peak bloom or when daylilies start to bloom.

• Plant **CUCUMBERS** and **SQUASHES** when lilac flowers fade.

• Plant **PERENNIALS** when maple leaves begin to unfurl.

• Plant **MORNING GLORIES** when maple trees have full-size leaves.

• Plant **PANSIES, SNAPDRAGONS,** and other hardy annuals after the aspen and chokecherry trees leaf out.

• Plant **BEETS** and **CARROTS** when dandelions are blooming.

WHEN TO . . .

	. . . FERTILIZE	. . . WATER
BEANS	After heavy bloom and set of pods	Regularly, from start of pod to set
BEETS	At time of planting	Only during drought conditions
BROCCOLI	3 weeks after transplanting	Only during drought conditions
BRUSSELS SPROUTS	3 weeks after transplanting	At transplanting
CABBAGE	3 weeks after transplanting	2 to 3 weeks before harvest
CARROTS	In the fall for the following spring	Only during drought conditions
CAULIFLOWER	3 weeks after transplanting	Once, 3 weeks before harvest
CELERY	At time of transplanting	Once a week
CORN	When 8 to 10 inches tall, and when first silk appears	When tassels appear and cobs start to swell
CUCUMBERS	1 week after bloom, and 3 weeks later	Frequently, especially when fruits form
LETTUCE	2 to 3 weeks after transplanting	Once a week
MELONS	1 week after bloom, and again 3 weeks later	Once a week
ONION SETS	When bulbs begin to swell, and when plants are 1 foot tall	Only during drought conditions
PARSNIPS	1 year before planting	Only during drought conditions
PEAS	After heavy bloom and set of pods	Regularly, from start of pod to set
PEPPERS	After first fruit-set	Once a week
POTATO TUBERS	At bloom time or time of second hilling	Regularly, when tubers start to form
PUMPKINS	Just before vines start to run, when plants are about 1 foot tall	Only during drought conditions
RADISHES	Before spring planting	Once a week
SPINACH	When plants are one-third grown	Once a week
SQUASHES, SUMMER	Just before vines start to run, when plants are about 1 foot tall	Only during drought conditions
SQUASHES, WINTER	Just before vines start to run, when plants are about 1 foot tall	Only during drought conditions
TOMATOES	2 weeks before, and after first picking	Twice a week

HOW TO GROW HERBS

HERB	START SEEDS INDOORS (WEEKS BEFORE LAST SPRING FROST)	START SEEDS OUTDOORS (WEEKS BEFORE/AFTER LAST SPRING FROST)	HEIGHT/ SPREAD (INCHES)	SOIL	LIGHT**
BASIL*	6–8	Anytime after	12–24/12	Rich, moist	○
BORAGE*	Not recommended	Anytime after	12–36/12	Rich, well-drained, dry	○
CHERVIL	Not recommended	3–4 before	12–24/8	Rich, moist	◑
CHIVES	8–10	3–4 before	12–18/18	Rich, moist	○
CILANTRO/ CORIANDER	Not recommended	Anytime after	12–36/6	Light	○◑
DILL	Not recommended	4–5 before	36–48/12	Rich	○
FENNEL	4–6	Anytime after	48–80/18	Rich	○
LAVENDER, ENGLISH*	8–12	1–2 before	18–36/24	Moderately fertile, well-drained	○
LAVENDER, FRENCH	Not recommended	Not recommended	18–36/24	Moderately fertile, well-drained	○
LEMON BALM*	6–10	2–3 before	12–24/18	Rich, well-drained	○◑
LOVAGE*	6–8	2–3 before	36–72/36	Fertile, sandy	○◑
MINT	Not recommended	Not recommended	12–24/18	Rich, moist	◑
OREGANO*	6–10	Anytime after	12–24/18	Poor	○
PARSLEY*	10–12	3–4 before	18–24/6–8	Medium-rich	◑
ROSEMARY*	8–10	Anytime after	48–72/48	Not too acidic	○
SAGE	6–10	1–2 before	12–48/30	Well-drained	○
SORREL	6–10	2–3 after	20–48/12–14	Rich, organic	○
SUMMER SAVORY	4–6	Anytime after	4–15/6	Medium-rich	○
SWEET CICELY	6–8	2–3 after	36–72/36	Moderately fertile, well-drained	○◑
TARRAGON, FRENCH	Not recommended	Not recommended	24–36/12	Well-drained	○◑
THYME, COMMON*	6–10	2–3 before	2–12/7–12	Fertile, well-drained	○◑

*Recommend minimum soil temperature of 70°F to germinate

** ○ FULL SUN ◑ PARTIAL SHADE

REFERENCE

GROWTH TYPE
Annual
Annual, biennial
Annual, biennial
Perennial
Annual
Annual
Annual
Perennial
Tender perennial
Perennial
Perennial
Perennial
Tender perennial
Biennial
Tender perennial
Perennial
Perennial
Annual
Perennial
Perennial
Perennial

DRYING HERBS

Before drying, remove any dead or diseased leaves or stems. Wash under cool water, shake off excess water, and put on a towel to dry completely. Air drying preserves an herb's essential oils; use for sturdy herbs. A microwave dries herbs more quickly, so mold is less likely to develop; use for moist, tender herbs.

HANGING METHOD: Gather four to six stems of fresh herbs in a bunch and tie with string, leaving a loop for hanging. Or, use a rubber band with a paper clip attached to it. Hang the herbs in a warm, well-ventilated area, out of direct sunlight, until dry. For herbs that have full seed heads, such as dill or coriander, use a paper bag. Punch holes in the bag for ventilation, label it, and put the herb bunch into the bag before you tie a string around the top of the bag. The average drying time is 1 to 3 weeks.

MICROWAVE METHOD: This is better for small quantities, such as a cup or two at a time. Arrange a single layer of herbs between two paper towels and put them in the microwave for 1 to 2 minutes on high power. Let the leaves cool. If they are not dry, reheat for 30 seconds and check again. Repeat as needed. Let cool. Do not overcook, or the herbs will lose their flavor.

STORING HERBS AND SPICES

FRESH HERBS: Dill and parsley will keep for about 2 weeks with stems immersed in a glass of water tented with a plastic bag. Most other fresh herbs (and greens) will keep for short periods unwashed and refrigerated in tightly sealed plastic bags with just enough moisture to prevent wilting. For longer storage, use moisture- and gas-permeable paper and cellophane. Plastic cuts off oxygen to the plants and promotes spoilage.

SPICES AND DRIED HERBS: Store in a cool, dry place.

COOKING WITH HERBS

A **BOUQUET GARNI** is usually made with bay leaves, thyme, and parsley tied with string or wrapped in cheesecloth. Use to flavor casseroles and soups. Remove after cooking.

FINES HERBES use equal amounts of fresh parsley, tarragon, chives, and chervil chopped fine. Commonly used in French cooking, they make a fine omelet or add zest to soups and sauces. Add to salads and butter sauces or sprinkle on noodles, soups, and stews.

HOW TO GROW BULBS

SPRING-PLANTED BULBS

COMMON NAME	LATIN NAME	HARDINESS ZONE	SOIL	LIGHT*	SPACING (INCHES)
ALLIUM	*Allium*	3–10	Well-drained/moist	○	12
BEGONIA, TUBEROUS	*Begonia*	10–11	Well-drained/moist	◐●	12–15
BLAZING STAR/ GAYFEATHER	*Liatris*	7–10	Well-drained	○	6
CALADIUM	*Caladium*	10–11	Well-drained/moist	◐●	8–12
CALLA LILY	*Zantedeschia*	8–10	Well-drained/moist	○◐	8–24
CANNA	*Canna*	8–11	Well-drained/moist	○	12–24
CYCLAMEN	*Cyclamen*	7–9	Well-drained/moist	◐	4
DAHLIA	*Dahlia*	9–11	Well-drained/fertile	○	12–36
DAYLILY	*Hemerocallis*	3–10	Adaptable to most soils	○◐	12–24
FREESIA	*Freesia*	9–11	Well-drained/moist/sandy	○◐	2–4
GARDEN GLOXINIA	*Incarvillea*	4–8	Well-drained/moist	○	12
GLADIOLUS	*Gladiolus*	4–11	Well-drained/fertile	○◐	4–9
IRIS	*Iris*	3–10	Well-drained/sandy	○	3–6
LILY, ASIATIC/ORIENTAL	*Lilium*	3–8	Well-drained	○◐	8–12
PEACOCK FLOWER	*Tigridia*	8–10	Well-drained	○	5–6
SHAMROCK/SORREL	*Oxalis*	5–9	Well-drained	○◐	4–6
WINDFLOWER	*Anemone*	3–9	Well-drained/moist	○◐	3–6

FALL-PLANTED BULBS

COMMON NAME	LATIN NAME	HARDINESS ZONE	SOIL	LIGHT*	SPACING (INCHES)
BLUEBELL	*Hyacinthoides*	4–9	Well-drained/fertile	○◐	4
CHRISTMAS ROSE/ HELLEBORE	*Helleborus*	4–8	Neutral–alkaline	○◐	18
CROCUS	*Crocus*	3–8	Well-drained/moist/fertile	○◐	4
DAFFODIL	*Narcissus*	3–10	Well-drained/moist/fertile	○◐	6
FRITILLARY	*Fritillaria*	3–9	Well-drained/sandy	○◐	3
GLORY OF THE SNOW	*Chionodoxa*	3–9	Well-drained/moist	○◐	3
GRAPE HYACINTH	*Muscari*	4–10	Well-drained/moist/fertile	○◐	3–4
IRIS, BEARDED	*Iris*	3–9	Well-drained	○◐	4
IRIS, SIBERIAN	*Iris*	4–9	Well-drained	○◐	4
ORNAMENTAL ONION	*Allium*	3–10	Well-drained/moist/fertile	○	12
SNOWDROP	*Galanthus*	3–9	Well-drained/moist/fertile	○◐	3
SNOWFLAKE	*Leucojum*	5–9	Well-drained/moist/sandy	○◐	4
SPRING STARFLOWER	*Ipheion uniflorum*	6–9	Well-drained loam	○◐	3–6
STAR OF BETHLEHEM	*Ornithogalum*	5–10	Well-drained/moist	○◐	2–5
STRIPED SQUILL	*Puschkinia scilloides*	3–9	Well-drained	○◐	6
TULIP	*Tulipa*	4–8	Well-drained/fertile	○◐	3–6
WINTER ACONITE	*Eranthis*	4–9	Well-drained/moist/fertile	◐●	3

REFERENCE

DEPTH (INCHES)	BLOOMING SEASON	HEIGHT (INCHES)	NOTES
3–4	Spring to summer	6–60	Usually pest-free; a great cut flower
1–2	Summer to fall	8–18	North of Zone 10, lift in fall
4	Summer to fall	8–20	An excellent flower for drying; north of Zone 7, plant in spring, lift in fall
2	Summer	8–24	North of Zone 10, plant in spring, lift in fall
1–4	Summer	24–36	Fragrant; north of Zone 8, plant in spring, lift in fall
Level	Summer	18–60	North of Zone 8, plant in spring, lift in fall
1–2	Spring to fall	3–12	Naturalizes well in warm areas; north of Zone 7, lift in fall
4–6	Late summer	12–60	North of Zone 9, lift in fall
2	Summer	12–36	Mulch in winter in Zones 3 to 6
2	Summer	12–24	Fragrant; can be grown outdoors in warm climates
3–4	Summer	6–20	Does well in woodland settings
3–6	Early summer to early fall	12–80	North of Zone 10, lift in fall
4	Spring to late summer	3–72	Divide and replant rhizomes every two to five years
4–6	Early summer	36	Fragrant; self-sows; requires excellent drainage
4	Summer	18–24	North of Zone 8, lift in fall
2	Summer	2–12	Plant in confined area to control
2	Early summer	3–18	North of Zone 6, lift in fall
3–4	Spring	8–20	Excellent for borders, rock gardens and naturalizing
1–2	Spring	12	Hardy, but requires shelter from strong, cold winds
3	Early spring	5	Naturalizes well in grass
6	Early spring	14–24	Plant under shrubs or in a border
3	Midspring	6–30	Different species can be planted in rock gardens, woodland gardens, or borders
3	Spring	4–10	Self-sows easily; plant in rock gardens, raised beds, or under shrubs
2–3	Late winter to spring	6–12	Use as a border plant or in wildflower and rock gardens; self-sows easily
4	Early spring to early summer	3–48	Naturalizes well; a good cut flower
4	Early spring to midsummer	18–48	An excellent cut flower
3–4	Late spring to early summer	6–60	Usually pest-free; a great cut flower
3	Spring	6–12	Best when clustered and planted in an area that will not dry out in summer
4	Spring	6–18	Naturalizes well
3	Spring	4–6	Fragrant; naturalizes easily
4	Spring to summer	6–24	North of Zone 5, plant in spring, lift in fall
3	Spring	4–6	Naturalizes easily; makes an attractive edging
4–6	Early to late spring	8–30	Excellent for borders, rock gardens, and naturalizing
2–3	Late winter to spring	2–4	Self-sows and naturalizes easily

REFERENCE

SUBSTITUTIONS FOR COMMON INGREDIENTS

ITEM	QUANTITY	SUBSTITUTION
BAKING POWDER	1 teaspoon	¼ teaspoon baking soda plus ¼ teaspoon cornstarch plus ½ teaspoon cream of tartar
BUTTERMILK	1 cup	1 tablespoon lemon juice or vinegar plus milk to equal 1 cup; or 1 cup plain yogurt
CHOCOLATE, UNSWEETENED	1 ounce	3 tablespoons cocoa plus 1 tablespoon unsalted butter, shortening, or vegetable oil
CRACKER CRUMBS	¾ cup	1 cup dry bread crumbs; or 1 tablespoon quick-cooking oats (for thickening)
CREAM, HEAVY	1 cup	¾ cup milk plus ⅓ cup melted unsalted butter (this will not whip)
CREAM, LIGHT	1 cup	⅞ cup milk plus 3 tablespoons melted, unsalted butter
CREAM, SOUR	1 cup	⅞ cup buttermilk or plain yogurt plus 3 tablespoons melted, unsalted butter
CREAM, WHIPPING	1 cup	⅔ cup well-chilled evaporated milk, whipped; or 1 cup nonfat dry milk powder whipped with 1 cup ice water
EGG	1 whole	2 yolks plus 1 tablespoon cold water; or 3 tablespoons vegetable oil plus 1 tablespoon water (for baking); or 2 to 3 tablespoons mayonnaise (for cakes)
EGG WHITE	1 white	2 teaspoons meringue powder plus 3 tablespoons water, combined
FLOUR, ALL-PURPOSE	1 cup	1 cup plus 3 tablespoons cake flour (not advised for cookies or quick breads); or 1 cup self-rising flour (omit baking powder and salt from recipe)
FLOUR, CAKE	1 cup	1 cup minus 3 tablespoons sifted all-purpose flour plus 3 tablespoons cornstarch
FLOUR, SELF-RISING	1 cup	1 cup all-purpose flour plus 1½ teaspoons baking powder plus ¼ teaspoon salt
HERBS, DRIED	1 teaspoon	1 tablespoon fresh, minced and packed
HONEY	1 cup	1¼ cups sugar plus ½ cup liquid called for in recipe (such as water or oil)
KETCHUP	1 cup	1 cup tomato sauce plus ¼ cup sugar plus 3 tablespoons apple-cider vinegar plus ½ teaspoon salt plus pinch of ground cloves combined; or 1 cup chili sauce
LEMON JUICE	1 teaspoon	½ teaspoon vinegar
MAYONNAISE	1 cup	1 cup sour cream or plain yogurt; or 1 cup cottage cheese (puréed)
MILK, SKIM	1 cup	⅓ cup instant nonfat dry milk plus ¾ cup water

ITEM	QUANTITY	SUBSTITUTION
MILK, TO SOUR	1 cup	1 tablespoon vinegar or lemon juice plus milk to equal 1 cup. Stir and let stand 5 minutes.
MILK, WHOLE	1 cup	½ cup evaporated whole milk plus ½ cup water; or ¾ cup 2 percent milk plus ¼ cup half-and-half
MOLASSES	1 cup	1 cup honey or dark corn syrup
MUSTARD, DRY	1 teaspoon	1 tablespoon prepared mustard less 1 teaspoon liquid from recipe
OAT BRAN	1 cup	1 cup wheat bran or rice bran or wheat germ
OATS, OLD-FASHIONED	1 cup	1 cup steel-cut Irish or Scotch oats
QUINOA	1 cup	1 cup millet or couscous (whole wheat cooks faster) or bulgur
SUGAR, DARK-BROWN	1 cup	1 cup light-brown sugar, packed; or 1 cup granulated sugar plus 2 to 3 tablespoons molasses
SUGAR, GRANULATED	1 cup	1 cup firmly packed brown sugar; or 1¾ cups confectioners' sugar (makes baked goods less crisp); or 1 cup superfine sugar
SUGAR, LIGHT-BROWN	1 cup	1 cup granulated sugar plus 1 to 2 tablespoons molasses; or ½ cup dark-brown sugar plus ½ cup granulated sugar
SWEETENED CONDENSED MILK	1 can (14 oz.)	1 cup evaporated milk plus 1¼ cups granulated sugar. Combine and heat until sugar dissolves.
VANILLA BEAN	1-inch bean	1 teaspoon vanilla extract
VINEGAR, APPLE-CIDER	—	malt, white-wine, or rice vinegar
VINEGAR, BALSAMIC	1 tablespoon	1 tablespoon red- or white-wine vinegar plus ½ teaspoon sugar
VINEGAR, RED-WINE	—	white-wine, sherry, champagne, or balsamic vinegar
VINEGAR, RICE	—	apple-cider, champagne, or white-wine vinegar
VINEGAR, WHITE-WINE	—	apple-cider, champagne, fruit (raspberry), rice, or red-wine vinegar
YEAST	1 cake (⅗ oz.)	1 package (¼ ounce) or 1 scant tablespoon active dried yeast
YOGURT, PLAIN	1 cup	1 cup sour cream (thicker; less tart) or buttermilk (thinner; use in baking, dressings, sauces)

TYPES OF FAT

One way to minimize your total blood cholesterol is to manage the amount and types of fat in your diet. Aim for monounsaturated and polyunsaturated fats; avoid saturated and trans fats.

MONOUNSATURATED FAT lowers LDL (bad cholesterol) and may raise HDL (good cholesterol) or leave it unchanged; found in almonds, avocados, canola oil, cashews, olive oil, peanut oil, and peanuts.

POLYUNSATURATED FAT lowers LDL and may lower HDL; includes omega-3 and omega-6 fatty acids; found in corn oil, cottonseed oil, fish such as salmon and tuna, safflower oil, sesame seeds, soybeans, and sunflower oil.

SATURATED FAT raises both LDL and HDL; found in chocolate, cocoa butter, coconut oil, dairy products (milk, butter, cheese, ice cream), egg yolks, palm oil, and red meat.

TRANS FAT raises LDL and lowers HDL; a type of fat common in many processed foods, such as most margarines (especially stick), vegetable shortening, partially hydrogenated vegetable oil, many commercial fried foods (doughnuts, french fries), and commercial baked goods (cookies, crackers, cakes).

Calorie-Burning Comparisons

If you hustle through your chores to get to the fitness center, relax. You're getting a great workout already. The left-hand column lists "chore" exercises, the middle column shows the number of calories burned per minute per pound of body weight, and the right-hand column lists comparable "recreational" exercises. For example, a 150-pound person forking straw bales burns 9.45 calories per minute, the same workout he or she would get playing basketball.

Chopping with an ax, fast	0.135	Skiing, cross country, uphill
Climbing hills, with 44-pound load	0.066	Swimming, crawl, fast
Digging trenches	0.065	Skiing, cross country, steady walk
Forking straw bales	0.063	Basketball
Chopping down trees	0.060	Football
Climbing hills, with 9-pound load	0.058	Swimming, crawl, slow
Sawing by hand	0.055	Skiing, cross country, moderate
Mowing lawns	0.051	Horseback riding, trotting
Scrubbing floors	0.049	Tennis
Shoveling coal	0.049	Aerobic dance, medium
Hoeing	0.041	Weight training, circuit training
Stacking firewood	0.040	Weight lifting, free weights
Shoveling grain	0.038	Golf
Painting houses	0.035	Walking, normal pace, asphalt road
Weeding	0.033	Table tennis
Shopping for food	0.028	Cycling, 5.5 mph
Mopping floors	0.028	Fishing
Washing windows	0.026	Croquet
Raking	0.025	Dancing, ballroom
Driving a tractor	0.016	Drawing, standing position

REFERENCE

FREEZER STORAGE TIME

(freezer temperature 0°F or colder)

PRODUCT	MONTHS IN FREEZER

FRESH MEAT
Beef . . . . 6 to 12
Lamb . . . . 6 to 9
Veal . . . . 6 to 9
Pork . . . . 4 to 6
Ground beef, veal, lamb, pork . . . . 3 to 4
Frankfurters . . . . 1 to 2
Sausage, fresh pork . . . . 1 to 2
Ready-to-serve luncheon meats . . . . Not
recommended

FRESH POULTRY
Chicken, turkey (whole) 12
Chicken, turkey (pieces) . . . . 6 to 9
Cornish game hen, game birds . . . 6 to 9
Giblets . . . . 3 to 4

COOKED POULTRY
Breaded, fried 4
Pieces, plain 4
Pieces covered with broth, gravy 6

FRESH FRUIT (PREPARED FOR FREEZING)
All fruit except those
listed below . . . . 10 to 12
Avocados, bananas, plantains 3
Lemons, limes, oranges . . . . 4 to 6

FRESH VEGETABLES (PREPARED FOR FREEZING)
Beans, beets, bok choy, broccoli,
brussels sprouts, cabbage, carrots,
cauliflower, celery, corn, greens,
kohlrabi, leeks, mushrooms, okra,
onions, peas, peppers, soybeans,
spinach, summer squashes . . . 10 to 12
Asparagus, rutabagas, turnips . . 8 to 10
Artichokes, eggplant . . . . 6 to 8
Tomatoes (overripe or sliced) 2
Bamboo shoots, cucumbers, endive,
lettuce, radishes, watercress . . . . . Not
recommended

CHEESE (except those listed below) . . . 6
Cottage cheese, cream cheese, feta, goat,
fresh mozzarella, Neufchâtel, Parmesan, processed cheese (opened) . . . Not
recommended

PRODUCT	MONTHS IN FREEZER

DAIRY PRODUCTS
Margarine (not diet) 12
Butter . . . . 6 to 9
Cream, half-and-half 4
Milk 3
Ice cream . . . . 1 to 2

FREEZING HINTS

FOR MEALS, remember that a quart container holds four servings, and a pint container holds two servings.

TO PREVENT STICKING, spread the food to be frozen (berries, hamburgers, cookies, etc.) on a cookie sheet and freeze until solid. Then place in plastic bags and freeze.

LABEL FOODS for easy identification. Write the name of the food, number of servings, and date of freezing on containers or bags.

FREEZE FOODS as quickly as possible by placing them directly against the sides of the freezer.

ARRANGE FREEZER into sections for each food category.

IF POWER IS INTERRUPTED, or if the freezer is not operating normally, do not open the freezer door. Food in a loaded freezer will usually stay frozen for 2 days if the freezer door remains closed during that time period.

PLASTICS

In your quest to go green, use this guide to use and sort plastic. The number, usually found with a triangle symbol on a container, indicates the type of resin used to produce the plastic. Visit **EARTH911.COM** for recycling information in your state.

NUMBER 1 · *PETE or PET (polyethylene terephthalate)*
IS USED IN . . . . microwavable food trays; salad dressing, soft drink, water, and juice bottles
STATUS . . . . hard to clean; absorbs bacteria and flavors; avoid reusing
IS RECYCLED TO MAKE. . . carpet, furniture, new containers, Polar fleece

NUMBER 2 · *HDPE (high-density polyethylene)*
IS USED IN . . . . household cleaner and shampoo bottles, milk jugs, yogurt tubs
STATUS . . . . transmits no known chemicals into food
IS RECYCLED TO MAKE. . . detergent bottles, fencing, floor tiles, pens

NUMBER 3 · *V or PVC (vinyl)*
IS USED IN . . . . cooking oil bottles, clear food packaging, mouthwash bottles
STATUS . . . . is believed to contain phalates that interfere with hormonal development; avoid
IS RECYCLED TO MAKE. . . cables, mudflaps, paneling, roadway gutters

NUMBER 4 · *LDPE (low-density polyethylene)*
IS USED IN . . . . bread and shopping bags, carpet, clothing, furniture
STATUS . . . . transmits no known chemicals into food
IS RECYCLED TO MAKE. . . envelopes, floor tiles, lumber, trash-can liners

NUMBER 5 · *PP (polypropylene)*
IS USED IN . . . . .ketchup bottles, medicine and syrup bottles, drinking straws
STATUS . . . . transmits no known chemicals into food
IS RECYCLED TO MAKE. . . battery cables, brooms, ice scrapers, rakes

NUMBER 6 · *PS (polystyrene)*
IS USED IN . . . . disposable cups and plates, egg cartons, take-out containers
STATUS . . . . .is believed to leach styrene, a possible human carcinogen, into food; avoid
IS RECYCLED TO MAKE. . . foam packaging, insulation, light switchplates, rulers

NUMBER 7 · *Other (miscellaneous)*
IS USED IN . . . . .3- and 5-gallon water jugs, nylon, some food containers
STATUS . . . . .contains bisphenol A, which has been linked to heart disease and obesity; avoid
IS RECYCLED TO MAKE. . . .custom-made products

REFERENCE

AROUND THE HOUSE

HOW MUCH DO YOU NEED?

WALLPAPER

Before choosing your wallpaper, keep in mind that wallpaper with little or no pattern to match at the seams and the ceiling will be the easiest to apply, thus resulting in the least amount of wasted wallpaper. If you choose a patterned wallpaper, a small repeating pattern will result in less waste than a large repeating pattern. And a pattern that is aligned horizontally (matching on each column of paper) will waste less than one that drops or alternates its pattern (matching on every other column).

TO DETERMINE THE AMOUNT OF WALL SPACE YOU'RE COVERING:

• Measure the length of each wall, add these figures together, and multiply by the height of the walls to get the area (square footage) of the room's walls.

• Calculate the square footage of each door, window, and other opening in the room. Add these figures together and subtract the total from the area of the room's walls.

• Take that figure and multiply by 1.15, to account for a waste rate of about 15 percent in your wallpaper project. You'll end up with a target amount to purchase when you shop.

• Wallpaper is sold in single, double, and triple rolls. Coverage can vary, so be sure to refer to the roll's label for the proper square footage. (The average coverage for a double roll, for example, is 56 square feet.) After choosing a paper, divide the coverage figure (from the label) into the total square footage of the walls of the room you're papering. Round the answer up to the nearest whole number. This is the number of rolls you need to buy.

• Save leftover wallpaper rolls, carefully wrapped to keep clean.

INTERIOR PAINT

Estimate your room size and paint needs before you go to the store. Running out of a custom color halfway through the job could mean disaster. For the sake of the following exercise, assume that you have a 10x15-foot room with an 8-foot ceiling. The room has two doors and two windows.

FOR WALLS

Measure the total distance (perimeter) around the room:

(10 ft. + 15 ft.) x 2 = 50 ft.

Multiply the perimeter by the ceiling height to get the total wall area:

50 ft. x 8 ft. = 400 sq. ft.

Doors are usually 21 square feet (there are two in this exercise):

21 sq. ft. x 2 = 42 sq. ft.

Windows average 15 square feet (there are two in this exercise):

15 sq. ft. x 2 = 30 sq. ft.

Take the total wall area and subtract the area for the doors and windows to get the wall surface to be painted:

400 sq. ft. (wall area)
- 42 sq. ft. (doors)
- 30 sq. ft. (windows)
328 sq. ft.

As a rule of thumb, one gallon of quality paint will usually cover 400 square feet. One quart will cover 100 square feet. Because you need to cover 328 square feet in this example, one gallon will be adequate to give one coat of paint to the walls. (Coverage will be affected by the porosity and texture of the surface. In addition, bright colors may require a minimum of two coats.)

METRIC CONVERSION

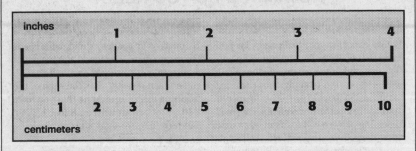

U.S. MEASURE	X THIS = NUMBER	METRIC EQUIVALENT	METRIC MEASURE	X THIS = NUMBER	U.S. EQUIVALENT
inch	2.54	centimeter		0.39	inch
foot	30.48	centimeter		0.033	foot
yard	0.91	meter		1.09	yard
mile	1.61	kilometer		0.62	mile
square inch	6.45	square centimeter		0.15	square inch
square foot	0.09	square meter		10.76	square foot
square yard	0.8	square meter		1.2	square yard
square mile	2.59	square kilometer		0.39	square mile
acre	0.4	hectare		2.47	acre
ounce	28.0	gram		0.035	ounce
pound	0.45	kilogram		2.2	pound
short ton (2,000 pounds)	0.91	metric ton		1.10	short ton
ounce	30.0	milliliter		0.034	ounce
pint	0.47	liter		2.1	pint
quart	0.95	liter		1.06	quart
gallon	3.8	liter		0.26	gallon

If you know the U.S. measurement and want to convert it to metric, multiply it by the number in the left shaded column (example: 1 inch equals 2.54 centimeters). If you know the metric measurement, multiply it by the number in the right shaded column (example: 2 meters equals 2.18 yards).

Where Do You Fit in Your Family Tree?

Technically it's known as consanguinity; that is, the quality or state of being related by blood or descended from a common ancestor. These relationships are shown below for the genealogy of six generations of one family. *–family tree information courtesy of Frederick H. Rohles*

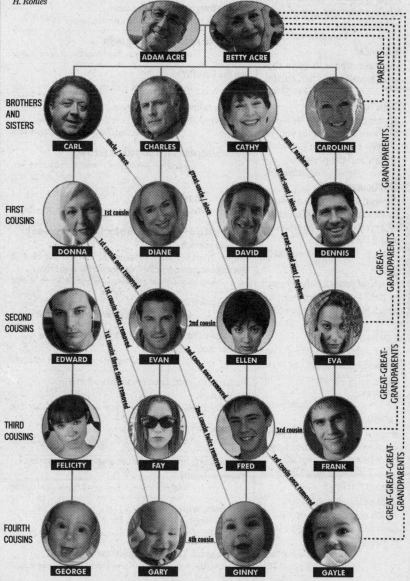

The Golden Rule
(It's true in all faiths.)

BRAHMANISM:

This is the sum of duty: Do naught unto others which would cause you pain if done to you.

Mahabharata 5:1517

BUDDHISM:

Hurt not others in ways that you yourself would find hurtful.

Udana-Varga 5:18

CHRISTIANITY:

All things whatsoever ye would that men should do to you, do ye even so to them; for this is the law and the prophets.

Matthew 7:12

CONFUCIANISM:

Surely it is the maxim of loving-kindness: Do not unto others what you would not have them do unto you.

Analects 15:23

ISLAM:

No one of you is a believer until he desires for his brother that which he desires for himself.

Sunnah

JUDAISM:

What is hateful to you, do not to your fellow man. That is the entire Law; all the rest is commentary.

Talmud, Shabbat 31a

TAOISM:

Regard your neighbor's gain as your own gain and your neighbor's loss as your own loss.

T'ai Shang Kan Ying P'ien

ZOROASTRIANISM:

That nature alone is good which refrains from doing unto another whatsoever is not good for itself.

Dadistan-i-dinik 94:5
–courtesy of Elizabeth Pool

FAMOUS LAST WORDS

Waiting, are they? Waiting, are they? Well–let 'em wait.
(To an attending doctor who attempted to comfort him by saying, "General, I fear the angels are waiting for you.")
–*Ethan Allen, American Revolutionary general, d. February 12, 1789*

A dying man can do nothing easy.
–*Benjamin Franklin, American statesman, d. April 17, 1790*

Now I shall go to sleep. Good night.
–*Lord George Byron, English writer, d. April 19, 1824*

Is it the Fourth?
–*Thomas Jefferson, 3rd U.S. president, d. July 4, 1826*

Thomas Jefferson–still survives . . .
(Actually, Jefferson had died earlier that same day.)
–*John Adams, 2nd U.S. president, d. July 4, 1826*

Friends, applaud. The comedy is finished.
–*Ludwig van Beethoven, German-Austrian composer, d. March 26, 1827*

Moose . . . Indian . . .
–*Henry David Thoreau, American writer, d. May 6, 1862*

Go on, get out–last words are for fools who haven't said enough.
(To his housekeeper, who urged him to tell her his last words so she could write them down for posterity.)
–*Karl Marx, German political philosopher, d. March 14, 1883*

Is it not meningitis?
–*Louisa M. Alcott, American writer, d. March 6, 1888*

How were the receipts today at Madison Square Garden?
–*P. T. Barnum, American entrepreneur, d. April 7, 1891*

Turn up the lights, I don't want to go home in the dark.
–*O. Henry (William Sidney Porter), American writer, d. June 4, 1910*

Get my swan costume ready.
–*Anna Pavlova, Russian ballerina, d. January 23, 1931*

Is everybody happy? I want everybody to be happy. I know I'm happy.
–*Ethel Barrymore, American actress, d. June 18, 1959*

I'm bored with it all.
(Before slipping into a coma. He died 9 days later.)
–*Winston Churchill, English statesman, d. January 24, 1965*

You be good. You'll be in tomorrow. I love you.
–*Alex, highly intelligent African Gray parrot, d. September 6, 2007*

REFERENCE